MANAGERIAL REALITY

Balancing Technique, Practice, and Values

MANAGERIAL REALITY

Balancing Technique, Practice, and Values

Peter J. Frost
University of British Columbia

Vance F. Mitchell
Embry-Riddle Aeronautical University

Walter R. Nord
Washington University

SCOTT, FORESMAN/LITTLE, BROWN HIGHER EDUCATION

A Division of Scott, Foresman and Company

Glenview, Illinois   London, England

To Nola, Fran, and Ann

Library of Congress Cataloging-in-Publication Data

Managerial reality: balancing technique, practice, and values /
  [edited by] Peter J. Frost, Vance F. Mitchell, Walter R. Nord.
     p.   cm.
  Includes bibliographical references.
  ISBN 0-673-38600-7
  1. Management. 2. Industrial management. I. Frost, Peter J.
II. Mitchell, Vance F. III. Nord, Walter R.
HD31.M29394 1990
658.4--dc20   89-10797
                                           CIP

123456-MPC-949392919089

Preface

Managerial Reality: Balancing Technique, Practice, and Values is directed toward students and practitioners of management. Like many others who teach management, each of us over the years has been confronted with the many discrepancies that seem to exist between what we teach about managing and management on the one hand and what our own experience and that of others tell us happens in so-called real organizations.

The enthusiastic reception our book *Organizational Reality: Reports from the Firing Line* received kindled the idea of someday preparing a book devoted to managers and the conflicts and challenges inherent in their roles. Accordingly, when our Executive Editor at Scott Foresman/Little Brown suggested that we do so, we happily agreed to undertake the task.

We surveyed reports by keen observers of management, self-reports of practitioners, fictionalized accounts of managerial behavior in novels and short stories, and on occasion, academic journals. Throughout our search we found a fundamental tension confronting managers between doing things right, doing the right thing, and doing what is right strategically and ethically. The perspectives that emerged from our search into this material provide the contents of this book.

It is important to realize that this book has a very different thrust from *Organizational Reality*. That book deals with people in a wide variety of organizational roles and thus has proven useful in connection with a number of subjects ranging from Organizational Behavior to Communication and Creative Writing. Here we are concerned exclusively with managers and managing.

Preparing this book has been a stimulating, intriguing, and educational experience. We hope that many readers likewise will find their perspectives on the practice of management revised as they make their way through the material in this book.

We are unanimous in our belief that the compilation of this book has been for us an enviable experience, a journey that has been interesting, exciting, and most rewarding. Since our contributions are distributed equally throughout the book, the ordering of names on the title page is alphabetical as in our previous work together.

No book is ever solely attributable to those who prepare it, and this book is no exception. We wish to thank Allan Cohen for providing an adaptation of his article with David Bradford, and Robert Berra, Diana Cawood, Sue Peterson, and Merle Welshans for bringing particular selections to our attention. Cathy Corrigan and Nita Ditchfield provided valuable assistance in searching out and organizing the material. Sandra Van Duyn and Peggy Smith provided efficient and enthusiastic administrative and secretarial assistance. Joe Dobson's help in the final stages is also greatly acknowledged. We owe a debt of gratitude to the many university and professional students in our courses whose healthy scepticism of what we teach inevitably served as reinforcement toward this undertaking. We also thank the many astute and articulate students of management whose reports comprise this book. We are grateful to Lyman Porter for his wise counsel and to Randall B. Dunham and Jon L. Pierce for acting as reviewers of the project. Finally, our deep thanks to Jane Steinmann, our Developmental Editor and Ginny Guerrant, our Project Editor, who shepherded this book through with grace, good humor, and skill.

Peter J. Frost
Vance F. Mitchell
Walter R. Nord

Contents

Introduction: "Doing Management"

Managers make a difference! The way they work with and through the activities of others in organizational settings impacts the lives of others and the fortunes of organizations they are entrusted to administer. Sometimes the difference is a negative one. Managers make mistakes, err in judgment, create problems for others, or behave selfishly or insensitively. As a result, people on the receiving end of the actions get hurt and organizational goals may be seriously impeded. At other times, the difference is positive. Managers anticipate errors or recover them, judge astutely, create and respond well to opportunities and behave honorably, sometimes even courageously. When this happens, people being managed blossom, organizational agendas are accomplished, and society benefits.

As Drucker observes ("The Emergence of Management" in Section 1, Managing: Its History, Challenge, and Nature) defining management is difficult . . . "it denotes a function but also the people who discharge it. It denotes a social position and rank but also a discipline and field of study." Drucker notes further that management "is the specific organ of the modern institution."[1] Organizations are characterized by formal sets of relationships imposed on less formal relationships among humans. They involve technical systems interacting with human activities. We believe that the primary function of management is the coordination of human effort in a world characterized by tensions between formality and informality, between technology and humanity.

At its core, we think that doing management involves a myriad of balancing acts which are needed to facilitate and secure coordination and cooperation between and among individuals and groups in organizations. We draw on the balancing image because it captures the type of actions managers must take to coordinate people with different values, self-interests, and intentions and departments with different agendas, tasks, goals, and criteria for effectiveness. It reflects the trade-offs managers must make between using structural mechanisms for achieving coordination and cooperation (such as plans, systems of control, and of organization) and more personal techniques of leadership. The balancing image captures the dilemmas managers must face and attempt to resolve in coordinating differing perceptions and beliefs about what is right or wrong strategically and morally in the affairs and direction of the organizations they administer. It is a dynamic process not a static function—we talk about balancing not balance, although there clearly are points of balance.

Managers must be part artist and part scientist—drawing on intuition and logic to get the organization's work done. They are inherently drawn into political behavior, dealing as they do with the interdependencies between people and departments with differing needs, resources, and expectations. Doing management requires an ability to envision the big picture, to "see the invisible" as Jonathan Swift put it. It requires the stamina to work through the long hours and the crises that occur inevitably in organizations, as well as a willingness to persevere and to engage in the repetitive mundane activities of daily organizational life. Managers need to anticipate the future, read the patterns in the present, and comprehend the lessons of the past.

All of this is a tall order! There is a real danger that one might draw the conclusion from the above that managers need to be like "Superman" or "Wonderwoman" and this might lead one to buy the fiction of the "Superboss." This also sets up expectations of performance that cannot easily or typically be met in the real world of organizations. In fact, chasing this goal of the perfect manager, creates, in the organizations (and business schools) of our modern post-industrial society, the addiction to work, and the workaholism of the professional manager that is much discussed in the media and is analyzed in the article "Hooked on Work" in Section 8, Managing Hazards.

Our point, made in a number of ways in the articles of *Managerial Reality,* is that doing management is complex, challenging, exacting, and exhausting but that the path to effective management is not that of the "Superboss." Clearly, to be successful, managers need to draw on their own particular skills and abilities. But they also need to work with and through the people (managers, employees, customers) *and* the systems (technical, legal, procedural) which are in and around their organizations. It is the interaction of the manager with people and systems that creates the challenge and also provides the opportunities for doing management effectively.

What is the primary focus of management? In our view it is the coordination of organizational activities and the securing of cooperation between and among organizational players (people and departments). Most textbooks deal with the functions managers engage in to establish and maintain such coordination. To help people learn about these functions, typical text headings and content deal with topics such as Planning, Organizing, Leading, Communicating, and Control. We have organized the material in *Managerial Reality* to reflect these traditional frameworks. As we have stated earlier, however, we believe that doing management is a complex balancing act and is much more dynamic than such functional categories suggest. Our choice of articles reflects this belief.

The essence of this balancing act can be understood by a simple framework that emphasizes three major organizational issues and the tensions between and among these issues. First, there is the issue of *doing things right,* that is, management that strives to use the logically correct techniques, plans, systems, and behaviors to coordinate the affairs of the organization. It involves an emphasis on managing "by the book," the book being whatever has been determined as the technically correct activity or procedure. These are the systems of selection, planning, appraisal, law developed in the abstract, in the laboratory, or in the "ivory tower." This is the realm of the manager as *technician.* Second, there is the issue of *doing the right thing,* of doing what is feasible, that is making the appropriate decisions and performing the appropriate coordinating activities, *given the circumstances in which the manager finds him or herself,* working with the personnel and resources available at a particular time and place. The manager takes action that is feasible given the contingencies of the actual situation. This is the realm of the manager as *pragmatist.*

Finally, there is the third issue—*What is right?* strategically and ethically, given the intentions of management and others (for example, employees, customers, stockholders, governments). What *should* the organization be doing to ensure its long-term effectiveness? What *should* managers be doing to ensure that everyone's rights, themselves included, are addressed? This is the realm of the manager as *strategist,* as *moralist.*

The articles in *Managerial Reality* capture these issues and the dilemmas managers face in deciding how, in doing management, they are to incor-

Figure 1

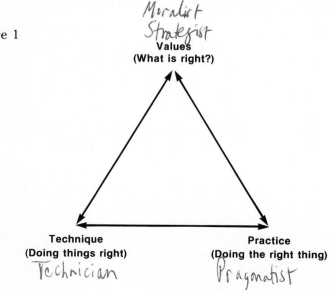

Moralist
Strategist
Values
(What is right?)

Technique   **Practice**
(Doing things right)   **(Doing the right thing)**
Technician   *Pragmatist*

porate logic (doing things right), pragmatic realities (doing the right things), and strategic and ethical pressures and considerations (deciding what is right).

Take, for example, the management of performance, and in particular, the appraisal of individual performance. Managers engaged in the appraisal of others must balance the technical requirements of appraisal (which are typically mandated by specialists in human resources and employment law) and the practical realities of their own objectives as managers, the circumstances surrounding the performance of their subordinates, and the particular qualities (skills, abilities, and intentions) of their subordinates.

Human resource managers typically want line managers to carry out performance appraisals that conform to the currently accepted behavioral theories and to company policy. Line managers on the other hand may want to bend, modify, or even ignore many of the technical and policy requirements of the performance appraisal system. They may do this to increase the performance of their subordinates, to make an example out of one subordinate so as to influence the actions of other subordinates, or even to move an unwanted employee out of their department. Managers acting in these ways act pragmatically, doing what they believe is the right thing in their efforts to meet personal and organizational goals.

Two excerpts from the article "Behind the Mask: The Politics of Employee Appraisal,"[2] (in Section 7, Managing Human Resources) illustrate this tension between the technical (doing it right) and practical (doing the right thing) aspects of managing performance appraisal.

Employee appraisal as a technique, as something to be done right is illustrated by the following statement:

> At some places the PA (performance appraisal) process is a joke—just a bureaucratic thing that the manager does to keep the IR (industrial relations) people off his back . . . (Longenecker, et al., 1987, p. 186)

The manager is expected to "do it right." "Right" in this case is seen to be rigid and narrow and of limited use to the operating manager.

On the other hand, to meet pragmatic realities (for example, to do the right things), managers sometimes choose to "adapt" techniques to suit the purposes they see as important, to meet the contingencies they face. For example . . .

> As a manager, I will do what is best for my people and the division. . . . I've used it to get my people better raises in lean years, to kick a guy in the pants if he really needed it, to pick up a guy when he was down or even to tell him he was no longer welcome here. It is a tool the manager should use to help him do what it takes to get the job done. I believe most of us here at _____ operate this way regarding appraisals. Accurately describing an employee's performance is really not as important as generating ratings that keep things cooking. (Longenecker, et al., 1987, p. 185)

The clash between the technical and practical requirements facing the manager quickly conjures up the What is right? question and thus, another balance point. What should the manager do? From a strategic point of view, the clash will likely be between those managers wanting to maintain an equitable and coherent system of evaluation (that is, the Human Resource or Personnel Managers) and those who will argue that anything goes to deal with what they face in the trenches. For example, line managers will likely argue that they are responsible for the bottom line, for making things happen, and should thus have the last word. The strategic aspect of employee appraisal is illustrated in the following statement by a manager:

> *This thing (the appraisal process) can really turn into an interesting game when the HR (Human Resource) people come out with a blanket statement like "Money for raises is tight this year and since superior performers get 7% to 10% raises there will be no superior performers this year." Talk about making things rough for us (raters)! . . . They try to force you to make the ratings fit the merit allowances instead of vice versa. (Longenecker, et al., 1987, p. 185)*

Resolution, in such a case, will come in part from which goals in the strategic plans of the organization are given more weight in practice and in part from who has more power in the organization, the technical specialists or the practical managers. Accomplishing balance between technique, practice, and strategy in managing performance appraisal is illustrated in the following excerpt from the same article:

> *At the last couple of places I've worked, the formal review process is taken really seriously; they train you how to conduct a good interview, how to handle problems, how to coach and counsel. . . . You see the things [appraisals] reviewed by your boss, and he's serious about reviewing your performance in a thorough manner. . . . I guess the biggest thing is that people are led to believe that* it is a management tool that works; it's got to start at the top! *(emphasis added) (Longenecker, et al., 1987, p. 186)*

One of the issues that frustrates human resource specialists in many organizations is that they are consistently caught in the tension between technique and practice but rarely invited to contribute to the resolution of the strategic question. Nor is their perspective on the morality of organizational action much listened to.

From an ethical point of view, what is right becomes an issue of fairness in the system, between and among individuals. Should exceptions be made to a system to meet individual requirements and circumstances? What are the consequences for the individuals concerned, for the manager, for the organization? (Section 9, Managing Ethically, deals squarely with these issues of doing management.) Of course, the growing importance of the legalities of management's activities provides a direct bridge between ethics and strategy as well as between the techniques and practices of management. Increasingly there are very real consequences for managers and organizations associated with their ignorance of, or noncompliance with, employment law.

In general, one can see that the dilemmas of "doing management" while facing these issues revolves around the following kinds of imbalance:

Overemphasis on the technical aspects of planning without taking into account the practical realities managers face in getting the job done can lead to such things as endless bureaucratic hoops, paper chases, "analysis-paralysis" and frequently a frustrated core of line managers. Some fine examples of this condition are included in "Business Fads: What's In and What's Out." In that article Donald Frey, CEO of Bell and Howell notes: "We went down to Wright Patterson Air Force Base, where they had PERT charting down to a science. They had more guys working on PERT charts than they had doing the job."

Overemphasis on the practical, day-to-day demands and contingencies of doing management, on the other hand, can lead to narrow, rigid behaviors and techniques and resistance to changes in systems and techniques that have become outmoded. This is part of the reason the automakers in Detroit got into such difficulties when the revolutionary change in oil prices hit North America in the 1970s (see "Maxwell's Warning" in Section 1).

Efforts to blend effectively the technical and practical requirements of work can be seen in many of the articles in the book, including those that discuss the systematic (rather than faddish) use of Quality Circles in organizations (see, for example, "Revolution by Evolution: The Changing Relationship between GM and the UAW" and "Quality Circle Leader").

Overemphasis on strategy without attention to plans and systems can lead to empty rhetoric or hollow vision. On the other hand, too much attention to plans and systems can kill the vision and cause people to lose sight of the strategy. Furthermore, the recognition of differences (differences in values, perceptions, and self-interests) that is implicit in a strategy can be lost when the attention is all on the mechanics of plans and on their implementation. We say more about this in later sections. Resolution of these tensions can come when managers with technical biases discover the role perception plays in organizational life (see "The Journey from Novice to Master Manager") and when leaders seek to link a vision or strategy with specific plans, techniques, and systems (see "The Greatest Capitalist in History").

Overemphasis on technique can also blind managers to the ethical implications of their behaviors. At the same time, a concern with ethics that does not establish a system for managing ethically is likely to confuse managers or to encourage them to discount ethical stances when dealing with organizational matters (see, for example, "James Gordon, Manager").

Finally, overemphasis on strategy in the absence of attention to practical realities facing managers and the organization is likely to yield ungrounded strategic plans, ones that misguide action or are ignored by managers (see, for example, "The Creation"). Conversely, an excessive concern with the day-to-day activities or a preoccupation with the short-run can prevent managers from seeing the big picture and from accurately interpreting how changes might affect their organizations in the long-run (see, for example, "Why Strategic Management Is Bankrupt"). Attempts to ground strategy in reality and to make what is present resemble what might be needed in the future are required (see "Ms. Raku" in Section 3).

In the real world of organizations, doing management requires attention to all these issues and their various interactions. Not all managers are responsible for determining strategy but all are involved in its implementation. All have a role to play in acting ethically (a complex issue in itself), being technically competent and practically effective. Balancing individual and organization, technical and human systems, social and organizational contexts and coordinating activities so that individual and organizational goals are met—is what doing management is all about.

About the Book

Managerial Reality is an anthology on management that is intended to portray through stories, anecdotes, reflections, and journalistic reports the richness, complexity, and excitement of management. We also hope to capture the diversity and challenge that managers face in their task of coordinating human effort in organizations. It chronicles the successes and failures of managers and the ethical and strategic dilemmas they wrestle with in getting their work done. It identifies some of the ways organizations penetrate the lives of managers at work and at home, at times creating opportunities for personal growth and career advancement but often creating hazards that managers must be alert to as they strive to balance organizational and personal agendas.

The book is organized around five basic principal elements of management frequently used in textbooks. These are Planning, Organizing, Leading, Controlling, and the Management of Human Resources. Emphasis is given to the broad contexts within which management takes place from its historical roots, and its social and political environments. Attention is also given to ethical issues affecting managers.

A fundamental theme of the book is that doing management involves finding balances between and among the technical, practical, strategic, and moral issues confronting today's managers. Management action in this context is illustrated at different levels from CEO to first-line supervisor.

Examples of management are drawn from a number of settings. In addition, two industries—automotive and computers—are featured in several articles spread throughout the book. These are major arenas of managerial activity in North America and in all post-industrial countries; they are of increasing importance in developing nations as well. The reader can easily isolate the automotive and the computer examples in the book and examine the many facets of managerial reality in them, treating them as complex case studies of management practice and experience.

We include articles that deal with both women and men. The organization of today and increasingly of tomorrow, involves women in key managerial roles. The experiences, successes, and failures of female managers in this book provide an opportunity to compare and contrast them with male managerial experiences and to explore the interaction between and among male and female managers.

We also give some attention in the choice of articles to the international management scene. We expect this to explode in the future and to create many new challenges and concerns for managers. What is learned from that experience will inform, in a significant way, the discussion of management, its role, functions, and activities.

We use a wide variety of sources including *Fortune, Business Week, U.S. News and World Report,* the *New York Times, Wall Street Journal, Harvard Business Review* as well as books and anthologies on management. The selections are durable and evocative.

We believe that this collection adds perspective to traditional books on management. In T. S. Eliot's "The Four Quartets" the statement is made that: "We had the experience but missed the meaning." We think that in trying to convey the meaning of management, textbook writers frequently miss or leave out the experience that provides the basis for the meaning they give to the activity. We believe that the articles, stories, and reports provided in *Managerial Reality,* in part, redress this imbalance by providing a sense of experience that illuminates the meanings given in management texts. We think the book also provides experiences that provide meaning that will carry us beyond the current academic wisdom we have about what management is all about.

We hope *Managerial Reality* proves informative and interesting to a wide range of readers (students, academics, managers) interested in a fascinating and important topic.

References

1. Drucker, P. F., *Management,* New York: Harper, 1973.
2. Longenecker, C. O., Gioia, D. A., and Sims, H. P., 1987, "Behind the Mask: The Politics of Employee Appraisal," *The Academy of Management Executive,* 1, 3, 183–193.

Balancing Technique, Practice, and Values

Managing: Its History, Challenge, and Nature

Peter Drucker is widely recognized as the world's leading authority on management. In our first article, Drucker observes that the rise of modern management is the most important development in recent history. The nature of our society and the quality of life are vitally linked to the knowledge, abilities, visions, and values of people who manage organizations.

Few people are apt to disagree with such an assertion. At the same time, unless we are followers of media that focus on the business world, the importance of management often remains latent in our everday awareness. Why do we pay so little attention to such important matters? What are the consequences of this inattention?

While there are many reasons for the inattention, several seem to stand out. First, most organizations are relatively private systems. It takes a great deal of effort to get "inside" them and see how they really operate. Even when we have a strong interest in a particular issue in an organization to which we belong, much of the vital information is protected. (For example, try to find out how the decision to deny a particular professor tenure or promotion was really made in your school.) Of course, if enough people were really interested in knowing, someone would find it profitable to hire a large number of investigators to bring such information into the open, as happens with respect to politics and governments. There are, however, many more business organizations than governments—it would take an enormous press corps to cover even a small percentage of these in any depth.

Second, the impact of any one organization seems less apt to have consequences for a large number of people than do most decisions made by governments. Even a proposal for a small increase in the admissions fee to a public park has a much more visible (but often less consequential) impact on a large number of people than all but a very small percentage of the decisions made by most private organizations.

Third, we believe there is a pervasive stereotype that management is a routine and hence not a very interesting process. Among other things we tend to see the enormous amount of quantitative and technical information that organizations have available to them. We assume that products are either desirable and well made or else the firm will fail. After all, the "bottom line" and the "invisible hand" appear to be pretty objective and exacting judges. Organizations that do not do the right things and/or do not do them correctly can be expected to fail. Consequently, it would *appear* that society can be reasonably confident that it is being well served by its organizations and those that run them and that there is not much exciting going on inside the organizations. In a society such as ours where prosperity is so observable, especially during the long period of prosperity which has spanned the total lives of most of us, it is easy to become quite complacent about management—even though, when we do think about it, we recognize its importance.

This complacency causes many members of society to fail to appreciate what management entails. As a result, the truly great achievements of men and women who do management are not appreciated. Moreover, the present and future issues that organizations need to address, if they are to serve society successfully, are overlooked. In short, the challenge of management is not recognized. We believe that the failure to recognize this challenge has potentially disastrous consequences for the future of society.

We also believe that the dimensions of the challenge can not be understood without getting inside of organizations and examining how they really operate. Once we get inside them, we find that the process is very exciting—sometimes as exciting as our favorite adventure stories and dramas and certainly as interesting as most of the events we see reported by the major media. The articles in this section were chosen to highlight the nature of management and its challenges. Taken together the articles show that doing things right, doing the right thing, and knowing what is right pose extremely difficult issues for managers.

The difficulties stem, in large measure, from the nature of organizations themselves. Two features are most salient. First, organizations need to achieve cooperation and coordination of a number of different individuals. Since each of these individuals is apt to have somewhat unique needs, emotions, and perceptions, achieving common direction is a very difficult challenge. Second, the context in which an organization exists (that is, its environment) is constantly changing. What is the right thing to do and the right way to do it are constantly changing. Similarly, what is right strategically and morally is not constant either.

Managers are responsible for achieving coordinated effort under these complex and changing conditions. Like other human beings who must take action but face complex and changing circumstances, managers often simplify the complexity. For example, they try to respond to today's problem using the same techniques that they used in the past or they search for a "quick fix"—the simple solution that will solve all the problems. To some degree, some simplification is essential. If the organization can never benefit from doing today what it learned to do yesterday, the costs would be enormous. Moreover, if every problem was approached in a way to take into account all its fine points and contingencies, action would be very slow if not impossible; by the time something was implemented, it would be obsolete. On the other hand, too much simplification or reliance on previous learning will lead the manager to navigate the organization according to a map that does not represent the terrain accurately.

Moreover, managers often lack precise instruments for directing the efforts of others. Most organizations have well-established procedures that they have used to move forward in the past. Neither they nor the people who operate them can be changed instantaneously. Even if one knows the right thing to do, what is right, and what is the right way to do it, does not mean that the organization is prepared to do any of the three.

Finally, there is the challenge of balancing the short run and the long run. Every individual, including the manager, will be part of an organization for a finite period of time. Since this period will often be shorter than the life of the organization, there are incentives for each individual to emphasize things that will produce benefits in a shorter period of time than might be good for the organization as an entity. The manager is responsible for the long-run well-being of the entity, but like any human being will be tempted to work in his/her own interests.

In short, the challenge of managing is to coordinate the actions of a variety of individuals who have different and often conflicting needs and perceptions, in order to achieve a viable organization that is able to respond to complex and changing environments. This result must be achieved using imperfect information and operating under the constraints imposed by structures and learning from the past. When we understand the nature of this challenge, it is hard to be complacent about managing. We hope these articles help you appreciate the nature of this challenge more deeply.

The Emergence of Management

Peter Drucker

During the last fifty years, society in every developed country has become a society of institutions. Every major social task, whether economic performance or health care, education or the protection of the environment, the pursuit of new knowledge or defense, is today being entrusted to big organizations, designed for perpetuity and managed by their own managements. On the performance of these institutions, the performance of modern society—if not the survival of each individual—increasingly depends.

Only seventy-five years ago such a society would have been inconceivable. In the society of 1900 the family still served in every single country as the agent of, and organ for, most social tasks. Institutions were few and small. The society of 1900, even in the most highly institutionalized country (e.g., Imperial Germany), still resembled the Kansas prairie. There was one eminence, the central government. It loomed very large on the horizon—not because it was large but because there was nothing else around it. The rest of society was diffused in countless molecules: small workshops, small schools, the individual professional—whether doctor or lawyer—practicing by himself, the farmer, the craftsman, the neighborhood retail store, and so on. There were the beginnings of big business—but only the beginnings. And what was then considered a giant business would strike us today as very small indeed.

The octopus which so frightened the grandparents of today's Americans, Rockefeller's giant Standard Oil Trust, was split into fourteen parts by the U.S. Supreme Court in 1911. Thirty years later, on the eve of America's entry into World War II, every single one of these fourteen Standard Oil daughters had become at least four times as large as the octopus when the Supreme Court divided it—in employment, in capital, in sales, and in every other aspect. Yet, among these fourteen there were only three major oil companies—Jersey Standard, Mobil, and Standard of California. The other eleven were small to fair-sized, playing little or no role in the world economy and only a limited role in the U.S. economy.

While business has grown in these seventy years, other institutions have grown much faster. There was no university in the world before 1914 that had much more than 6,000 students—and only a handful that had more than 5,000. Today the university of 6,000 students is a pygmy; there are even some who doubt that it is viable. The hospital, similarly, has grown from a marginal institution to which the poor went to die into the center of health care and a giant in its own right—and also into one of the most complex social institutions around. Labor unions, research institutes, and many others have similarly grown to giant size and complexity.

In the early 1900s the citizens of Zurich built themselves a splendid City Hall, which they confidently believed would serve the needs of the city for all time to come. Indeed, it was bitterly attacked by conservatives as gross extravagance, if not as megalomania. Government in Switzerland has grown far less than in any other country in the world. Yet the Zurich City Hall long ago ceased to be adequate to house all the offices of the city administration. By now, these offices occupy ten times or more the space that seventy-five years ago seemed so splendid—if not extravagant.

The Employee Society

The citizen of today in every developed country is typically an employee. He works for one of the institutions. He looks to them for his livelihood. He looks to them for his opportunities. He looks to them for access to status and function in society, as well as for personal fulfillment and achievement.

The citizen of 1900 if employed worked for a small family-type operation; the small pop-and-mom store employing a helper or two; the family household; and so on. And of course, the great majority of people in those days, except in the most highly industrialized countries—such as Britain or Belgium—worked on the farm.

Our society has become an employee society [emphasis added]. In the early 1900s people asked, "What do you do?" Today they tend to ask, "Whom do you work for?"

We have neither political nor social theory for the society of institutions and its new pluralism. It is, indeed, incompatible with the political and social theories which still dominate our view of society and our approach to political and social issues. We still use as political and social model what the great thinkers of the late sixteenth and seventeenth centuries, Bodin, Locke, Hume, and Harrington, codified: the society which knows no power centers and no autonomous institution, save only one central government. Reality has long outgrown this model—but it is still the only one we have.

A new theory to fit the new reality will be a long time coming. For new theory, to be more than idle speculation and vague dreaming, must come after the event. It codifies what we have already learned, have already achieved, have already done. But we cannot wait till we have the theory we need. We have to act. We have to use the little we know. And there is one thing we do know: management is the specific organ of the new institution, whether business enterprise or university, hospital or armed service, research lab or government agency. If institutions are to function, managements must perform.

The word "management" is a singularly difficult one. It is, in the first place, specifically American and can hardly be translated into any other language, not even into British English. It denotes a function but also the people who discharge it. It denotes a social position and rank but also a discipline and field of study.

But even within the American usage, management is not adequate as a term, for institutions other than business do not speak of management or managers, as a rule. Universities or government agencies have administrators, as have hospitals. Armed services have commanders. Other institutions speak of executives, and so on.

Yet all these institutions have in common the management function, the management task, and the management work. All of them require management. And in all of them, management is the effective, the active organ.

The institution itself is, in effect, a fiction. It is an accounting reality, but not a social reality. When this or that government agency makes this ruling or this decision, we know perfectly well that it is some people within the agency who make the ruling or the decision and who act for the agency and as the effective organ of the agency. When we speak of General Electric closing a plant, it is not, of course, General Electric that is deciding and acting, it is a group of managers within the company.

Georg Siemens, who built the Deutsche Bank into the European continent's leading financial institution in the decade between 1870 and 1880, . . . once said, "Without management, a bank is so much scrap, fit only to be liquidated." Without institution there is no management. But without management there is no institution. Management is the specific organ of the modern institution. It is the organ on the performance of which the performance and the survival of the institution depend.

Management Is Professional

We further know that *management is independent of ownership, rank, or power* [emphasis added]. It is objective function and ought to be grounded in the responsibility for performance. It is professional—management is a function, a discipline, a task to be done; and managers are the professionals who practice this discipline, carry out the functions, and discharge these tasks. It is no longer relevant whether the manager is also an owner; if he is, it is incidental to his main function, which is to be a manager. Eiichi Shibusawa's Confucian ideal of the "professional manager" in the early days of modern Japan . . . has become reality. And so has Shibusawa's basic insight that the essence of the manager is neither wealth nor rank, but responsibility.

From Business Society to Pluralism

The rhetoric of the New Left talks of our society as being a big-business society. But this is as outdated as the rhetoric of the New Left is altogether. Society in the West *was* a business society—seventy-five years ago. Then business was, indeed, the most powerful of all institutions—more powerful even than some governments. Since the turn of the century, however, the importance of business has gone down steadily—not because business has become smaller or weaker, but because the other institutions have grown so much faster. Society has become pluralist.

In the United States in the 1970s, no businessman compares in power or visibility with the tycoons of 1900, such as J. P. Morgan, John D. Rockefeller, or—a little later—Henry Ford. Few people today even know the names of the chief executive officers of America's biggest corporations; the names of the tycoons were household words. Not even the largest corporation today can compare in power and even in relative wealth with those tycoons who could hold the U.S. government for ransom.

It makes little sense to speak of the "military-industrial complex." The high level of defense spending in the United States has for many years been an economic depressant. It would make more sense to speak of the "military-university complex." No business today—in fact, no business in American history—has a fraction of the power that today's big university has. By granting or denying admission or the college degree, the university grants or denies access to jobs and livelihoods. Such power no business—and no other institution—ever had before in American history. Indeed, no earlier institution would ever have been permitted such power.

In Europe things are only slightly different. Business careers have become respectable to a degree unknown in 1900. They have gained equality with careers in government, in academic life, or in the military—all of which ranked socially much higher seventy-five years ago. But still there is no one in French business today whose influence and power can compare with that of the DeWendel family of steelmakers in the France of the Third Republic, or with the power which a few families of the Haute Banque exercised through their control of the Banque de France and of French money and credit policy. There is no businessman and no business enterprise in Germany today that can compare in power and influence with the Krupps and other steel barons of 1900, or with I. G. Farben in the 1920s. There is no business executive in today's England who can compare in power and influence with the merchant banking families who, almost down to the 1930s, ran the Bank of England and, through it, the British Treasury, as family fiefs.

Of all contemporary societies, Japan can most nearly be described as a business society. Business management has greater influence in Japan than in any other developed country. But even in Japan, there is no business manager today and no business enterprise whose power and influence stand comparison with the power and influence which the great Zaibatsu concerns of 1900 or 1920—Mitsubishi, Mitsui, Sumitomo, and Yasuda—exerted on economy and society alike.

In the United States of 1900, almost the only career opportunity open to the young and ambitious was business. Today there are untold others, each promising as much (or more) income, and advancement as rapid as a career in business.

Around the turn of the century, whatever of the gross national product did not go to the farmer went in and through the private business economy. The nonbusiness service institutions, beginning with government, accounted probably for no more than 10 percent of the nonfarm gross national product of the United States at the turn of the century and up till World War I. Today, while farming has largely become a business, more than half of the gross national product goes to or through service institutions which are not businesses and which are not held accountable for economic performance nor subject to market test.

Well over a third of the gross national product in the United States today goes directly to governments, federal, state, and local. Another 3 to 5 percent goes to nongovernmental schools, that is, private and parochial, including the nongovernmental colleges and universities. Another 5 percent of GNP, that is, two-thirds of the total health-care bill, is also nongovernmental, but also nonbusiness. On top of this, there is a great variety of not-for-profit activities, accounting maybe for another 2 to 5 percent of gross national product. This adds up to 50 or perhaps as much as 60 percent of the GNP which does not go to the business sector but to, or through, public-service institutions.

Indeed, while the New Left talks of the big-business society, its actions show a keen awareness that business is not the dominant institution. Every period of public unrest since the end of the Napoleonic Wars began with uprisings against business. But the revolt against authority that swept the developed countries in the sixties centered in the institutions—especially the university—which were most esteemed by yesterday's radicals and which were, so to speak, the good guys of organization thirty or forty years ago.

The nonbusiness, public-service institutions do not need management less than business. They may need it more.

There is growing concern with management in nonbusiness institutions.

Among the best clients of the large American management consulting firms these last ten or fifteen years have been government agencies such as the Department of Defense, the city of New York, or the Bank of England. When Canada in the late sixties first created a unified military service, with army, navy, and air force all combined, the first conference of Canadian generals and admirals was not on strategy; it was on "management by objectives." The venerable orders of the Catholic Church are engaged in organization studies and in management development, with the Jesuits in the lead.

A generation or two ago, the German civil service knew that it had the answers. But now, the city of Hamburg—long known for its excellence in public administration—has created a management center for its civil service and has made management the responsibility of one of the senior members of the city's government. Even the British civil service has been reorganized with the objective of introducing "management."

An increasing number of students in advanced management courses are not business executives but executives from hospitals, from the armed services, from city and state governments, and from school administrations. The Harvard Business School even runs an increasingly popular advanced management course for university presidents.

The management of the nonbusiness institutions will indeed be a growing concern from now on. Their management may well become the central management problem—simply because the lack of management of the public-service institution is such a glaring weakness, whether municipal water department or graduate university.

And yet, *business management is the exemplar.* And any book on management, such as this one, has to put business management in the center.

Why Business Management Has to Be the Focus

One reason is history. Business enterprise was the first of the modern institutions to emerge. From the beginning, that is, from the emergence of the railroads and the "universal banks" as large businesses in the late nineteenth century, business enterprise was unmistakably a new and different institution rather than an outgrowth of older ones, as were apparently government agency, university, hospital, and armed service. There was, of course, concern about management in other institutions.* But until recently it was sporadic and undertaken usually in connection with an acute problem and confined to it. But the work on management in business and industry was from the beginning meant to be generic and continuous.

Another reason why the study of management to this day has primarily been a study of business management is that so far the economic sphere alone has measurements both for the allocation of resources and for the results of decisions. Profitability is not a perfect measurement; no one has even been able to define it, and yet it is a measurement, despite all its imperfections. None of the other institutions has measurements so far. All they have are opinions—which are hardly an adequate foundation for a discipline.

The most important reason for focusing on business management is that it is the success story of this century. It has performed within its own sphere. It has provided economic goods and services to an extent that would have been unimaginable to the generation of 1900. And it has performed despite world wars, depressions, and dictatorships.

The achievement of business management enables us today to promise—perhaps prematurely (and certainly rashly)—the abolition of the grinding poverty that has been mankind's lot through the ages. It is largely the achievement of business management that advanced societies today can afford mass higher education. Business both produces the economic means to support this expensive undertaking and offers the jobs in which knowledge can become productive and can be paid for. That we today consider it a social flaw and an imperfection of society for people to be fixed in their opportunities and jobs by class and birth—where only yesterday this was the natural and apparently inescapable condition of mankind—is a result of our economic performance, that is, of the performance of business management. In a world that is politically increasingly fragmented and obsessed by nationalism, business management is one of the very few institutions capable of transcending national boundaries.

---

*The work of Elihu Root as Secretary of War on the organization of the General Staff of the U.S. Army is an American example; the work of Adickes and Micquel as big-city mayors and ministers of the Crown on local government in Germany is another; both were done between 1900 and 1910.

The multinational corporation brings together in a common venture management people from a great many countries with different languages, cultures, traditions, and values, and unites them in a common purpose. It is one of the very few institutions of our world that is not nationalistic in its world view, its values, and its decisions; but truly a common organ of a world economy that, so far, lacks a world polity.

It is also business management to which our society increasingly looks for leadership in respect to the quality of life. Indeed, what sounds like harsh criticism of business management tends often to be the result of high, perhaps unrealistically high, expectations based on the past performance of business management. "If you can do so well, why don't you do better?" is the underlying note. . . .

The emergence of management may be the pivotal event of our time, far more important than all the events that make the headlines. Rarely, if ever, has a new basic institution, a new leading group, a new central function, emerged as fast as has management since the turn of the century. Rarely in human history has a new institution proven indispensable so quickly. Even less often has a new institution arrived with so little opposition, so little disturbance, so little controversy. And never before has a new institution encompassed the globe as management has, sweeping across boundaries of race and creed, language and traditions, within the lifetime of many men still living and at work.

Today's developed society, sans aristocracy, sans large landowners, even sans capitalists and tycoons, depends for leadership on the managers of its major institutions. It depends on their knowledge, on their vision, and on their responsibility. In this society, management—its tasks, its responsibilities, its practices—is central: as a need, as an essential contribution, and as a subject of study and knowledge.

———————————————●———————————————

Business Fads: What's in—and out

*Executives Latch on to Any Management Idea
That Looks Like a Quick Fix*

John A. Byrne

Allan A. Kennedy had just delivered his $5,000, 90-minute pep talk on corporate culture to a select group of top executives of an industrial-service corporation.

The show was slick. Kennedy, a former McKinsey & Co. consultant and co-author of *Corporate Cultures,* had run through his chat on company rituals some 200 times. "By now I've got an act that could play on Broadway," he says.

Yet even Kennedy was taken aback by the audience's enthusiasm when the curtain came down. "This corporate culture stuff is great," the chairman raved at dinner following the talk. Then, turning to his president, he demanded, "I want a culture by Monday."

Astonishing as it may seem, the executive was serious. There is, of course, merit in Kennedy's belief that a corporation's culture—its shared values, beliefs and rituals—strongly influences its success or failure. But it would seem obvious to most executives that a culture must be built over years, not ordained overnight.

Or would it? Like Kennedy's client, a lot of American executives these days seem eager to latch on to almost any new concept that promises a quick fix for their problems.

Having trouble developing new products? Try "intrapreneurship," the process for getting entrepreneurial juices flowing in a big company.

Having a tough time competing against the Japanese? Try "quality circles," the managerial export from Japan that has U.S. workers and managers sitting around tables finding ways to increase productivity and ensure quality.

Having problems with employee productivity? Try "wellness," the new buzzword for fitness programs that encourage managers to exercise, eat healthy foods, and stop smoking.

Facing the threat of a hostile takeover? Restructure your company by writing off a mature business and taking on a mountain of debt. Wall Street will almost surely respond by jacking up your stock price, and that should keep the raider at bay.

Hollow Symbols. There's nothing inherently wrong with any of these ideas. What's wrong is that too many companies use them as gimmicks to evade the basic challenges they face. Unless such solutions are well thought out and supported by a sincere commitment from top management, they are doomed to fail. They quickly become meaningless buzzwords, hollow symbols, mere fads.

Even more disturbing is how these fads change, often by 180°. In the 1960s it seemed everyone wanted to diversify, to become a conglomerate. Today, an opposite trend has emerged under the fancy rubric of "asset redeployment." It's the term for conceding that a past diversification spree was a mistake, for spinning off businesses and getting back to the basics.

Or take strategic planning. In the late 1970s it was all the rage. Following the lead of General Electric Co., many companies hired planners at corporate headquarters to chart the future plans of their businesses. Today corporate planning staffs have been substantially reduced or eliminated, because it makes more sense for line managers, closer to the business, to plot strategy.

Business fads are something of a necessary evil and have always been with us. What's different—and alarming—today is the sudden rise and fall of so many conflicting fads and how they influence the modern manager.

What's hot right now? "Touchy-feely" managers who are "demassing." Translation: Nice-guy bosses are laying off still more workers. Other companies are forming "strategic alliances"—launching a joint venture with their No. 1 competitor, perhaps, to plug a product or technology void. The thoroughly modern corporation wants to turn its managers into "leaders" and "intrapreneurs" through "pay for performance." Those same managers flock to Outward Bound expeditions to learn survival skills.

On the other hand, autocratic bosses are out. So are the corporate planners and economists who not long ago pontificated on "reindustrialization," "synergy," and "management by objectives." On the way out: the hostile takeover wave that has dominated business for the past two years, the raiders who used junk bonds, and the golden parachutes that managers devised to protect themselves from the raiders.

And so it goes, to the consternation of those whose task it is to run a business. "Last year it was quality circles," says Harvey Gittler, a Borg-Warner Corp. manager in Elyria, Ohio. "This year it is zero inventories. The truth is, one more panacea and we will all go nuts."

He is not alone in this feeling. A marketing manager with a big Midwest equipment maker feels whipsawed. "In the past 18 months, we have heard that profit is more important than revenue, that quality is more important than profit, that people are more important than profit, that customers are more important than our people, that big customers are more important than small customers, and that growth is the key to our success," he recounts. "No wonder our performance is inconsistent."

One new fad seems to be an attempt to clear up some of this confusion. Some large companies, including General Motors Corp. and Ford Motor Co., have issued managers glossy, pocket-sized cards to remind them of their companies' guiding principles—a key ingredient of their changing corporate cultures. Ford's mission statement—handed out last March—was two years in the making, involved hundreds of employees, and was O.K.'d by its board of directors. Some GM managers have been issued as many as three reminders, each adorned with a mug shot or two of the top brass. Call it Management by Card.

Why the proliferation of business fads? And why have they become more ephemeral than ever? Perhaps it's because many managers are frustrated by their inability to compete in a world marketplace. Or perhaps it's because they are under intense pressure from Wall Street to perform short-term miracles. The result is a mad, almost aimless scramble for instant solutions. "We're all looking for magic," explains Thomas R. Horton, president of the American Management Assn. "If you tell me I can avoid a cold by taking half a pound of Vitamin C, I'll want to believe you even if it only gives me indigestion."

The search has fueled an industry of instant management gurus, new-idea consultants, and an endless stream of books promising the latest quick fix. Indeed, when it came time for Ralph H. Kilmann, a University of Pittsburgh business professor, to concoct a title for his new management book, he settled on *Beyond the Quick Fix,* in itself a reflection of how faddishness has come to dominate management thinking.

The book's point will probably be lost on many managers, however. A major corporation recently asked Kilmann if he could give its top 50 officers a seminar on his new book in only 15 minutes. "You mean you want me to do *Beyond the Quick Fix* quickly," he responded. The author declined the invitation.

Tangled Webs. It is not clear how big a threat this rash of palliative trends poses. Business fads have waxed and waned through the decades, yet corporations survive. Faddish ideas began to influence U.S. executives in a major way with the emergence of the professional manager in America after World War II. Seat-of-the-pants management was becoming old hat. Instead it became popular to follow the principles of Frederick Winslow Taylor, the inventor of time-and-motion studies 50 years earlier. He contended that running a company should be more a science than an art.

Managers rushed to try scientific methods, such as observation, experimentation, and reasoning. They immersed themselves in quantitative analysis. "Operations research" became the rallying cry. By itself, not a bad idea. But the success of operations research begat a series of unintelligible acronyms and buzzwords and an avalanche of charts, curves, and diagrams.

Remember PERT? Program Evaluation & Review Technique charts were spiderweb-like diagrams to ensure that projects would be completed on time. "We all did them," recalls Donald N. Frey, chief executive of Bell & Howell Co. "But it took so much effort to get the charts done, you might as well have spent the time getting the job done."

Frey, then a young manager at Ford, had a rude awakening about PERT's pitfalls. "We went to Wright Patterson Air Force base, where they had PERT charting down to a science. They had more guys working on PERT charts than they had doing the job. It was an enormous overhead cost just to allow the generals to show visitors their PERT charts."

Executives also found that management by objectives, another 1950s invention, often tangled them in paper. "We got so balled up in the details that we spent more time on paperwork than the whole damn thing was worth," says George W. Baur, president of Hughes Tool Co.'s tool division.

Mainframe Monkeys. When the mainframe computer came along in the 1950s, it contributed to the mounting pile of paper. Many companies installed computers in rooms with huge display windows to show them off. "A lot of people got computers because GE got them," says Ian Wilson, a 26-year GE veteran now with the Stanford Research Institute. "It was monkey see, monkey do."

When GE decentralized its operations in 1950, scores of companies followed, thinking that this was the antidote for corporate bureaucracies. Similar moves became so fashionable that almost no executive could be heard advocating centralized management. That is, until some companies discovered that decentralizing led to more vice-presidents who built up their own cumbersome fiefdoms and gave line managers even less autonomy.

Centralized companies decentralized and then some decentralized corporations centralized. "It depended on which consultant you hired," remembers Donald P. Jacobs, dean of Northwestern's Kellogg School of Management.

In the 1960s a wave of "people-oriented" management thinkers gained prominence. Many of the fads they promoted mirrored social trends. T-Groups, group encounter sessions for executives, came into vogue as the Beatles and Bob Dylan sang to a new, less bridled generation. Their popularity heralded the start of the touchy-feely approach to business; "sensitive," participative managers started sharing the spotlight with the management-by-numbers conglomerateurs who dominated the times. The new managers espoused Theory Y, a model for participative management created by a Massachusetts Institute of Technology management professor, Douglas McGregor, in the 1950s. It was the beginning of the end for Theory X, an authoritarian form of governance that grew out of managers' World War II military experiences.

Oh, how the times had changed. John Clemens, then a young, freshly scrubbed manager for Pillsbury and now a Hartwick College professor, remembers it well. Along with 20 or so colleagues, he was summoned to a country-club meeting room to face a bearded, rather hip, psychiatrist. The T-Group trainer, Clemens recalls, instructed them to take off their ties, shoes, and name tags. Then the lights went out.

"We began crawling on the floor in the dark when I bumped into our president," he says. "It was atrocious. We would have done better figuring out how to sell more brownie mix."

Tens of thousands of managers from such companies as IBM, TRW, Union Carbide, and Weyerhaeuser trekked to T-Group sessions in search of self-awareness and sensitivity. The concept, popularized by National Training Laboratories, was simple: Mix a dozen or more people together in a room without a leader or an agenda and see what happens. Often, delegates would hurl personal insults across a room. The resulting "feedback," it was hoped, would make Theory X managers less bossy and more participative.

Plotting People. As the decade came to an end, T-Groups gave way to Grid-Groups. And T-Grouped managers such as Clemens became G-Grouped quickly enough. Launched by Robert R. Blake and Jane S. Mouton's *The Managerial Grid* in 1964, the grid rated managers on two characteristics—concern for people vs. concern for production. "The beauty of it is that you could plot people all over the place," adds Clemens. "If you scored a high concern for people and a low concern for production, people would say, 'This guy's a wimp. He's a 1-9.' If you had a high concern for production (9-1), you were a dictator."

In the decade of the MBA, the 1970s, it was perhaps inevitable that the numbers-oriented students turned out by the B-schools would help to make strategic planning *de rigueur*. Another approach pioneered by GE, it caught the fancy of many executives. "After we put in our strategic planning system

Management Lingo: How to Read Between the Lines

What's Out	*What's In*
Centralization Father knows best.	**Asset Redeployment** Divest losers; put your money where the growth is. Redeal. Pray for a better hand.
Conglomerates Napoleon tried it, so did Harold Geneen. Enough said.	
Consultants Company doctors. At least they still make house calls.	**Back to Basics** Where you go when your synergistic move into high tech flops.
Corporate Planners Worrying about tomorrow's problems. It's more fun than worrying about today's.	**Chapter 11** A new way to break labor contracts or to sidestep liability suits.
Decentralization Then again, maybe Father doesn't know best.	**Corporate Culture** Get everybody singing the same song and hope they're in key.
Experience Curve Fight for market share. What you lose on each sale, you'll make up on volume.	**Demassing** Slimming down at the top. The latest euphemism for firing people.
Factory of the Future Robot heaven. Not yet available on earth.	**Intrapreneurship** Discovering the entrepreneurs in your own ranks. That may be easier than keeping the bureaucracy at bay once you do.
Golden Parachutes The executive safety net. The problem is, not everybody's a highflier.	**Leveraged Buyouts** Trading the short-term expectations of your stockholders for the short-term expectations of your bankers and bondholders.
Management by Objectives Here an objective, there an objective, everywhere an objective.	
Management by Walking Around The ultimate open-door policy. A few steps too far?	**Niches** Markets your competitors haven't found. Yet.
One-minute Managing Balancing reward and punishment in managing your employees. The executive equivalent of paper-training your dog.	**Out-sourcing** When you can't afford to make it yourself.
	Pay for Performance It used to be known as piecework.
Quantitative Management The numbers tell it all. Except what to do next.	**Restructuring** Writing down and leveraging up.
Raiders The thrill is gone. Ask Carl Icahn.	**Skunk Camp** Officially, a management seminar. Unofficially, it's a boot camp with Tom Peters.
Reindustrialization The crusade to revive Smokestack America. Back to the future?	**Strategic Alliances** Losing market share? Sign on with the competition.
Synergy Genetic engineering for corporations. But don't forget, when you cross a horse with a donkey, the result is a mule.	**Touchy-Feely Managers** The boss is a really nice guy. He's also still the boss.
T-Groups Building team spirit. . . .	**Wellness** Part of the health craze. You'll know it's arrived when they stop serving lemon meringue pie in the company cafeteria.
Theory Y A form of participatory management. You really do have a say in how things are run. Sure you do.	
Theory Z The art of Japanese management. For those who've forgotten the ABCs of American management.	

By Stuart Jackson in New York

in 1970, we were deluged with people from around the world wanting to talk to us about it," recalls GE alumnus Walker.

Some of these visitors failed to distinguish between form and substance. They became engrossed in the mechanics of setting up a planning system rather than focusing on finding the answers, says Harvard business school's Michael E. Porter. "Too often it became a function of shuffling papers with no underlying value."

Dog Stars. Porter was one of the many consultants who helped make strategic planning a buzzword. Consultants have always had a role in launching fads. They sold managers on psychological tools such as the Thematic Apperception Test in the 1950s. (Executives were told to conjure up stories based on series of pictures.) They also peddled sensitivity training in the 1960s. But consultants have been working overtime to roll out new fads since the 1970s.

One of the most rapidly spreading and widely used theories ever to emerge was the gospel according to Bruce D. Henderson's Boston Consulting Group Inc. Henderson put cows, dogs, stars, and question marks on matrix charts in hundreds of executive suites. Businesses were put into such categories as cash cows (mature companies that could be milked) and dogs (marginal performers in a market with poor prospects).

Fads multiplied in the 1980s as U.S. executives grappled for ways to contend with foreign competition—so much so that management by best-seller came into vogue . . . . William Ouchi's *Theory Z* and Richard Pascale and Anthony Athos' *The Art of Japanese Management* were the first such best-sellers when published in 1981. Both books pushed U.S. companies to adopt such Japanese management techniques as quality circles and job enrichment.

Some wags wondered if U.S. managers would soon be issued kimonos and be required to eat with chopsticks. "There wasn't an American manager who wasn't talking about it four years ago," says James J. O'Toole, a management professor at the University of Southern California. But when O'Toole's *New Management* magazine recently asked readers to name the most influential management books in recent years, not a single reader mentioned *Theory Z.*

Theory Z is still having an impact, however. Quality circles, an updated version of the employee suggestion programs and labor-management councils of the 1950s, are still in. In 1979, the International Association of Quality Circles had only 200 members. Now membership is almost 8,000.

Immortality. Why such mass popularity? Edward E. Lawler III, director of the University of Southern California's Center for Effective Organizations, says that QCs are partly a fad. "In a number of cases we studied," says Lawler, "the CEO of the company had seen a TV program or read a magazine article on QCs and decided to give them a try. Circles were simply something the top told the middle to do to the bottom."

Quality circles may be helping some companies improve productivity, though they have received mixed reviews. Koppers Co. installed QCs in 1981 at a plant in Follansbee, W. Va. They flopped when Koppers axed half the work force. Now it's trying a program called PITCH—for People Involved in Totally Changing History. The jury is still out on PITCH, but outsiders wonder how seriously employees will take a program that seems to promise immortality for working at a plant that makes creosote roofing tar.

Taking the best-seller even further were consultants Thomas J. Peters and Robert H. Waterman Jr. Their *In Search of Excellence,* published in 1982, added Skunk Works, Management By Walking Around, and Stick to Your Knitting to the manager's vocabulary.

One *Excellence*-type slogan caught on more widely than any other: "People are our most important asset." But how seriously did executives take it? One major property and casualty insurer adopted this motto two years ago, promoting it in its annual report and in management memos. Yet as one divisional manager grouses, there was no real commitment. "Since the introduction of that campaign, our training budget has been cut in half and our employee profit-sharing plan has been eliminated," he says. "We've laid off 1,000 staff members. Our tuition reimbursement program has been dissolved, and the athletic center has been closed. A lot of those important assets are looking for new jobs."

Pies and Salads. Some of the folks who promote new management ideas will even call a fad a fad. Take wellness, fitness programs that attempt to get employees to eat salads instead of hamburgers. "We feel it probably has a two- to three-year life cycle," figures Robert G. Cox, president of PA Executive Search Group. Cox's consulting outfit tells potential clients that managers who smoke cost them $4,000 annually in lower productivity and higher absenteeism.

On a recent engagement, PA's consultants stood duty in a corporation's cafeteria. "We noticed they picked up a lot of desserts when they went through the cafeteria line," relates Cox. "We also noticed that the lemon meringue pie was at the beginning of the line and the salads were in the back." The consultants' solution: switching the pies and the salads.

In many cases, a fad lasts as long as the boss is interested. "Our CEO got very excited about wellness two years ago," confides a personnel manager for a major transportation company. "We all went through stress-management programs, got rewarded for stopping smoking, and had to read *Fit or Fat.* But last year wasn't profitable, and now all of that has stopped."

And today there is intense competition for the executive's attention. A slew of instant gurus have emerged to spread the differing gospels, each with a proprietary lexicon of his own. Gifford Pinchot talks of intrapreneurship. Allan Kennedy talks of corporate culture. Ichak Adizes, a self-styled "organizational therapist" based in Santa Monica, Calif., advocates consensus-building meetings and brainstorming sessions.

Dirty Hands. Adizes has the ear of BankAmerica President Samuel H. Armacost. The banker was introduced to the Yugoslavia-born consultant by board director Charles R. Schwab in 1983 via cassette tape. Armacost, says

Adizes, listened to his "Adizes Method Audio Series" until 2 A.M. one night and was so impressed that he arranged a retreat with the consulting whiz for top management at the posh Silverado Country Club in Napa County.

The upshot? The Adizes method cost BofA an estimated $3 million. Top managers, figures one BofA officer, spent much of their time trying to build consensus under the method. "Several senior guys were spending half their time in these meetings for months on end," says one insider. Adds a consultant who worked with the bank: "The real fix would have been to fire five levels of management so the top guys could get their hands dirty." A bank spokesman says Adizes helped reorganize the bank into two divisions.

The impact goes well beyond the waste of time and resources. Companies risk losing the support and confidence of their people. "The people below are often laughing at the senior management," says consultant Kilmann. "They are saying, 'How stupid can you be?'"

A little faddishness may be helpful because it makes managers think about new ways to do their jobs better. In earlier decades, fads appear to have had that effect. They tended to be in fashion for years, if not decades, and did less harm. They seemed less goofy, too.

Today, the bewildering array of fads pose far more serious diversions and distractions from the complex task of running a company. Too many modern managers are like compulsive dieters: trying the latest craze for a few days, then moving restlessly on.

The Journey from Novice to Master Manager

Bob Quinn

As I listened to the man sitting in front of me, my mind ran backwards across the interviews that I had just completed. His subordinates and peers had given him glowing reviews: "Born to manage." "A great role model." "He is one person I am glad to work for."

As I tried to ask him questions that would unlock the mystery behind his success, an interesting story began to unfold. It seemed to involve both a crisis and a transformation.

After graduating from a five-year engineering program in four years, he had taken a job with his current organization. He had made a brilliant start and was promoted four times in eight years. He had the ability to take a complex technical problem and come up with a better answer than anyone else could. Initially he was seen as an innovative, action-oriented person with a bright future.

After his last promotion, however, everything started to change. He went through several very difficult years. For the first time he received serious negative feedback about his performance. His ideas and proposals were regularly rejected, and he was even passed over for a promotion. In reflecting on those days, he said:

> *It was awful. Everything was always changing and nothing ever seemed to happen. The people above me would sit around forever and talk about things. The technically right answer didn't matter. They were always making what I thought were wrong decisions, and when I insisted on doing what was right, they got pissed off and would ignore what I was saying. Everything was suddenly political. They would worry about what everyone was going to think about every issue. How you looked, attending cocktail parties—that stuff to me was unreal and unimportant. . . .*

On several occasions, the engineer's boss commented that he was very impressed with one of the engineer's subordinates. Finding the comment somewhat curious, the engineer finally asked for an explanation. The boss indicated that no matter how early he himself arrived at work, the subordinate's car was always there.

The engineer went to visit the subordinate and relayed that he had noticed that the subordinate always arrived at work before he did. The subordinate nodded his head and explained: "I have four teen-agers who wake up at dawn. The mornings at my house are chaotic. So I come in early. I read for awhile, then I write in my personal journal, read the paper, have some coffee, and then I start work at eight."

When the engineer left his subordinate's office, he was at first furious. But after a couple of minutes, he sat down and started to laugh. He later told me, "That is when I discovered perception." He went on to say that from that moment everything started to change. He became more patient. He began to experiment with participative decision making. His relationships with superiors gradually improved. Eventually he actually came to appreciate the need to think and operate in more complex ways at the higher levels of the organization. . . .

> *In the end, the frustration and pain turned out to be a positive thing because it forced me to consider some alternative perspectives. I eventually learned that there were other realities besides the technical reality.*
>
> *I discovered perception and long time lines. At higher levels what matters is how people see the world, and everyone sees it a little differently. Technical facts are not as available or as important. Things are changing more rapidly at higher levels, you are no longer buffered from the outside world. Things are more complex, and it takes longer to get people on board. I decided I had to be a lot more receptive and a lot more patient. It was an enormous adjustment, but then things started to change. I think I became a heck of a lot better manager.*

As a manger this man was not perfect. Clearly he had his share of bad days, and during the preceding year, a bad one for the industry, he had his share of defeats. There were occasions when he got discouraged and there were times when his subordinates felt he still acted too impulsively. Nevertheless, he had a wide range of capacities and most of the time displayed an ability to call upon them in successful ways. For the most part, he had become, with considerable effort, a master of management, a person with the capacity to create excellence.

---●---

Maxwell's Warning

David Halberstam

There had been plenty of warnings. Some experts had pointed out that the sources of oil were not limitless, that consumption was rising faster than production. Some noted that certain of the oil-producing countries were politically unstable and hostile to the United States. The men of the auto industry had never heeded the warnings. They dismissed them as veiled criticisms of the cars they were making.

In June 1973, a young man named Charley Maxwell flew from New York to Detroit to talk to the top executives of the three main auto companies. A decade later astute observers would mark that particular time, mid-1973, as the last moment of the old order in the industrialized world. It was a time when energy was still remarkably cheap and in steady supply, a time when the great business captains could still make their annual forecasts with some degree of certainty. Detroit was still Detroit in those heady days. It regularly sold eight million cars a year, and in a good year, a boomer's year, the kind loved by everyone in the business from the president of a company to the lowliest dealer, it sold ten or eleven million. More, these were precisely the kind and size of cars Detroit wanted to sell—big heavy cars loaded with expensive options. In those days no one talked about energy conservation except a few scholarly types. The average American car got about thirteen miles per gallon then, a figure far below that expected of cars in most other modern countries. Detroit's cars were large, weighty, and powerful. Comfort and power, rather than economy, seemed important in the marketplace. Americans were a big people, and they liked to drive long distances. If the cars were no longer of quite the quality many of the company engineers and manufacturing men wanted, this was deemed a matter of no great consequence, for they still sold. Anyone who complained about the quality of the cars was a quibbler, more than likely an egghead who subscribed to *Consumer Reports.* After all, a car need last no more than the three years before the owner turned it in for a brand-new model, which would be equally large, or, given the American presumption of rising social status, even larger. As the new car reflected the owner's climb, so the old car now began its own journey down the social scale, ending up an owner or two later in some ghetto inhabited by members of the American underclass. There, patched and repatched, it would consume even greater quantities of gas.

The intelligentsia of America, much given to driving small, fuel-efficient, rather cramped foreign cars, often mocked Detroit for the grossness and gaudiness of its product. To many liberal intellectuals Detroit symbolized all that was excessive in the materialism of American life (just as to many small-town American conservatives, the companies' partner, the United Auto Workers, symbolized everything that was excessive about the post-New Deal liberal society). None of this carping bothered Detroit. It was a given that Americans preferred big cars—and only Detroit made big cars. There was a seldom-spoken corollary to this axiom: Big cars meant big profits, and small cars meant small profits. In early 1973 the fact that Detroit was selling what it wanted to sell was considered proof that Detroit, rather than its critics, truly understood the American customer. The future looked brighter than ever. An ugly war in Southeast Asia which had sapped the nation's strength and resources was finally ending, and Detroit was bullish about the auto economy just ahead. That bullishness seemed to be based on good reason. For if there was one benign economic certainty, as far as American industrialists and American consumers were concerned, it was the low price of gas and oil, a price that seemed almost inflation-proof in the postwar era. In 1950 the price of a gallon of gas at the pump had been 27 cents, 20 cents of it for the gas itself and the rest for taxes. Twenty years later, the price of virtually every other basic consumer commodity had approximately doubled, but the price of gas had remained, tantalizingly, almost the same. At the moment that Charley Maxwell set out for Detroit, in 1973, a gallon of gas cost 37 cents at the pump, 26 of it for the gas itself. The price seemed a blessing so constant that everyone had come to take it for granted.

That was the premise of the city to which Charley Maxwell was traveling. He was thirty-five years old and had spent all of his adult life in the oil business, mostly with Mobil in the Middle East and Nigeria. He was by nature scholarly, and those long years in the field had added practical experience to his theoretical expertise, a rare combination. In the late sixties, when Mobil had started replacing its American overseas employees with foreign nationals, Maxwell had been sent back to the United States. It seemed to him that his career opportunities in the oil industry had been drastically reduced, and, looking for a way to exploit his knowledge, he had become an oil analyst for a Wall Street firm called Cyrus Lawrence.

Every field has its awesome experts, but there was something about Charley Maxwell's professional authority that was almost chilling. Part of it was his appearance, the hair plastered down over his forehead and parted in the middle, the old-fashioned, almost prim wire-rimmed glasses, the slightly stooped posture, the preoccupied manner; he looked like the sort of person who as a sixth-grader had been doted upon by his teachers because he had always gotten the right answer to every question, who had been good at what his teachers wanted rather than at what mattered to his peers. . . .

In those June days of 1973, however, he was not yet well known outside his field, and his field was not yet a hot one. Americans believed that their own domestic supplies of oil were plentiful and that there were virtually limitless sources in the Persian Gulf. What Charley Maxwell intended to tell the top-level auto executives he believed he would meet in Detroit was what he had been telling his superiors for some time now—that there would soon be dramatic, indeed revolutionary, changes in the price of energy. The assumption of the past, that energy would remain cheap because it had always been cheap and its price would increase only at small, acceptable, noninflationary increments, had to be discarded. America's own resources were rapidly proving inadequate, and the nation would thus become far more dependent upon the oil-producing nations of the Middle East. But the American oil companies would no longer be able to control the prices set for Arab oil, as they had so easily in the past. The Arabs would set the prices themselves. Since oil was in those days significantly underpriced in terms of its true market value, the loss of that control would have serious consequences for American heavy industry in general and Detroit in particular.

Maxwell had seen all this coming for a number of years. As early as 1970 he had started using the phrase "energy crisis"—apparently his coinage. He used it to refer to a crucial, ominous shift in the supply and demand of oil. He calculated that worldwide oil consumption was climbing 5 to 6 percent annually, and there was no reason to believe the surge would abate. If anything, it was likely to accelerate. New nations, recently graduated from their colonial past, were fast becoming both industrialized and urbanized and demanding far greater amounts of energy. Throughout the underdeveloped world, people were leaving their tribal huts and moving into cities, and, as they did, they took new jobs in factories which required energy, they lived in apartments which required energy, and to get to work they used transportation which also required energy. It was revolution taking place, a revolution of people who were changing their way of life and of nations that were expanding and modernizing their economies. The world, Maxwell concluded, had changed dramatically and was going to continue to change as more and more nations moved toward industrial economies. Ten and sometimes fifteen additional countries were leaving the preindustrial age each year and coming into the mechanical age. But there had not as yet been any reflection of this trend in the price of the ingredient most precious to the modern industrialized state, oil. There was going to be one terrible moment, Maxwell was sure, when the price would simply shoot up, out of anyone's control, the oil seeking its true market value. . . .

Maxwell knew that he was not alone in his pessimism, that a number of other energy experts, using much the same research, had come to similar conclusions. But most of these experts worked for the large oil companies, where the darker view had not yet been accepted. Maxwell's own superiors at the Wall Street investment firm of Cyrus Lawrence, however, had been greatly impressed by his estimates and the dispassionate way in which he presented his evidence. Both as a courtesy and also out of their own self-interest, for it would not hurt to lend out so brilliant a man with such original and important perceptions, they decided to send him to Detroit. There, the Cyrus Lawrence people proposed, he would talk to executives at the highest level, who surely would be more than anxious to hear these findings that had such fateful implications for their companies.

Maxwell himself was not so sure. He knew Detroit and he knew it well. He had grown up there, his stepfather had been employed at a middle level by Ford, he himself had even gone to Cranbrook, the city's elite prep school, where many of his classmates were sons of auto titans. Maxwell knew how stratified the city was, how isolated and insular. It was, he believed, a place of bedrock beliefs, a place where new truths did not seep easily from the bottom to the top. In Detroit, truth moved from the top to the bottom.

Maxwell had been promised meetings with the high auto executives, people who operated at the ultimate level of power. He was dubious about that. He might be well known in the world of oil, but he was young, and Detroit did not readily listen to junior people. Detroit believed in hierarchy and seniority rather than in individual brilliance. One advanced in Detroit not necessarily by being brilliant—brilliance meant that someone might be *different* and implied a threat—but by accommodating oneself with attitudes of those above one. Maxwell, because of his age and the nature of his message, would almost surely be looked upon as impertinent. These men would have their own sources of information, among them the men who headed the great oil companies, the men still resistant to the pessimistic vision of Maxwell and his kind. Powerful, successful, and conventional, typical of the corporate class, they believed that tomorrow would be like today because it had always been like today and because they wanted it to be like today. In their view, if the price of oil went up, it would go up slowly over many decades. They had controlled the oil world—and thus the price of energy—in the past. They would control that world and the price of energy in the future. So Charley Maxwell had been skeptical from the start that he would get the very top people as promised. If his supporters thought so, he knew better, and he had automatically translated his prospects downward. He would be lucky, he decided, to meet people at the 65 percent level of power. That, he soon learned, was too sanguine an expectation.

He did not do badly at the start. He went first to Chrysler, where Tom Killefer, the senior financial officer, had assembled a group of upper-middle-level executives. They listened quietly as Maxwell made his solemn little speech, saying in effect that all their estimates about what kind of cars Americans could and would drive were about to fly out the window. Killefer himself had been pleasant; he was a Rhodes scholar, different from the average

Detroit executive, less narrow, in better touch with the outside world. When Maxwell finished, Killefer thanked him and said, "Well, what you say is very, very impressive, very impressive indeed, and of course if it's true, then we're going to have to give it a hard, hard look." There were questions, and bright young men in the group, perhaps less complacent because Chrysler was already a shaky company, were clearly interested. But even as he was finishing his presentation, Maxwell had a sense that it was all to no end, that these men would leave the meeting and shake their heads and say how interesting it had been, what a bright fellow Maxwell was, maybe a bit rash, something of an alarmist, didn't they think, but bright and interesting nonetheless. Worth thinking about. That would be it, Maxwell thought, possibly a letter or two thanking him, but no real penetration of the process.

Chrysler, unfortunately, turned out to be by far the best of the three meetings. He had been taken seriously there, and Killefer was, whatever else, a representative of top management. Ford was a good deal worse. At Ford he met two people at the lower planning level. They were junior executives, making, he suspected, about $25,000 a year, which was a very small salary in executive Detroit. They were, he knew instantly, completely without power, and they had been sent there because a steadily descending series of Ford executives had told their immediate subordinates that someone had to go and cover the meeting, until finally, far down the line, there had been two men so unimportant that they had no subordinates to send. These two were there precisely because they were powerless. Maxwell felt a bit odd, standing in that room saying that Detroit was going to have to change its whole line of cars and that an entire era had ended, and saying this to men who could not change the design of an ashtray. Somehow that thought made his presentation more impassioned than ever.

General Motors, of course, was the worst. There were no high-level meetings scheduled. In fact, there were no meetings scheduled at all. Someone very junior asked Maxwell if he would like to drive out to the testing grounds and meet with some GM people there. He did, encountering no one in any position of responsibility, though for his troubles he was able to see some of GM's new models. They looked rather large to him, cars that would surely use a great deal of gas.

Such was Charley Maxwell's trip to Detroit. He had not even gotten across the moat. Detroit was Detroit, and more than most business centers it was a city that listened only to its own voice. But he left town worried about what he was sure was going to happen to a vital American industry. Maxwell did not think that the coming change in price would necessarily be so great that even a Detroit that was prepared for change would be severely damaged. Rather, he was worried because Detroit was unprepared—because no one in America seemed willing to practice even the most nominal kind of conservation, which suggested that the country was psychically unready for major increases. A big jump in price might trigger a panic, which would compound the difficulty of entering a new economic order. Those who were set up for change could deal with it, he suspected; those who were not were likely to come apart. Detroit, he feared, was going to have to learn its new truths the hard way.

A few months later, on October 6, 1973, on the eve of Yom Kippur, the holiest of Jewish holy days, Egypt tried a military strike on Israel. Eventually Israel struck back and once again, for the third time since World War II, defeated the Egyptians. To the Arab world this humiliation was one more demonstration of its powerlessness. The Arabs blamed Israel's existence on its American sponsorship. Thwarted both militarily and politically, the Arabs now turned at last to their real strength, their economic leverage. They began an oil embargo on the West. Before it was over, the price of oil had rocketed from $3 a barrel to $12 a barrel. The United States, long accustomed to cheap energy, was completely unprepared to respond to the Arab move. Unwilling to increase the taxes on gasoline and oil and thus at least partially stabilize the price of energy, it had in effect permitted the Arabs to place a tax not just on the American oil consumer but on the entire country. The effects on the American economy at every level were dramatic. The era of the cheap energy upon which so much of America's dynamism and its broad middle-class prosperity was premised was beginning to end. A new era with profound implications for the industrial core of America, the great Middle Atlantic and Midwestern foundry of the nation, had arrived. Occasionally in later years Charley Maxwell would run into Tom Killefer, who by then had left Chrysler to become the chairman of the United States Trust Company, and when he did, Killefer would shake his head and say, "You—you're the one man I hate to see. God, I still remember that warning." . . .

---•---

Quality

John Galsworthy [1867–1933]

I knew him from the days of my extreme youth, because he made my father's boots; inhabiting with his elder brother two little shops let into one, in a small by-street—now no more, but then most fashionably placed in the West End.

That tenement had a certain quiet distinction; there was no sign upon its face that he made for any of the Royal Family—merely his own German name of Gessler Brothers; and in the window a few pairs of boots. I remember that it always troubled me to account for those unvarying boots in the window, for he made only what was ordered, reaching nothing down, and it seemed so inconceivable that what he made could ever have failed to fit. Had he bought them to put there? That, too, seemed inconceivable. He would never have tolerated in his house leather on which he had not worked himself. Besides, they were too beautiful—the pair of pumps, so inexpressibly slim, the patent leathers with cloth tops, making water come into one's mouth, the tall brown riding boots with marvellous sooty glow, as if, though new, they had been worn a hundred years. Those pairs could only have been made by one who saw before him the Soul of Boot—so truly were they prototypes incarnating the very spirit of all foot-gear. These thoughts, of course, came to me later, though even when I was promoted to him, at the age of perhaps fourteen, some inkling haunted me of the dignity of himself and brother. For to make boots—such boots as he made—seemed to me then, and still seems to me, mysterious and wonderful.

I remember well my shy remark, one day, while stretching out to him my youthful foot:

"Isn't it awfully hard to do, Mr. Gessler?"

And his answer, given with a sudden smile from out of the sardonic redness of his beard: "Id is an Ardt!"

Himself, he was a little as if made from leather, with his yellow crinkly face, and crinkly reddish hair and beard, and neat folds slanting down his cheeks to the corner of his mouth, and his guttural and one-toned voice; for leather is a sardonic substance, and stiff and slow of purpose. And that was the character of his face, save that his eyes, which were gray-blue, had in them the simple gravity of one secretly possessed by the Ideal. His elder brother was so very like him—though watery, paler in every way, with a great industry—that sometimes in early days I was not quite sure of him until the interview was over. Then I knew that it was he, if the words, "I will ask my brudder," had not been spoken; and, that, if they had, it was his elder brother.

When one grew old and wild and ran up bills, one somehow never ran them up with Gessler Brothers. It would not have seemed becoming to go in there and stretch out one's foot to that blue iron-spectacled glance, owing him for more than—say—two pairs, just the comfortable reassurance that one was still his client.

For it was not possible to go to him very often—his boots lasted terribly, having something beyond the temporary—some, as it were, essence of boot stitched into them.

One went in, not as into most shops, in the mood of: "Please serve me, and let me go!" but restfully, as one enters a church; and, sitting on the single wooden chair, waited—for there was never anybody there. Soon, over the top edge of that sort of well—rather dark, and smelling soothingly of leather— which formed the shop, there would be seen his face, or that of his elder brother, peering down. A guttural sound, and tip-tap of bast slippers beating the narrow wooden stairs, and he would stand before one without coat, a little bent, in leather apron, with sleeves turned back, blinking—as if awakened from some dream of boots, or like an owl surprised in daylight and annoyed at this interruption.

And I would say: "How do you do, Mr. Gessler? Could you make me a pair of Russia leather boots?"

Without a word he would leave me, retiring whence he came, or into the other portion of the shop, and I could continue to rest in the wooden chair, inhaling the incense of his trade. Soon he would come back, holding in his thin, veined hand a piece of gold-brown leather. With eyes fixed on it, he would remark: "What a beaudiful biece!" When I, too, had admired it, he would speak again. "When do you wand them?" And I would answer: "Oh! As soon as you conveniently can." And he would say: "To-morrow fordnighd?" Or if he were his elder brother: "I will ask my brudder!"

Then I would murmur: "Thank you! Good-morning, Mr. Gessler." "Goot-morning!" he would reply, still looking at the leather in his hand. And as I moved to the door, I would hear the tip-tap of his bast slippers restoring him, up the stairs, to his dream of boots. But if it were some new kind of foot-gear that he had not yet made me, then indeed he would observe ceremony—divesting me of my boot and holding it long in his hand, looking at it with eyes at once critical and loving, as if recalling the glow with which he had created it, and rebuking the way in which one had disorganized this masterpiece. Then, placing my foot on a piece of paper, he would two or three times tickle the outer edges with a pencil and pass his nervous fingers over my toes, feeling himself into the heart of my requirements.

I cannot forget that day on which I had occasion to say to him: "Mr. Gessler, that last pair of town walking-boots creaked, you know."

He looked at me for a time without replying, as if expecting me to withdraw or qualify the statement, then said:

"Id shouldn'd 'ave greaked."

"It did, I'm afraid."

"You goddem wed before dey found demselves?"

"I don't think so."

At that he lowered his eyes, as if hunting for memory of those boots, and I felt sorry I had mentioned this grave thing.

"Zend dem back!" he said; "I will look at dem."

A feeling of compassion for my creaking boots surged up in me, so well could I imagine the sorrowful long curiosity of regard which he would bend on them.

"Zome boods," he said slowly, "are bad from birdt. I can do noding wid dem, I dake them off your bill."

Once (once only) I went absent-mindedly into his shop in a pair of boots bought in a emergency at some large firm's. He took my order without showing me any leather, and I could feel his eyes penetrating the inferior integument of my foot. At last he said:

"Dose are nod by boods."

The tone was not one of anger, nor of sorrow, not even of contempt, but there was in it something quiet that froze the blood. He put his hand down and pressed a finger on the place where the left boot, endeavoring to be fashionable, was not quite comfortable.

"Id 'urds you dere," he said. "Dose big virms 'ave no self-respect. Drash!" And then, as if something had given way within him, he spoke long and bitterly. It was the only time I ever heard him discuss the conditions and hardships of his trade.

"Dey get id all," he said, "dey get id by adverdisement, nod by work. Dey dake it away from us, who lofe our boods. Id gomes to this—bresently I haf no work. Every year id gets less—you will see." And looking at his lined face I saw things I had never noticed before, bitter things and bitter struggle—and what a lot of gray hairs there seemed suddenly in his red beard!

As best I could, I explained the circumstances of the purchase of those ill-omened boots. But his face and voice made so deep impression that during the next few minutes I ordered many pairs. Nemesis fell! They lasted more terribly than ever. And I was not able conscientiously to go to him for nearly two years.

When at last I went I was surprised to find that outside one of the two little windows of his shop another name was painted, also that of a bootmaker—making, of course, for the Royal Family. The old familiar boots, no longer in dignified isolation, were huddled in the single window. Inside, the now contracted well of the one little shop was more scented and darker than ever. And it was longer than usual, too, before a face peered down, and the tip-tap of the bast slippers began. At last he stood before me, and, gazing through those rusty iron spectacles, said:

"Mr. _____, isn'd it?"

"Ah! Mr. Gessler," I stammered, "but your boots are really *too* good, you know! See, these are quite decent still!" And I stretched out to him my foot. He looked at it.

"Yes," he said, "beople do nod wand good boods, id seems."

To get away from his reproachful eyes and voice I hastily remarked: "What have you done to your shop?"

He answered quietly: "Id was too exbensif. Do you wand some boods?"

I ordered three pairs, though I had only wanted two, and quickly left. I had, I do not know quite what feeling of being part, in his mind, of a conspiracy against him; or not perhaps so much against him as against his idea of boot. One does not, I suppose, care to feel like that; for it was again many months before my next visit to his shop, paid, I remember, with the feeling: "Oh! well, I can't leave the old boy—so here goes! Perhaps it'll be his elder brother!"

For his elder brother, I knew, had not character enough to reproach me, even dumbly.

And, to my relief, in the shop there did appear to be his elder brother, handling a piece of leather.

"Well, Mr. Gessler," I said, "how are you?"

"I am breddy well," he said slowly; "but my elder brudder is dead."

And I saw that it was indeed himself—but how aged and wan! And never before had I heard him mention his brother. Much shocked, I murmured: "Oh! I am sorry!"

"Yes," he answered, "he was a good man, he made a good bood; but he is dead." And he touched the top of his head, where the hair had suddenly gone as thin as it had been on that of his poor brother, to indicate, I suppose, the cause of death. "He could nod ged over losing de oder shop. Do you wand any boods?" And he held up the leather in his hand: "Id's a beaudiful biece."

I ordered several pairs. It was very long before they came—but they were better than ever. One simply could not wear them out. And soon after that I went abroad.

It was over a year before I was again in London. And the first shop I went to was my old friend's. I had left a man of sixty, I came back to one of seventy-five, pinched and worn and tremulous, who genuinely, this time, did not at first know me.

"Oh! Mr. Gessler," I said, sick at heart; "how splendid your boots are! See, I've been wearing this pair nearly all the time I've been abroad; and they're not half worn out, are they?"

He looked long at my boots—a pair of Russia leather, and his face seemed to regain steadiness. Putting his hand on my instep, he said:

"Do dey vid you here? I 'ad drouble wid dat bair, I remember."

I assured him that they had fitted beautifully.

"Do you wand any boods?" he said. "I can make dem quickly; id is a slack dime."

I answered: "Please, please! I want boots all round—every kind!"

"I will make a vresh model. Your food must be bigger." And with utter slowness, he traced round my foot, and felt my toes, only once looking up to say:

"Did I dell you my brudder was dead?"

To watch him was painful, so feeble had he grown; I was glad to get away.

I had given those boots up, when one evening they came. Opening the parcel, I set the four pairs in a row. Then one by one I tried them on. There was no doubt about it. In shape and fit, in finish and quality of leather, they were the best he had ever made me. And in the mouth of one of the Town walking-boots I found his bill. The amount was the same as usual, but it gave me quite a shock. He had never before sent it in till quarter day. I flew downstairs, and wrote a cheque, and posted it at once with my own hand.

A week later, passing the little street, I thought I would go in and tell him how splendidly the new boots fitted. But when I came to where his shop had been, his name was gone. Still there, in the window, were the slim pumps, the patent leathers with cloth tops, the sooty riding boots.

I went in, very much disturbed. In the two little shops—again made into one—was a young man with an English face.

"Mr. Gessler in?" I said.

He gave me a strange, ingratiating look.

"No, sir," he said, "no. But we can attend to anything with pleasure. We've taken the shop over. You've seen our name, no doubt, next door. We make for some very good people."

"Yes, yes," I said; "but Mr. Gessler?"

"Oh!" he answered; "dead."

"Dead! But I only received these boots from him last Wednesday week."

"Ah!" he said; "a shockin' go. Poor old man starved 'imself."

"Good God!"

"Slow starvation, the doctor called it! You see he went to work in such a way! Would keep the shop on; wouldn't have a soul touch his boots except himself. When he got an order, it took him such a time. People won't wait. He lost everybody. And there he'd sit, goin' on and on—I will say that for him—not a man in London made a better boot! But look at the competition! He never advertised! Would 'ave the best leather, too, and do it all 'imself. Well, there it is. What could you expect with his ideas?"

"But starvation——!"

"That may be a bit flowery, as the sayin' is—but I know myself he was sittin' over his boots day and night, to the very last. You see I used to watch him. Never gave 'imself time to eat; never had a penny in the house. All went in rent and leather. How he lived so long I don't know. He regular let his fire go out. He was a character. But he made good boots."

"Yes," I said, "he made good boots."

And I turned and went out quickly, for I did not want that youth to know that I could hardly see.

•

Revolution by Evolution: The Changing Relationship Between GM and the UAW

Donald F. Ephlin
United Automobile Workers Union

The mid-1930s were indeed a time of revolution in America. While workers were engaging in sit-down strikes at General Motors the winter of 1936–1937, the company tried to block food shipments into the plant, turned off the heat, and called in police (who used tear gas and billy clubs) and tried to use court injunctions to remove striking workers from plant premises. After a bitter 44 days, GM finally acceded to the UAW's demand to negotiate a contract for its workers.

From The Academy of Management, *EXECUTIVE*, Vol. II, No. 1, 1988, pp. 63–65. Reprinted by permission of the author.

Since then, the union's progress has been decidedly evolutionary—a steady succession of gains in bread-and-butter issues that were supplemented year in and year out with progress in achieving other goals, particularly in social issues such as pensions and health care. More recently, we have made substantial gains in the areas of long-term job and income security, workplace health and safety, and greater input into the corporate decision-making process for our members.

But when we step back and look over the span of some 50 years—a wink in the eye in man's long struggle to improve his lot—we can identify change that is cumulatively as dramatic and at least as far reaching as the bitter battles of the 1930s that established a beachhead for the United Auto Workers.

In the 50 years since the UAW negotiated its first contract with General Motors, our relationship has evolved from one that was strictly adversarial to one that is more reasoned and geared toward problem solving. This change has occurred on both sides and I, for one, believe it works to the advantage of the union, its members, and the corporation. As we look to the future, I think it worthwhile to take a brief glance at the past and to examine how we got to where we are today.

The Growth of the UAW

Since the UAW first gained the right to represent hourly workers at GM, we have seen a dramatic change in the relationship between both parties. What began as a revolution in Flint, Michigan over 50 years ago has evolved into a working relationship that has ultimately benefited all involved.

When the UAW and GM signed that first one-page contract in 1937, it was with an initial goal of getting the company to agree to negotiate a labor agreement with the union. The issue was simple: recognition of the then fledgling UAW as the bargaining agent for GM employees. GM was, by the standards of the day, a huge corporation, with assets of $1.5 billion and 69 plants in 35 cities. By 1937, the UAW's total membership was 375,000, up from 35,000 just two years before.

The early years were important in that the UAW won significant protections for the workers. Just two years after winning the right to represent GM workers, the union established seniority rights and laid the groundwork for an apprentice program. While significant progress had been made in a short time, the union had a broad and long-term agenda for improving the lives and ensuring the security of its members. Our work had just begun.

Times were good, the companies were enormously profitable, and the union pressed hard to ensure that the GM workers shared in that success. This was first achieved with the establishment, in 1940, of 40 hours of annual paid vacation for employees with at least one year on the job. The amount of annual paid vacation was doubled in 1942 for employees with five years of seniority. That same year (1942) the contract provided a 4-cent-per-hour raise for workers.

It was also during that time—World War II—that the union's leadership adopted a no-strike clause. The day after the attack on Pearl Harbor the union's governing body, the International Executive Board, met and voted to place a moratorium on strikes for the duration of the war, a position that was affirmed by union membership. The UAW also sought to convert auto plants into "arsenals of democracy" and called for the adoption of a plan, authored by then UAW Vice-President Walter Reuther, for "Five Hundred Planes a Day." Reuther saw this as a way to put idle workers to work and feed the economy. During this period, the union developed a reputation as being committed to world peace and full employment. Reuther also had a plan to replace production for war by production for peace. Its centerpiece was a program to put America's industrial capacity to work building homes, transportation systems, and meeting other "social needs" that had been neglected during the war. Reuther reasoned that such a plan could ensure the employment of not only the "Rosie the Riveters"—the tens of thousands of women who joined the workforce during the war years—but the returning GIs as well.

When union members returned from the war and to their old jobs at GM, they found a union that had matured and was committed to pursuing an agenda for economic and social justice for its members. They also faced a corporation that had weathered the war in fine shape and was again highly profitable. It was in that first postwar contract negotiation with General Motors that the union had demanded that the corporation "open its books." After a 113-day strike in 1945–1946, an agreement was signed with GM giving workers an 18-cent-an-hour raise. This brought the average hourly wage for an autoworker to $1.44. Within the next two years the union negotiated six paid holidays and the first annual improvement factor (AIF), which acknowledged workers' contributions to regular productivity increases. A cost-of-living allowance (COLA) to offset the impact of inflation was also negotiated for the first time.

The union, however, had an agenda far broader than traditional bread-and-butter matters. Having achieved a measure of economic security for its members, it turned its efforts to the area of social issues. Reuther, who was by then UAW President, took up the banner of "Too Old to Work, Too Young to Die" and, marshaling public opinion, negotiated the first UAW-employer-paid pension program in 1950. That same year the union closed the gap and was able to negotiate a fully paid hospitalization plan for employees.

Although the auto companies were relatively strong, they were also plagued by cyclical downturns in the industry. Workers often found themselves out on the street during these downturns and during the then-annual changeover of models. In 1955 the union took a major step in guaranteeing an annual wage with the adoption of the Supplemental Unemployment Benefit (SUB) program, an income cushion for laid-off workers. This layoff protection plan has stood the test of time by providing hundreds of thousands of workers with an economic safety net during some lengthy interruptions of work.

It is worth noting that during the 1950s and 1960s, while the union made progress in both economic and social programs, management's treatment of workers was building to a crisis point. Nothing illustrated that better than the bitter 67-day strike at GM in 1970 over a myriad of so-called traditional issues—most notably maintaining an adequate cost-of-living program and establishing early retirement under the "30 and Out" program. Relations between the management at GM and the UAW were so bad that GM's Lordstown, Ohio plant became synonymous with worker dissatisfaction. Studs Terkel, in his book *Working,* immortalized the plant in a chapter entitled "The Blue Collar Blues."

During the 1960s and 1970s, local contract issues became a critical battleground. In each round of bargaining, negotiations were conducted simultaneously at over 150 local units, and in many of these local negotiations costly strikes resulted. To some, the issues seemed insignificant in economic terms, but in reality they related directly to working conditions on the shop floor, matters relating to dignity in the workplace, and the human factors involved in mass production. It took years for both the corporation and the union to understand fully how critical these issues had become.

It was against that backdrop that former UAW Vice-President Irving Bluestone pressed hard for the establishment of a "Quality of Worklife" (QWL) program. Bluestone's goal, and the goal of all of us who support the notion of QWL, was to address the issues of dignity in the workplace and how to achieve a greater measure of democracy on the shop floor.

While QWL has not been a panacea, it has fostered greater communication among many in management and the union and in some cases has served as a beginning point for a joint approach in many locations. In retrospect, I believe that the establishment of Quality of Worklife programs laid an important foundation in the evolution of the relationship between workers and managers. It was the first major acknowledgment by management that workers and their union had a contribution to make to the operation of a company.

In the 1970s the auto industry was on a boom-or-bust roller coaster, caused in large part by huge price increases at the gasoline pumps and Detroit's inability to meet growing consumer demand for small cars. Nothing, however, could have prepared either the union or the automakers for what was to come. In 1978, just as everyone thought an upswing was in place with record sales and profits, the following year brought the overthrow of the shah in Iran. This led to an even bigger surge in gasoline prices and subsequent economic chaos, which hit the auto industry first and hardest.

While Ford, GM, and especially Chrysler were reporting record losses, workers in the plants were being hit hard as well, a result of the exhaustion of unemployment funds, plant closings, depleted or dwindling SUBs, and the uncertainty about the future.

When the auto companies came to the UAW in late 1981 and asked us to reopen contract negotiations, it was against a backdrop of ⅓ of our members at Ford and GM on layoff, 22 Big Three plants having been closed during the previous two years, and a growing loss of confidence in the domestic auto industry. There were many factors beyond our control that contributed to the financial woes of the companies, most of which had to do with skyrocketing sales of imports—helped by the strong dollar—and a national economic policy of a deliberately engineered recession, soaring general unemployment, and double-digit inflation.

It should be noted that we in the union never viewed ourselves as being in the business of "bailing out" the companies where our members work. Our primary concern has always been to protect jobs, seek reasonable wage and benefit improvements, and to ensure a safe and healthy workplace. All that changed in the early 1980s, when workers in the plants were being made to bear the brunt of the depression in the automotive industry and were being singled out for much of the blame. These charges ranged from unfair accusations of excessive wage and benefit levels to poor product quality and an inability to compete with the Japanese.

When we agreed for the first time in our history to reopen the contracts with Ford and GM, the label "concessionary bargaining" was attached to what we ultimately did. The UAW has a long and proud history of bargaining in accordance with the circumstances of the time. We did what was right and responsible in 1982 and we met our main objectives of preserving the long-term job and income security of our members. I have always viewed that contract as "reciprocal bargaining," for in the long run we won far more than we gave up. Yes, workers did accept a wage freeze for the term of the contract, but in return we established in perpetuity several important provisions that have served as a foundation upon which to build in the years since—most notably, the job and income protection provisions and the establishment of profit sharing. (The profit-sharing formula we negotiated at Ford has paid over $5,000 to the average worker in the last five years. While profit sharing at GM has not been as lucrative for the employees, the principle is carved in stone.) From that agreement grew this new and expanded role for workers and their union in the day-to-day operation of the company, as well as a myriad of training, education, and health and safety programs that have enhanced life on the plant floor and have given workers a greater say in defining and performing their jobs. Perhaps the most significant aspect of the contracts reached that year was that the agreement was based on an overriding principle—the total acceptance of our union.

In our next round of contract talks in 1984, the UAW expanded on the job and income security programs negotiated during the previous round of bargaining. While the auto companies were not out of the woods financially, they appeared to be on the road to stability. We had, however, established the critical principles of jointness and greater plant democracy; there was no turning back the clock. That year we also negotiated a far-reaching and comprehensive job security program at GM, the Job Opportunity Bank Security (JOBS) program, which guaranteed protection against layoffs caused by outsourcing, new technology, or negotiated productivity improvements. The program, part of of the pattern set at GM, was replicated at Ford. Since the programs were implemented three years ago, some 12,500 workers at GM have participated in the JOBS program. Another 2,000 workers at Ford who would have otherwise lost their jobs and income have participated in a comparable program.

When we went to the table in 1987 to negotiate a new national agreement with GM and Ford, our primary goal was enhanced job security. In the summer of 1987, GM faced declining market share, eroding sales, the announcement of nearly a dozen plant closings, a loss of public and investor confidence, and a crisis in its in-house components operations. Moreover, we in the union made clear our position that we felt a large measure of GM's problems resulted directly from the company's lack of a uniform labor policy and an absence of clear direction and follow-through from its top management.

Major improvements in our job security program, which protects employees from layoffs except in well-defined, volume-related situations, were the result of this round of negotiations. Gains were also made in the areas of wages, pensions, and health care and in strengthening the solvency of the SUB fund.

We have also expanded the scope of our current joint activities at GM and won a greater level of involvement for the union in numerous areas. Not enough can be said about our union's input into and impact on the day-to-day operation of the General Motors Corporation. None of us could have imagined the across-the-board involvement we now have. For example, one year ago I was invited to serve on the corporation's Quality Council, a group of top GM executives who regularly review and make recommendations on all aspects of quality. During the 1987 contract talks Bob Stempel, the new president of GM, asked me to co-chair the Council. In addition to our involvement with the Quality Council, the union and GM management have jointly developed a corporatewide Quality Network. This network is comprised of representatives of the company and the union who will participate, on the group and plant levels, in quality efforts, from design to final assembly. This is significant because for the first time in the history of General Motors, union and management are working together to address the issues of quality and customer satisfaction.

———————————————●———————————————

Women: World-Class Managers for Global Competition

Mariann Jelinek
Case Western Reserve University
Nancy J. Adler
McGill University

It is no secret that business faces an environment radically different from that of even a few years ago, the result of increasingly global competition. The Commerce Department estimated in 1984 that in U.S. domestic markets some 70% of firms faced "significant foreign competition," up from only 25% a decade previously. By 1987, the chairman of the Foreign Trade Council estimated

From The Academy of Management, *EXECUTIVE*, Vol. II, No. 1, 1988, pp. 11–19. Reprinted by permission of the authors.

the figure to be 80%. In 1984, U.S. exports to markets abroad accounted for 12.5% of the GNP; by comparison, Japan's 1984 exports were 16.5% of its GNP.[1] Global competition is serious, it is pervasive, and it is here to stay.

More stringent competition is an important result of this global economy. (See Exhibit 1.) Because markets are increasingly interconnected, "world-class standards" are quickly becoming the norm. New products developed in one market are soon visible in markets around the world, as initial producers use their advantage, forcing competitors to meet the challenge or lose market share. Product life-cycle has been reduced by 75%. Product development and world-wide marketing are becoming almost simultaneous. For example, recent developments in superconductivity, initially demonstrated in Zurich, were quickly replicated in The People's Republic of China, the United States, Japan, and in Europe. Similarly, U.S. automobile customers quickly learned to demand improved quality from U.S. automakers, once the Japanese autos had demonstrated it. Standards for price, performance, and quality have been permanently altered worldwide.

Exhibit 1 Focus of Competition

When Focus of Competition is:

Local or Regional	*National*	*Export Sales*	*Sourcing or Manufacturing Abroad*	*Global Business Arena*
Managerial Focus is:				
Home Country Focus		←	→	Global Focus
Managerial Relations Tend to Depend on:				Depend on a Variety of Views,
Own Views				
Own Resources		←	→	Others' Resources
"Lone Ranger"				"Team Spirit"
Personnel Policy Emphasizes:				
Home Country		Some	Some Foreign	Multicultural &
Personnel		Expatriates	Nationals	Multinational
Policy				Personnel Policy
		←	→	

Thus North American companies in locally oriented competition tend to focus on the home country, with managers generally depending on their own resources and home country personnel. In contrast, a firm sourcing or manufacturing abroad is much more likely to have an international focus and to have moved toward seeing a variety of views and others' resources as essential to team-spirited management, deliberately using multicultural personnel.

New Competitive Strategies

The problem for Americans, who historically have enjoyed the luxury of a large and generally protected domestic market, is how to respond to all these changes. Global competition means much more than sending excess domestic production abroad. Today, many formerly eager markets are contested by well-entrenched locals or by competing foreign companies. The new competition does not involve simply sales abroad, or even foreign competitors here and abroad. Rather, its varied faces are likely to include the following circumstances—none of them typical for most business even a few years ago:

- Extensive on-going operations within foreign countries. This means a vastly increased demand for sophisticated, multiculturally adept managers. Foreign operations and markets are neither temporary nor trivial, but essential for long-term survival.
- Strategic management across cultures. Global management necessitates working in numerous countries at once. Yet what works at home, or in one foreign country, may not work in another. Cultural norms and expectations differ. Sensitivity and finesse must be brought to bear on strategic intentions, to transliterate them sensibly. In many cases a straight translation probably will not do, whether of a product name or the more complicated matters of market attack, strategic intent, or mission.
- More foreign personnel throughout the company. Foreign personnel are both necessary and valuable to a firm seeking to penetrate global markets. Even within the United States a broadly pluralistic personnel pool with substantial ethnic identity—most notably Hispanic and Asian, but others as well—belies the mythical "melting pot" image of prior decades. Effectively managing multicultural organization dynamics is a prerequisite for success today and tomorrow, not merely an indulgent gesture or a legal requirement.
- More joint ventures and strategic alliances to gain access to new technology, new markets or processes, and to share costs and lower risk. Indeed, not only are U.S. firms increasingly becoming involved in joint ventures with foreign firms, but more and more the U.S. firm is not the dominant partner. Today, "we" often need "them" as much as or more than "they" need "us." Thus, cross-cultural management is becoming increasingly critical to success—even survival.

Each of these new competitive strategies demands new skills. Improved ability to communicate across profound differences in approach and expectations, assumptions and beliefs—to say nothing of languages—is key. Because culturally based beliefs, perceptions, expectations, assumptions, and behaviors are deeply held, they are especially sensitive issues, requiring exceptional tact. (See Exhibit 2.)

Exhibit 2

Some Alternative Values Orientations:

	Culture A	Culture B	Culture C
Individuals seen as:	Good	Both Good & Evil	Evil
World is:	To Be Conquered	Lived With in Harmony	To Be Endured
Human Relations center on:	Individuals	Extended Groups	Hierarchical Groups
Time orientation:	Future	Present	Past
Action Basis is:	Free Will & Facts	Cultural or Social Norms	Biological or Theological

Adapted from ideas in Nancy J. Adler and Mariann Jelinek, "Is 'Organization Culture' Culture Bound?", *Human Resource Management* 25:1 (Spring 1986), 73–90; as based on F. Kluckhohn and F. L. Strodbeck, *Variations in Values Orientations* (Evanston, IL: Row, Peterson, 1969).

In short, managing globally calls upon an array of cross-cultural skills not readily at hand for most American managers, and not widely taught in most American business schools. To address these nontraditional problems we suggest a nontraditional resource: women managers. Our case is not based on altruism, nor equal opportunity under the law, nor even fairness, although all of these should be mentioned. Our case is based on the pragmatic self-interest of firms facing a challenging global environment.

But can women make it, especially in foreign cultures that presumably do not consider women men's equals? Won't they be ignored, mistreated, or intimidated? Shouldn't we respect foreign countries' cultural norms—even if they appear discriminatory to us? And do American women managers really want to take on this challenge? These are valid concerns, and an emerging body of research suggests some surprising answers. We will look at the special skills women bring to the new global competition and at the results women are achieving abroad, particularly in the fastest growing market in the world, the Pacific Rim. The conclusions may surprise you at first. However, upon reflection, they are utterly comprehensible and point to a powerful resource for a sustainable competitive advantage not readily available or duplicable in other cultures.

A Nontraditional (but Increasingly Valuable) Resource

All cultures differentiate male and female roles, expecting males to behave in certain ways, females in others; anticipating that men will fill certain roles, and women others. In many cultures, including America's, the traditional female role supports many attitudes and behaviors contradictory to those defined as managerial. This has been one of the key barriers to women's entry into managerial careers in the U.S. domestic arena: it operates both in terms of self-selection and differential difficulty.

After two decades of women's liberation movements and despite legislation and education, women remain different from men, even in the United States, arguably one of the most assertively egalitarian countries in the world. Men are still typically raised to be more aggressive and independent; women are still typically raised to be social and more communal.[2] Of course, there have been visible changes in sex roles and norms in North America as elsewhere in the world. There is also substantial debate over how much of the difference in behaviors can be attributed to biology and how much to acculturation factors. Nevertheless, in general, men still tend to be more aggressive than women.[3]

Melvyn Konner makes a strong argument that male aggression has biological roots in puberty, but that thereafter, greater aggression may be a learned and socially reinforced pattern. He notes that males commit the vast majority of violent crimes in every known society. Women, whose biochemistry does not initially encourage aggression at puberty, according to Konner, tend to evolve behavior patterns that emphasize sensitivity, communication skills, community, inclusion, and relationships.[4]

Research on sex roles and managerial characteristics has tended to reinforce the rather limited view of management skills and leadership most of us have acquired, a view identifying leadership with power and potency with adversarial control. In study after study, undergraduates, MBAs, and managers (male and female) in the United States have tended to identify stereotypically "masculine" (aggressive) characteristics as managerial and stereotypically "feminine" (cooperative and communicative) characteristics as unmanagerial.[5]

Yet American women now make up about half the U.S. workforce, and occupy over a quarter (27.9%) of all managerial and administrative positions,[6] although as late as the mid-1980s they represented only 5% of top executives.[7] In international management, women are rarer still, less than 3%.[8] Yet their achievements call into question some widely held beliefs about women and about management. Their unconventional achievements suggest a resource difficult for others to match.

Women Abroad

American women have been pursuing graduate education in management in increasing numbers, now accounting for about 50% of the enrollment at some large state schools and about a third of the enrollment at the most prestigious private schools. More and more are developing an interest in international postings. It would be surprising if they did not, as international business is so clearly "where the action is" in many companies today. To investigate the role of North American women as expatriate managers, Adler undertook a four-part study. In the first part, 686 Canadian and American firms were surveyed to identify the number of women sent abroad. Of 13,338 expatriates, 402 or 3% were female.[9] Other parts of the study sought to explain why so few North American women work abroad. The second part of the study surveyed 1,129 graduating MBAs from seven management schools in the United States, Canada, and Europe. Overall, 84% said they would like an international assignment at some point in their career; there were no significant differences between males and females.[10] While there may have been a difference in the past, today's male and female MBAs appear equally interested in international work and expatriate positions.

One need not depend on opinion or assumptions for assessing women's performance internationally; there are documentary research results. In the working world, women are beginning to be assigned abroad. In another part of the study a survey of 60 major North American multinationals revealed that over half (54%) of the companies were hesitant to post women overseas. This is almost four times as many as were hesitant to select women for domestic assignments (14%). Almost three-quarters of the personnel vice-presidents and managers believed that foreigners are prejudiced against female managers (73%), and that prejudice could render women ineffective in international assignments. Seventy percent believed that women in dual-career marriages would be reluctant to accept a foreign assignment, if not totally disinterested. For certain locations, the personnel executives expressed concern about women's physical safety, hazards involved in traveling in underdeveloped countries and, especially for single women, isolation and potential loneliness.[11] These findings agreed with those of a survey of 100 top managers in *Fortune 500* firms operating overseas: The majority believed that women face overwhelming resistance when seeking management positions in the international division of U.S. firms.[12]

No Welcome Mat?

There is certainly evidence to suggest that women are discriminated against as managers worldwide; women managers in foreign cultures are very rare indeed.[13] In many societies, local women are systematically excluded from managerial roles. Japan offers an excellent case in point; there are almost no Japanese women managers higher than clerical supervisors, especially in large, multinational corporations. In general, Japanese society expects women to work until marriage, quit to raise children, and return, as needed, to low-level and part-time positions after age 40. In Japan, the workplace remains a male domain.[14] Similarly, while women from prominent families in the Philippines can hold influential positions in political and economic life, overall only 2.7% of working women hold administrative or managerial positions in business or government.[15] The picture is similar in India, where women are constitutionally equal to men, but are culturally defined as primarily responsible for the home and children. Women have fared somewhat better in Singapore, where government policy and a booming economy between 1980 and 1983 helped raise women to 17.8% of managerial and administrative positions, up from 7% in 1980.[16] Only recently, and as yet rarely, do women fill managerial positions in these countries.[17]

Women in International Management

Clearly, it is the cultures of these foreign countries that perpetuate this scarcity of indigenous female managers in most Asian countries. If so, how can North American companies successfully send female managers to Japan, Korea, Hong Kong, the Philippines, the People's Republic of China, Singapore, Thailand, India, Pakistan, Malaysia, or Indonesia? Is the experience of these countries' women—most specifically their relative absence from managerial ranks—the best predictor of what expatriate women's experiences will be?

Research results suggest that local women's experience is not a good predictor of North American women's reception, experiences or success in Pacific Rim countries.[18] Indeed, it seems that North American predictions confuse the noun "woman" with the adjective "female," as in "female manager." The research disconfirms a set of North American assumptions predicting how Asians would treat North American female managers based on the North Americans' beliefs concerning Asians' treatment of Asian women. Confusing? Yes. Fundamentally important? Also yes. The problem with these assumptions, and the conclusions they lead to, is that they have been proven wrong.

Fifty-two female expatriate managers were interviewed while on assignment in Asia or after returning from Asia to North America as part of the larger study described earlier. Because of multiple foreign postings, the 52 women represented 61 Asian assignments. The greatest number were posted in Hong Kong (34%), followed by Japan (25%), Singapore (16%), the Philippines and Australia (5% each), Indonesia and Thailand (4% each), and at least one each in Korea, India, Taiwan, and the People's Republic of China. Since most of the women held regional responsibility, they worked throughout Asia, rather than just in their country of foreign residence. The majority of the women were posted abroad by financial institutions (71%), while the others were sent by publishing, petroleum, advertising, film distribution, retail food, electronic appliances, pharmaceuticals, office equipment, sporting goods, and soaps and cosmetics firms, and service industries (including accounting, law, executive search, and computers).

On average, the women's expatriate assignments lasted two and a half years, ranging from six months to six years. Salaries in 1983, before benefits, varied from US $27,000 to US $54,000 and averaged US $34,500. The women supervised from zero to 25 subordinates, with the average being 4.6. Titles and levels varied considerably; some held very junior positions (such as trainee and assistant account manager), while others held quite senior positions (including one regional vice-president). In no case did a female expatriate hold her company's number-one position in any region or country.

The Expatriate Experience

These expatriates were pioneers. In the majority of cases, the female expatriates were "firsts," with only 10% having followed another woman into her
international position. Of the 90% who were first, almost a quarter (22%)
represented the first female manager the firm had ever expatriated anywhere;
14% were the first women sent by their firms to Asia, 25% were the first sent
to the country in question, and 20% were the first women abroad in their
specific job. Clearly, neither the women nor their companies had the luxury
of role models; there were no previous patterns to follow. With the exception
of a few major New York-based financial institutions, both women expatriates and their firms found themselves experimenting, with no ready guides
for action or for estimating the likelihood of success.

The companies decided to send women managers to Asia only after a process that might be described as "education." In more than four out of five
cases (83%), it was the woman herself who initially introduced the idea of
an international assignment to her boss and company. For only six women
(11%) had the company first suggested it, while in the remaining three cases
(6%) the suggestion was mutual.

The women used a number of strategies to "educate" their companies. Many
women explored the possibility of an expatriate assignment during their initial job interview, and simply turned down firms that were totally against the
idea. In other cases, women informally introduced the idea to their bosses
and continued to mention it "at appropriate moments" until the assignment
finally materialized. A few women formally applied for a number of expatriate positions before finally being selected. Some women described themselves
as having specifically planned for international careers, primarily by attempting to be in the right place at the right time. For example, one woman predicted
that Hong Kong would be her firm's next major business center and arranged
to assume responsibility for the Hong Kong desk in New York, leaving the
rest of Asia to a male colleague. The strategy paid off: within a year the company sent her, rather than her male colleague, to Hong Kong.

Overall, the women described themselves as having had to encourage their
companies and their bosses to consider the possibility of expatriating women
in general and themselves in particular. In most cases, they confronted and
overcame numerous instances of corporate resistance prior to being sent. For
example:

(Malaysia) *"Management assumed that women don't have the physical stamina
to survive in the tropics. They claimed I couldn't hack it."*

(Thailand) *"My company didn't want to send a woman to 'that horrible part of
the world.' They think Bangkok is an excellent place to send single men, but not
a woman. They said they would have trouble getting a work permit, which wasn't
true."*

(Japan and Hong Kong) *"Everyone was more or less curious if it would work.
My American boss tried to advise me, 'Don't be upset if it's difficult in Japan and*

Korea.' The American male manager in Tokyo was also hesitant. Finally the Chinese boss in Hong Kong said, 'We have to try.' "

(Japan) *"Although I was the best qualified, I was not offered the position in Japan until the senior Japanese manager in Tokyo said, 'We are very flexible in Japan'; then they sent me."*

In some instances, the women faced severe company resistance. Their companies sent them abroad only after all potential male candidates for the post had turned it down.

(Thailand) *"Every advance in responsibility is because the Americans had no choice. I've never been chosen over someone else."*

(Japan) *"They never would have considered me. But then the financial manager in Tokyo had a heart attack and they had to send someone. So they sent me, on a month's notice, as a temporary until they could find a man to fill the permanent position. It worked out and I stayed."*

(Hong Kong) *"After offering me the job, they hesitated. 'Could a women work with the Chinese?' So my job was defined as temporary, a one-year position to train a Chinese man to replace me. I succeeded and became permanent."*

This cautiousness and reluctance are particularly interesting because they tend to create an unfortunate self-fulfilling prophecy. As a number of women reported, if the company is not convinced you will succeed (and therefore offers you a temporary position rather than a permanent slot, for instance), this will communicate the company's lack of confidence to foreign colleagues and clients as a lack of commitment. Foreigners will then mirror the home company's behavior, also failing to take the temporary representative seriously. Assignments can become substantially more difficult. As one woman in Indonesia put it, "It is very important to clients that I am permanent. It increases trust, and that's crucial."

Outcomes Abroad: Did it Work?

Ninety-seven percent of the North American women described their experiences as successful, despite the difficulties and the reluctance on the part of their firms. While their descriptions were strictly subjective, a number of objective indicators suggest that most assignments did, in fact, succeed. For example, most firms decided to send another woman abroad after experimenting with their first female expatriate. In addition, many companies offered the pioneer women a second international assignment upon completion of the first. In only two cases did women describe failures: one in Australia and one in Singapore. The Australian experience was the woman's second posting abroad, preceded by a successful Latin American assignment and followed by an equally successful post in Singapore. The second woman's failure in Singapore was her only overseas assignment to date.

Advantages

Perhaps most astonishing was that, above and beyond their descriptions of success, almost half the women (42%) reported that being female served more as an advantage than a disadvantage in their foreign managerial positions. Sixteen percent found being female to have both positive and negative effects, and another 22% saw it as irrelevant or neutral. Only one woman in five found the professional impact of gender to be primarily negative abroad.

The women reported numerous professional advantages to being female. Most frequently, they described the advantage of being highly visible. Foreign clients were curious about them, wanted to meet them, and remembered them after the first meeting. It was therefore somewhat easier for the women than for their colleagues to gain access to foreign clients' time and attention. Examples of this high visibility included:

> **(Japan)** *"It's the visibility as an expat, and even more as a woman. I stick in their minds. I know I've gotten more business than my two male colleagues. They are extra interested in me."*

> **(Thailand)** *"Being a woman is never a detriment. They remembered me better. Fantastic for a marketing position. It's better working with Asians than with the Dutch, British, or Americans."*

> **(India and Pakistan)** *"In India and Pakistan, being a woman helps for marketing and client contact. I got in to see customers because they had never seen a female banker before. . . . Having a female banker adds value for the client."*

Visibility was not the only advantage. The women also described the advantages of good interpersonal skills and their observation that men could talk more easily about a wider range of topics with women than with other men. This ease of interchange was especially important in cross-cultural situations, where difficulties of nuance and opportunities for miscommunication abound. The women's ease was unforced and quite sincere, since it springs from fundamental socialization patterns. For example:

> **(Indonesia)** *"I often take advantage of being a woman. I'm more supportive than my male colleagues. . . . Clients relax and talk more. And 50% of my effectiveness is based on volunteered information."*

> **(Korea)** *"Women are better at treating men sensitively, and they just like you. One of my Korean clients told me, 'I really enjoyed the lunch and working with you.'"*

> **(Japan)** *"Women are better at putting people at ease. It's easier for a woman to convince a man. . . . The traditional woman's role . . . inspires confidence and trust, there's less suspicion, and I'm not threatening. They assumed I must be good if I was sent. They became friends."*

In addition, many of the expatriates described a higher status accorded them in Asia. That status was not denied them as foreign female managers; on the contrary, they often felt that they received special treatment not accorded their male colleagues. Clearly, it was always salient that they were women, but being women did not appear to prohibit them from operating effectively as managers. Moreover, most of the women claimed benefits from a "halo effect." Most of their foreign colleagues and clients had never worked with a female expatriate manager. At the same time, the foreign community was highly aware of how unusual it was for North American firms to send female managers to Asia. Thus, the Asians tended to assume that the women would not have been sent unless they were the best. Therefore, they expected them to be "very, very good."

The problems the women did experience were most often with their home companies rather than their Asian clients. For instance, after obtaining a foreign assignment, some women experienced limits to their opportunities and job scope imposed from back home. More than half the female expatriates described difficulties in persuading their home companies to give them latitude equivalent to that given their male colleagues, especially initially. Some companies, out of concern for the women's safety, limited their travel (and thus their role and often their effectiveness), excluding very remote, rural, and underdeveloped areas.

Other companies made postings temporary, or shorter than the standard male assignment of two to three years. This temporary status was often an important detriment: One Tokyo banker warned potential foreign competitors,

"Don't go to Japan unless you're ready to make a long-term commitment in both time and money. It takes many, many years."[19]

Business relationships and the effective development of "comfort levels" center on personal relationships and reliability over the long haul, especially in Japan, but also in many other "slow clock" cultures that focus on the long term.[20] It takes time to build relationships, and time to learn the culture. The contrast to the infamous American emphasis on "fast tracks" and quarterly results could not be more stark.

Managing foreign clients' and colleagues' initial expectations was a key hurdle for many of the women. Since most Asians had previously never met a North American woman in a managerial position, there was considerable curiosity and ambiguity about her status, level of expertise, authority, and responsibility—and therefore the appropriate form of address and demeanor to be used with her. In these situations, male colleagues' reactions were important. Initial client conversations were often directed at male colleagues, rather than at the newly arrived female manager. Senior male colleagues, particularly from the head office, became important in redirecting the focus of early discussions toward the woman. If well done, smooth, on-going work relationships were quickly established.

Women as *Gaijin*

Throughout the interviews, one pattern emerged persistently. First and foremost, foreigners are seen as *foreigners*. Like their male colleagues, the female expatriates are categorized as *gaijin* (foreigners) above all, and not locals. Foreign female managers are not expected to act like local women. Thus, the rules governing the behavior of local women, potentially limiting their access to management and managerial responsibilities, do not apply to the expatriate women. The freedom of action this identification carries is substantial:

> **(Japan)** *"The Japanese are very smart: they can tell that I am not Japanese, and they do not expect me to act as a Japanese woman. They will allow and condone behavior from foreign women which would be absolutely unacceptable from their own women."*

As Ranae Hyer, a Tokyo-based vice-president of personnel of the Bank of America's Asia Division said, "Being a foreigner is so weird to the Japanese that the marginal impact of being a woman is nothing. If I were a Japanese woman, I couldn't be doing what I'm doing here. But they know perfectly well that I'm not."[21]

Ultimately, of course, the firm's product or service and the woman herself must be acceptable in business terms. Simply sending a female will not carry an inadequate product or too-costly services:

> **(Hong Kong)** *"There are many expat and foreign women in top positions here. If you are good at what you do, they accept you. One Chinese woman told me, 'Americans are always watching you. One mistake and you are done. Chinese take a while to accept you and then stop testing you.'"*

> **(Hong Kong)** *"It doesn't make any difference if you are blue, green, purple, or a frog. If you have the best product at the best price, they'll buy."*

Nevertheless, the incremental advantages of easier communication and visibility, greater facility at relationships *per se,* and greater trust and openness often allow a female expatriate to enjoy significant pluses in a highly competitive atmosphere. Perhaps even more important, women's advantage in succeeding abroad draws on characteristics that have traditionally been a fundamental part of the female role in many cultures—their greater sensitivity, communication skills, and ability to establish rapport. Women need not buy into the competitive game. They can subtly shift the interaction out of the power and dominance modes so typical of business interchange—and so highly dysfunctional in cross-cultural relations—into the sort of cooperative, collaborative modes becoming increasingly important today.

Global competition is a tough game, and "world class" standards are a genuine challenge. Our opponents are worthy foes, strong competitors with numerous advantages. Foreign firms now control state-of-the-art technology, producing top-quality, low-cost products and services that respond quickly and effectively to worldwide clients' rapidly changing needs. Moreover, they often enjoy lower costs for capital and personnel, concerted government support and, in some cases, nontariff, cultural barriers to foreign firms' entry into their domestic markets and long-established relationships with other foreign nations. These advantages must be overcome if North American firms are to prosper in the future. Yet the traditional image of business as warfare and the character of the relationships based on it are increasingly dysfunctional. New modes of "collaborative competition" require traditionally "female" skills. The new competition is so challenging that only the best can stay in the game; we need all the advantages we can muster—including full usage of the best of our resources, male and female.

Alliances and Cooperative Competition

In businesses from automobiles to semiconductors, insurance and financial services to brokering and steel, competition is very often a matter not only of global enterprise but of collaboration with other firms, foreign as well as domestic. Collaborative competition succeeds by making common cause, by cooperation rather than the independence so typical of North American business behavior. Alliances may be essential to navigating the intricacies of, for instance, nontariff barriers to entering the Japanese market; making the connections required to do business in foreign lands; and especially sharing the increasingly substantial investment required to develop new technologies. Global operations require coordinated activities across the whole spectrum of business activity, not merely sales or marketing. Success rests upon relationships, including those at the most senior executive levels—relationships made far more difficult by cultural differences.

Among the more important differences between North America and the cultures of the Pacific Rim, South America, the Middle East, Africa, and most of Europe are the different cultural "clocks" and norms, particularly regarding the depth and strength of relationships *per se:*

> *"In Germany, your product is most important to your success; in Japan, it is the human relationships you build. Without them, you will not succeed." (Manager of a trading company)*[22]

> *"The Japanese don't want people who do a good job but have a bad attitude." (Japanese CEO, automobile industry)*[23]

> *". . . strict adherence to personal loyalty is at the core of Japanese concern for people rather than for principles."*[24]

The Bottom Line

In a highly competitive world, especially one generating new norms of business behavior that are counterintuitive to past practice, only the most canny organizations will prosper. Where many competitors form alliances and cooperative ventures, firms that cannot or will not, will operate at a significant disadvantage. They will have to struggle along, "reinventing the wheel" with each new culture.

The sorts of collaborative alliance we have described go far beyond selling or buying abroad. They encompass a broad spectrum of joint activities and common endeavors united by a common thread: the need to negotiate, communicate, cooperate closely over an extended period of time, and build enduring professional relationships across significant intercultural barriers. Such relationships are a very serious matter in other cultures, where longevity and trust accrue together and where the nuances of communication can make or break a deal.

Often, simply because so much of "business" is, in the context of other cultures, really a "relationship," it may be invisible to those North Americans most intent on "business, first and last," and most impatient with "socializing." In many other cultures, what we may see as purely social is for them a crucial testing process—to discover whether a relationship can be created that might be the foundation for doing business. Failure to invest the time and energy needed to build the relationship may well doom any attempt to establish a business arrangement. Without a firm basis of trust, cross-cultural suspicion will find many reasons to feel insulted or challenged by a "rude" foreigner. Failure to comprehend that friendship may have important strategic consequences is equal folly.

Within such a context, women represent a significantly underutilized resource. With good management school credentials and business performance, women are a readily trainable, highly useful source of talent—and the international arena suggests a particularly apt new application for the relationship skills still more highly developed among women than among men today. We believe that women are perfect candidates for expatriate positions and international careers both because they perform so well, and because their skills are the skills of the future.

Of course, there are men who are sensitive and skilled in communication; and of course there are women who are insensitive. In general, however, it is women who tend to possess greater sensitivity and relationship skills. Does this mean that these skills cannot be taught to males? On the contrary: the socialization process most women experience is, indeed, a form of "teaching."

Women who are successful abroad can provide role models and coaching for their male colleagues. This means that the women will have to be seen as resources, consulted and relied upon for their special expertise. Business school curricula can also help. Both specialized coursework and cross-cultural elements in all courses can highlight the importance of the international arena. Organizational behavior, organizational development, international management, and cross-cultural experiential activities can all present far broader perspectives than the standard BBA or MBA work focused completely on United States business practices.

American business already faces a global marketplace and global competition. This world is too small and too interconnected for "Lone Ranger" business practices; no single view encompasses all of its reality, and intolerance is a luxury we cannot afford. Traditional U.S. business approaches to competition as battle, which build arm's length business relationships on this basis, seem very risky indeed. Alliances, cooperative efforts, joint ventures, collaborations, and even business more or less as usual but carried out across cultural lines, can be facilitated by skills traditionally thought of as "female."

Global competition is a tough league, so challenging that we must employ all our skills and advantages, and the best of our people. We believe women possess a crucial advantage in social relationship and communication skills. Increasingly, the best of our male managers too will be working to acquire and hone important skills formerly seen as "female"—those centering on relationships, communication, and social sensitivity.

Endnotes

1. Discussions of competition are widespread in the business press and current management literature. See, for instance, Thomas J. Peters' "Competition and Compassion," *California Management Review*, 28(4), Summer 1986, pp. 11–26. Several sources for comparison figures on the U.S. economy and those of our trading partners can be found in Lester Thurow's *The Zero Sum Solution*. New York: Simon and Schuster, 1985; and Bruce Merrifield, U.S. Department of Labor, cited in Lester Thurow's "Why We Can't Have a Wholly Service Economy," *Technology Review*, March 1985.

    For a thought provoking look at some of the changes, see also Thomas J. Peters, "A World Turned Upside Down," *Academy of Management Executive*, 1(3), August 1987, 231–242.
2. Carol Gilligan, *In a Different Voice*. Cambridge, MA: Harvard University Press, 1982.
3. See "Women, Men and Leadership: A Critical Review of Assumptions, Practices and Change in the Industrialized Nations," by Jeff Hearn and P. Wendy Parkin. *International Studies of Management & Organization*, v. 16 (Fall-Winter 1986), pp. 33–60 for a useful discussion from a thoughtfully international perspective.
4. Melvin Konner, *The Tangled Wing: Biological Constraints on the Human Spirit*. New York: Harper Colophon, 1982.
5. Gary N. Powell and D. Anthony Butterfield, "The 'Good Manager': Masculine or Androgynous?", *Academy of Management Journal* 22: 2 (1979), pp. 395–403.
6. U.S. Department of Labor, 1982.
7. A. Trafford, R. Avery, J. Thornton, J. Carey, J. Galloway, and A. Sanoff, "She's Come a Long Way—Or Has She?". *U.S. News and World Report*, August 6, 1984, 44–51.
8. Nancy J. Adler, "Women in International Management: Where Are They?". *California Management Review*, 26(4), Summer 1984, 78–89.
9. See Footnote 8 above.
10. See Nancy J. Adler's "Do MBAs Want International Careers?", *International Journal of Intercultural Relations*, 10(3), 1986, 277–300 and "Women Do Not Want International Careers and Other Myths About International Management," *Organizational Dynamics*, 13(2), Autumn 1984, 66–79.
11. Nancy J. Adler, "Expecting International Success: Female Managers Overseas." *Columbia Journal of World Business*, 19(3), Fall 1984, 79–85.
12. N. Thal and P. Cateora. "Opportunities for Women in International Business," *Business Horizons*, 22(6), December 1979, 21–27.
13. There are a number of useful resources for information on women in Japanese management, including the following: Tracy Dahlby, "In Japan, Women Don't Climb the Corporate Ladder," *New York Times*, September 18, 1977; M.M. Osako, "Dilemmas of Japanese Professional Women," *Social Problems*, 26, 1978, 15–25; Marguerite Kaminski and Judith Paiz, "Japanese Women in Management: Where

Are They?" *Human Resource Management,* 23(3), Fall 1984, 277–292; and Patricia G. Stinhoff and Kazuko Tanaka, "Women Managers in Japan," *International Studies of Management and Organization,* 17(3–4), Fall-Winter 1987, 108–132. Reprinted in Nancy J. Adler and Dafna N. Israeli (Eds.) *Women in Management Worldwide.* Armonk, NY: M.E. Sharpe, 1988.

14. Blas F. Ople, "Working Managers, Elites," *The Human Spectrum of Development.* Manila, the Philippines: Institute for Labor and Management, 1981.
15. Audrey Chan, "Women Managers in Singapore: Citizens for Tomorrow's Economy," in Nancy J. Adler and Dafna N. Israeli (Eds.) *Women in Management Worldwide.* Armonk, NY: M.E. Sharpe, 1988.
16. Nancy J. Adler (Ed.) *Women in Management Worldwide,* special issue of *International Studies of Management and Organization,* 17(3–4), Fall-Winter 1987, and Nancy J. Adler and Dafna N. Israeli (Eds.) *Women in Management Worldwide.* Armonk, NY: M.E. Sharpe, 1988.
17. Nancy J. Adler, "Pacific Basin Managers: A *Gaijin* Not a Woman," *Human Resource Management,* 26(2), Summer 1987, 169–192.
18. Eric Morgenthaler, "Women of the World: More U.S. Firms Put Females in Key Posts in Foreign Countries," *Wall Street Journal,* March 16, 1978, 1, 27.
19. Edward T. Hall and Mildred Reed Hall, *Hidden Differences: Doing Business with the Japanese.* Garden City, NY: Anchor Pres/Doubleday, 1987.
20. See Footnote 12 above.
21. See Footnote 15 above.
22. See Footnote 16 above.
23. See Footnote 16 above.
24. Mark Zimmerman, *How to Do Business with the Japanese.* New York: Random House, 1985.

The Wall Street Journal, March 8, 1988.

They Wouldn't Hire Them

Of 197 chief executives interviewed by recruiter Canny, Bowen Inc., 54% think that most presidential candidates since World War II haven't had sufficient managerial experience to be the nation's CEO.

Planning

Many words we use to discuss work and management have moralistic connotations. For example, in our society, to describe a person as not motivated to work often implies a basic character or moral flaw. Consequently many of us feel guilty when we shirk or even think of shirking.

In our view, the idea of planning has similar moral connotations. We are taught very early how important it is that we plan our time. A little later in life we are urged to plan our careers. In college, we are admonished—often as freshmen—to make a plan of what courses we will take. In fact, if we showed evidence of not taking planning seriously, we may have been screened out of certain colleges because we appeared to lack direction or did not seem to know what we wanted to do. In the workplace we are taught to plan ahead whether that be for the day, the week, the year, or longer. To be criticized as failing to plan is a telling criticism.

This stress on planning has spawned many techniques to help motivate us to plan and to plan effectively. Clearly these efforts have been of great benefit to many people. Given limited time and resources and many competing demands for them, planning helps individuals to focus on what they judge to be important and to know what things to say no to. Moreover, planning can increase the likelihood that needed resources will be available when needed. (The advantages that Japanese manufacturers obtain from their "just-in-time" system, where parts arrive at exactly the time they are needed, are a prime example of the benefits of systematic and careful planning.) There is no doubt that planning deserves much of the homage we pay it—"Apple Computer's Debi Coleman" certainly demonstrates this.

On the other hand, like most virtues, piety can replace substance. Mechanistic rituals (filling out forms; sorting tasks into piles by priority; holding daily, weekly, annual planning meetings) demonstrate to oneself and to others that planning has been done. With this mind set we often think that once the plan has been created and agreed to, planning has been done.

When approached in this way, planning is often suboptimal. For one thing, in a rapidly changing world, we recognize that what we assume today may be very different tomorrow. Consequently, it is difficult to motivate ourselves to plan—"What's the use?" we ask ourselves. Moreover, the plan sometimes takes on a life of its own. Having forced ourselves to do all the work of developing a detailed plan, people often resist changing it. Later, when we see how far off our previous plan was, we find it difficult to motivate ourselves to plan again. Our mistake has been to substitute the thought or the idea for the action by equating the development of a plan with planning.

Because plans developed with this mind set have often yielded disappointing results, planning has gotten a bad name. (See the first article in this section—"The Creation.") In fact, C. Northcote Parkinson, a most astute observer of organizations, has concluded that " . . . perfection of planning is a symptom of decay."[1] Focusing on the planning of buildings, Parkinson found that perfection of planned layout by organizations " . . . is achieved only by institutions on the point of collapse."[2] Why should this be so? Parkinson explained that an organization engaged in discovery and progress has no time to plan its corporate headquarters. More recently, another astute observer, Karl Weick wrote " . . . plans have been overrated as a crucial component for accomplishment of effective actions."[3]

Weick, however, argued that plans are still important, but for reasons other than what people normally think. He suggested, for instance, that plans function as advertisements that can attract potential investors. In this sense, plans help people who read them (that is, managers, customers, or shareholders) to see ways that their needs can be met. Moreover, plans can serve as symbols that signal new directions to members or outsiders. Plans also serve as screens to evaluate the strength of commitments of people. In this sense, Weick views them as games—if people in the system want something badly enough they can demonstrate this by embedding their energies in a plan. Finally, Weick notes that plans are excuses for interaction; creating plans requires that actors from various parts of the system (often those who would need to work together to implement the plan) talk with each other. This interaction helps people get to know each other and learn from each other. As a result, the organization becomes better prepared to implement the plan as well as respond to other problems. In Weick's words, "Plans are a pretext under which several valuable activities take place in organizations."[4]

Weick's ideas lead directly to the view of planning we advanced in this section. Planning is not an end in itself; rather it is a process that facilitates making things happen in an organization. For example, planning influences the knowledge and motivation people have about the organization and a particular project or task. Moreover, the planning process is intricately related to other processes within the organization. For example, the communication process in an organization influences how much and what kind of information people have available for deciding what is the right thing to do. (Many of these ideas are effectively illustrated in David Hurst's paper in this section entitled "Why Strategic Management Is Bankrupt".)

When we view planning as a process perspective, we can appreciate why the ritualistic approach that focuses on creating "the plan" is so inadequate. In some sense that approach leads to the activity of planning and the plan itself becoming ends in themselves. People become more concerned with technique—doing planning right rather than with doing the right thing. A plan can also become detached from the strategic questions that underpin it in the first place. People lose sight of what issues the plan was designed to address. In short, the planning becomes separate from the real activity of the organization.

In the articles that follow, we see many of the outcomes of this divorce. We see top level managers and corporate staffs becoming so far removed from the concrete needs of the organization that they misunderstand what is happening. Somehow the sophisticated planning techniques of the specialists must be harmonized with the realities of implementation. In other instances, we see how the very techniques that people use to communicate successfully in some ways make it difficult for them to develop an effective strategic plan. They become wedded to past techniques and processes. On the other hand, we see many instances where planning is an integral part of other activities, and that the *way* planning is done can communicate the mission of an organization. Moreover, it should become clear that planning never stops and, since plans will often fail, organizations need to be prepared to respond to these failures. It is our view that such responses will be most apt to be effective when the plans themselves have been developed organically—that is, as a process that is fully integrated with the ongoing activities of the organization.

Finally, plans do not automatically become reality. As Drucker put it so well, "The best plan is *only* a plan, that is, good intentions, unless it *degenerates into work*."[5] To make a plan more than a hope—to implement it—often requires considerable skill and effort. There are always conflicting objectives and preferences within an organization, and plans can become the stimulus for forcing these conflicts to be recognized and addressed. Throughout these selections we see various ways—force, commitment to mission, skill in framing decisions—that are used to make plans become reality.

To reiterate, planning is a process that is integrally related to other organizational processes. To fail to recognize this organic relationship is to misunderstand an important part of how effective managers manage. To accept the more mechanistic view is to increase one's vulnerability to either not planning and feeling guilty, or planning and being frustrated by not seeing one's hopes become real. We hope the following articles help cement the more organic view.

References

1. C. N. Parkinson, *Parkinson's Law* (Boston: Houghton Mifflin, 1957), p. 61.
2. *Ibid.*, p. 60.
3. K. E. Weick, *The social psychology of organizing*, 2d ed. (Reading, MA: Addison-Wesley, 1979), p. 10.
4. *Ibid.*, p. 11.
5. P. F. Drucker, *Management* (New York: Harper & Row, 1974), p. 128.

The Creation

Anonymous

In the beginning was the plan
and then came the assumptions
and the assumptions were without form
and the plan was completely without substance
and darkness was upon the faces of the workers.
And they spake unto their group heads, saying:
"It is a crock of shit, and it stinketh."
And the group heads went unto their section heads, and sayeth:
"It is a pail of dung, and none may abide the odour thereof."
And the section heads went unto their managers, and sayeth unto them:
"It is a container of excrement, and it is very strong,
such that none here may abide by it."
And the managers went unto their Director, and sayeth unto him:
"It is a vessel of fertilizer, and none may abide its strength."
And the Directors went unto their Director-General, and sayeth:
"It contains that which aids plant growth, and it is very strong."
And the Director-General went unto the assistant Deputy Minister,
and sayeth unto him:
"It promoteth growth, and it is very powerful."
And the ADM went unto the Deputy Minister, and sayeth unto him:
"This powerful new plan will actively promote the growth and
efficiency of the department, and this area in particular."
and the Deputy Minister looked upon the plan,
and saw that it was good,
and the plan became policy.

Why Strategic Management Is Bankrupt

David K. Hurst

*The strategic management paradigm, the dominant management paradigm in
North America, fails when it comes to helping a company move successfully
into new ventures. The author proposes placing strategic management within
the larger "creative management" paradigm. . . .*

One Company's Experiences

Our experiences over the past 25 years with the strategic management model are instructive and, as the reader will see, appear to parallel those of many North American corporations. When our company first went public in 1962, it was a tiny steel distribution business with five branches and $14 million in sales. The management group consisted of the president, the only member of the founding family working in the company, and his manager, a seasoned steel operator who had spent 20 years in the business. Both men were intimately involved with the day-to-day activities of the steel distribution operation, and their objectives and strategy reflected a determination to stick to that business.

The early 1960s was a good time to be in the steel service-center industry in Canada. Driven by the demands of the baby boom, the country was developing an infrastructure with the necessary manufacturing industries, and steel users were poorly serviced by distributors. The general economy appeared in excellent shape, and there was much talk of economists' newly found ability to fine tune the important variables. Government at last seemed to have solved the perennial problems of cyclical recessions and unemployment. In the private sector the talk was all of growth and planning.

Sometime between 1962 and 1964 our company president caught that growth bug and resolved to make the company grow. His operating manager, a tough, hard-nosed taskmaster from the old school, was clearly not the man to make this happen. But the president found an individual who fitted the requirements perfectly. An engineer with a Harvard M.B.A., this man had spent 15 years at Proctor and Gamble. He was organized, understood strategic planning, and was determined to make businesses grow. He joined the company in 1965 as executive vice-president.

The organization changed in several ways after he joined. First, it became a good deal more formal, with written policies and plans. Second, a split was created between operating units and the holding entity—a split between managers and investors, between divisions and the head office.

At this time, comprehensive planning was introduced into the corporation. Divisions were asked to submit five-year forecasts to the corporate office which, faced with competing demands for scarce funds, would then allocate capital using various financial tests and minimum requirements for return on investments.

Two groups with distinctly different perspectives and interests began to emerge in the company: the operating managers who ran the profit centers and the "investors," the corporate office heads who ran the holding company on behalf of the public shareholders. This second group acted as a kind of mediating investment group, investing on behalf of the shareholders in a portfolio of divisions.

To give themselves the perspective and space needed to plan for growth, the president and executive vice-president moved their offices away from the steel operations. They saw themselves as "informed directors," supplying advice and counsel to the divisions as required. They recognized that they could not be operators and could not provide general management support. Their management function was limited to the assessment, reward, and replacement, if necessary, of the operating management.

This form of organization, dubbed *federal decentralization* by Peter Drucker, is undoubtedly good for operating managers. In our company it gave them the necessary space to operate without interference, even though at times their autonomy bordered on complete independence. But federal decentralization creates a head office of powerful, driven managers who have no businesses to run, only a group of autonomous divisions to oversee. The head office makes decisions in the areas of portfolio structure, capital allocation, and senior personnel, but these activities are not enough to engage the full attention of top executives. The temptation for the corporate office to buy something is nearly irresistible. Thus, when the president and executive vice-president moved to a corporate office, the stage was set for the company to grow by acquisition.

Lessons from Acquisitions

Between 1964 and 1980, when we were acquired by another firm, our corporation made 27 separate acquisitions, which involved more than 40 distinct businesses. This program expanded the company's size tremendously through the 1970s; but in the process, the investment function and its needs totally overpowered the management function and its concerns. The situation made the company vulnerable to a takeover and was a major factor in the subsequent collapse of the organization.

Specifically, the initial four acquisitions were failures. The first company bought was a small manufacturer of precision equipment, primarily for the auto industry. Since the owner/manager wanted to retire, our vice-president of administration was put in charge "to introduce the necessary organization and control" and to work with the acquired company's existing management. However, the acquired company's management was in turmoil for the next 18 months: All managers were replaced, and many skilled workers were lost.

Fortunately, a surge in the marketplace brought the business back into the black. At that time, our corporation decided to acquire a similar business and merge the two. This led to the second disaster.

On paper the numbers look impressive. It seemed that a combination of cost savings and margin improvements would result in a significant profit. Instead the combination of the two businesses became almost instantly unprofitable. Sales sagged and margins shrank as the business cycle turned down. It became clear that the businesses were not nearly as similar as they had appeared. Each one served slightly different markets and had different ways of operating. The complete merging of the two businesses led to a predictable loss of good people. The combined business never did make an operating profit. In 1972 we were relieved to sell it to ITT Canada.

Early in the game we also acquired a steel distribution operation very similar to those in our core business. We planned at the outset that this business would be run by our own operating managers. In fact the returns were predicated upon their ability to turn the business around. The first year was expected to be tough, but the medium- and longer-range view called for the acquisition to be an important source of new income. The purchase appeared to involve little financial risk because the major asset being acquired was steel inventory. The deal proceeded.

A year later only one member of the acquired company's original management team was left. It would take five years and a good deal of help from the 1973–1974 economic boom before the business again became profitable. During that time the operating management was so preoccupied with problems that it missed out on most of the considerable growth in the markets served by the acquisition. The employees who had left in the first year formed their own business, and with new equipment and financing they became very successful. They outstripped the business we had acquired in both size and profitability—a very perverse outcome.

Our fourth acquisition in this "program of planned corporate growth" was in high technology. The business was "in applications engineering in the field of process control and instrumentation," as the acquisition recommendation put it. Reasons for the acquisition of the business included:

- The high growth rate of the industry
- The presence of an undeveloped niche in the marketplace.
- Large potential markets, of which a small share would generate significant sales volumes.
- Diffuse and scattered competition.
- Technical synergies available to other businesses.
- The parent company's ability to provide financial management and policy direction.

The investment was made by way of a debenture in March 1968. We were forced to call the loan and put in a receiver to wind up the company's affairs. The problem was that this high-tech company had never really been an organization; rather, it had been a group of technical experts, all doing whatever interested them. There had been no core of competence.

A Reevaluation

Following these inauspicious beginnings senior managers in the corporate office took stock. They again asked themselves what business they were in and concluded that it was "industrial distribution." This new definition coincided (unfortunately, as it turned out) with their first successful acquisition.

This time a family-owned distributor of ballbearings and power transmission equipment was acquired. The family, keen to sell but concerned that the employees and the business be well looked after, approached us through a mutual friend. The business had always been profitable, and several other buyers were wiling to pay the asking price. However, we were selected as the buyer because of the closer personal rapport the family felt it had with our company's senior management.

The existing management team stayed with the business after we acquired it. The business continued to be profitable, growing steadily by branch network expansion, and became a major contributor to our results. Unfortunately, this success was attributed to the "industrial distribution" strategy. After making two more steel-related acquisitions, we set off on what was to become a disastrous course, a series of acquisitions in the building supplies industry.

The Grand Design

By 1972 we were still earning less than $100 million in revenue. Outside of the steel business, our only successful acquisition was the bearings distribution operation. This industry continued to be extremely attractive to us, but in both Canada and the United States few of the distributors were for sale. Those that were for sale were quickly snapped up by Bearings Inc. and Genuine Parts, the two largest operators in the industry.

In its search for new growth opportunities, senior management came upon a hardware supply business in eastern Canada. Run by a self-made man, a political figure in the region, the business had an astonishing growth record. This man had parlayed a bank loan and his political contacts into a small group of assorted trading companies. With the sale of his business he became financially independent. In addition, he was given a mandate to make the new division grow—and grow it did. Between 1972 and 1976 we invested more than $50 million (much of it borrowed) in the Building Supplies Group, as it came to be called. Twelve business units, located between Nova Scotia and British Columbia, were acquired.

Acquisition was piled on acquisition without any attempt on our corporation's part to digest what were essentially small family businesses. Unfortunately, the businesses were not particularly profitable; rampant inflation and FIFO accounting (which allows increases in inventory costs to be reflected in profits) made them appear much more profitable than they really were. The profit picture for each acquisition developed into a pattern. The business would generate profits for the first one or two years after acquisition and then slump badly. Economic forecasts for each unit began to show the "hockey stick" effect—losses for the short term followed by a steady recovery to handsome profits in the long term.

Even though senior management accepted this outlook, the stock market did not. Our share price, after many years of trading at around book value, began to fall below that range.

Why did corporate management allow this acquisition activity to continue? One of the chief opponents of this course, a steel operator, argued that cash was being siphoned off from his steel operations to finance a reckless acquisition spree. Nevertheless, dedication to growth undoubtedly made the corporate office amenable to strategies that promised growth. Perhaps even more important, at the root of corporate management's inability to see reality was a grand strategic design developed by the management of the Building Supplies Group.

The grand design culminated in a national chain of supplies stores linked by a sophisticated on-line computer system and operating at several levels of distribution—retail, wholesale, commercial. Numerous examples of this kind of organization were cited, including Lowes and Hechinger (two successful U.S. regional building supplies distributors) and (one trembles to remember it) Wickes (which went into Chapter 11 in 1981, the second largest U.S. company ever to do so). Because of the emphasis on formal, written communications and the investor-manager distinction, these strategies, which looked good on paper, were never tested in practice. Corporate management never went into the field to talk to employees without the filter of senior management.

Much later while walking around a particularly dilapidated Building Supplies Group operation in 1979, I was reminded of Liddel Hart's report of the World War I general visiting the battlefield: "This highly placed officer from general headquarters was on his first visit to the battlefront—at the end of the four months' battle. Growing increasingly uneasy as the car approached the swamp-like edges of the battle area, he eventually burst into tears, crying, 'Good God, did we really send men to fight in that?' To which his companion replied that the ground was far worse ahead."

For us, the further we proceeded with the acquisition(s) program, the harder it became to get out of it. In theory the investor role of the corporate office allowed it to divest itself of a business, but in practice this did not work. There were always objections from the various group managements, the inevitable "hockey stick" forecasts, and the arguments that one more acquisition would complete the puzzle and fulfill the grand design. The company had become trapped in its own conceptual framework.

The pace of acquisitions continued, with profits coming primarily from the steel operations and the bearing distribution companies. The inflationary growth of the late 1970s, together with the Canadian government's reckless investment incentives designed to encourage energy self-sufficiency, helped sustain the trend. The steel cycle peaked in 1979: The company produced a net income of $14 million on revenues of $535 million, with the Building Supplies Group producing 7% of the profit on 30% of the revenue. The steel cycle faltered in 1980 and recovered briefly in 1981 before plunging into its steepest decline since the Great Depression.

After the Fall

The downward plunge in the business cycle caused problems in all of our businesses, but the failure of our strategic frameworks was brought home to us most forcibly in the collapse of the Building Supplies Group. This group of operations, which had been acquired at such great cost over the previous ten years, collapsed in two senses: financially and conceptually. The severe recession battered the entire economy, and many marginal businesses failed. On the conceptual level, the entire grand design, the coast-to-coast network of distribution operations, was suddenly revealed to be a management delusion, a paper plan without substance. In hindsight, every strategic view taken by the management team of the Building Supplies Group seemed to have been a wishful pattern imposed upon the future by a small number of managers at the top.

Now the reader may well feel that these corporate disasters are indicative of management incompetence, faulty analysis, and misdirected strategy. Indeed the proponents of strategic planning usually make this argument. "There is nothing wrong with the model," they say. "All you have to do is apply it properly." Well, there *is* something wrong with the model.

The problem with the strategic paradigm is the assumptions underlying it. The paradigm assumes that businesses are like complex, mechanical clockworks operating in an environment that can be objectively determined by senior managers of the business. It is supposed that this knowledge, together with the managers' assessment of their organizations' strengths and weaknesses, can be used to devise a strategy of objectives, plans, and so forth. These strategies are meant to allow managers to structure their organizations and adapt to and/or take control of the environment.

But these strategic structures are built on retrospective foundations. They work for the future only so long as the pattern of the future mimics that of the past. Such stability is unusual and does not last for long. The last such period was the 30 or 35 years after World War II. This largely benign economic environment caused the strategic view of business to become extremely popular. Like the economists' ability to "fine tune" the economy, the strategic method appeared to work—at least for a while.

A deeper problem with the strategic model is the economic framework upon which it is based. This framework assumes that capital is the scarce resource to be rationed among many competing investment opportunities. In fact, the current situation in North America is quite the opposite: Opportunities are scarce, while capital is plentiful. I shall argue that the inability of the strategic model to create such opportunities lies at the heart of its problems.

Toward an Alternative Model

Alfred North Whitehead once wrote that "understanding has two modes of advance, the gathering of detail within assigned pattern, and the discovery of novel pattern with its emphasis on novel detail." This is also the case with the progress of business organizations. On the one hand is the strategic mode, with its gathering of data within an existing conceptual framework. On the other hand is a more naive mode, by which data are gathered apparently without pattern, and in that process new patterns are formed. In contrast to the strategic mode, this might be called the mission mode—a search for mission, purpose, and meaning for both the organization and its employees.

Exhibit 1 shows clearly the contrast between the two modes, although the reader is cautioned that the conceptual problem lies less with the nouns and the verbs than it does with the conjunctions used to connect them. Western

Exhibit 1 Two Organizational Processes

Strategy	Mission
Planned	Spontaneous
Analysis	Synthesis
External	Internal
Things	Phenomena
States	Relationships
Strengths/weaknesses	Competencies/preferences
Reduction	Emergence
Fundamentals	Purpose
Designed	Evolves
Objectives	Values
Precise	Vague
Targets	Directions
Set	Appear
Focus	Awareness
Search	Recognition
Means	Ends
How	Why
Make it happen	Let it happen
Today's business	Tomorrow's business

thought is biased toward "either . . . or" rather than toward "both . . . and." This bias is largely the result of our failure to reconnect the conceptual categories to which we have reduced reality by our exclusive use of rational thought structures. It reflects our penchant for linear thought and notions of cause and effect, as opposed to cyclical, interactive concepts. The key to understanding strategy and mission rests primarily on our ability to grasp the complex dynamic relationship that exists between the two.

The Task of Strategy

The lists in Exhibit 1 can be read both horizontally and vertically. The strategic management mode is a conscious, deliberate activity that focuses on a particular organization in a particular environment. The strategic manager stands outside of these "objects" and analyzes them, reducing them to some fundamental categories. This analysis is achieved, of course, by the use of complex conceptual frameworks that allow managers to generalize and manipulate aspects of reality. Targets are set to measure the corporation's progress toward objectives. The focus is on programs—how to "make it happen."

Now this is a very valuable process, but not for the purposes for which many managers use it. The strategic mode is helpful for looking *backward* rather than *forward,* for what it *excludes* rather than what it *contains.* The strategic mode cannot tell managers where they are going, only where they have been. It is useful for managing today's business, the business that already exists. The strategic mode requires some content that can be analyzed.

An organization has to exist *before* the strategic mode can be applied. Otherwise, there is nothing on which to focus and from which to generalize.

This requirement of the strategic mode interferes with the strategic manager's ability to discover new business opportunities. Discovery is only partially a problem of search; it is mainly a problem of recognition. The history of product innovation in business abounds with examples of this. After a comprehensive study carried out in the early 1950s, Arthur D. Little assured IBM that there would never be a market for more than 5,000 copiers of the kind then being developed by Haloid (which later became Xerox), and IBM rejected the license to the new process. In the 1980s both Parker Brothers and Milton Bradley turned down the opportunity to market Trivial Pursuit.

Thus exclusive use of the strategic mode leads to discovery of only what is recognized. A historical pattern is imposed on reality and, unless the world stays very stable, this pattern may not be appropriate in the future. This was what our company discovered during our acquisition years. Our view of the future was continually determined by our interpretation of past events.

Even though the strategic mode may not be very useful for creating new businesses, it is invaluable for getting rid of old ones, for "sloughing off yesterday's business," as Peter Drucker has put it. Any manager who has been through a turnaround can testify to the power of formal, strategic analysis applied to existing businesses. Without its use, organizations become complacent and overweight. To use a farming analogy, strategic management is a weeding device that allows healthy, productive crops to grow unharmed by weeds. But in the process it ensures that a different crop will never be grown.

The task of strategy is to "make it happen," but too often all the emphasis is put on the *make* and none on the *it*. To make anything happen, a person must first know what *it* is. When dealing with an existing business, managers may know what *it* is; but when they try to bring about change and develop new businesses, they usually don't know. The question "What is *it*?" is crucial. The role of the mission mode is to answer that question.

The Role of Mission
The mission mode consists of a process that is spontaneous rather than planned. It involves the gradual synthesis of phenomena internal to the organization, a growing awareness on many levels of relationships, competencies (things a person does well), and preferences (things a person likes to do). As the process proceeds, ideas begin aggregating in clusters around particular people and groups. Visions of what *could* be and a sense of purpose become clearer to the members of the organization. Values are discussed openly; as they are spread, refined, and shared, they begin to allow a *recognition* of what directions to take. The external environment of opportunity begins to crystallize, and these directions appear.

The role of the mission process, then, is to open up the organization to new opportunities by relaxing the tight downward focus of the existing strategy. The process releases to the surface deeply, perhaps unconsciously, held convictions and beliefs about what the organization means to its members. These values form a soft framework in which new opportunities at the periphery of vision may be netted. In other words, the role of the mission process is the "let it happen," when "it" is the process leading to the "it" of strategy.

The Interaction Between Mission and Strategy

The interaction between the mission and strategy modes is extraordinarily difficult for members within an organization to see, for the processes are "nested" inside one another. The processes of the mission mode precipitate strategic actions which, in turn, trigger mission processes, and the two modes are present simultaneously. A somewhat simplified model of the organization (Exhibit 2) shows the two processes connected by spirals. The power for the spin is provided by the twin processes of mission and strategy: Mission pulls while strategy pushes. Of course strategy can also be generated by the lone genius who knows just what to do. This method is a more direct process.

The mission process can be thought of as a way to pull the organization into the future. It brings opportunities (by ensuring that they are recognized) into the vortex of the organization, where they are transformed from ideas into innovations and from innovations into new products, services, or whatever. This transformation is accomplished by the strategy process, which cuts out old, unprofitable products and services and reduces innovations to practical programs. Mission supplies the form to which strategy can give substance.

This part of the process can be compared to the precipitation of crystals from a supersaturated solution. A liquid (people in the organization) is heated and stirred so that an amorphous powder (potential opportunities) can be dissolved (assimilated). As the liquid stops moving (changes mode) and cools (becomes rational), large crystals (good ideas) will appear out of the solution, solidify, and grow.

Exhibit 2 A Model of Organization Processes

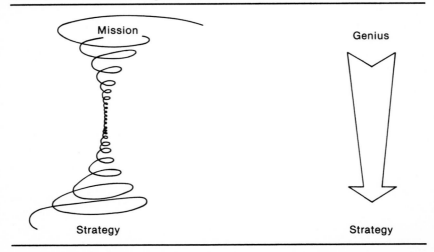

Mission

Genius

Strategy

Strategy

The analogy is fine as far as it goes, but it does not reflect the reverse process in which the decisions made affect the opportunity-recognition process. The organization's understanding of what has happened in the past will have an important influence over the way it sees the future.

This aspect of the process is best illustrated by Exhibit 3, which shows a returning outer set of spirals connecting strategy to mission. The inner and outer spirals combine to create a swirling toroidal, or donut, shape (the layers of the donut will be explained shortly). Thus an organization can be conceived of as being dynamic. Like the vortex that forms in bath water when one pulls out the plug, the structure of the organization is sustained only so long as energy is poured through the system. In this model the donut shape of the organization is sustained by mission (supplied either by process or genius) and strategy. Like Janus, the Roman god of the threshold, the organization looks forward to the future and back to the past. Mission prospects while strategy retrospects. The two meet in the present. The potentially perceivable environment is all around, but the environment actually perceived is represented by the "skin" of the donut. Thus the organization grows (learns) by expanding its perceived environment—by recognizing and processing opportunities. . . .

Why Strategic Management Is Bankrupt

The test of business solvency is not the size of assets but the relative balance of assets and liabilities. Strategic management has enormous assets, but often

Exhibit 3 A Dynamic Model of Organization Processes

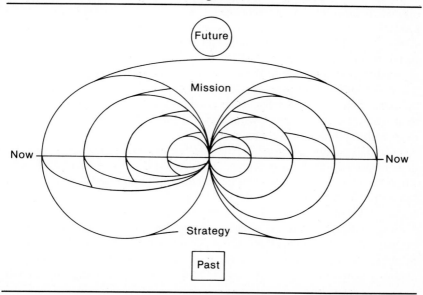

the claims against it exceed those assets. Instead of recognizing it as a rational tool for managing stability—for elaborating on success and culling failure—too many advocates view strategic management as a way to create innovation and lead change. Our experience suggests that this is not the case. The strategic management model is essential for managing today's business, but it cannot create tomorrow's because the strategic paradigm is sterile.

The strategic model also runs into trouble when it is used as an instrument to manage managers by objectives. By starting with the concept of objectives, the paradigm ignores the critical roles of imaginative vision and shared values. As a result, instead of growing from within the organization, vision and values turn into extensions of the personality of senior managers. The prevalence of the "tool" or "instrument" metaphor in strategic management is illustrative of this tendency. The manager is seen as a rational tool user who stands outside the situation. Objects are changed by the tool user but do not affect either the tool or its user. Thus the strategic management of people can easily become manipulative and elitist. In the absence of genius, purpose and meaning will be lost. So will the organization's ability to innovate—that is, to evolve.

Strategic management is a fine methodology with which to pursue given ends. But it functions poorly as a philosophy for reaching an agreement within an organization as to what those ends should be.

Leadership

In the past many writers on management have described leadership in terms of the qualities a single individual may possess. These qualities bear a striking resemblance to the various stages of the creative management process. Leaders, they say, have vision and values, conceptualize rapidly, and act decisively. We can now see that leadership is really a process, an ongoing dynamic relationship among a number of individuals in search of meaning. If leadership is effective, then these individuals will develop a shared vision, a sense of common purpose, and the ability to make their own unique contributions. Their work will satisfy their need for both identity and community, their striving both to become what they are and, at the same time, to belong to something larger than themselves.

Leadership is the process by which each individual is allowed to play his or her best role at the appropriate stage. We call the effective mingling of strengths a team. The achievement of teams within an organization is the result of true leadership. "When the great leader has done his work, the people will say 'We did it ourselves,'" wrote Lao Tzu in the fifth century B.C.

Too few business leaders today are innovators and developers of new industries. Most of our heroes are either paper entrepreneurs, assisted mightily by our tax laws, or technicians. (Keep in mind Maslow's definition: "A technician is a man who understands everything about his job except its ultimate purpose and its place in the order of the universe.") The result has been a profound loss of meaning for both the managers and the managed.

This loss of meaning is not restricted to business organizations. It pervades our social institutions, churches, governments, universities, and families. We have the answers but we have forgotten the important questions. This "freedom" from the important has made us slaves to the urgent. Too many managers have lost the vision of what they can become, of their sense of purpose.

The search for and the recognition of purpose and meaning are the mainsprings of all motivation. In this way, the processes discussed here are at the heart of both the most glorious and the most infamous periods in human history. When great leaders released these processes within their people, philosophy and art flourished and societies had their golden age. When great tyrants used the same processes for their own purposes, they led their people into darkness and disaster.

In business, the point at which everything starts to go wrong is also the point at which management believes that it can stand outside the system and manipulate the processes for its own benefit. Such actions generate perverse reactions because management is not outside the system looking in; it is inside the system looking at itself. The perverse outcomes of many acquisitions and mergers have been documented repeatedly. Following acquisitions, hundreds of major corporations have attempted to restructure their operations, usually by shedding the acquired businesses and returning to their core operations. Many acquisitions, especially those carried out by the large integrated oil companies, were based on the most rational and logical of reasons. Yet the results have often been the opposite of those intended.

Perverse outcomes are also endemic to government at all levels. Government housing programs have usually achieved results opposite those intended. Energy self-sufficiency programs lead to line-ups and shortages. Efforts to prop up foreign governments often succeed in alienating them from the people that they govern.

We persist with our efforts to achieve unilateral control and domination over complex systems. But we are part of these systems, and the systems are alive. They react *and* respond to our efforts to change them. In the short term we may get the logical results of our actions. In the longer run these results may be overwhelmed by natural consequences.

To change complex systems we need to start by changing ourselves. We do not have to change to anything *different*. We need only to stop trying to be things that we are not.

The change begins with the recognition that reality is not a given that is accessible to clear-eyed, rational perception. To be sure, parts of the world are accessible in this way, but reality is mostly multidimensional, and we as individuals are intimately involved in its construction. The business environments that strategists scan are as much an *output* of our culture as they are an *input* from reality. The recognition of this must have profound effects on our understanding of the meaning of objectivity. C. West Churchman has put it well: "Instead of the silly and empty claim that an observation is objective if it resides in the brain of an unbiased observer, one should say that an observation is objective if it is the creation of many inquirers with many different points of view."

These different points of view correspond to the different stages of the creative process. We need to abandon our notions of the lone manager as hero, who rationally solves the problems of the world. We must assemble teams to handle the total process. We need to combine the two great human gifts, reason and passion, the head and the heart, and we need to stand at the threshold of the present, looking at both the past and the future. Now is the only time. In that process our organizations may realize their potential. We may become what we are.

------------------●------------------

Goodbye, Corporate Staff

Thomas Moore

General Foods administers its empire from a gleaming monument of corpocracy that rises like an Aztec temple over a pond in Rye Brook, New York. But today the imposing architecture of the building and the headquarters organization it housed have become relics. Acquired by Philip Morris two years ago, General Foods recently announced it would dismantle its corporate staff hierarchy and eliminate most of its 2,000 headquarters jobs. An operating president will move his executives into the vacated offices; he and two other presidents will hire about half the people dumped by headquarters.

A corporation can slim down in lots of ways. U.S. companies seem to have tried them all, from selling off businesses to closing redundant plants. But an increasingly popular route to greater efficiency is cutting the corporate staff. That is the often vast collection of planners, economists, marketers, central purchasing agents, real estate managers, human-resources specialists, futurologists, other analysts, and deep thinkers who sit at headquarters and often annoy the operating executives by offering to help them. Says Robert Tomasko, author of the new book *Downsizing* and a partner at management consultants Temple Barker & Sloane: "Corporate staff is becoming an endangered species."

Some companies hack away indiscriminately, weakening critical control functions or lopping off valuable services. Others trim insufficiently or simply smoosh people around from one organization chart to another. But a few have shown how to slough off staff neatly. In many cases the employees who remain inhabit a strange new world in which decisions are quick, accountability is clear, and everyone is working harder.

Life in the new minimalist corporation is tougher but simpler. The small corporate headquarters may be located a thousand miles or more from principal operating units, as the Charlotte, North Carolina, office of steelmaker Nucor is. The new head office decides how to allocate corporate capital among internal and external investments, watches the investments closely, and replaces managers who do not meet budgets. Freed to manage their businesses, general managers decide what services they need and whether they should get them from corporate headquarters, from their own staffs, or from outside suppliers.

Many chief executives never felt comfortable with the entourages they allowed to grow around them. In 1953, in the early days of America's postwar managerial revolution, John L. McCaffrey, then chief of International Harvester, told FORTUNE: "We sit at our desks all day while around us whiz and gyrate a vast number of special activities, some of which we only dimly understand. And for each of these activities, there is a specialist. . . . All of them, no doubt, are good to have. All seem to be necessary. All are useful on frequent occasions. But it has reached the point where the greatest task of the president is to understand enough of all these specialties so that when a problem comes up he can assign the right team of experts to work on it."

Today, with U.S. corporations under pressure from foreign competition, these doubts have swelled into a managerial counterrevolution. Partners at McKinsey & Co., the management consultants often brought in to do hatchet work by bloated corporations too timid to draw their own blood, argue that the large staffs of traditional multibusiness corporations no longer serve much purpose in the U.S., Britain, and other developed economies.

Big corporations historically created value by recruiting and training talent and providing capital to invest in operations, explains Stephen Coley, a McKinsey principal in Chicago. They still do in developing countries. But in efficient economies, with sophisticated headhunters, investment bankers, and consultants for just about anything, corporations can buy these services and no longer need full-time staffs to provide them. "Our view is that value is created only in the operating units," says Coley. "The role of the corporation in a developed economy is to act as a demanding and farseeing parent, but not one that tries to do everything for the businesses it is trying to nurture."

Few companies have shown how to do that as successfully as Anglo-American conglomerate Hanson Trust (1986 revenues: $6 billion). "What Hanson does is go out and find corporate anachronisms—top-heavy, widely diversified companies—and then bust them up and get rid of corporate staff," says Coley. In the past 14 years its U.S. arm, Hanson Industries North America, has taken over ten companies, including two big industrial conglomerates, U.S. Industries and SCM Corp. Between 1982 and October's stock market crash, Hanson shares more than quadrupled in value; they have since fallen by a quarter. Hanson's latest move: a just-consummated $2.2 billion deal to buy

Large Companies with Small Staffs

It pays to keep lean at the top: Most of these abstemiously staffed giants have performed admirably in recent years.

Company	1986 Sales (millions)	Employees		Sales (millions) Per Headquarters Employee
		Total	Headquarters	
Burlington Northern	$6,941	43,000	77	$90
Transamerica	$7,120	15,200	100	$71
CSX	$6,345	52,000	100	$63
Dana	$3,695	36,000	72	$51
Nucor	$ 755	3,700	17	$44
Hanson Industries	$3,769	33,000	89	$42
Henley Group	$3,172	18,000	75	$42
Heinz	$4,366	45,000	175	$25
Borg-Warner	$3,623	82,000	175	$21
James River	$2,607	35,500	175	$15
Brunswick	$1,717	18,700	180	$10

Source: Temple Barker & Sloane

Kidde Inc., another conglomerate that makes everything from Jacuzzis to pots and pans.

Sir Gordon White, Hanson Industries' jetsetting chairman, holes up in an elegant Park Avenue office with a staff of 12, including secretaries and the company's one public relations officer. But the home of most of Hanson's top U.S. executives, which Sir Gordon rarely visits, is back-to-basics chic. The company leases part of the third and fourth floors of a modest four-story building in an exurban industrial park near the Amtrak train station in Iselin, New Jersey. Inside, Hanson's headquarters has the panache of an insurance company's back office. Almost all the furniture, right down to the framed prints and potted plants, are leftovers from USI and SCM.

As Hanson Industries has quadrupled in size in the past four years, its headquarters has grown only from 29 people to 89. That is a fraction of what many smaller U.S. companies employ. USI, for instance, had 172 and SCM 182 at headquarters. Hanson pools a dozen or so personal computers and does not own or lease a mainframe; it uses an outside payroll service. The company's total corporate expense, including salaries and office space, was $17 million last year—about one-quarter the combined corporate expenses of USI, SCM, and Hanson at the time of their mergers.

Hanson's organization chart is something a child can understand. Sir Gordon and President David Clarke are at the top. Reporting to Clarke are five corporate vice presidents in charge of law, finance, organization development, acquisitions, and operations. Six group vice presidents, each overseeing a batch of individual operating companies, report to the corporate VP for operations. The senior management group of 12 at Iselin is supported by 42 middle managers and 35 secretaries and clerks.

Clarke, 46, an avid sailor who used to own a fishing business, professes to be astonished by the excess corporate baggage carried by most big companies, not to mention the grand life to which many top executives have become accustomed. That's a major reason he cites to explain American companies' loss of their competitive edge. He likens the atmosphere at pre-Hanson USI to a country club's. The company had moved from New York to a spacious new building with a view on Dolphin Cove, a picturesque inlet of Long Island Sound in Stamford, Connecticut. In the summer the staff knocked off at 5:30 P.M.—a half hour earlier than normal—and at noon on Fridays. "That is not an appropriate way to run a company," says Clarke. "We are fighting a war with the Japanese, the Taiwanese, and the Europeans, and you don't want your people sitting on a golf club green."

Quickly Clarke homed in on superfluous staff specialties. "We start out with a zero-base premise," he says. "We want to keep nothing more than what it takes to get the job done." His first act: firing the four-person economics department. "I don't want economists taking away the authority of managers," he says. "As CEO, I want my managers to sign in blood what *they* think housing starts will be."

Then he got rid of 30 outside consultants: "Why should the company spend another $2 million a year to help me do my job?" He eliminated a central marketing department and the real estate department, which had not sold a parcel of property in three years. Clarke explains: "The problem with an in-house capability for something like real estate is that this guy puts himself out of business if he achieves his goal, which is to liquidate property." Within a year Clarke sold USI's headquarters building for $9.4 million.

At SCM he pulled the plug on an immense data services center in North Carolina that cost $8 million a year. Though many streamlining companies are letting computer services grow, Clarke felt the center was overloading his executives with information, making it harder for them to reach decisions, not easier. He also jettisoned SCM's management training center on the Hudson River and its 26 staffers. "Hiring and developing the right people is the most important thing I do as a manager," he says. Strategic planners are another group of employees that bit the dust. Clarke reasons that strategy is too important to be left to experts; managers must do it themselves. Like most other executives, he says he gets no kick from firing people, but adds, "You shouldn't let the human element affect the basic business decision." He tolerates lawyers as a necessary evil and instructs them to resolve issues rather than prolong them.

Clarke maintains that keeping an organization streamlined is second in importance only to creating an excellent product at the right price. It's like sailboat racing, he says. He won the Newport-Bermuda race last year in part by staying lighter than most other boats. As competing craft loaded up on beer and food, sinking farther into the water, he took only the required five gallons of water per crew member plus dehydrated food to save weight. Rather than getting a good sleep below deck, the off-watch crew often clipped themselves to lifelines on deck to keep the boat sailing flat and fast.

"There was nothing in that boat that we didn't need to get to St. David's Lighthouse in Bermuda," Clarke says. "The old guard at the yacht clubs say minimalists like me are ruining the sport by making sailing unpleasant. But I'm not in it to be comfortable. The winning is the fun. That's the whole point."

A company that runs an even tighter ship than Hanson is Nucor, the feisty mini-mill company in North Carolina that is fast becoming a maxiplayer in steel manufacturing. Its big advantage is that it did not have to streamline— Nucor never built a giant staff. With revenues that will pass $800 million this year, it maintains a corporate staff of 17 people. "That's up 6% this year too, because we added a person," says Chief Executive Ken Iverson. Total corporate costs, including office space: $8.6 million last year, or a minuscule 1.3% of all costs. Corporate costs that rise above 5% begin to put an excessive burden on operating units, according to McKinsey. Nevertheless, some companies are hard put to keep them below 15%.

How does Nucor do it? Iverson says CEOs ask him this question more than any other. He has decentralized his 14 divisions to the point where they could probably run themselves if they had to. Each business operates as an autonomous company in a regional market, making all its operating decisions. The tiny central office monitors budgets, cash flow, and operations. Iverson occasionally employs consultants for economic forecasting but more often uses published forecasts on the steel industry he can consult for next to nothing. Strategic planning? He sits down three times a year with his general managers to discuss how to allocate the company's capital.

Hanson and Nucor are models for many of America's corporate behemoths as they begin the tough job of eliminating long-embedded staff. The simplest and most radical approach, many chief executives have concluded, is to let operating managers decide what corporate services—from public relations to real estate management—they are willing to pay for out of their own budgets. That's what General Foods is doing. "We wanted to make it easier for each of our operating companies to decide exactly what resources it needs to pursue its business interests," says Chairman Philip Smith. "They alone will decide what they need to be competitive."

One of the dangers of decentralizing corporate staff is that a number of oversize staffs can bloom lower down in the organization. Example: Mobil. In its oil and gas operations Mobil long maintained some two dozen regional centers, a half dozen divisional offices, plus its New York corporate headquarters, all of which were staffed as if they were separate companies. As though guided by some internal genetic structure, each of these management centers cloned the staff group of the office to which it reported. Each generally employed 175 to 200 planners, lawyers, controllers, human-resources people, systems experts, and so on—some 6,000 altogether.

The little-company syndrome, as some Mobil executives referred to their bureaucratic malady, was costly, laborious, and a drag on decision-making. According to Don McLucas, head of human resources and the man who coordinated Mobil's cutback program, staff specialists often created their own lines of authority parallel to the operating hierarchy's. With staff matrices on top of matrices, decisions could take months, even years, as each management center conducted its own review and added its own recommendations to be considered by the next level. McLucas recalls that a $1 million decision by Mobil Française to buy a gas station in downtown Paris, for example, was reviewed by four additional management layers. The four: Mobil Europe, the international marketing and refining division, the worldwide marketing and refining division, and finally Mobil Oil Corp. in New York.

Trying to limit the staff at each center would often lead to long debates about precisely how many planners or accountants were necessary. McLucas says: "We concluded that if we didn't eliminate some of these management offices entirely—get rid of the whole goddamn thing—our reduction program wouldn't work."

Mobil has halved its 24 regional offices to 12 in the past five years and reduced the duplication of staff at its six division offices and headquarters. Overall it has cut corporate staff by one-quarter—the same proportion by which it has reduced total employment. Staff jobs should be even fewer by 1990, when the oil giant expects to finish moving its corporate headquarters and divisional offices into one complex in Fairfax, Virginia.

As companies scale back corporate hierarchies, many are redefining the role of the head office. The notion of an elaborate system of checks and balances with parallel lines of reporting—which found its most extreme expression at ITT under Harold Geneen—is out. The new trend is to think of the corporate center as a small merchant bank or holding company, investing capital among various enterprises, monitoring the profitability of each against projections, replacing underachieving top managers, and constantly looking for new investment opportunities. As McKinsey's Coley says, "It doesn't take a cast of thousands to do that."

Burlington Northern, the railroad and natural resources company, reorganized itself six years ago. It changed from a traditional integrated American corporation into a holding company. The headquarters staff, 50 to 60 managers, moved from St. Paul to Seattle. One reason: so they would not dabble in everyday operational problems back in St. Paul or worry general managers by looking over their shoulders. The operating managers compete for capital allocation—the best performers get the most capital—creating new pressures to run as lean as they can. Total employment at the railroad has fallen from 57,000 to 33,000. Its management group has shrunk from 6,000 to 3,700, with corporate staff sustaining a disproportionate share of the cuts. Computer services is the only area that has grown.

Even big, vertically integrated firms that don't want such a radical transformation are narrowing their corporate focus to basic strategic goals rather than tactics. Says Ford's human-resources chief, Peter Pestillo: "The corporate role at Ford has changed from audit and review, or the oversight of other people, to corporate strategy, or what the company ought to be doing."

Some companies have handed to corporate staff the job of reducing corporate staff. That arrangement rarely works well. AT&T tried it and has eliminated at least 12,000 staff jobs; it still has 18,300 left. The company is decentralizing, though perhaps not enough. It is dispersing many corporate functions, such as public relations and marketing, to seven regional hubs, each of which will serve AT&T's various businesses in that region. But ultimate authority remains firmly in New York. Hub staffs report to counterparts at headquarters, which also decides how to allocate corporate overhead costs to each of the units. "The operating managers don't have the choice to do without all staff services," admits Charles Marshall, AT&T's vice chairman for personnel, who adds that the managers often blame their skinny bottom lines on overhead charges.

Yet left alone—and with powerful motivation—AT&T operating managers have shown they can cut staff as well as anyone. After deregulation, fierce competition nearly drove out of business the division that makes and markets phone products. With the blessing of the New York headquarters, its operating manager, Victor Pelson, turned the business around by short-cutting corporate channels. "There was not time to go through the traditional organization and prepare reports and fancy review graphs," he says. "We had to toss the problems right in the laps of the line people."

They changed the entire product mix in 18 months, opened a factory in Singapore within a year, closed half the business offices and phone stores, and cut division staff by half, or some 10,000 people. Pelson says, "The traditional staffs were cut the most. We reduced senior vice presidents by two-thirds." Up to then such bold actions in such a short time were unheard of at AT&T. But no longer. Pelson has been promoted to head AT&T's general business systems division, where he is doing more of the same.

While staff reduction begins as a cost-cutting exercise, it usually accomplishes much more. Decisions are made faster; managers get closer to their markets. Companies that have shrunk staff find that these effects are almost always more valuable than the initial cost savings. Above all, paring the staff highlights a lesson that is often forgotten in good times and relearned in bad: Line managers are the stars of business. They probably know what they need to do their jobs. If they need help, let them ask for it—and pay for it.

●

How Coke's Decision to
Offer 2 Colas Undid 4½ Years of Planning

After Successful Introduction Of New Coke, Firm
Began To See Market Slip Away

Which One Will Be Flagship?

John Koten and Scott Kilman

ATLANTA—In a stuffy hotel meeting room here last Monday, Brian Dyson, the president of Coca-Cola Co.'s domestic soft-drink operation, listened patiently as a group of company bottlers voiced their frustrations.

One told how his deliverymen were being harassed by grocery shoppers who disliked the "new" Coke. Another said he had become too embarrassed to tell people what he did for a living. Still another declared, "We've got to cut our losses."

Top executives of Coca-Cola had pretty much decided on their course of action by that time, but the bottlers' solidarity clinched matters.

A Public Apology

On Wednesday, as everyone in America must know by now, the soda-pop giant made its startling announcement. In one of the most stunning flip-flops in marketing annals, Coke publicly apologized for scrapping a 99-year-old product that had perhaps become more American than apple pie. Henceforth, it said, the old Coca-Cola would be revived as Coca-Cola Classic and would be sold right alongside the sweeter, reformulated new Coke introduced in April.

Thus, in one stroke, Coke largely undid what 4½ years of elaborate planning and market research had dictated was the right move. The abrupt decision, without any detailed marketing and advertising plans, surprised industry analysts and Coke's competitors alike. Coke executives, in fact, were still huddling Friday to try to settle such basic issues as whether its advertising agency should handle the two Cokes as one account or two.

The company felt it had little choice in its action. After the initial success of the reformulated Coke, company executives suddenly sensed that the expected howls of diehard old-Coke drinkers were possibly being adopted by the public at large. Coca-Cola's own weekly surveys showed that a major swing in consumer sentiment had begun on Memorial Day. By early July, antagonism toward the new Coke was so great that it was losing heavily in the Thursday-night surveys not only to old Coke but to Pepsi as well.

The company's quick decision to cut its losses drew immediate praise from many quarters. But Coke's troubles are far from over. Besides the blow to the company's reputation as one of the nation's premier marketing machines, Coca-Cola still faces the difficulty of making its new two-cola strategy work.

Not a Panacea

"We know we can't treat this as the silver bullet that solves all our problems," concedes Sergio Zyman, the senior vice president for marketing at Coke's domestic soft-drink arm. "We have a major job ahead of us."

The marketing of two versions of Coke, for example, raises far different problems than the 1982 decision to market Diet Coke, the first product to borrow the prized Coke trademark. Diet Coke quickly became the nation's No. 3 soft drink.

One danger repeatedly mentioned in the company's own discussions is the prospect that the return of original Coke might irreparably discredit the newer version. The company wants the improved product as its flagship, but there already are signs that some bottlers will fight to give old Coke the main prominence. Meanwhile, Pepsi officials can laughingly gloat that the actions show that Coke obviously has doubts about both products.

Coke's most optimistic view is that having two colas with its famous trademark will allow it to capture more customers than it could with just one. At the same time, though, it also recognizes that it now is a long way from the strategy it laid out for itself only a few months ago. Says Ira Herbert, Coke's executive vice president for marketing: "There are a lot of questions we have to talk our way through."

Coke's original plan, hatched only after one of the most exhaustive research projects ever for a consumer-goods company, was intended to break what for several years has been Pepsi's biggest advantage in the market: its ability to win taste tests against Coke consistently. "The idea," says one of Coke's top ad strategists, "was to take all the positive qualities associated with the current product, its heritage and so on, and transfer that to an improved tasting product."

Misjudging the Public

What Coke misjudged, however, was the willingness of consumers to go along with that concept. The company's change of heart wasn't just an attempt to satisfy a few disgruntled loyalists; Coke's research and sales figures suggested a far more broad-based rejection of its strategy. In some important markets, shipments fell as much as 15% in June. And when company researchers two weeks ago asked 900 consumers which Coke they liked better, 60% said "old" and only 30% "new."

Toward the end of June and in the first week of July, the company gradually began to feel it was losing control of how the public perceived its product. As the numbers in the weekly surveys grew worse, Roy Stout, the head of Coke's market-research department, began giving regular briefings to the company's top management. During one, the company president, Donald Keough, wondered whether a broader study might show a different trend. The following week the company surveyed 5,000 consumers, but the results only further confirmed the bad news.

Coke officials put some of the blame on the press for fanning public discontent. After an Atlanta newspaper quoted him as critical of new Coke, Franklin Garrett, a retired Coke public-relations executive, received an angry call from Roberto Goizueta, Coke's chairman.

Until the end of May, however, Mr. Goizueta had little reason to be upset. In the first month after its introduction, new Coke showed every sign of fulfilling the chairman's declaration that the decision was "one of the easiest we ever made." Shipments to Coke bottlers during the month rose by the highest percentage in five years. New Coke was tried by a record number of people for any product, and more than three-quarters of those who tried it indicated they would eagerly buy it again.

But suddenly the mood of consumers changed. "It started all at once,' says Mr. Stout. "At one point we were ahead of schedule with all of our targets. Then, it went completely the other way."

Bottlers, who are Coke's front-line contact with consumers, were the first to feel the heat. At a regional convention in Dallas June 18, a petition was circulated demanding the return of the old formula. F. M. Bellingrath, a Pine Bluff, Ark., bottler, took the message to Coke's chairman.

Meanwhile, top Coca-Cola executives in Atlanta considered alternatives, including changing the new Coke. Mr. Zyman, the marketing executive, ordered all members of his staff to monitor telephone calls coming in from consumers, to look for ideas on how the company might counter the trend.

The Customers Speak

Mr. Zyman also watched through one-way mirrors as Coke researchers interviewed focus groups of consumers about why they didn't like new Coke. After one such session in New Jersey, he decided to ask what Coke could do to get consumers to be happy with the new product. "All they could say was to bring back old Coke," Mr. Zyman says.

Coke's agonizing neared a peak just before Thursday, July 4. On Wednesday, the company's top executives met privately with the five bottlers who represent the company's largest markets. All worried that the company was confronted with a potentially dangerous situation: If the sales slide accelerated, the company might not be able to reverse the trend.

Resting at home on Thursday, says Mr. Keough, the Coke president, he decided that regardless of what embarrassment it might cause, the company had to bring back its old formula. On Friday, he began ordering departments of the company to prepare for a relaunch of the product as though a final decision had already been made.

In market research, Mr. Stout began testing alternative names for the product. Among the suggestions: Original Coke, Coke 100, Coke 1886, Old Coke and Coke 1. Several dummy commercials also were filmed announcing the move, one featuring Mr. Keough and two featuring professional actors.

Calling In the Admen

Unlike its elaborate preparations for the introduction of reformulated Coke, the company didn't include outside consultants or ad agencies in its decision making until the last minute. As a result, when the company filmed the ads, it asked McCann Erickson to send a video crew to Atlanta without explaining why.

The design of the Coke Classic package wasn't begun until two days before the announcement, requiring the company to create a phony paper label for the can it used in the commercial.

Having told Mr. Keough that he would submit his final recommendation on what the company should do last Monday, Mr. Dyson, the president of Coca-Cola U.S.A., waited until the weekend of July 6 and 7 to decide. While training for a triathalon under the Confederate monuments at Stone Mountain, Ga., he decided that the return of old Coke was the company's best option.

Last Monday, some Coke executives still wanted to wait and see whether the hostile feelings toward the company would die down. One argument held that the furor would subside once the company proceeded with plans to remove the word "new" from the label on the Coke can.

"In some ways, I think the sentiment already had begun to turn (for the better)," says Mr. Stout, the Coke market researcher. "But there also was a feeling the experience might leave deep scars."

Loss of Faith?

Another potential problem was a loss of faith, mainly among the company's bottlers, in Coke's research. At the bottler meeting with Mr. Dyson on Monday, a number of those present said they were tired of hearing the company's projections. It was shortly after that meeting that Mr. Dyson relayed his final recommendation to Mr. Keough.

Coca-Cola was forced to announce its plans on Wednesday, a day sooner than it wanted to, because of leaks on Wall Street. But even as they finished plans for a formal news conference last Thursday, Coke executives were just beginning to look at some important aspects of how they could make the new strategy work.

It wasn't clear whether the company would want to keep its current "Coke is It" advertising campaign or to what extent the company would run ads broadcasting the reappearance of old Coke.

Over the past weekend, Mr. Stout began an elaborate research effort to determine how the announcement has affected the company's reputation, its products and its credibility with consumers.

"This company is exposed in a way that it never has been before," one of the company's top ad officials says. "There's a good reason, though, why we earned a reputation as smart marketers. If any company can work its way out of this mess, we can."

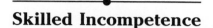

Skilled Incompetence

Chris Argyris

There is great skill in knowing how to conceal one's skill.

La Rochefoucauld

The ability to get along with others is always an asset, right? Wrong. By adeptly avoiding conflict with coworkers, some executives eventually wreak organizational havoc. And it's their very adeptness that's the problem. The explanation for this lies in what I call skilled incompetence, whereby managers use practiced routine behavior (skill) to produce what they do not intend (incompetence). We can see this happen when managers talk to each other in ways that are seemingly candid and straightforward. What we don't see so clearly is how managers' skills can become institutionalized and create disastrous side effects in their organizations. Consider this familiar situation:

> The entrepreneur-CEO of a fast-growing medium-sized company brought together his bright, dedicated, hardworking top managers to devise a new strategic plan. The company had grown at about 45% per year, but fearing that it was heading into deep administrative trouble, the CEO had started to rethink his strategy. He decided he wanted to restructure his organization along more rational, less ad hoc, lines. As he saw it, the company was split between the sales-oriented people who sell off-the-shelf products and the people producing custom services who are oriented toward professionals. And each group was suspicious of the other. He wanted the whole group to decide what kind of company it was going to run.
>
> His immediate subordinates agreed that they must develop a vision and make some strategic decisions. They held several long meetings to do this. Although the meetings were pleasant enough and no one seemed to be making life difficult for anyone else, they concluded with no agreements or decisions. "We end up compiling lists of issues but not deciding," said one vice president. Another added, "And

it gets pretty discouraging when this happens every time we meet." A third worried aloud, "If you think we are discouraged, how do you think the people below us feel who watch us repeatedly fail?"

This is a group of executives who are at the top, who respect each other, who are highly committed, and who agree that developing a vision and strategy is critical. Yet whenever they meet, they fail to create the vision and the strategy they desire. What is going on here? Are the managers really so incompetent? If so, why?

What Causes Incompetence

At first, the executives in the previous example believed that they couldn't formulate and implement a good strategic plan because they lacked sound financial data. So they asked the financial vice president to reorganize and reissue the data. Everyone agreed he did a superb job.

But the financial executive reported to me, "Our problem is *not* the absence of financial data. I can flood them with data. We lack a vision of what kind of company we want to be and a strategy. Once we produce those, I can supply the necessary data." The other executives reluctantly agreed.

After several more meetings in which nothing got done, a second explanation emerged. It had to do with the personalities of the individuals and the way they work with each other. The CEO explained, "This is a group of lovable guys with very strong egos. They are competitive, bright, candid, and dedicated. But when we meet, we seem to go in circles; we are not prepared to give in a bit and make the necessary compromises."

Is this explanation valid? Should the top managers become less competitive? I'm not sure. Some management groups are not good at problem solving and decision making precisely because the participants have weak egos and are uncomfortable with competition.

If personality were really the problem, the cure would be psychotherapy. And it's simply not true that to be more effective, executives need years on the couch. Besides, pinpointing personality as the issue hides the real culprit.

The Culprit Is Skill
Let's begin by asking whether counterproductive behavior is also natural and routine. Does everyone seem to be acting sincerely? Do things go wrong even though the managers are not being destructively manipulative and political?

For the executive group, the answer to these questions is yes. Their motives were decent, and they were at their personal best. Their actions were spontaneous, automatic, and unrehearsed. They acted in milliseconds; they were skilled communicators.

How can skillful actions be counterproductive? When we're skillful we usually produce what we intend. So, in a sense, did the executives. In this case, the skilled behavior—the spontaneous and automatic responses—was meant to avoid upset and conflict at the meetings. The unintended by-products are what cause trouble. Because the executives don't say what they really mean or test the assumptions they really hold, their skills inhibit a resolution of the important intellectual issues embedded in developing the strategy. Thus the meetings end with only lists and no decisions.

This pattern of failure is not only typical for this group of managers. It happens to people in all kinds of organizations regardless of age, gender, educational background, wealth, or position in the hierarchy. Let me illustrate with another example that involves the entire organizational culture at the upper levels. Here we'll begin to see how people's tendency to avoid conflict, to duck the tough issues, becomes institutionalized and leads to a culture that can't tolerate straight talk.

Where the Skillful Thrive

The top management of a large, decentralized corporation was having difficulty finding out what some of its division presidents were up to. Time and time again the CEO would send memos to the presidents asking for information, and time and time again they'd send next to nothing in return. But other people at headquarters accepted this situation as normal. When asked why they got so little direct communication from their division heads, they'd respond, "That's the way we do things around here."

Here is an organization that isn't talking to itself. The patterns that managers set up among themselves have become institutionalized, and what were once characteristic personal exchanges have now become organizational defensive routines. Before I go on to describe what these routines look like, let's look at how this situation arose.

Built into decentralization is the age-old tug between autonomy and control: superiors want no surprises, subordinates want to be left alone. The subordinates push for autonomy; they assert that by leaving them alone, top management will show its trust from a distance. The superiors, on the other hand, try to keep control through information systems. The subordinates see the control devices as confirming their suspicions—their superiors don't trust them.

Many executives I have observed handle this tension by pretending that the tension is not there. They act as if everyone were in accord and trust that no one will point out disagreements and thereby rock the boat. At the same time, however, they do feel the tension and can't help but soft-pedal their talk. They send mixed messages. . . .

The CEO in this example kept saying to his division presidents, "I mean it—you run the show down there." The division presidents, wanting to prove their mettle, believed him until an important issue came up. When it did the CEO, concerned about the situation and forgetting that he wanted his division chiefs to be innovative, would make phone calls and send memos seeking information.

Defensive Routines Emerge

One of the most powerful ways people deal with potential embarrassment is to create "organizational defensive routines." I define these as any action or policy designed to avoid surprise, embarrassment, or threat. But they also prevent learning and thereby prevent organizations from investigating or eliminating the underlying problems.

Defensive routines are systemic in that most people within the company adhere to them. People leave the organization and new ones arrive, yet the defensive routines remain intact.

To see the impact of the defensive routines and the range of their effects, let's return to the division heads who are directed by mixed messages. They feel a lack of trust and are suspicious of their boss's intentions but they must, nonetheless, find ways to live with the mixed messages. So they "explain" the messages to themselves and to their subordinates. These explanations often sound like this:

"Corporate never really meant decentralization."

"Corporate is willing to trust divisions when the going is smooth, but not when it's rough."

"Corporate is more concerned about the stock market than about us."

Of course, the managers rarely test their hypotheses about corporate motives with top executives. If discussing mixed messages among themselves would be uncomfortable, then public testing of the validity of these explanations would be embarrassing.

But now the division heads are in a double bind. On the one hand, if they go along unquestioningly, they may lose their autonomy and their subordinates will see them as having little influence with corporate. On the other, if the division executives do not comply with orders from above, headquarters will think they are recalcitrant, and if noncompliance continues, disloyal.

Top management is in a similar predicament. It senses that division managers have suspicions about headquarters' motives and are covering them up. If headquarters makes its impression known, though, the division heads may get upset. If the top does not say anything, the division presidents could infer full agreement when there is none. Usually, in the name of keeping up good relations, the top covers up its predicament.

Soon, people in the divisions learn to live with their binds by generating further explanations. For example, they may eventually conclude that openness is a strategy that top management had devised intentionally to cover up its unwillingness to be influenced.

Since this conclusion is based on the assumption that people at the top are covering up, managers won't test it either. Since neither headquarters nor division executives discuss or resolve the attributions or the frustrations, both may eventually stop communicating regularly and openly. Once in place, the climate of mistrust makes it more likely that the issues become undiscussable.

Now both headquarters and division managers have attitudes, assumptions, and actions that create self-fulfilling and self-sealing processes that each sees the other as creating.

Under these conditions, it is not surprising to find that superiors and subordinates hold both good and bad feelings about each other: "They are bright and well intentioned but they have a narrow, parochial view"; or "They are interested in the company's financial health but they do not understand how they are harming earnings in the long run"; or "They are interested in people but they pay too little attention to the company's development."

My experience is that people cannot build on their appreciation of others without first overcoming their suspicions. But to overcome what they don't like, people must be able to discuss it. And this requirement violates the undiscussability rule embedded in the organizational defensive routines.

Is there any organization that does not have these hang-ups and problems? Some people suggest that getting back to basics will open lines of communication. But the proffered panacea does not go far enough; it does not deal with the underlying patterns. Problems won't be solved by simply correcting one isolated instance of poor performance.

When CEOs I have observed declared war against organizational barriers to candor and demanded that people get back to basics, most often they implemented the new ideas with the old skills. People changed whatever they could and learned to cover their asses even more skillfully. The freedom to question and to confront is crucial, but it is inadequate. To overcome skilled incompetence, people have to learn new skills—to ask the questions behind the questions.

Defensive routines exist. They are undiscussable. They proliferate and grow underground. And the social pollution is hard to identify until something occurs that blows things open. Often that something is a glaring error whose results cannot be hidden. The recent space shuttle disaster is an example. Only after the accident occurred were the mixed messages and defensive routines used during the decision to launch exposed. The disaster made it legitimate for outsiders to require insiders to discuss the undiscussable. (By the way, writing a tighter set of controls and requiring better communication won't solve the problem. Tighter controls will only enlarge the book of rules that William Rogers, chairman of the president's committee to investigate the Challenger disaster, acknowledged can be a cure worse than the illness. He pointed out that in his Navy years, when the players went by the book, things only got worse.)

Managers do not have the choice to ignore the organizational problems that these self-sealing loops create. They may be able to get away with it today, but they're creating a legacy for those who will come after them.

How to Become Unskilled

The top management group I described at the beginning of this article decided to learn new skills by examining the defenses they created in their own meetings.

First, they arranged a two-day session away from the office for which they wrote a short case beforehand. The purpose of these cases was twofold. First, they allowed the executives to develop a collage of the problems they thought were critical. Not surprisingly, in this particular group at least half wrote on issues related to the product versus custom service conflict. Second, the cases provided a kind of window into the prevailing rules and routines the executives used. The form of the case was as follows:

1. In one paragraph describe a key organizational problem as you see it.
2. In attacking the problem, assume you could talk to whomever you wish. Describe, in a paragraph or so, the strategy you would use in this meeting.
3. Next, split your page into two columns. On the right-hand side, write how you would begin the meeting: what you would actually say. Then write what you believe the other(s) would say. Then write your response to their response. Continue writing this scenario for two or so double-spaced typewritten pages.
4. In the left-hand column write any of your ideas or feelings that you would not communicate for whatever reason.

The executives reported that they became engrossed in writing the cases. Some said that the very writing of their case was an eye-opener. Moreover, once the stories were distributed, the reactions were jocular. They enjoyed them: "Great, Joe does this all the time"; "Oh, there's a familiar one"; "All salespeople and no listeners"; "Oh my God, this is us."

What is the advantage of using the cases? Crafted and written by the executives themselves, they become vivid examples of skilled incompetence. They illustrate the skill with which each executive sought to avoid upsetting the other while trying to change the other's mind. The cases also illustrate their incompetence. By their own analysis, what they did upset the others, created suspicion, and made it less likely that their views would prevail.

The cases are also very important learning devices. During a meeting, it is difficult to slow down behavior produced in milliseconds, to reflect on it, and to change it. For one thing, it's hard to pay attention to interpersonal actions and to substantive issues at the same time. . . .

The cases written by individuals who supported the product strategy did not differ much. They too were trying to persuade, sell, or cajole their fellow officers. Their left-hand columns were similar.

In analyzing their left-hand columns, the executives found that each side blamed the other for the difficulties, and they used the same reasons. For example, each side said:

"If you insist on your position, you'll harm the morale I've built."

"Don't hand me that line. You know what I'm talking about."

"Why don't you take off your blinders and wear a company hat?"

"It upsets me when I think of how they think."

"I'm really trying hard, but I'm beginning to feel this is hopeless."

These cases effectively illustrate the influence of skilled incompetence. In crafting the cases, the executives were trying not to upset the others and at the same time were trying to change their minds. This process requires skill. Yet the skill they used in the cases has the unintended side effects I talked about. In the cases, the others became upset and dug in their heels without changing their minds.

Here's a real problem. These executives and all the others I've studied to date can't prevent the counterproductive consequences until and unless they learn new skills. Nor will it work to bypass the skilled incompetence by focusing on the business problems, such as, in this case, developing a business strategy.

The Answer Is Unlearning

The crucial step is for executives to begin to revise how they'd tackle their case. At their two-day seminar each manager selected an episode he wished to redesign so that it would not have the unhappy result it currently produced.

In rewriting their cases, the managers realized that they would have to slow things down. They could not produce a new conversation in the milliseconds in which they were accustomed to speak. This troubled them a bit because they were impatient to learn. They had to keep reminding themselves that learning new skills meant they had to slow down.

Each manager took a different manager's case and crafted a new conversation to help the writer of the episode. After five minutes or so, they showed their designs to the writer. In the process of discussing these new versions, the writer learned a lot about how to redesign his words. And, as they discovered the bugs in their suggestions and the way they made them, the designers also learned a lot.

The dialogues were constructive, cooperative, and helpful. Typical comments were:

"If you want to reach me, try it the way Joe just said."

"I realize your intentions are good, but those words push my button."

"I understand what you're trying to say, but it doesn't work for me. How about trying it this way?"

"I'm surprised at how much my new phrases contain the old messages. This will take time."

Practice is important. Most people require as much practice to overcome skilled incompetence as to play a not-so-decent game of tennis. But it doesn't need to happen all at once. Once managers are committed to change, the practice can occur in actual business meetings where executives set aside some time to reflect on their actions and to correct them.

But how does unlearning skilled incompetence lead to fewer organizational snafus? The first step is to make sure executives are aware of defensive routines that surround the organizational problems that they are trying to solve. One way to do this is to observe them in the making. For example, during a meeting of the top line and corporate staff officers in our large decentralized organization, the CEO asked why the line and staff were having problems working effectively. They identified at least four causes:

The organization's management philosophy and policies are inadequate.

Corporate staff roles overlap and lead to confusion.

Staff lacks clear-cut authority when dealing with line.

Staff has inadequate contact with top line officers.

The CEO appointed two task forces to come up with solutions. Several months later, the entire group met for a day and hammered out a solution that was acceptable to all.

This story has two features that I would highlight. First, the staff-line problems are typical. Second, the story has a happy ending. The organization got to the root of its problems.

But there is a question that must be answered in order to get at the organizational defensive routines. Why did all the managers—both upper and lower—adhere to, implement, and maintain inadequate policies and confusing roles in the first place?

Why open this can of worms if we have already solved the problem? Because defensive routines prevent executives from making honest decisions. Managers who are skilled communicators may also be good at covering up real problems. If we don't work hard at reducing defensive routines, they will thrive—ready to undermine this solution and cover up other conflicts.

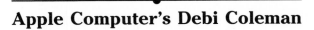

Apple Computer's Debi Coleman

Mark Dowie

When Debi Coleman was appointed vice president of Apple Computer, Inc., in 1985, she went out and bought every sports magazine she could find. Being the first woman to penetrate the all-male inner sanctum of Apple's top management, she wanted to be prepared for every conceivable conversation. There were women in management at Apple, more than at many computer companies, in fact. But none had reached the executive level before Coleman, who is vice president, operations, with responsibilities that include worldwide manufacturing.

By staying up late and studying arcane technical manuals and engineering textbooks, she had already made herself enough of an expert on conveyors and robots to break into industrial America's last bastion of male dominance— manufacturing. Now she had to survive in the executive suite, and not, she wants you to know, "the way Mary Cunningham did."

Since she had mastered the complexities of manufacturing, surely she could comprehend the world of sport. She began studying. Her deadline was an upcoming executive retreat, where it would be just her and the boys for the weekend. Coleman spent the night before the retreat rehearsing the jargon and memorizing names of the fast and famous in a world she had completely ignored for 32 years.

The first day of the retreat Coleman discovered she had wasted her time. "At the luncheon break [Apple president] John Sculley was wearing this gorgeous sweater," she recalls. "One of the vice presidents noticed it and said, 'John, that's a very attractive sweater you're wearing.' 'Thank you,' he said, 'I bought it at Nordstrom's.' 'Oh, really,' said another exec, 'I shop at Nordstrom's, too. I like it much better than Macy's.' The others were saying, 'Oh? I buy mine at Lands' End.' 'Well, I'm really into L.L. Bean,' and I'm stting at this table thinking, 'When is the sports going to start?' "

One senses, on meeting Debi Coleman that she wishes there was a little more testosterone on the top floor at Apple. Lee Iacocca is, after all, her personal role model.

Coleman, who has the memory of a 10-megabyte RAM chip, is vintage Silicon Valley—young, single, brilliant, and perpetually high on technology. Work is her passion and "Macs are my babies," she says of the magnificent little computers she helped develop and now manufactures—a million of them out there, one made every 27 seconds—at a robotized factory in Fremont, California, across the bay from Apple's Cupertino world headquarters. Coleman's Valley image is completed with a fairly strict "fifty-five-hour workweek" (with occasional workaholic binges), a Mercedes-Benz sedan, and a remodeled home in the bucolic hills of Los Altos.

"Resistors," "capacitors," "transistors," and "flyback transformer" roll comfortably off the tongue as she raps with engineers and technicians. But Coleman is neither technician nor engineer—not even a scientist. She is an English major from Brown University with an MBA from Stanford. Her hands-on business training, acquired at General Electric, where she worked immediately after graduating from Brown, and at Hewlett Packard, where she went after Stanford, is in finance, not manufacturing. She learned about making computers by watching, listening, and reading about manufacturing. But that background is not unusual at Apple, where almost everyone is kept at least a little out of their field and business cards hide true credentials behind titles like

"Software Evangelist," "Hardware Wizard," and "Product Champion." It all seems to work, says John Livingston, Apple's manufacturing technology director. "I have learned more about manufacturing from Debi Coleman in three years at Apple than I did in my previous twelve years in the business."

Six months after Coleman first arrived at Apple from Hewlett Packard in mid-1981, Apple's founder, chairman of the board, and enfant terrible Steve Jobs asked her to join the small clandestine team of specialists he had created to develop a new computer (the Macintosh). He asked Coleman to become team controller. She accepted. "This was definitely a soft landing for me," she recalls. "The excitement was totally infectious. There wasn't much financial work to do so I sat around the labs learning about chips and boards. We were also building the machine to build the machine"—a completely new automated factory. "I had my eye on that factory."

A few months later, when the Mac was in full production, Coleman took Jobs for a walk on the beach, where she offered him a deal that was hard to refuse. If she could get enough Macs out of the new factory in Fremont at the right price, she asked, would he let her run the factory? Already impressed with her tough enforcement of costs and quick grasp of things mechanical, Jobs rose to the challenge. Coleman made the quota and in 1984 Jobs gave her the factory.

It is in Fremont that the future of Apple, perhaps of the whole personal computer industry, might well be determined—largely by the initiative of Debi Coleman. If there is a hope of keeping any aspect of computer manufacturing in the United States, it is, according to Coleman, in the kind of computer-controlled robotic assembly that is being developed at that plant.

Early in the morning, while the shifts are changing, Coleman takes me to the factory she used to run. "You will never read about inventory excesses at Apple again," she boasts as we begin the tour. "Computers will not be made until they are preordered by the marketing division, and parts will be brought in on a 'just-in-time' basis."

As we wend our way past tote trays, under overhead conveyors, she explains that labor is no longer a significant factor in the final assembly of computers. "There are about thirty minutes of human labor in this machine," she says, pointing to a Mac as it rolls past another robot, which places another component in the now classic chassis, "and most of that time is in material handling, not assembly. . . . Some of it is in testing," she adds. "We still need human judgment in testing." She doesn't say whether that is good or bad. She also says she doesn't know how much human labor is in her competitors' products. "There are no industry standards for these things. It's all trade secret," she says, but she is confident that "Apple is one of the best in the industry."

After Steve Jobs was run out of the company by John Sculley (whom Jobs had hired from PepsiCo), Coleman stayed at Apple and was promoted by Sculley to the top manufacturing job at $200,000 a year. Sculley, who calls Coleman "a national treasure," says he could have put someone "safe" in the job but decided to take a "risk with Debi . . . not because she was a woman, but because she was not technically trained. She would be the youngest member of the executive staff. But she had strong ideals, commitment, and a very fast mind." For Sculley, the risk paid off.

In the summer of 1985, Coleman continued her quest for efficiency by recommending the closure of a large plant in Dallas and the selling of another in Garden Grove, California. Sculley accepted her recommendation, and the plants were closed. About 700 people were out of work and Apple was running close to capacity again. Coleman, however, did not close the Dallas operation until everyone who had worked for her there had found another job.

The Apple II line is assembled in Singapore, and Apple products for the European market are made in Cork, Ireland. Coleman travels frequently to those sites, en route visiting the hundreds of overseas vendors that supply the chips, wires, tubes, drives, transistors, knobs, and circuit boards that go into Apple products. The Fremont plant is now Apple's only American manufacturing facility, and even there, less than half the parts assembled are manufactured in this country.

Unlike many of her peers in the multinational corporate world, however, Coleman denies being an internationalist. At the drop of a gavel she will orate passionately on the repatriation of American manufacturing. Her ultimate goal in life, she says, is to bring product manufacturing home again—not just Apples, or even just personal computers, but also cars, steel, watches, and television sets. She doesn't seem wildly patriotic about it. It is simply a matter of prestige.

And how do we accomplish the repatriation of manufacturing? With women.

"One of the key ways we are going to regain our global competitiveness is to use one hundred percent of our brainpower. The Japanese don't do that," she says. "By keeping women out of management, they limit their resources."

While she would love to bring all of Apple's manufacturing back to the United States, she still defends her expanding offshore operations and overseas vendor base. She even pushes the shopworn company line that Singapore was originally set up to meet the Southeast Asian demand for Apple IIs. In fact, there has barely ever been a market for American computers in Asia (particularly not 8-bit Apples), and Singapore has from its opening shipped more of the Apple IIs made there back to the United States than to anywhere else.

This is not to suggest that Debi Coleman is a heartless corporado chasing cheap labor into the underdeveloped world and running away from safety legislation. Apple has an exemplary personnel and safety record in the United States, acknowledged by Silicon Valley labor organizers and toxics activists alike. Nor does it suggest that she is callous about working people's lives. Her friends and fellow workers say they never saw her more depressed than the day she flew to Texas to announce the closing of the Dallas plant—something she didn't need to do in person, but did anyway. As we tour the Fremont plant together, it is clear that she is well liked at every level of the company. Not by everybody, of course, but then who in a workplace of 5,000 people is? She is described by some as overambitious and pushy ("a porcupine with hives"). But most of the feedback is positive. "Debi is very much one of the guys," a former coworker tells me. "Not one of the *boys*," she makes clear, "one of the *guys*." But like so many well-meaning young executives before her, Coleman ultimately defers to boardroom values.

"Unions, what's a union?" she gibes when I ask if there have been any attempts to organize Fremont. "Actually, I was in a union once. When I worked as a check-out clerk in a supermarket—Amalgamated Meatcutters and Butcher Workmen of North America. I hated it. The only thing they fought for was the advancement of incompetents. I have never worked in a union company since. Nor have I talked to a union official since I worked in the computer industry."

Union officials in Silicon Valley, who have yet to organize a major employer, admit that if they ever succeed, "Apple would probably be the last to fall." Coleman's human resources assistant Joan Murosky claims the subject of unions has never even been raised at Apple. "If you're treating people right, then unionization doesn't enter the picture."

That shows, not only in the bustling Cupertino offices of Apple, where, despite some creeping bureaucratization, one still senses an exuberance uncommon in the American workplace, but also in the Fremont plant, where workers tell me they regard Coleman's robotics as a challenge rather than a threat. Of course, most of the "workers" who appreciate the robots are in fact young, college-educated men who are there to develop, control, and improve the machines that are displacing less skilled, less educated women who work the few remaining assembly stations that have not yet been automated.

At one such station there is an older woman hand-inserting a delicate capacitor into an integrated circuit board. As quick and nimble as her hands are, this is still evidently a bottleneck in the assembly line. "We haven't figured out how to automate this function yet," Coleman tells me, her Luciano Pavarotti voice booming over the background clatter. "I have offered $5,000 to anyone who does." The woman on the line turns briefly and flashes a quizzical smile. Fremont, like so many manufacturing plants in America, is becoming, in Coleman's own words, "a white-collar factory."

While Coleman relates affectionately to the people who work for her—"So how are the kids, Fred?" "Fine, Debi. How's your mom?"—she is also very fond of her robots. She is particularly proud of an experimental one-armed assembler encased in a large glass box. The device is speedily performing several intricate functions in the short, jerking, but terribly precise movements that endeared R2-D2 to us all. "This is a prototype that is performing functions no one else has been able—" She stops herself, steps in front of the glass box, and hides the busy device behind her strong, wide body. "I don't think I should be showing you this," she says, laughing nervously. "Please don't report the manufacturer's name."

I dutifully cross it out of my notebook.

Coleman has created a special robotics task force at Apple, a team of super-skilled technicians whose mandate it is to advance the automation of Fremont and other Apple plants. While she admits that robotics is on her list of factors that will help save manufacturing for America, she is quick to point out that it is low on her list, reminding me that labor represents "only about one to two percent" of the total cost of a personal computer. It is for this reason that labor and labor unions remain on the periphery of her consciousness. It is machines, not people, that make computers, and it is manufacturing technology, not labor relations, that will keep Apple Computer afloat.

Before leaving Cupertino, I visit with Jean-Louis Gassée, the brilliant French technician who emigrated from France to head Apple's worldwide product development team. Gassée sports a T-shirt imprinted with an Apple and the latest company battle cry: "The Power To Be Your Best." He speaks fondly of an "intricate relationship" with Coleman, who tells him often and bluntly that his new products can't be manufactured efficiently. "She is crazy, but she's one of the most startling intellects we have at Apple. Whether she is giving us crap or kudos, we always listen with interest." Gassée says he recommended Coleman to Sculley when the top manufacturing job opened up, but he stops short of taking credit for her success.

"Where then is Debi's power base?" I ask.

Gassée is angered by the question. "What do you mean 'power base'?" he asks in a thicker than usual French accent. "We do not think that way at Apple. Debi is where she is because she is brilliant."

"So her power base is between her ears?" I ask, squirming away from my repugnant line of inquiry.

"Exactly," says Gassée. He, too, is relieved and waits for the next question. Where will Debi end up? IBM? Tokyo? CEO at Apple?

Anywhere she wants, says Gassée. "but I want her to stay here."

Coleman herself says she has no interest in running Apple or IBM. "Apple is already well managed," she says. "I know people aren't supposed to have missions anymore, but I have one. I would really like to be the person they said saved manufacturing for the United States in the late twentieth century. And the way I think I could do this best would be to run General Electric . . . within the next ten years."

Oil Spill in the Midwest Provides Case Study in Crisis Management

Clare Ansberry

Ever since John R. Hall answered an early Sunday morning phone call, the Ashland Oil Inc. chief executive has become the latest study of the ups—and downs—of crisis management.

For the 55-year-old Mr. Hall, who has weathered several corporate storms, the massive oil spill from one of the company's storage tanks into two major Midwestern rivers could be his most serious ordeal. The effects of the accident are spreading as swiftly as the 100-mile-long oil spill itself, raising the specter of huge liability claims against the Ashland, Ky. based oil refiner.

Like other chief executives confronting public-relations nightmares, Mr. Hall has had to make quick and risky decisions in a constantly changing crisis. He originally decided, for instance, that the disaster was contained enough so that he didn't have to devote all his attention to it. He subsequently opted to fly to Pittsburgh to take the heat himself by apologizing and admitting the company has made mistakes. For that, Ashland is winning plaudits.

"They're doing a commendable job from a PR point-of-view," says Gerald C. Meyers, a former American Motors Corp. chief executive and crisis-management expert.

But that in turn could also backfire. Already, disclosures that the company might not have had necessary permits for the collapsed storage tank raise questions about the responsible corporate image Mr. Hall is trying to project.

What follows is a capsule chronology of how Mr. Hall has managed the oil slick and its public spillover.

SUNDAY: As soon as the president of Ashland Petroleum Co. told Mr. Hall that one million gallons of diesel fuel had spilled into the Monongahela River, Mr. Hall knew he had a serious problem. "But I didn't know how serious," says the chemical engineer.

He spent much of Sunday trying to answer that. Rushing to his office, he and president Charles J. Luellen sat in front of a speaker phone talking with colleagues at the accident site and elsewhere.

Almost immediately, Mr. Hall believed that although this was a massive environmental problem, it could be controlled. He also quickly discarded the idea of going to the disaster site himself. His emergency-management team there could handle the logistical decisions, and it was still unclear what had caused the spill. "He didn't want to make an official appearance until he could provide some answers," says vice president and media chief J. Dan Lacy.

He also isolated himself from distractions, allowing subordinates to handle all outside queries. And he didn't issue a press release under his name. Says Mr. Lacy: "I didn't recommend a press release. When a situation is evolving so rapidly, a release isn't good enough." About the only non-company contact Mr. Hall made was to a concerned Pennsylvania Gov. Robert Casey late Sunday. "I told him we intended to clear up the mess as fast as we could," Mr. Hall recalls.

MONDAY: Mr. Hall arrived at work at 6:30 a.m., about a half-hour earlier than usual. He decided against devoting his regular three-hour Monday morning meeting with top executives solely to the spill. He believed the crisis was being handled well and didn't demand all his attention—although he dashed in and out of the meeting for periodic updates.

He was wrong. By mid-morning, things were unraveling. "Phones were ringing off the wall," says one company executive, with calls coming from public officials, reporters and local water companies, as well as members of Ashland's own emergency management team.

Emerging were several troublesome discrepancies about the spill. Reporters initially had been told that the storage tank was new and the company held a permit to construct it. But, Mr. Hall learned, his spokesmen had spoken too soon; in fact, the tank was reconstructed from 40-year-old steel without a written permit. (Mr. Lacy says new information Monday "from several sources" made Ashland aware "that what we said previously wasn't exactly right.") In addition, Mr. Hall discovered less-complete-than-usual testing had been conducted on the tank.

A cautious executive, Mr. Hall pondered each of these new facts and became more quiet than usual—a clear sign to colleagues that he was angry at them. "It was obvious that he was frustrated, upset and eager to get the right information," an Ashland vice president says.

The situation soon worsened when the crisis turned from just an environmental mess to a public-health-and-safety concern. With river currents unusually fast, crews couldn't trap all the spill and, consequently, 750,000 Pennsylvania residents faced having no water—a scenario Mr. Hall hadn't anticipated.

"That changed the situation completely," says Mr. Lacy. "It was no longer a situation in which we could simply do everything to clean up the river. All of a sudden people were involved very directly, and they needed answers."

For Mr. Hall, that sparked the feeling that he ought to make a public statement at the accident site. By late Monday, he was debating that with his staff.

His lawyers advised against it, arguing Mr. Hall shouldn't admit any mistakes. The liability issue was a worry. But Mr. Hall felt he had to be candid. "Our company had inconvenienced the lives of a lot of people, and I felt it was only right to apologize," he says.

TUESDAY: On his corporate jet, en route to Pittsburgh, Mr. Hall rehearsed for his press conference ("How long will it take to clean up the spill?" a press relations manager tested him; "How much will it cost?").

The first stop was the spill site at Jefferson Borough, outside Pittsburgh, where he surveyed the collapsed tank and commended tired workers on their "good job." Then he traveled to downtown Pittsburgh to confront dozens of reporters, who barraged him with questions about whether Ashland met government regulations. Ignoring his lawyers' advice to sidestep questions about permits and testing procedures, Mr. Hall admitted Ashland didn't have a written permit for the tank and had conducted tests that met federal standards, but that were less extensive than is typical for the company.

He was troubled about flaws in the company's operating procedure, and felt the only way to clear the slate was to divulge everything he knew.

"If we made mistakes, we have to stand up and admit them," he says. "I would have preferred that we had done some things differently—like (not) using 40-year-old steel."

During the oft-hostile press conference, he perspired heavily, and laughed nervously when asked if he would forgo a shower to help conserve water supplies.

WEDNESDAY & THURSDAY: Mr. Hall canceled business trips to Lexington, Ky. and Washington, D.C., to stay in Pittsburgh for a whirlwind public relations campaign. He met with the city's political leaders, the editorial boards of local papers and telephoned the governors of Ohio and West Virginia, where the spill was making its way. Mr. Hall, says a colleague, "wanted to reinforce the view that even though mistakes may have been made, we want to do what's right."

With water supplies restored for most Pittsburgh-area residents and the crisis eased, Mr. Hall planned to fly back to Ashland last night, where he must now face the legal aftermath.

In retrospect, what would Mr. Hall have done differently? "He would have wanted more accurate information faster," says Mr. Lacy. Says Mr. Hall: "I suppose you always should be prepared for the unexpected—and are never as prepared as you'd like to be."

The New York Times, March 17, 1988.

Philadelphia Mayor Challenges Sanitation Union

William K. Stevens

PHILADELPHIA, March 15—Two years ago, Mayor W. Wilson Goode won widespread applause when he broke an unpopular 20-day strike by a union so powerful, in the view of many Philadelphians, that it actually ran the city sanitation department—and none too well, at that.

Now Mr. Goode has thrown down another challenge to the union, one that promises to bring about an important test of his political resolve and skill. He is asking the sanitation workers' union, in effect, to give the city enough control over trash collection to do the job as well and as cheaply as private enterprise. Otherwise, he vows, private enterprise will take over from the union's members.

Contract Expires in June

With the labor contract that emerged from the 1986 strike nearing expiration, the city opened bids last week from private trash-collection companies that, the Mayor says, could replace the city workers. On first inspection, the bids indicated that private collection would be cheaper than having the sanitation union's members do the job, Mayor Goode said.

To match or better the contractors' offer, Mr. Goode maintains, the union would have to agree to changes in work rules to allow the city to save money by deploying workers more effectively and using new and more efficient equipment, like bigger garbage trucks.

The present contract expires June 30, and the private companies would go to work on July 1—either as part of a negotiated arrangement or as part of the city's response if a strike occurs.

The 2,400-member union, Local 427 of the American Federation of State, County and Municipal Employees, is "absolutely" opposed to private contracting and "unalterably" opposed to any loss of jobs or status, said Jack Collins, a spokesman for the local.

Mr. Goode, in a recent interview, said, "I'm not talking about firing anyone or laying anyone off." He said any displaced trash collectors—there could be 1,000 or so—would be put to work "on brooms or mechanical equipment," cleaning the city's streets and sidewalks.

Mr. Goode said that one way or another, "my goal is to significantly change the way the sanitation union operates" so "we can respond to the basic service needs of an old, deteriorating city."

The Mayor says he is "dead serious" about shifting to private trash-collection contractors if the union does not allow changes in work rules so that the city can determine what size trucks to use, how many workers are needed on them, how many hours they should work and what new technology should be introduced.

Mr. Collins says the union is taking him at his word, but beyond that would not comment on the contract negotiations. The union president, James Sutton, has said he was willing to discuss the Mayor's ideas.

Both Mr. Sutton and his union live with the memory of the three-week 1986 strike. Mounds of uncollected trash and garbage then became a fixture in national news reports. The strike was called by

A.F.S.C.M.E. District Council 33, which represents the city government's 13,000 blue-collar workers, including the 2,400 sanitation workers under Mr. Sutton.

Fight Within Union

Earl Stout, the president of District Council 33 since 1974, directed and controlled the strike, whose major sticking point was his refusal to let the city audit the books of the union's medical and welfare fund, to which the city contributes. All other city unions had previously submitted to such audits.

After Mr. Goode successfully sought an injunction against Mr. Sutton's union and threatened to dismiss its members if they did not return to work, the sanitation workers capitulated and returned. The larger strike thereupon collapsed and Mr. Stout agreed to open the welfare fund's books. Mr. Goode, having defeated a labor leader who was thought to be so powerful that no earlier Mayor had dared challenge him, won praise for his strength and adroitness.

Since then, Mr. Stout's fortunes have fallen. He has been reprimanded by his international union three times for violating the union's constitution. Lately he has been contending with allegations that he bought new cars with union funds, then resold them within a short time to himself and members of his family for as little as $100 apiece.

Mr. Sutton is challenging Mr. Stout for leadership of District Council 33 in an election scheduled for May 10. And in any case, some union insiders say, Mr. Sutton rather than Mr. Stout appears to be controlling the sanitation workers' dealings in its talks with the city this time.

Organizing

Organizations have been so prevalent in the lives of most of us that we simply take their existence for granted. As a result, we fail to appreciate their relationship to other dimensions of human activity and their newness in human history. To be sure, organizations have played a significant role in many religious, military, and governmental activities for centuries. The dominant role in economic activities played by formal organizations—social systems that have been deliberately designed to achieve stated objectives—has been a relatively recent phenomenon. In the United States, for example, even late in the 19th century, most work was done in very small and personally run structures, such as the family- and owner-run and managed enterprises. Today, even though small businesses are a major source of employment, when people think and talk about managing, they are usually envisioning some large, complex organization—the modern corporation being the prototype.

What people know about these organizations is often gathered through "snapshots." An organization's mammoth physical plant or its palatial headquarters is very visible. Certain key events such as the introduction of a new product or service are also easily seen as a result of media coverage. The processes, however, behind these observables are obscure to outsiders. Only rarely are we cognizant of the previous facilities that the existing ones replaced or of the history associated with the organization's growth (see, for example, Henry Mintzberg's "Ms. Raku") that a movie or even a series of snapshots would reveal. Even though we hear of mergers and bankruptcies, the number and size of the buildings and of the organizations that own them, often lead us to assume that the organizations are permanent fixtures on the earth's surface. We see them as stable objects that have existed and probably will continue to exist for a long time. From this perspective we tend to see organizations *only* as "things"—as concrete entities. We suggest that such a viewpoint leads us to overlook how the constantly changing nature of organizations and the numerous events that threaten an organization's survival complicate the balancing act managers must perform (see, for instance, the story of IBM in "The Greatest Capitalist in History").

We suggest the importance of an alternative perspective that emphasizes two elements. First, when thinking about management, it is better to view organizations as being processes rather than as things. While for some purposes it may be useful to think of organizations as "things," such as considering them as legal entities when writing or enforcing laws, for managing them it is often far more useful to think of them as processes. In other words, any given organization is constantly evolving as it interacts with its environment. As information and resources move in and out of an organization, the fabric of the organization changes. Moreover, organizations get older; they grow and contract; they appear to go through cycles of one type or another. They may add new parts (for example, departments, personnel, technologies) and/or rearrange the relationship among their parts as shown in "Flambeau Corp." and "IBM's Plan to Decentralize." A snapshot simply cannot capture such developments.

Secondly, we believe it is important to view modern organizations in the context of economic and social history. Successful economic activity requires that individual human beings coordinate their actions. At a very basic level, organizations function to help humans attain effective coordination. In some sense, this assertion simply states the obvious. On the other hand, it calls attention to the fact that organizations are but *one* of a number of ways of coordinating. Human actions are also coordinated through the institution we call markets which rely on people influencing each other's actions through prices they are willing to pay and demand for their goods and services. Likewise, they are coordinated through negotiation and by contracts enforced by governments and other third parties. Also, as in the case of the smaller economic enterprises, actions are coordinated through individual leadership and/or face-to-face communication. As the size of the enterprise gets very large, however, such approaches become less effective. Moreover, organizations based on personal relationships are extremely vulnerable to all types of individual failings such as greed, corruption, sickness, and death. While organizations never completely rid themselves of such dependencies, they attempt to reduce their significance by *adding* other forces to make coordination more predictable—that is, less dependent on any particular individual(s).

For successful coordination, a number of things must take place. For example, information needs to be exchanged among people. Likewise, people need to pay attention to the "right" elements at the "right" time; if they do not, their collective performance will be disjointed and ineffective. Moreover, people need to know what they are supposed to do, have the competence to do it, and be motivated to behave accordingly. Some tasks, such as a tug of war, require everyone to do pretty much the same thing. Successful performance of other tasks, such as football, depends upon different individuals doing complementary tasks. Despite these contrasts, the

managerial tasks are similar—disseminating knowledge of requirements, as-
suring proper timing and competence, or motivating.

The managerial work can be accomplished in a variety of ways. In some
cases, one person who we might call a leader can see that all these things
are done by giving directions and announcing rewards and punishments.
In other cases, we might need an extensive system of contracts or simply
provide a market place where individuals can transact their business. At other
times, it seems that developing rules and procedures, hiring people to supervise others, establishing formal communication and authority relationships among employees, training people and monitoring performance of
assigned tasks, and so forth are needed to achieve coordination. It is this
latter set of approaches that we call organizing and that, when used, produce the type of systems we call organizations. Generally, a combination
of these approaches is found.

So far, our discussion of organizing has centered on formalizing interactions that previously were less formal or did not exist at all. Today, however, the problems managers face are not simply adding these types of formal
mechanisms to informal relationships. Instead, they are attempting to change
the formal relationships that already exist. In essence, they are trying to
*re*focus attention or change established communication patterns among people. These changes are better seen as reorganizing rather than organizing.
Most of the articles included in this section suggest (see "Detroit vs. the UAW,"
among others) that many of the problems modern managers face require
reorganization rather than simply organization.

In some ways, reorganizing may be more difficult than organizing. (See
"Bitter Survivors" for instance). Reorganizing requires that old established
ways be discarded. Some people, however, may have a vested interest in
the old ways. For example, a professor whose status (and perhaps even whose
job) depends upon being a skilled lecturer is apt to resist a new curriculum
and teaching assignments that emphasize coaching and experiential learning. Reorganizing requires redirecting the efforts of professors who may have
strong and very rational (as well as less rational) commitments to the previous approach. If organizations are to grow and are to respond effectively
to changing environmental conditions, reorganizing is essential.

The first couple of articles in this section deal with the task of organizing, but most of the others reveal why reorganizing is so important to today's managers. These reasons include: changes brought about by new
technologies, changes induced by competition, and changes in the nature
of customer desires which alter the nature of the products and services a
firm produces. These articles also show additional problems that reorganizing introduces: learning and unlearning, battles over turf, and responding
to new demands without sacrificing the organization's traditional strengths.
It should be clear that efforts to organize are closely interrelated with other
ways that coordination is achieved in an organization. Moreover, they demonstrate the even greater challenges that confront contemporary managers
whose task in reorganizing is balancing the old and the new.

Ms. Raku

Henry Mintzberg

Ms. Raku made pottery in her basement. That involved a number of distinct tasks—wedging clay, forming pots, tooling them when semidry, preparing and then applying the glazes, and firing the pots in the kiln. But the coordination of all these tasks presented no problem: she did them all herself.

The problem was her ambition and the attractiveness of her pots: the orders exceeded her production capacity. So she hired Miss Bisque, who was eager to learn pottery. But this meant Ms. Raku had to divide up the work. Since the craft shops wanted pottery made by Ms. Raku, it was decided that Miss Bisque would wedge the clay and prepare the glazes, and Ms. Raku would do the rest. And this required coordination of the work, a small problem, in fact, with two people in a pottery studio: they simply communicated informally.

The arrangement worked well, so well that before long Ms. Raku was again swamped with orders. More assistants were needed, but this time, foreseeing the day when they would be forming pots themselves, Ms. Raku decided to hire them right out of the local pottery school. So while it had taken some time to train Miss Bisque, the three new assistants knew exactly what to do at the outset and blended right in; even with five people, coordination presented no problem.

As two more assistants were added, however, coordination problems did arise. One day Miss Bisque tripped over a pail of glaze and broke five pots; another day Ms. Raku opened the kiln to find that the hanging planters had all been glazed fuchsia by mistake. At this point, she realized that seven people in a small pottery studio could not coordinate all of their work through the simple mechanism of informal communication. (There were 21 possible channels by which two people could communicate.) Making matters worse was the fact that Ms. Raku, now calling herself president of Ceramics Limited, was forced to spend more and more time with customers; indeed, these days she was more likely found in a Marimekko dress than a pair of jeans. So she named Miss Bisque studio manager, to occupy herself full-time with supervising and coordinating the work of the five producers of the pottery.

The firm continued to grow. Major changes again took place when a work study analyst was hired. He recommended changes whereby each individual performed only one task for one of the product lines (pots, ashtrays, hanging planters, and ceramic animals)—the first wedged, the second formed, the third tooled, and so on. Thus, production took the form of four assembly lines. Each

From Henry Mintzberg, THE STRUCTURING OF ORGANIZATIONS: A Synthesis of the Research, © 1979, pp. 1–2. Reprinted by permission of Prentice-Hall, Inc., Englewood Cliffs, NJ.

person followed a set of standard instructions, worked out in advance to ensure the coordination of all their work. Of course, Ceramics Limited no longer sold to craft shops; Ms. Raku would only accept orders by the gross, most of which came from chains of discount stores.

Ms. Raku's ambition was limitless, and when the chance came to diversify, she did. First ceramic tiles, then bathroom fixtures, finally clay bricks. The firm was subsequently partitioned into three divisions—consumer products, building products, and industrial products. From her office on the fifty-fifth story of the Pottery Tower, she coordinated the activities of the divisions by reviewing their performance each quarter of the year and taking personal action when their profit and growth figures dipped below that budgeted. It was while sitting at her desk one day going over these budgets that Ms. Raku gazed out at the surrounding skyscrapers and decided to rename her company "Ceramico.". . .

And it should be told that one day in her aging years, when Ms. Raku came down from her fifty-fifth story office to preside at the groundbreaking ceremony of Ceramico's largest-ever factory, she slipped on her shovel and fell in the mud. Her sense of revulsion at having dirtied her dress was suddenly replaced by one of profound nostalgia, for she realized that this was her first real contact with the earth since her days in the studio. There came the sudden revelation that making pots was more important than making money. And so the organization took on a new mission—the hand-making of beautiful yet functional pots—and it developed a new structure to reflect its new ideology. As her last act as president, Ms. Raku changed the name of the organization one last time—to Potters of the Earth.

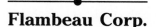

Flambeau Corp.

Richard Daft

"I was killing myself trying to manage 500 employees spread out in five plants around the country, running three shifts a day," says Bill Sauey, sitting in an office cluttered with plastic toys, housewares, sporting goods, and industrial parts. "After twenty-five years of keeping everything under my control, I decided there had to be a better way."

The better way Sauey found was to chop his company, Flambeau Corp., into pieces and turn over control of the pieces to a group of independent general

Reprinted by permission from ORGANIZATION THEORY AND DESIGN 2/e by Richard Daft. Copyright © 1986 by West Publishing Company. All rights reserved.

managers. Before Sauey made the change at the beginning of 1979, Flambeau was highly centralized. The company, which manufactures plastic products, had grown steadily to $24 million with Sauey running the whole show. But as Flambeau got larger and larger, the pressure to continue that growth became too much for one man to handle. Today, Sauey presides over a company with six independent divisions under six managers—and sales have jumped to $35 million.

Sauey started Flambeau Corp. in 1947. From that point on, he guided Flambeau singlehandedly. By 1965, it had reached $10 million in sales. Sauey signed all the checks, bought all the plant equipment, interviewed all potential employees, and played a role in developing and selling all Flambeau's products. The company was a testament to his persistence and his conviction that he could solve any business problem. So he continued to manage the company in his own tightly controlled way even though there were signs that this style wasn't working so well anymore. . . .

"I didn't want to decentralize authority," says Sauey, "because I thought I'd lose the ability to get my message across and get the job done effectively." Sauey continued to make all important budgetary, sales, marketing, and production decisions for both the Georgia and Wichita plants, and he couldn't find a manager who wanted to work under those conditions.

It was the sheer weight of details Sauey wanted to keep under his control that finally led to an uncharacteristic decision—he gave up control over one part of the company. This happened in 1977 when Flambeau acquired Vlchek Plastics Co. in Middlefield, Ohio. In the past, Sauey had always merged acquisitions into the central organization. "But I didn't this time," he says, "because I was so busy with the rest of the company—which by now had 500 employees working in five plants—that I knew if I brought it into our system I'd screw it up."

Two things happened. Vlchek's sales began doubling annually, and for once, Sauey didn't feel insecure about his lack of direct control. "I was really surprised at how little I worried about what went on at Vlchek," he says, his voice still registering amazement.

Unlike the early days, Sauey couldn't just work harder to make things go; he was already overworked and tired, and he was feeling the pressure of trying to hold the company together while the forces of growth were pulling things apart.

"I was sitting at home one night after a frantic day at work, and I made up my mind. I just said to myself, 'By god, I've got to do it.' "

Things moved very fast after that. Sauey wrote up a reorganization manual that spelled out how he was going to decentralize Flambeau and give authority to general managers who would report to him but have the freedom to run their divisions as they saw fit. It had taken him seven years, though, to decide that it was fundamental to Flambeau's growth.

The Greatest Capitalist in History

Thomas J. Watson Jr. got his job from his father, but built IBM into a colossus big enough to satisfy even the wildest of the old man's dreams. Here he tells in his own words how he did it.

Peter Petre

High-growth companies dominated by entrepreneurial leaders inevitably face the difficult transition to professional management. For IBM, already a $600-million-a-year giant when Watson Sr. stepped aside, this maturing process was long overdue. It was up to Watson Jr. to develop a cadre of capable executives while fighting to maintain a breakneck rate of growth.

We tackled the question of organization in 1956. Until the mid-1950s the company was run essentially by one man, my father. If IBM had had an organization chart at that time, there would have been a fascinating number of lines—perhaps 30—running into his office. As a consequence, people were constantly waiting outside his door, sometimes for as long as a week or two, before they could see him. He saw the important ones, of course, but when I complained about people wasting time in his anteroom, he said, "Oh Tom, let them wait. They're well paid."

This chaotic style had worked exceedingly well since 1914, but it couldn't support the scale of operations many of us anticipated. After several months of study in 1956, we called the top 100 people or so to a three-day meeting in Williamsburg, Virginia, where we distributed responsibility for running the company. We installed a check-and-balance arrangement that later became famous as the IBM system of contention management, in which staff officials would challenge the views of operating men. No decision was final without a staff man's concurrence—and if he signed, his job was just as much at stake as the executive's who made the decision. When an executive and a staff man couldn't agree, the problem got kicked upstairs to senior management, which didn't suffer indecisiveness gladly.

I never varied from the managerial rule that the worst possible thing we could do would be to lie dead in the water with any problem. Solve it, solve it quickly, solve it right or wrong. If you solved it wrong, it would come back and slap you in the face and then you could solve it right. Lying dead in the water and doing nothing is a comfortable alternative because it is without immediate risk, but it is an absolutely fatal way to manage a business.

My way of doing business was never entirely scientific, but I think the emotional, dramatic kind of manager can hold his own with a scientific manager. I never hesitated to intervene if I saw the company getting bogged down.

For instance, we were having a dreadful time in the late 1950s moving the development people into transistors. The Japanese were already making cheap transistor radios by the millions, and we were putting our computers together with acres and acres of vacuum tubes. The transistor was obviously the wave of the future: It was faster than the tube, generated less heat, and had great potential for miniaturization. But our people had labored to master the tube. This new invention shocked them and they resisted it. Williams and I finally wrote a memo that said, after June 1, 1958, we will design no more machines for electronic tubes. Signed, Tom Watson, Jr. The development people were awfully mad. But I kept giving them transistor radios. I ordered 100 of them, and whenever an engineer told me transistors were undependable, I would pull a radio out of my bag and challenge him to wear it out.

I managed with a council of eight to ten executives, and I had a good deal more respect for the opinions of several of these people than for my own conclusions. I would dissolve this committee whenever it reached a point where I thought some people couldn't keep up as IBM grew. Then I would establish a new committee with a different name and most, but not all, the same people. By changing those committees I was able to keep them staffed with the hottest boys in town.

My most important contribution to IBM was my ability to pick strong and intelligent men and then hold the team together by persuasion, by apologies, by financial incentives, by speeches, by chatting with their wives, by thoughtfulness when they were sick or involved in accidents, and by using every tool at my command to make that team think that I was a decent guy. I knew I couldn't match all of them intellectually, but I thought that if I used fully every capability that I had, I could stay even with them.

My younger brother, Dick, was the leader who made the company live up to the "international" part of the name our father gave it in 1924. Father organized the IBM World Trade Corp. as a wholly owned subsidiary in 1950, and Dick soon became chief executive. He spoke fluent French, learned Spanish and Italian, and traveled the world to develop businesses in 80 countries. By 1970, World Trade's net earnings matched those of the domestic company, at about $500 million each.

In IBM's domestic business I depended most heavily on Williams and Red LaMotte, to whom I turned on delicate issues of personnel. The most able operating man in IBM was Vin Learson, who eventually succeeded me as chief executive. Learson was an imposing figure, 6 feet 6 inches tall, and his mere presence in a room was enough to get people's attention. He came from a Boston Irish family and put himself through Harvard. For 20 years I gave him IBM's toughest assignments, such as selling off our time-clock company and rescuing a new line of mainframes that had gotten bogged down, and he did each task successfully.

I never hesitated to promote someone I didn't like. The comfortable assistant—the nice guy you like to go on fishing trips with—is a great pitfall. Instead I looked for those sharp, scratchy, harsh, almost unpleasant guys who see and tell you about things as they really are. If you can get enough of them around you, and have patience enough to hear them out, there is no limit to where you can go.

With so much contention built in, why did IBM's management work? For one thing, with rare exceptions we promoted from within. Virtually every IBM executive started as a salesman. Because we were growing so fast, promotions came quickly. All of our senior executives, including me, knew what it felt like to be thrown into deep water not knowing if you could swim.

When the Williamsburg reorganization created dozens of slots for staff specialists in such areas as manufacturing, personnel, finance, and marketing, we "made" the expert simply by naming the man to the job. This method worked in the main because, as young and inexperienced as these executives might be, they had come up from the bottom. They knew what IBM stood for as well as they knew their own names.

IBM employees all had job security, dating back to the days when my father refused to fire people during the Depression. Instead, he kept the factories running and made parts for the bins, which stood us in good stead when the Social Security Act passed and we landed the contract to supply the accounting equipment the government needed. If you proved ineffectual at a job, you were not put out on the street; you were reassigned to a level where you were known to perform well. In doing this we would sometimes strip a man of a fair amount of dignity, but we would then make a great effort to rebuild his self-respect.

Money was another reason the system of contention worked. On one occasion I was ranting in an executive committee meeting about something, I hope something worthwhile, and this rather unusual, sarcastic, and outspoken fellow from my office named Tom Buckley leaned over to Spike Beitzel, later a senior vice president, and asked, "Do you know why they all take this bunk from him?" Beitzel, who was anxious not to attract my attention just then, shrugged. Buckley said, "Because they're all getting filthy rich!"

In 1955 I persuaded my father to give stock options for the first time. He was conservative about anything having to do with the company's stock. Although he never actually owned more than 5%, he always operated the company very much as though it were his. The very mention of selling more stock would sometimes send him into a rage. Dad never had options and didn't believe in them. Instead he paid high salaries and urged his employees—and everyone else he met—to buy IBM stock. Some of the people who made sandwiches behind the counter at Halper's drugstore underneath IBM's old headquarters in Manhattan, where Dad occasionally had coffee, ended up with fortunes.

Despite the dim view he took of options, my father stopped objecting as soon as I told him they had become accepted practice and that we couldn't hang on to the best people without them. The options we gave were liberal, about seven times the employee's salary. People making $50,000 got $350,000 in options that were probably worth $10 million eventually. In the first two rounds about 40 people got them, and each one ended up a wealthy man. . . .

To survive and succeed in a hot market, a company must be willing to change everything about itself except its basic beliefs. IBM operated for decades on a simple set of principles: Give the individual full consideration, spend a lot of time making customers happy, go the last mile to do a thing right. Everyone shared these values, but we never got around to codifying them until the early 1960s.

You would be surprised how primitive our training methods were up until the late 1950s. We looked up to General Electric, which had an excellent school. We had our sales school and machine school, but nothing to teach a man how to be someone's boss. A branch manager would call a salesman in and say, "You're promoted to assistant manager. Be careful with people, don't swear, and wear a white shirt." Not until 1966 did we pass a rule that people could never manage unless they had been to management school.

When we started the program, we used cases straight from the Harvard Business School. I took the head of the program aside one day and said, in my usual undiplomatic way, that if we were really going to do something unique, we had to teach something unique.

He said, "Don't you want them educated to be good managers?"

"You don't understand," I said. "We are going to educate them in *IBM* management: communications, supreme sales and service efforts, frequent meetings, going to a guy's house if his wife is ill and seeing if you can help out, making post-death calls." You don't read that in anybody else's manual. Those were things we'd built up over the years, and new IBM managers have to know them in addition to technology.

For disgruntled workers we had the Open Door Policy, a practice tracing back to the early 1920s. Employees had to first take up their gripes with their managers. If they got no satisfaction, they could come to my office. I spent about one-fifth of my time on Open Door complaints or walking through plants, talking to salesmen, and chatting with customers. I asked what was right and, more important, what was wrong. You don't hear things that are bad about your company unless you ask. It is easy to hear good tidings, but you have to scratch to get the bad news.

My father strove to blur the distinction between white-collar and blue-collar workers. Not only did he pay well, but he eliminated piecework in the factories. For many years IBM's retirement package was identical for all employees, with pensions based solely on length of service, not salary or position. This philosophy stood my father in good stead during the period where there was a lot of labor unrest in America. Organizers were hitting pretty hard at the lush retirement plans some companies offered their executives. I don't think we were primarily driving to stay unorganized, but it had that effect.

In 1958 Jack Bricker, our manager of personnel, suggested that we shift all of our employees to salaries, eliminating the last difference between factory and office work. Although this move came off well, it was thought at first to be very risky. The joke went around that on the first day of hunting season no one would show up for work at our Rochester, Minnesota, plant.

I considered taking even more radical steps to increase our employees' commitment to IBM. When I talked to my wife at night, I would speak of various ways of sharing our success more broadly. Those at the top were doing fantastically well on stock options. This despite the fact that Williams and I stopped taking options in 1958, after Williams said, "We don't want to look like pigs." While IBM's workers were making high salaries, they weren't making the kind of capital gains that employees with options were.

I even asked myself whether our present system of corporate ownership is the system that will support the free American way long term. Though I never found a practical way to achieve it on a meaningful scale, I looked for ways to increase employee ownership of the business. Historically even the employee stock purchase plan has done little to encourage long-term investment by employees, because people sell when the stock rises. And the plan can create bad morale problems whenever the stock value is declining. We decided we could do the best for our employees by developing benefits such as major medical coverage and matching grants for charities and schools. Those we worked very hard on.

I disliked applying a double standard to managers and employees. A business is a sort of dictatorship. You have the antitrust laws that tell you what you can do, and you know you shouldn't be a thief. But the top man has wide discretion. He can give unfair bonuses, he can suggest policies that are not right, he can run airplanes to golf resorts. I never criticized my contemporaries publicly, but there are a lot of things that IBM did differently from other businesses during my watch. Maybe they didn't have my philosophies— or my markups, either.

I thought that the head of a business has responsibilities almost like the head of a country—without a supreme court and without the checks and balances, except for the checks and balances that the marketplace and the annual report impose on his operation. For that reason you cannot treat management differently from the employees. If a manager does something unethical, he should be fired just as surely as a factory worker.

It took me a number of years to realize that a CEO has to spot-check decisions made by his subordinates. Early in my career some managers in one of our plants started a chain letter. The idea was that one manager would write to five other managers, and each of those would write to five more, who would each send some money back to the first guy and write to five more, and so on. Pretty soon they ran out of managers and got down into employees. It ended up that the employees felt pressure to join the chain letter and pay off the managers.

I got a letter of complaint about this and brought it to the attention of the boss of the division. I expected him to say, at a minimum, "We've got to fire a couple of guys. I'll handle it." Instead he simply said, "Well, it was a mistake." I couldn't persuade him to fire anybody. Now you could admire him for defending his team, but I think there is a time when integrity should take the rudder from team loyalty. He was in many ways a capable manager, but from then on I thought he had a blind spot, and it retarded his career.

If it had happened a few years later, I would have fired the managers involved myself. I did this in perhaps a dozen cases when managers broke rules of integrity. Each time I overruled a lot of people who argued that we should merely demote the man, or that the operation would fall apart without him. The company was invariably better off for the decision and the example, but the decisions were lonely. . . .

●
_____

Corporations Reshaped by Computer

The traditional organizational chart—the familiar pyramid-shaped, hierarchical diagram of interconnected boxes and lines emanating from the boss's office and branching down to the lowliest clerk—is being reshaped in today's climate of mergers, acquisitions and restructurings.

Head of groups as diverse as the Republican Party and Big Eight accounting firms are turning to computer-generated circular diagrams to analyze power structures and informal information flow within a company, often discovering strengths and weaknesses that are hidden in today's increasingly complex organizations.

How should the company be restructured after a merger? Why doesn't marketing know what engineering is working on? How would the company change if a new president is named from sales, rather than from financial? Who has his feet up on the desk?

Increasingly, such questions are being posed to Netmap International Inc., a San Francisco-based software company that is a leader in the use of computers to analyze organizational structure.

"Netmap substitutes objective data for the confusing and self-serving anecdotes about who did what or was supposed to do what," said Donald G. Livingston, director of human resources for the customer service division of TRW Inc. a Netmap client.

Leslie J. Berkes, Netmap's chief technical officer, uses the analogy of a medical scanner to describe the process. Just as a CAT scan looks deep inside the body for tumors that could otherwise be seen only through surgery, he said, Netmap shows a chief executive the inner workings of his organization. Companies can also use Netmap to evaluate minority promotion policies and determine the average age of top decision makers.

"We look for the tumor but gain other insights serendipitously," said Mr. Berkes, who holds a Ph.D. in organizational behavior.

One major facet of the Netmap process that is gaining attention is its ability to identify the informal communication network that many business analysts have concluded is integral to effective management. Netmap officials cite studies showing that most internal communication is lateral, and thus is not reflected in chain-of-command organization charts. Netmap says its diagrams show group leaders which employees are actually making decisions and where greater interaction is needed.

"The informal network is an enormously helpful way of looking at an organization," said E. Patrick Marfisi, manager of the electronics practice support staff at McKinsey & Company, a consulting firm. "The C.E.O. is hamstrung until he knows the informal links."

One Netmap client was the manufacturing division of a large telecommunications company in the throes of deregulation. (Netmap does not disclose the identities of its clients because the analysis is considered confidential.) This division thought that by increasing its sales and marketing employees, it could transform itself from a technical to a marketing-oriented company. It hired Netmap to verify this shift.

Netmap first asked the 101 top executives to determine which co-workers they had regular contact with and how important that interaction was on a scale of 1 to 10. The program throws out all links not confirmed by both sides, and removes biases so that egocentric employees who rated all associations as 9's would have their scores lowered if the other person thought the links were only 2's.

Netmap then arranges the data for interpretation, grouping employees in networks where they had the most proven contacts. These networks are represented by circles, and employees with confirmed links are connected by lines. Those who interact with many are dubbed "bleeders" because the ink by their names is so thick. Those with no links are called "detached isolates," who often become prime candidates for reassignment or dismissal.

In the case of the telecommunications company, the principal message was that the engineering department was still the dominant division. Netmap showed no links between the marketing department and that of finance, and only limited communication among marketing, sales and production. The chief financial officer was linked to only one other individual in his department, and the chief executive's network group consisted almost entirely of engineers.

"Netmap shows companies whether they have achieved an effective marriage of strategy and structure," Mr. Berkes said. "If not, the strategy is just smoke."

The advantage of the computer is not only the speed of data compilation, but also the ability to say "what would happen if?" This allows management to see how closing a plant, naming a new president or department head, or

The New Organization Chart

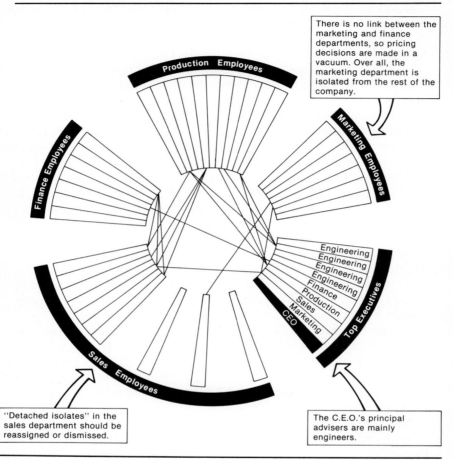

There is no link between the marketing and finance departments, so pricing decisions are made in a vacuum. Over all, the marketing department is isolated from the rest of the company.

"Detached isolates" in the sales department should be reassigned or dismissed.

The C.E.O.'s principal advisers are mainly engineers.

selling or buying a company would change the organization. The different outcomes can be seen in the new groups that emerge when employees are rearranged, for example, or when departments are added or subtracted.

Using the data it collects, Netmap also can determine whether the company ignores its female or minority workers and how many years it typically takes to become a senior manager. One disadvantage, Mr. Livingston of TRW said, can be the overwhelming amount of information.

Netmap officials said they had done more than 200 such diagnoses worldwide, for fees ranging from $15,000 to $175,000.

"We are just the diagnosticians," said James L. Kelly, Netmap's president and chief executive officer. "It's up to the client to do what he will."

Often, that is quite a lot. One executive responsible for making acquisitions for a multibillion-dollar office products company estimated that he would have saved several million dollars in acquisition costs had he discovered Netmap sooner. Mr. Livingston of TRW said Netmap would be used to "shorten the learning curve" for the division's new general manager.

Meanwhile, the telecommunications company dismissed three sales executives who had no links, reorganized its marketing department, and the chief executive vowed to meet regularly with all department heads.

IBM's Plan to Decentralize May Set a Trend— but Imitation Has a Price

Larry Reibstein

Since International Business Machines Corp.'s announcement that it would decentralize its management structure, management consultants have been predicting that other companies will follow.

For many companies, it could be an expensive imitation.

In recent years an increasing number of companies have learned that pushing decision-making down the ranks is a management luxury they can't always afford, especially in a competitive environment. The benefits can be undermined by staff duplication, marketing confusion and out-of-control local units. That's been especially true as companies shed units and return to a single, core business.

As a result, many companies, including Hewlett-Packard Co. and Minnesota Mining & Manufacturing Co., are in fact moving slightly in the other direction— either consolidating functions or reining in their divisional managers.

"The worst thing is companies will decide IBM has done it, and that makes it right for them," says Robert M. Tomasko, a consultant with Temple, Barker & Sloan, of Lexington, Mass. "But there's no right or wrong reason for everyone."

What IBM Did

IBM, hoping to become more responsive to customers and spur innovation, shifted broad responsibility from corporate headquarters to six product and marketing groups that will have wide latitude in decision-making. In addition, the company says that over the next couple of years "many thousands" of corporate staff members will be moved into positions that put them closer to customers.

Students of corporate history have plenty to look at in gauging the effectiveness of such a move. For the past 50 years, decentralization has come and gone several times as a management trend. And so its pitfalls are well known.

The first is that it can lead to costly duplication. Hewlett-Packard, for instance, has since 1959 allowed its units to operate as minicompanies, each with its own manufacturing, marketing, finance and personnel staffs. But about three years ago, the company decided that sometimes such duplication was too expensive.

For example, each of Hewlett-Packard's units manufactured circuit boards for its particular product—even though the boards are often interchangeable. This setup allowed unit managers flexibility and control over volume and quality. But the company says that system was "redundant" and a cost it no longer could afford in the face of strong competition. To eliminate the overlap, the company has consolidated the circuit-board manufacturing at fewer sites, says Lewis E. Platt, executive vice president of Hewlett-Packard's technical-systems sector.

Stiffer global competition has forced companies like Johnson & Johnson, cited by management experts as a model of a well-run decentralized company, to make adjustments to trim duplication. Last year, it consolidated about 75% of the manufacturing of sanitary-protection products in Europe into a single plant in Germany.

The products had been made at plants run by previously autonomous units. But as more and different types of sanitary-protection products were developed, a spokesman says, the company could no longer afford installing in each plant the necessary sophisticated machinery.

"To compete with the products consumers want, we can't afford to manufacture locally," a company spokesman says.

Companies have also found that small decentralized sales forces can be inefficient when dealing with large customers.

3M used to sell products like stethoscopes, elastic bandages, scrub brushes and plastic hospital drapes out of two different medical-products divisions. That worked well when individual doctors made buying decisions, because 3M's slew of sales agents could contact each one and tout the products' features.

But when buying decisions began to be made by hospital groups, 3M's decentralized sales strategy became inefficient. Hospitals were more interested in price and bulk purchases, and they preferred buying from one sales representative rather than dealing with sales agents from two divisions.

So the company merged the two divisions in 1984. "We can now offer bundles of products to large hospital groups and have fewer people in the field," says Jerry E. Robertson, executive vice president, life sciences sector.

Another problem with decentralization has arisen when companies find that their units are competing with each other. While that may spur innovation and aggressiveness at some companies, sometimes it leads to confused customers.

Hewlett-Packard, for instance, had at least three autonomous divisions making different—and incompatible—computers aimed at the professional and office markets. "The fact is, those products were being sold competitively against one another by the various divisions," a spokesman says. "Customers were telling us we didn't have a coherent strategy."

So last year the company stripped the divisions of their autonomy, placing them under one group, reporting to one manager. Among the first changes: Products were made technologically compatible.

Companies that have decentralized also have found that managers tend to make decisions in the best interests of their units, but that doesn't always coincide with what's best for the corporation.

John Hoffman of Cresap, the consulting arm of Towers Perrin Co., says it's common to find "an operating unit taking care of its short-term needs at the expense of the corporation's long-term needs." For example, he says, a chemical division looking to pump up immediate profits sells its product to an outside customer at a price higher than it could have gotten from a sister division. But the corporation ultimately loses because the sister division would have made even higher profits by adding greater value to that product.

Example of Wall Street

Wall Street firms in particular have been plagued by maverick units, with headquarters exercising little oversight, says Robert B. Lamb, a New York University management professor. "There were a number of prima donnas who were able to create their own departments, expand their staffs on their own, decide their own capital-risk exposure and, because they were so successful, the corporate parent was reluctant to monitor," he says.

Some companies have the opposite problem with decentralization: It fails because managers prefer the security of corporate control. They are therefore reluctant to embrace the newfound freedom.

As part of a decentralization plan begun in 1984, for example, many managers at TRW Inc. are required to submit financial forecasting and reporting plans only once a year instead of monthly. But some managers are resisting, continuing to require their subordinates to submit the plans more frequently, says Howard Knicely, TRW's vice president for human relations. "To get them to get rid of that detailed financial reporting is a tough sell," he says. As a result, employees are tied up with providing unnecessary information.

Despite all the problems, however, nobody thinks decentralization will go away—if only because of the image it presents.

"Nobody wants to admit to being centralized," says Jay Lorsch, a Harvard Business School professor. "The American feeling is it's good to let people make decisions and be autonomous."

Bitter Survivors

Thomas J. Murray

On the face of it, William Jeffries (not his real name) was a lucky guy—the only one of seven loan officers at a Los Angeles area branch of Crocker National Bank who wasn't fired after Crocker was taken over by Wells Fargo & Co. last year. Jeffries, a 35-year-old MBA, had made his reputation as a crack salesman, and that was why Wells Fargo kept him on. But he was so grateful to survive the company's massive layoffs, he willingly took on the daunting task of converting all of Crocker's commercial accounts to Wells Fargo's accounting and operating systems. With no guidelines or support staff to help him, he toiled away seven days a week for six months to complete the job.

It was a mistake. While Jeffries was slaving over the conversion, his fellow loan officers were out drumming up new business. In January, his job performance was rated unsatisfactory, and since then he has been given only the smallest and most troublesome accounts to manage—"the junk work," as he puts it. "All they are interested in is developing new accounts, which I had no time for during those hectic months," he says bitterly.

Becoming increasingly agitated as he discusses his plight, Jeffries exclaims heatedly, "I've been watched closely for the past several months, I have to account for every trip out of the office while my peers don't, and I'm being tested all the time for every move I make."

Unfortunately, variations of Bill Jeffries' tale are being heard in companies across the industrial spectrum. For middle managers who have survived the corporate takeovers and restructuring of the last few years, elation has turned to frustration, anger and a sense of helplessness. As survivors, they had figured they were among the elite, with unique opportunities to catch top management's eye and advance their careers. Now their hopes have crumbled, and many fear their careers have come to a dead stop. "I get depressed just walking into the office every morning," says one. "My only hope is that I have enough self-esteem and drive left to convince some other company to hire me."

Of course, no one faults industry for its massive drive to reorganize and downsize. Faced with intense competition from abroad, the profound effects of deregulation and technological change, hundreds of major corporations had no choice but to slash fat payrolls. In their zeal to streamline management ranks, however, few companies gave any thought to how drastically the relationships between managers and the organization would change as responsibilities were shifted and subordinates were swept out. "Old bonds have been shattered and new ways of operating introduced," says Myron Roomkin, professor of human resources management at Northwestern's Kellogg School of Management. "But all that many companies tell their managers is, 'You're a professional. Get the job done!' "

The "survivor" problem has hardly been recognized by corporate America, let alone tackled. But management experts believe it will haunt industry over the next decade and cause untold long-term damage to many companies. By undermining the competitive spirit of their middle managers now, they say, companies are sacrificing the development of top-notch senior managers for the future. In the process, they are undermining their long-term growth and productivity.

A case in point: AT&T. Some observers think it will take the communications giant years to recover from the management disruptions caused by its reorganization and wholesale layoffs (some 60,000 employees in all). Internally, staff psychologist Joseph Moses recently issued a hard-hitting report charging that top management's neglect of "people issues" has led to a middle-management morale crisis that threatens "irreparable damage" to the company. According to Moses' evaluation, "Survivors are often disillusioned, frustrated, bitter and most of all, lacking in hope." He concluded: "The amount of suppressed, covert hostility lurking just below the surface is truly frightening."

It's ironic to think that the survivors may actually be the biggest losers in this era of restructuring. Certainly, many companies have treated the middle managers they let go better than those who remain. As President William Bridges of California management consulting firm Pontes Associates points out, "Those who left often received handsome severance packages and outplacement assistance, while those still on the job have been overworked and given little or no guidance during a difficult transition period."

Getting the survivors to talk about their travails is difficult. Convinced there will be another bloodletting, they are extremely anxious about their job security. As a result, all of the dozen or so managers who were willing to be interviewed by BUSINESS MONTH agreed to tell their stories only after being assured of anonymity.

What becomes clear in talking to these managers is that they are being forced to take on a huge work load. Most claim they are doing the job of two or three managers, with sharply reduced staff and clerical support. And to a man, they say, they are getting no help from top management.

A typical example is Randolph Smith (not his real name), manager of new-product development at a unit of Atlantic Richfield Co. Following a company-wide reorganization and deep personnel cutbacks, Smith says, he lost four of his six subordinates virtually overnight and had to put in an additional twenty-to-thirty hours a week to keep pace with a growing number of new assignments. "Upper-level management wouldn't acknowledge that so many people had left, yet it kept on wanting more results every time we increased our work load," he says. "I wanted to be aggressive and crank out the best products possible, but without the people to back you up and support your efforts, you just can't do the job right. I'm getting more and more frustrated every day."

Some managers have so much additional work and responsibility thrown at them that their positions are, in effect, completely changed. And with no guidance from above, many quickly find themselves in over their heads. The branch manager at one AT&T California unit explains that his job has changed dramatically over the past few years to accommodate not only management cutbacks but the introduction of new technology in the office and the consolidation of the company's communications and information organizations. "In my heart I know it makes sense to present our new markets with a solid front," he says, "but I've gotten so little direction from upstairs that it's endless confusion for me. And all the time I'm sweating out the chance I'm on the hit list for the next layoff."

Perhaps most disheartening, reorganization has meant actual demotion for many of the survivors. Scores of managers at Exxon, E.I. du Pont and Telex Corp., among others, have been dropped several grades, with little or no chance for advancement.

Ward Bell (not his real name), for one, saw his position as a national operations manager at a Raytheon Co. division vanish the day after Telex acquired the unit in 1985. While two security guards stood by and a locksmith changed desk and door locks, four managers were fired on the spot. This eliminated two whole levels of management, and Bell was reduced to running a Los Angeles area branch. "After working my way up from technician to national ops manager, Black Friday comes along and I'm pushed back two layers," he sighs. "The company keeps putting on these PR campaigns telling us what great career opportunities we have, but that's a laugh. There's very little upward mobility around this company anymore, and I'm out of here as soon as I can land something decent."

Those are brave words, but most of the managers interviewed show little confidence in their ability to find new, meaningful jobs. For most, it is evident, their biggest fear is joining their former co-workers on the unemployment line. Many have lost their mentors, as well as their industry contacts. "I feel lost since my main man took early retirement," says the AT&T branch manager. "He was always there when I needed a pep talk or wanted guidance on my career moves."

Most damaging, insecurity is affecting middle managers' job performance. Consultants warn of early "burnouts," and many survivors admit they are increasingly afraid to make decisions. "I see lots of dispirited managers who are no longer contributing 100% to the job," says Telex' Bell. "They're scared their jobs will go up in smoke if they pop their heads out of their foxholes, and I'm afraid a lot of us will need therapy to get our careers going again."

Eastman Kodak Co., which has let more than 10,000 employees go over the past few years, is already paying the price for middle-management insecurity, according to one insider. To help regain its dominance in the camera market against severe new competition, in 1984 Kodak started up several small business units to speed up new-product development. However, according to one technology director, some of the managers heading up the units have been so apprehensive about making decisions that the businesses are floundering, and many key personnel have quit. "They know they have only so much time to produce a winner or they will be shut down," he explains. "But they're also scared they will make a wrong decision too soon and be terminated overnight."

Job pressures, needless to say, are shaking up the survivors' personal lives. Many worry about how little time they get to spend with their families and complain of fatigue and various physical ailments. Robert McCarthy, who heads his own outplacement firm in Los Angeles, has seen many of these "walking wounded" come through his door. "They're losing the balance in their lives," he says. "I'm afraid many of them will become victims of alcoholism, drugs and divorce."

These experiences seem to confirm what a number of critics are saying: that industry could be defeating the whole purpose of downsizing. To begin with, it is no secret that a number of companies have let some of their best managers slip through the net; du Pont and Atlantic Richfield are just two that unexpectedly lost many top performers when they offered attractive financial packages for voluntary resignations and retirements.

As for those unhappy managers who tough it out and stay, the cumulative effects of overwork, fear and top management indifference could be devastating over the long term. Joseph Moses' speculations about AT&T's survivors says it all: "One can't help wondering what kind of managers they will be like in the future when they populate senior levels at AT&T."

Despite the army of executives on the street, some large corporations are already finding it more difficult to get top talent. Many job-hunting managers are deliberately avoiding the giants with tarnished reputations, recruiters report.

Equally ominous, big business is less attractive these days to promising young university graduates and MBAs. College placement officers at UCLA, Stanford and Duke University's Fuqua School of Business all say that more and more of their graduates are rejecting careers with large corporations in favor of smaller companies, where they perceive greater stability, entrepreneurial spirit and opportunities for rapid advancement.

In fairness, it must be allowed that the survivor problem is so new that many top managements have yet to realize that they could have a full-blown crisis on their hands. But there's no doubt that most companies are simply closing their eyes to the situation. "Too many companies think business will just go back to normal without any positive action on their part," says Lucia Cappachione, a Los Angeles consultant who has been helping Walt Disney Co. solve transition problems since its big layoffs in 1984.

Amid the general neglect, two companies that stand out for their early recognition of the survivor problem are Ford Motor Co. and Apple Computer, Inc. Ford CEO Donald Peterson and Apple CEO John Sculley were quick to introduce new training programs to help managers cope with added responsibilities and staff cutbacks in the aftermath of massive layoffs and corporate restructuring.

A few other companies have begun to tackle the problem. At du Pont, where 35,000 employees have been let go since 1982, H. Gordon Smyth, senior vice president of employee relations, claims that managers have reacted well for the most part to increased authority and responsibility. They were helped substantially, he says, by the company's adoption of a new team concept that calls for every department to set its own goals. Du Pont is also holding seminars to teach marketing skills to all managers.

At AT&T, John C. Petrillo, director of human resources, says that top management is responding to the Moses report and earlier internal studies. It is providing counseling for managers with psychological problems. And it is offering one- and two-week education and training programs to all personnel, including managers, to indoctrinate them in the new corporate environment and strategy and help them rethink their jobs. "It's not easy to accomplish because we're dealing with deep-set ways of thinking and behaving at this company," he says. "But we realize the frustrations our people are feeling and believe we can help them through this turbulent time."

There are other signs of movement. The Conference Board, in tandem with Northwestern's Myron Roomkin, is launching the first major study on the survivors. Several concerned CEOs on the Board's Research Council urged the group to look into the issue and try to come up with some answers, according to a spokesman. Du Pont's Smyth also is urging senior executives to use industry meetings as a forum for swapping ideas. Besides that, a number of outplacement firms say they plan to expand their assistance programs for disgruntled survivors.

Too little, too late? Roomkin blames "stupid top management" for failing to predict the current "debacle" ten years ago and plan for it. He argues that the demographics available at that time, mainly the flood of baby-boomers into middle-management jobs, clearly indicated that a crunch was coming with the first major recession. Even now, after all the layoffs of recent years, he says disgustedly, "No one has figured out how to run a company well with fewer managers."

According to the experts' prognosis, the problem of middle-management stagnation could fade away on its own by the mid-1990s. By then, a new and much smaller generation of young people will be entering the managerial work force, and opportunities for advancement will speed up again. But for now, it seems, shortsighted companies are creating a generation of alienated middle managers, with all the implications that holds for corporate growth and stability.

Detroit vs. the UAW: At Odds Over Teamwork

*Even the union is split over a move for
Japan-style production*

Aaron Bernstein and Wendy Zellner

It sounded like a reasonable request last fall when General Motors Corp. asked the 9,000 workers at its Pontiac (Mich.) truck and bus plant to accept a production system based on Japanese-style teams. GM wanted a new local contract easing union work rules that impede such changes. In return, it promised to consider giving Pontiac a new truck to build. Local leaders of the United Auto Workers say that after they rejected GM's proposal, the company went ahead with teams anyway. GM also announced that it would build the new truck at another plant that has agreed to work rule changes. This and other issues boiled over into a four-day strike last March that blocked teams at Pontiac. Declares Local 594 President Donny G. Douglas: "The traditional system can work."

The dispute highlights what is fast becoming a central issue in current negotiations at GM and Ford Motor Co., whose labor pacts expire on Sept. 14. GM, Ford, and Chrysler have toyed for years with the team concept. Now, based in part on the astonishing productivity achieved at a Toyota-GM joint venture in Fremont, Calif., Detroit has settled on teams as a key way to compete with imports and new U.S. factories owned by Japanese carmakers,. GM wants UAW President Owen F. Bieber to make a commitment to teams in the national contract—paving the way for GM in negotiations at local plants where work-rule changes are decided.

Steep Price. This prospect is causing turmoil in the union. Donald F. Ephlin, the UAW's chief negotiator at GM, believes that teams can make work more fulfilling and save jobs by making the industry more competitive. His position has provoked a severe attack from UAW dissidents who blame union leaders for letting GM pit one plant against another. The split ensures that the companies will have to pay dearly to win an endorsement in the national contracts.

In early August the UAW added a dramatic new job security proposal to its demands. Going beyond its traditional goal of protecting current workers, the union said it wants to guarantee a specific number of jobs—an idea long rejected by Detroit as too risky. Surprisingly, GM responded Aug. 12 by offering some job guarantees for a UAW commitment to plant-level efficiency gains—most of which would come from teams.

Teams really are just one element of a more efficient alternative to the mass production system popularized by Frederick Winslow Taylor 85 years ago. He argued that work should be chopped into small, repetitive tasks simple enough to be done by "a child or a gorilla." As unions organized, their contracts codified work rules governing these employer-designed job classifications. This produced a rigid system that employers have been trying to change for several decades.

By contrast, worker participation and flexibility are bywords of the team philosophy. At its heart is the idea of training workers to perform several jobs instead of just one, so that they'll be less bored and more motivated. Management also hands over some control of production on the theory that employees will design a workplace more efficiently than management can. Coupled with this is a range of new manufacturing methods such as just-in-time inventory control. A key ingredient is the guarantee that if an employee finds a more efficient way to work, he won't be laid off.

A number of U.S. manufacturers have experimented with teams recently, including General Electric, Goodyear, and Procter & Gamble. Detroit started in 1973, when the UAW suggested giving workers more control through a process known as quality of work life. But companies remained cool to such approaches until they realized that giving workers more control would improve productivity.

This, indeed, has happened. The GM-Toyota venture, New United Motor Manufacturing Inc. (NUMMI), makes fewer models and less complex cars than when it was just a GM plant. But most experts say teams are a main reason NUMMI makes about the same number of units with about half the workers. Mark Hogan, NUMMI's general manager, says his plant is some 20% less productive in man-hours per vehicle than Toyota, which may be the world's most efficient carmaker. But that's 10 points better than a year ago, and Hogan expects to catch up in time. More important, the consensus is that NUMMI is 20% to 40% more efficient than most GM plants.

Actually, GM learned about teams before NUMMI. The going was bumpy after the company opened its Shreveport (La.) light-truck assembly plant with teams in 1981. But by 1984 management and the union agreed to persuade, rather than force, workers to learn multiple jobs with an approach called pay-for-knowledge. As workers learn more jobs, their hourly pay goes up, to a maximum of 50¢ over the base wage of $12.82 an hour. The flexibility this creates makes it easy to operate more efficiently.

Job-Swapping. Recently, management wanted to cut a job from the team of Dave Smith, who installs rear bumpers. "The team experimented with different ways to get rid of the work," says Smith, who came to Shreveport in 1984 from GM's Tonawanda (N.Y.) plant. "We all switched jobs and came up with four or five different plans for cutting a job." The team is still deciding which

of the two best schemes to adopt, and whoever's job goes will move to another part of the plant. "But at my old plant, management would just have
told us to do it their way," says Smith.

The flexibility of teams also holds down the need for relief workers, and
it reduces boredom. Earnest Hilliard, who's been at Shreveport since 1981,
says that it's easy to cover for an absent comrade—or just switch jobs for a
while—as long as some team members know several jobs. "I used to switch
jobs for half a day with one of my buddies just because we were bored," he
says. "It makes the day go by faster."

Today, Shreveport is one of GM's best plants. GM's weekly internal Labor
Performance Report rates each plant according to its overall labor efficiency.
"We're not first every week, but on average we are," says Thomas Dennig,
the plant's production manager. The report also measures the number of hours
needed to build a vehicle. In the week ended Aug. 2, Shreveport's hourly and
salaried work forces averaged 23.2 hours—the lowest in GM and the same as
NUMMI's.

Coming off such successes, "GM has decided to spread teams to all its 175
plants," says NUMMI's Hogan. GM has started teams in a dozen or more components plants. Since January, 30-odd assembly plants have sent groups of
managers and UAW officers to study NUMMI. GM also set up an executive task
force headed by Richard M. Donnelly, to develop a "common" GM production system involving everything from materials handling to teams. GM already has decided to use NUMMI's five-member teams as its model instead of
those in Shreveport, which average 15 people.

Though many UAW members welcome teams as a way to achieve industrial democracy, GM's impatience has provoked mounting resistance. Some
workers feel teams are a company trick to get them to work harder. A vocal
minority has railed at UAW conventions against what it calls "whipsawing,"
or management playing one local against another, as the union claims occurred at Pontiac.

The dissidents point to GM's decision to close its Norwood (Ohio) assembly plant as another example. Both Norwood and GM's Van Nuys (Calif.) plant
made the same car, but Norwood made them for about $600 a car cheaper.
Nonetheless, last year, GM decided to shut down its Norwood plant and keep
Van Nuys open, largely because Van Nuys has agreed to switch to teams. Alfred
S. Warren Jr., GM's vice-president of labor relations, denies that this consti-
tutes whipsawing. A longtime supporter of teams, he insists that worker cooperation can't be forced. But, he adds, "if I have to put a new product somewhere,
I'm going to put it where the attitude is most cooperative."

Resistance also stems from lower-level managers' reluctance to give up
power. Most team systems replace foremen with team leaders, who are union
members. Remaining managers must suggest and discuss rather than issue
orders, which is a major cultural change for many. Says Ken Norden, a manager "at an old-style, dog-eat-dog GM plant in Baltimore" before he moved to
Shreveport: "The adjustment was a little hard for me at first. It's difficult to

share respect with others. I got used to it, but many managers can't who grew up in the old, dictatorial role."

The bigger problem is GM's need to move fast as its profits sink—which creates something of a catch-22. Management is growing more desperate to get productivity gains from teams. But by pushing too hard for the union to accept them, GM risks causing so much worker resentment that much of the new system's motivational benefits could be lost.

Big Risks. The Japanese avoid this problem by exchanging job security for worker cooperation—and that may be what's in the works in current auto talks. NUMMI managers reduced the UAW's fear of job losses by promising that they would bring work now subcontracted to outside companies back into the plant and even to take pay cuts themselves before laying off workers. Both GM and Ford could bring in subcontracted work if their plants were more productive.

The big question is how far they'll go to meet the union's demand for a guaranteed number of jobs. The UAW may be content to establish that principle without insisting on the 370,000 jobs Ephlin has mentioned—the UAW employment at GM before it recently idled 41,000 workers indefinitely. But the risks are large. With a high guarantee, an economic downturn could leave the companies paying many employees for whom there was no work. Detroit's willingness even to discuss such a deal is one indication of the promise of teams.

"We see domestic and foreign manufacturers making significant quality and productivity improvements by adopting more flexible systems," says Stanley J. Surma, Ford's chief labor negotiator. "We think this notion needs to be discussed at the national level."

Quality Circle Leader

Being a QC leader has permanently altered my supervisory style.

Jim Wall

Quality circles are advised to attack smaller problems first, to get the feel of it. We didn't. We went with a large problem that had a large cost saving. It took us a long time to put everything together. There was a lot of data gathering required. And there were times when I think the circle, the members of the circle, were getting a little frustrated because we weren't moving. But the closer it got, when everything started fitting together, when the charts we were

Reprinted by permission of the publisher, from BOSSES by Jim Wall (Lexington, Mass.: Lexington Books, D. C. Heath and Company, Copyright 1986, Jim Wall).

making were prepared, and when we were getting to the point that we were having dry runs on our presentations, then the enthusiasm really started building. Once we had our presentation, everyone just had a great feeling about it.

The problem was one of automating a job that previously had been done by hand. We get an engineering order to make some sort of engineering change, and on the back of the order you've got a place to indicate what you did to comply. So what we did, okay, was to come up with a way to get that indication into the computer so you could punch a button and the computer would flash up the engineering order and what was done to respond to it.

We calculated out the savings, and from what we know about future business over the next three years, we calculated that we would be saving right around $650,000 a year. The cost for implementing this entire system is going to be about $450,000, so we're actually paying for the implementation of that system in the first year. The reason we went with this big, complex problem was that the further we got into it, the more cost savings we could see. We were really thrilled with what we could save the company.

There are ten men in my quality circle. What I did when I set it up was to take the names of everyone who volunteered and put them into piles, one for each department, so I would have a cross section from all departments. Then I just drew a name out of each pile, so that in my quality circle I have some of my own people but most come from other departments and are under other supervisors.

Once we're in the QC meeting, my job is to keep the meeting moving. I'm not supervising that group. I am a member just like they are, but I'm the chairman, who makes sure that things keep moving rather than getting bogged down. I'm both a supervisor within the department and the leader of the QC. I don't want to say I'm a QC supervisor because I don't want to impose my feeling on the circle. If they want recommendations from me, I want them to ask for them because of my experience. I can help them in making a decision, but I want the decision to be made by the circle, not by me.

The circle members and I work with the facilitator, who sits in on all our meetings. We meet once a week, and if we're having a problem somewhere— say we need help from another department somewhere, or we're not getting cooperation somewhere—it's his job to get with these people and straighten things out so that we can get some cooperation. He is a liaison for us and for the other QC's that he works with.

I'll tell you what I have done. I read about this really good idea in my quality circle training manual. I liked it, and I don't know of too many circles that use it. Using an alphabetical system, we have a new leader every week. Each person in my circle takes a turn at leading a session. So I think the members are finding out what it takes to lead somebody. For instance, you get ten or eleven people trying to say something at the same time and nobody is getting anywhere. They find out for themselves that somebody has to keep things organized, going, moving forward. So when a meeting starts, one person knows he is going to be the leader, so he just starts it. My role—I try to sit back and watch the circle move. If we get bogged down on an issue, I try to solve the issue so we can keep moving, so that we don't use the whole hour arguing a particular thing.

I serve as a mediator, pointing out that this is a problem here, and suggesting that we take some guys, investigate it, get some feedback on it, and move on to something else. Let's keep going. I don't want them to try and please me with their ideas; they're there to solve problems in the areas with their own techniques.

When we make our presentations to management, the whole circle does it. What I generally do is make the introduction; that is, I give a little speech as to what we're going to present to them. Then my circle members—we've already gone through our presentation several times to get all the bugs worked out before we actually give the real presentation—make the actual presentation. And I think this helps, too, because it exposes the members to upper management, who remember their names. They say, "Hey, this guy did a good job in there." And it follows the opposite way also. The members feel good being able to look a top manager they normally wouldn't see straight in the eye and say that we need this, this, and this. They get to see the persons behind some of the names they read and hear.

Savings—like our $1.5 million in three years—is one reason I am so enthusiastic about leading a quality circle. It also gives the average employee more visibility, more opportunity to do something about his conditions, and it is a "people-building" program. I think people building is the most important thing other than the cost savings. We are building people. It makes people better. It makes their job better, and it makes them feel better about themselves.

The circle, as it improves quality, really develops the personnel. The members of the circle learn problem-solving techniques: how to investigate problems, brainstorming, and other investigation approaches. They're becoming better decision makers and problem solvers on the job, not just in the circle. So it's beneficial to the company from that standpoint.

The QC is also good for me. It's good exposure, and along with the younger members, I've developed. If nothing else, it's a refresher to me on problem solving and solution finding. And I'm finding that it's broadening me, exposing me to technical areas that I previously knew little about.

My leadership position is a delicate one within the circle. I am in a dual role—a supervisor within the department but a leader in the QC. While we're in a room, just us—the QC—I try not to come on as a supervisor. I try to treat them as equals and don't overpower them. But a lot of subjects come up as we're leaving the room, walking down the hall, or coordinating during the week that require me to act as supervisor. Then they perceive or recognize that I have a great deal of power. The dual role doesn't confuse them, but it does create some stress for me.

I don't know how much the QC members appreciate the fact that I come down and give up my power in the QC. I think they might. But more importantly, out of that room they all know they can come up to me and talk to me about any problem, not just one related to our QC. Maybe it's a father image that I've achieved [laughs].

I am sure they appreciate the number of free hours I spend at night working on presentations. I'm not stating, "You guys do this, you do that." I'm in there doing. It's not participative management, it's participative QC, equalism.

I think my mode of managing my own group has changed since I've started being a leader in the QC. As a supervisor, I know my people have a firm, set schedule to meet, and we're almost constantly behind schedule. So here I have to be a little more firm in my direction. With a QC it's freer. Number one, it's voluntary and there's no schedule. There's no deadline to meet in the circle. You can drag opinions out from people. If you take the time frequently to draw out opinions, people will start to present the opinion along with the problem. That is, when they present the problem, they'll say, "I think we should do this or that to solve it." And they'll indicate how they personally feel about the problem and the solution.

Learning this has really changed me; its made me more participative. Because I get so participative with the circle (I see benefits from participation—my QC people are so free to let their ideas flow) I say, "Why can't it work over here in my group?" I've changed and developed a different vocabulary, a different way to express myself, and now I conduct myself interpersonally in a way that better taps the resources of my subordinates.

Now, when time is available, when people in my group ask me questions, I'll say, "What do you think?" or "Why don't you go here, there, or wherever, and find that out." I've always found that if you've got to dig it out yourself, you'll remember it. If someone just tells you, it's too easy. You'll just be back in a week asking the same question.

QC has not only affected my style; it's had an effect on my superiors. The company's management has preached participative management for a number of years and put us through seminars on it, but they never used it or gave us the opportunity to use it. They were just beating the drums. Now, with QC, it's starting to seep in to all levels of management. And it eases some of that shockwave. Instead of the vice president coming in, beating the fist, and saying, "You *will* have participative management"—you know, the old Theory X—they're helping us to ease into it. They still expect the same quick response [*laughs*], but the way it is presented and supported is different.

In a nutshell, and no one expected this, having quality circles around and being a leader of a quality circle has changed my supervisory style on the job and has even changed the supervisory style of my superiors.

———————————————●———————————————

Keeping the Fires Lit Under the Innovators

Christopher Knowlton

Around this time of year, the noonday temperature in St. Paul, Minnesota, is three degrees below freezing, so it seems an unlikely spot for a caldron of innovation. Nonetheless, new products bubble up at a rate of more than 200 a year from the research labs that crowd Minnesota Mining & Manufacturing's 435-acre St. Paul campus. Many of 3M's innovations are modest variations of such ordinary but ubiquitous industrial and consumer items as masking tape, coatings for highway reflectors, and sandpaper.

Some 6,000 scientists and engineers are continually stirring the pot, primarily in chemistry and applied science. In all, the company makes some 60,000 products that last year produced revenues of $9.4 billion, up 10% from the year before. Operations in 50 other countries accounted for 40% of those sales. Assisted by the ailing dollar, earnings rose 18% to $918 million. In FORTUNE's annual survey of America's most admired corporations, 3M most recently ranked No. 6—out of 306 entries. The company is often cited for its ability to keep innovation alive in a large, necessarily bureaucratic organization.

The man responsible for seeing that the fires don't go out is Allen F. Jacobson, 61, known as Jake, who joined 3M as a chemical engineer straight out of Iowa State University in 1947. In contrast with his popular predecessor, Lewis Lehr, Jacobson is strict and a little cold. He once rebuked the minister at his Presbyterian church for preaching that one person's profit is another's loss. Collaring the young man after the service, Jacobson informed him tersely that his remarks were "not in line with our country's best economic thinking."

While hardly the type to encourage the entrepreneurial whims of 3M's researchers, this Calvin has a dash of the Good Shepherd. To be sure that his flock of innovators share their ideas, Jacobson keeps his organization relatively decentralized. Information flows to the top from clearly defined reporting relationships and lots of shoptalk. He says, "You can't make too many of the decisions on the executive floor. You have to depend on the people who are close to the market and the technology."

Under Jacobson, 3M continues to codify many of the practices that preserve the innovative spirit of its scientists and engineers. Researchers are encouraged to spend 15% of their time pursuing pet projects that might have a payoff for the company down the road—a pastime they call "bootlegging." The stick behind that carrot is that 25% of each division's annual sales are expected to come from products developed in the prior five years.

Small groups staffed with a researcher and a market push inventions through the design and development stage. It takes an average of seven years from a product's invention to its successful introduction, although the trek can be made in less. Though Post-it notes took six years, some tapes take only one. Ultimately, 60% of the ideas wind up on the lab floor, but Jacobson wryly notes, "Outsiders say we are very lenient in rewarding failure."

One superior product fresh from the labs is the first videocassette tape for the Super VHS video recorder. The tape, which 3M hopes will be the industry standard by the 1990s, improves picture resolution by capturing 400 lines of broadcast information vs. the standard 230.

Besides coming up with new products, the labs are also supposed to protect and extend the product line against the encroachments of competitors. A case in point: In 1980, 3M developed the first water-activated synthetic casting tape used to set broken bones, but by 1982 eight other companies had brought out copycat products. When 3M researchers discovered that some of these tapes were actually easier to apply than 3M's, they retreated to their labs to develop and test 140 new versions in a variety of fabrics, before introducing the next year an improved product that was stronger and easier to use.

In 1985, 3M's earnings declined 9.5% when the lofty dollar pummeled sales. Though Jacobson responded by cutting costs 35%, he spared R&D spending. Through this period, it actually rose from 4.5% of sales in 1980 to 6.6% today, a figure roughly twice the U.S. average for manufacturers. Now the company is reaping the benefits of that investment.

Every so often the caldron produces a witch instead of a winner. Recently a line of air ionizers used to remove dust from the air in factory production facilities began leaking radiation. Though 3M maintains that the ionizers pose no serious health threat, it recalled them, fearing they would taint the company's reputation. When asked about that reputation, Jacobson dismisses all the business buzzwords and phrases save innovation and the pursuit of quality. "These are the tools for staying ahead in our increasingly competitive society," he says. For a man who goes one on one with God's anointed, he practices what he preaches.

4

Influencing

In introducing the previous chapter, we asserted that organizations are one of several ways that human beings coordinate their efforts. Organizing can, but seldom does fully replace other means of integrating human action. Over the last century or so, however, as the more traditional personal means of influencing people to cooperate were insufficient, the importance of formally organized procedures increased dramatically.

Despite this increase, even within highly formalized organizations, the traditional and more personal modes of influence continue to play a major role. They grease the wheels of the organization's machinery and give life to the processes of its systems. In fact, the abilities of managers to employ these modes has much to do with the success of a group or an organization as well as the personal advancement of the individual.

In many ways the personal aspects of influencing are probably similar to what they were centuries ago, before organizations became so important. While perhaps brute physical force plays a less central role than it did in earlier times, in almost all social systems individuals attempt to alter the behavior of others to the advantage of one or more individuals or to the group as a whole. What is radically different, however, is that these traditional and less formal actions take place in organizations—in social systems that are formally structured. This context creates new elements that managers must balance; here we consider two of them.

First, the organization is superimposed on informal interpersonal processes. The organization assigns individuals to formal positions and these formal positions have remarkable effects on how people interact with each other. For example, consider a group of people who are at the same organizational level working together on a task. Now, without changing anything else, appoint one of them supervisor or leader. What will happen? It has been our experience that this label can have an astonishingly dramatic impact on the interaction. The individual appointed leader often takes more responsibility for the job and becomes more authoritarian in relating to the others. The other members of the group often become more passive than before, waiting for directions from the "leader." Moreoover, the leader is now treated as an outsider—"It is us against her." Clever experiments by David Kipnis[1] and Elliot Aronson[2] provide supporting evidence for these general patterns. Giving people some formal power over others has dramatic effects on how they relate to each other.

Second, while the organization is superimposed on a less formal set of relationships, it also helps to create informal social systems. In particular, by organizing people into departments or other formal units, the organization creates groups that work together. In this way, organizing gives rise to new sets of interpersonal interactions and to new sets of needs and interests. Since, in such departmentalized systems, the achievement of a person's own ends depends on the success of his/her department, people develop interests in advancing the interests of their own departments—sometimes over and above the goals of the organization. In essence, the organization has created a new set of needs. Similarly, the interests of individuals often are best achieved by advancing in the hierarchy that organizing often introduces. Again, the organization itself has created a new set of interests which somehow managers must balance.

Many influence attempts within an organization are motivated by these organizationally created interests. The time and energy devoted to battles for formal position and status within an organization can easily become nearly as great (if not greater) than that devoted to outstripping the firm's competitors in the market place. Similarly, interdepartmental struggles can account for a large amount of time that managers spend attempting to influence other people. Battles over transfer prices are a prime example.

Transfer prices are literally the price that one unit of an organization charges another unit of the organization for supplying it with some good or service. Since these are often simply paper transactions, it is useful to think of the transfer price as the amount of credit one supplying unit receives. Of course, the credit it receives is a debit on the accounts of the other organizational unit. If both units are evaluated on the basis of such debits and credits, as they are in many accounting systems, the department that supplies the good will look better (that is, more profitable) if the transfer price it receives is high; conversely, the department that receives the good will appear better if the transfer price it has to pay is low. Each department has an incentive to try to make the terms of exchange favor itself. Accordingly, the departments attempt to influence each other and third parties (for example, the accountants who conceived the transfer price). Note that this particular conflict takes the form it does because of elements created in the organizing process—the departments and the transfer pricing system. People in organizations spend a great deal of time trying to influence each other over such internally generated problems. In short, the organization itself creates numerous conditions for conflict and hence for people to attempt to influence each other. In many of the articles in this section, pressures people are responding to are those organizationally spawned problems.

Regardless of whether the need to influence others is produced directly by some task or was created by the organization itself, the associated human drama is fascinating. The drama is constructed by the personal characteristics of those involved—human emotions, beliefs, values, and the behavioral skills of the actors (see, for example, "Situations that Promote Organization Politics" and "Taking the Hype out of Leadership"). The outcomes are often determined by the abilities of the actors to sense and appeal to what others believe, feel, and value as strategically or morally right. Of course, the whole play takes place on a stage set by history and current events.

Given the nature of the drama as we have portrayed it, leadership (which we define as the ability to influence others to act in accordance with one's preferences) is not well understood. It is no wonder that people who have sought a simple list of characteristics of successful leaders or have advanced models of leadership that consist of a very few dimensions are often looked upon by managers as not providing very useful answers for them as they try to lead others or to deal with leaders in the organization. Although much is known about leadership, most treatments of the topic for managers do not give sufficient emphasis to the elements of the influence process that lead us to characterize it as drama. The articles in this section attempt to highlight some of these components.

We see that leadership is far more than simply an interpersonal event. Leadership takes places in a larger human system and is affected by the "whole." We also see how personal characteristics (gender, positive and negative orientations, and emotions) affect the influence process. Similarly, just as on the stage, timing is essential. Moreover, there are a variety of audiences (see, for example, "Airline Field Manager") watching the performance and moving them emotionally and behaviorally depends on playing to their consciousness.

Further, we see how when the situation changes new roles are demanded. Of special interest is a fact pointed out in several of the selections (most clearly in "The Plateauing Trap") that it is relatively easy to influence during a period of growth or perhaps even during a period of crisis where everyone recognizes that something needs to be done. The greatest challenge may come, however, during ordinary periods when there is little stimulus to draw on to energize people. These periods may be very common—nothing needs to be done differently; people need to be induced to do what they have always done well. In this sense, although transformational leadership may be very important, perhaps recently too little attention has been given to what we might call revival leadership—renewing energy and commitment under conditions where stability and routine are the order of the day.

There is a great deal to learn about influencing and leading. The following articles capture some of the drama often omitted by writers of textbooks who are just writing about management rather than about doing management. They reflect on the conflicting pressures managers experience and provide some clues for successful leadership under such conditions.

References

1. D. Kipnis, *The Powerholders* (Chicago: University of Chicago Press, 1976).
2. A Pirandelian Prison, *New York Times Magazine*, 8 April 1973, pp. 38–40, 49.

Wreckers

Anonymous

I watched them tearing a building down,
A gang of men in a busy town,
With a hi-heave-ho and a lusty yell,
They swing a beam and the side walls fell.
I asked the foreman, "Are those men skilled
As the men you hire if you had to build?"
He gave me a laugh and said, "No indeed!
Just common labor is all I need.
I can easily wreck in a day or two
what builders have taken years to do."
I thought to myself as I went my way,
Which of these roles have I tried to play?
Am I a builder who works with care,
Measuring life by the rule or square?
Am I shaping my deeds to a well made plan,
Patiently doing the best I can?
Or am I wrecking like he who walks the town
Content with the labor of tearing down?

The Wallenda Factor

Warren Bennis

One of the most impressive and memorable qualities of the leaders I studied
was the way they responded to failure. Like **Karl Wallenda,** the great tight-
rope aerialist, who once said, "The only time I feel truly alive is when I walk
the tight-rope," these leaders put all their energies into their task. They simply don't think about failure, don't even use the word, relying on such syno-
nyms as *mistake* or *glitch* or *bungle* or countless others, such as *false start,
mess, hash, bollix,* or *error.* Never *failure.* One of them said during the course
of an interview that "a mistake is just another way of doing things." Another
said, "I try to make as many mistakes as quickly as I can in order to learn."

Shortly after Wallenda fell to his death in 1978 (traversing a 75-foot-high
tight-rope in downtown San Juan, Puerto Rico, his wife, also an aerialist, discussed that fateful San Juan walk, "perhaps his most dangerous." She recalled,

> *"All Karl thought about for three straight months prior to it was* falling. *It was the
> first time he'd* ever *thought about that, and it seemed to me that he put all his energy
> into* not falling, *not into walking the tight-rope."*

"The Wallenda Factor," by Warren Bennis, from New Management, Vol. 1, No. 3, pp. 46–47,
copyright © 1986 by New Management. Reprinted by permission of John Wiley & Sons, Inc.

Mrs. Wallenda went on to say that her husband even went so far as to personally supervise the installation of the tight-rope, making certain that the guy-wires were secure, "something he had never even thought of before."

From what I learned from my interviews with successful leaders, I can say that when Karl Wallenda poured his energies into *not falling* rather than walking the tight-rope, he was virtually destined to fail. Indeed, I call that peculiar combination of vision, persistence, consistency, and self-confidence necessary for successful tight-rope walking—the combination I found in so many leaders—the Wallenda Factor.

An example of the Wallenda Factor comes in an interview with **Fletcher Byrom,** who retired recently from the presidency of the Koppers Company, a diversified engineering, construction, and chemicals company. When asked about the "hardest decision he ever had to make," he said,

"I don't know what a hard decision is. I may be a strange animal, but I don't worry. Whenever I make a decision, I start out recognizing there's a strong likelihood I'm going to be wrong. All I can do is the best I can. To worry puts obstacles in the way of clear thinking."

Or consider **Ray Meyer**—perhaps the winningest coach in college basketball—who led DePaul University to 40 straight years of winning seasons. When his team dropped its first home game after 29 straight home-court victories, I asked him how he felt about it. His response was vintage Wallenda: "Great! Now we can start concentrating on winning, *not* on not losing." And then there is **Harold Prince,** the Broadway producer. He regularly calls a press conference the morning after one of his Broadway plays opens—before reading any reviews—in order to announce plans for his *next* play.

Effective leaders overlook error and constantly embrace positive goals. They pour their energies into the task, not into looking behind and dredging up excuses for past events. For a lot of people, the word "failure" carries with it a finality, the absence of movement characteristic of a dead thing, to which the automatic human reaction is helpless discouragement. But, for the successful leader, failure is a beginning, the springboard of hope.

One CEO I interviewed, **James Rouse,** the famed city planner and developer, said that when he was dissatisfied with the looks of some housing in his Columbia, Maryland, project, he tried to influence the next design by nagging and correcting his team of architects. He got nowhere. Then he decided to stop correcting them and tried to influence them by demonstrating what he wanted, *what he was for.* Inspired by Rouse's vision, the architects went on to create some of the most eye-catching and functional housing in the country. What this illustrates is that the self-confidence of leaders is *contagious.* Two more examples: In the early days of Polaroid, **Edwin Land** continually inspired his team to "achieve the impossible." Land's compelling self-confidence convinced his managers and researchers that they couldn't fail. When **William Hewitt** took over Deere and Company in the mid-1950's, he turned a sleepy, old-line farm implements firm into a leader among modern multinational corporations. His secret? Commitment. Confidence. Vision.

And always asking, "Can't we do this a little better?" And the employees rose to the occasion. As one long-time Deere employee put it: "Hewitt made us learn how good we were." Because they know where they are going, great leaders inspire the people who work for them so that they, too, can walk the tight-rope. That is one of the reasons why organizations run by great leaders often appear so productive.

Although leading is a "job" for which leaders are handsomely paid, where their rewards come from—and what they truly value—is a sense of adventure and play. In my interviews, they describe work in ways that scientists and other creative types use: "exploring a new space," "solving a problem," "designing or discovering something new." Like explorers, scientists, and artists, they seem to focus their attention on a limited field—their task—forget personal problems, lose their sense of time, feel competent and in control. When these elements are present, leaders truly enjoy what they're doing and stop worrying about whether the activity will be productive or not, whether their activities will be rewarded or not, whether what they are doing will work or not. They are walking the tight-rope.

I've wondered, from time to time, if this fusion of work and play, where, quoting from a **Robert Frost** poem, "love and need are one," is a positive addiction. My guess is that it is a healthy addiction, not only for individual leaders but for society. Great leaders are like the Zen archer who develops his skills to the point where the desire to hit the target becomes extinguished, and man, arrow, and target become indivisible components of the same process. That's good for the leaders. And when this style of influence works to attract and empower people to join them on the tight-rope, that's good for organizations and for society. Hail the Wallenda Factor!

●
———————————————

Taking the Hype out of Leadership

Forget the tracts extolling the singular virtues of leaders. A CEO offers more practical advice.

Andrew S. Grove

One of our divisional marketing managers recently asked for a meeting with me. A man in his mid-30s, he reports to a division general manager, who reports to the group general manager, who in turn reports to me. I know that this fellow works hard at his job, and also that he pays attention to his progress up the ladder. As he said quite openly when asking for the meeting, the purpose of the session was to have a "career checkup": He wanted to know if he was doing all the right things for the company to continue his rise through the ranks.

Our discussion went smoothly at first. He told me of some things he had done in the past year that he was particularly proud of, and a bit about what he planned to do. Then he asked what I thought he should be working on. I countered with another question: What were his strengths? He quickly replied that he prided himself on his organizational skills, his understanding of his product area and the market, and his rapport with the corporate sales force—the people who, while not under his authority, use his marketing strategies to sell the division's products. Next I asked where he thought he was lacking. After considerable hesitation, he gave an answer that didn't mean a whole lot to me: "I am afraid I don't provide enough leadership."

He isn't the only one thinking about leadership these days. Whether the question is our national competitiveness, the decay of ethics in government, or just about any other problem facing our society, sooner or later someone will identify the root cause as a lack of leadership. Leaders, we are told, embrace change. They transform their organizations with bold actions based on their abiding vision of the shape of how things need to be. In the avalanche of books and articles on the subject that have come down around our heads recently, most of the commentary centers on the President or on the chief executives of major corporations.

So how does all this relate to my divisional marketing manager?

He is one of perhaps five million American middle managers. For the most part, these people don't possess grand visions for their companies, but instead worry about procedures for approving loans, methods of reducing the set-up time for some newfangled and terribly expensive piece of machinery, approaches for introducing new products, and the like. Can such managers be leaders? Do they need to be?

A few weeks after my meeting with the man, I happened to see him in action. He was giving a presentation—an important one—to a group of corporate sales managers, explaining his division's marketing plans for the next six months: what to sell, to whom, how, and for how much. His aim was to ensure that his products would receive a healthy "share of mind" among the sales managers, who sell products from all of Intel's divisions.

This was no piece of cake. As I listened from the back row, one sales manager after another raised objections to the plans being presented. "How can we sell against the competition if we don't have the such-and-such feature?" one demanded. "Unless we have a complete family to offer, we are wasting our time," another said. And so it went, each comment just stimulating another even more critical one.

The young marketing manager acted as if he basically agreed with the comments, even when they were obviously exaggerated. It seemed to me that the sales managers were mainly trying to make their own lives easier. The perfect product is easy to sell; no salesman enjoys having to make up for a product's imperfections by dint of extra work. But the marketing exec was so bent on appeasing this group that he just went with the flow, agreeing with whatever they said. When his time was up, he left behind a very disgruntled group of sales managers.

As I watched this scene, a picture of what had gone wrong formed in my mind. It struck me that most famous examples of military leadership arise in situations where the Great Leader spurs his underarmed and bedraggled followers, on their last legs and with no ammunition left, to great feats of valor. Winston Churchill's greatest moment came when London was being bombed and an invasion of England seemed imminent. Leaders, I thought to myself, are individuals who make ordinary people do extraordinary things in the face of adversity.

What the marketing manager needed to do was to make this ordinary group of salesmen commit themselves to do their extraordinary best in selling his imperfect and incomplete product line. The more his products were underdogs to the competition, the more he needed to elicit such a commitment. But he didn't rise to the occasion. His earlier comment about his lack of leadership skills was, unfortunately, quite correct, perhaps even more true than he realized.

Nonetheless, I hope the man will not try to go about improving himself by reading too much of the current literature on leadership. Being told that leaders and managers are inherently different people would be less than helpful; indeed, the message might discourage him from trying to develop his skills. Nor would the suffocating preoccupation with larger-than-life business figures like Lee Iacocca and Jack Welch do him much good: His role in the business world is so far removed from theirs that he might as well read about the exploits of Alexander the Great.

The lesson my young marketing executive must learn is that an effective manager needs to blend altogether different skills but does not need to be superhuman. On the one hand, he needs administrative skills, skills based on logic and used according to predictable rules. On the other hand, he also needs an ability to convey his strong feelings about a subject when that's appropriate, as it would have been with the sales managers. What he should have said, and with obvious conviction, is something like this: "Here's our product line. We know it's not perfect and we will work to improve it continually. But, for now, this is what we—and you—have to work with, and what you must sell. I *know* it can be sold because I have sold it myself. You can call me anytime, day or night—here is my home phone number—if you need help to work out an approach that's right for your customer. Give me 24 hours and I will be there to go with your salespeople to call on any account that needs it."

My would-be leader also needs to learn to gauge the right moment to inject his emotion into a business situation. Leaders get the timing right. Had he burst into his speech too early, he would have come across to the sales managers as insincere. As it happened, he missed the right time altogether and came across as a weak, wishy-washy, uncommitted manager. The perfect moment probably would have been after he replied strongly to the first couple of objections.

How will my subordinate learn such things? Not by reading about great leaders whose experience is so foreign as to make it impossible for him to identify with them. Nor, in my view, by going to wilderness retreats and climbing poles and rafting down white-water rivers. He will learn the same way each of us has learned the important, unteachable roles in our lives, be they that of husband or wife, father or mother: by studying the behavior of people who have made a success of it and modeling ourselves after them.

I went back to the divisional marketing manager after the sales presentation and told him that he was right, he did indeed lack in leadership skills. I described how I saw him come across at the meeting, and the opportunity he had missed. He wasn't at all happy to have his suspicions confirmed, but, knowing him, the next time he makes a presentation to the sales managers, I'm expecting a major display of leadership.

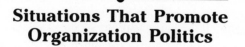

Situations That Promote Organization Politics

Samuel A. Culbert and John J. McDonough

. . . Politics is an inevitable by-product of each individual's struggle to gain context. In the process, however, we did not intend to leave the impression that high levels of political activity are desirable. Nothing could be further from the truth. High levels of political activity, particularly of the tactical kind, are major forms of distraction that drain energy and spirit from the workplace. . . .

Involvement in politics is necessary—each individual's success depends on articulating the framework that allows others to comprehend what he or she is attempting to create and its value to the institution. But when nothing an individual does produces enduring appreciation, his or her political needs take on a significantly different cast. Then people engage in politics primarily to force others to see them, their units, and/or their production in a way that will enable them to accomplish their immediate objectives. Progress made today has to be repeated tomorrow. Excessive politics is the result. . . .

In our work we come across many excessively politicized situations. And when we talk with those managers who have the position and the power to affect them we are continually amazed. We are amazed that they are so blind to what is going on! They look around them and see the obvious symptoms—rumors, morale problems, credit stealing, firings, attempts to fix accountability by putting excessive blame on people when goals are not met—with little insight into what people need and why they are acting so political. . . . We believe that organization politics result from people lacking context, or feeling the threat of having their context taken away (notwithstanding the fact that some people are excessively greedy and compulsive in their desire for power and for them politics is a way of life). The rest of this chapter is devoted to identifying the circumstances that systematically deprive people of context and create the need for politics irrespective of the personalities involved. We have identified six such situations which will be discussed in turn.

1. Competition at the Top

In our experience the most frequent source of organization politics is excessive competition at the top. This competition may be over advocacy of specific viewpoints or values, or over people's desires for power and interests in being number one. In any event a domino effect is created whereby competitive dynamics at the top set off pressures to act politically at each echelon below. And amazing to us is the capacity of those on the top for believing that their conflict and competition is contained and not a problem for those below. So often their reactions are like those of feuding parents. They wonder what's wrong with their troubled children without realizing that their kids' problems relate to their own. Competing executives often view their own behavior as irrelevant to solving the political problems they see in the ranks below and this attitude tends to squeeze the people beneath them all the more. We've seen this attitude in the public sector, we've seen it in the private, and we wanted to include an example of each since the political forces are somewhat different.

One instance of an organization with internal political turmoil created by competition at the top occurred within an important state energy commission during the late 1970s. At the top of the commission were five governor-appointed commissioners who, as stipulated by legislation, were appointed to represent different points of view. There was an environmental appointee, whose responsibility was to advocate the conservation of natural resources; there was an industrial expansion appointee, whose responsibility was to advocate policies that provided cheap and plentiful power for industrial consumption; and there were three public appointees, each of whom was charged with representing a discipline such as economics or law along with the well-being of the general public in whatever ways they individually felt that might best be accomplished.

In concept and on paper the commission structure seemed like a wonderful idea. Energy policy would be decided in a forum in which varied and competing interests would be represented and in which no parochial point of view would dominate. However, in practice having five commissioners presented big problems for those who had the job of performing commission work.

Working for the commission was a professional staff of 400 with its own management hierarchy. While the commissioners had the job of framing issues, considering facts, and setting policy, the staff's job was to collect the data, perform the analyses, and implement the decisions taken by the commissioners as a group. The staff organization was supposed to be free to work independently of a commissioner's persuasion except that the commissioners' policy-setting rights extended to voting on key personnel appointments including those of all managers. On any given day anyone who aroused the enmity of three of the five commissioners could be voted out of a job. Of course most were protected by civil service and had a fall-back position in another agency. Nevertheless, any manager from the executive director on down could lose his or her managerial rank with barely a day's notice.

From this structure one can easily visualize the type of competition that could break out if individual commissioners failed to respect the stance another felt obligated to take. And as luck would have it, the particular mix of commissioner personalities produced just such a lack of respect and there were many times when the arguments became heated, when personalities were attacked, and when expression of different points of view became the occasion for open warfare. Adding even more pressure was the fact that this commission was often in the public limelight; it was the first to address nuclear energy issues that were to set national precedents.

Thus, whenever the competition became keen, relationships between the commissioners and the staff became especially political. Commissioners would sequester staffers, inquire how their analytic work was coming, ask what preliminary conclusions were being drawn, and then present their own interpretations with innuendos that anyone seeing the results differently ought to have his or her head examined. Then they implied that just such an examination might take place during a closed-door hearing of the five commissioners.

From the staff perspective, the situation was an organizational nightmare. As one manager put it, "It's like having five different bosses, each with his own independent viewpoint, with the added twist that none of the commissioners takes any responsibility for the fact that we have to deal with an associate's points of view." Predictably, staff members became quite cautious and began spending a high percentage of their work time trying to figure out how to keep each of the commissioners happy, and thinking about how to defend themselves against those from within their own ranks who had aligned themselves with a particular commissioner. The result was a staff that often took refuge in verbose, highly technical language and bland reports. Staff relations with the commissioners degenerated into a game of pretending that each commissioner's interests came first. In effect the staff attempted to play off one commissioner's biases against another's.

We recognize that an organizational setting in which each manager has five bosses who don't get along represents an extreme situation. Nevertheless it's a situation that illustrates the problems associated with developing self-context when one lacks a stable frame of reference at the top. People need context, and when it's not forthcoming from the organization, they attempt to get it by erecting a framework of their own. But, because they cannot be explicit about the role they are pursuing and the stance they are taking, they act politically. They develop alliances to protect them while they covertly follow a substitute direction which, in their own minds, is superior to, or at least as good as, the directions given to them by the top. Thus the commissioners' inability to articulate a coherent point of view rendered the organization vulnerable to covert views that, in many instances, were excessively self-indulgent and at odds with a direction that even the commissioners had agreed to among themselves. Apparently there is a level of participation in which politics take on a runaway dimension where people can no longer discriminate between what's necessary in order to cope and political behavior as a way of life.

In the private sector politics rarely have their origins in situations like the one described above. If there is one thing that top managers in the private sector know, it's how to isolate and center responsibility and to hold operating levels accountable. Nevertheless, when competition breaks out at the top, it produces political binds that people in the levels below find every bit as intense and unnerving. For instance, we are intimately familiar with a conglomerate that put its entire operating management through a painful exercise when two top-level executives started fighting. The circumstances were straightforward and easily understandable—each of these men needed different contexts in order to feel secure and powerful.

The conglomerate was a group of sixteen companies with a strong-willed founder/chairman of the board who was past retirement age. There were two senior managers, one in charge of operations and the other in charge of finance; one of them would become the chairman's successor. The operations man held the title of corporation president and had been raised in the parent industry, which for the sake of anonymity we'll call the transportation business. He was using that industry's accounting framework as the basis for monitoring and overseeing each of the acquired businesses. The finance man held the title of executive vice-president. He was relatively new to the corporation, had never worked in the transportation business, and had experience in several industries. He contended that the transportation model was wrong for the conglomorate as a whole and that each of the acquired businesses had distinctive components and facets to which the transportation experience was insensitive and which his department was well equipped to handle if only operations would accept a new system.

Behind this dispute was the ambivalence of the chairman of the board about letting go. As long as his top level executives fought, his presence was essential. His support of each and refusal to declare his own deciding point of view kept the competition going. Each executive had to dig in or be seen as capitulating. There was nowhere to retreat. In an attempt to settle this conflict the finance man created an organizational exercise. Under the guise of "business systems planning," a task force was created to conduct an in-depth study of each of the company's sixteen businesses and to recommend whether or not a new set of categories should be used in monitoring the activities, results, and profits of each of the groups. To insure that its findings would be seen as valid, only people with the most impeccable credentials were appointed to the task force.

Once the finance man created the task force the president might as well have started packing. There was no way a group of managers with different businesses would agree with the transportation model. They didn't, and when the study was concluded the president was allowed to resign. So were several senior executives who had been schooled in the transportation business and who had relocated in other divisions. The finance man immediately succeeded the president, but the recommendations for a new system were only partially implemented. Today it's a new situation. There's another fight, with the new president holding the line on the modified system he instituted, and a new protagonist arguing for a different model. The Chairman is still holding on, unconsciously fueling the flames. And the pressures continue to filter down. Today's pressure is for short-term immediate profits with deep cutbacks in personnel, moratoriums and ceilings on salary increases, and curtailment of internal functions that have long-term payback periods such as R&D.

In our experience top-level shootouts are never contained. We've never seen them take place without affecting a large part of an organization. For instance, in the aforementioned example there are senior managers in each of the sixteen companies who are so afraid of becoming a fatality in the next purge that they shun lining up with any identifiable viewpoint that might later place them in conflict with a new perspective that emerges at corporate head-quarters. Most are biting their tongues and running their businesses as if monthly statements are the only navigational tools needed to chart a course or to measure their division's progress.

Common to both of these illustrations is instability at the top. Organization politics are a common response when people find themselves in situations where disagreements at the top deprive them of organizational context—of a stable framework against which they can reference their organization actions and link them to the good of the whole. In its absence people devise statements of function for themselves which are born in self-interests, covertly pursued, and which become sources of daily political tension. Thus people engage in the machinations that they believe will provide the self-context needed to be an organizational and personal success. The lack of a stable point of view, however, need not result from multiple bosses using different perspectives. It can just as easily result from the erratic behavior of a single boss.

2. The Erratic Boss

Some months ago a colleague asked us to counsel a friend of his who was spending sleepless nights worrying about his new job. We agreed and made a date to see him. When the friend came over he gave us all the cues that he expected a long conversation and was surprised when the conversation concluded twenty-five minutes later.

> *The friend came in, took out his cigarettes and lighter and arranged them along with his keys on the table. He accepted our offer of coffee, discovered he had two cigarettes lit at once, looked extremely anxious, thanked us for seeing him, and got right into relating his predicament. He was a professional photographer who had been working for three months as a photographic editor of a female-oriented equivalent of* Playboy *magazine. He told us that he was heterosexual, had never photographed men before, didn't know women's tastes in beefcake, and had a too-short boss who seemed to enjoy pushing him, at six feet two, around. We asked how others got along with the boss? When he said, "They think the boss is crazy and complain he is always changing his mind about what he wants," we said, "Quit."*

We told "the friend" to quit because it was clear that he was in a situation in which self-context could never be attained. He had an essential function he did not feel competent to perform, lacked the skill to perform his role distinctively, and did not have an orientation that would allow him to be confident that his activities would eventually accumulate to accomplish a distinct role and essential function. What's more, he had a boss who would not lend him a stable frame of reference to use until he could develop his own. What could be worse than not being confident of the judgments one has to make, having a boss whose framework seems more dependent on internal emotional processes than on external facts, and lacking the experience needed to take a stand when one thinks him- or herself correct?! It puts an individual in a situation where his or her bearings and success totally depend on the whims of an inconsistent evaluator. This forces a person to cultivate that relationship on far less than honest grounds.

The pervasiveness of problems with erratic bosses was demonstrated to us through a peculiar set of circumstances. We had consented to an interview by a *Los Angeles Times* reporter who was developing an article on "crazy bosses" and the effect their erratic behavior had on the people who worked for them. Once we figured out what she was up to we advised her to change the title from "Crazy Bosses" to "Crazy-Making Bosses." We reasoned that bosses with deep emotional problems are relatively easy to spot and, once recognized, relatively easy to discount. On the other hand, those we label "crazy-making" have a style that makes it very difficult for people to achieve context and their destructive impact is often difficult to see. We reasoned that individuals are emotionally vulnerable when they depend on a boss who either lacks the ability to affirm their context or is competitive with them and has no interest in doing so. We described how a boss with a need for a context that is incompatible with a subordinate's could drive that person nuts while not posing a particular problem for others whose needs for context are more compatible.

Fortunately for the reporter, she decided to stick with the Crazy Boss title and her article was a big success. Not only did it appear on the front page of the *Times* but it was syndicated in at least twenty other major publications. Despite our errant advice, our views were given prominent attention with the result that we were deluged with calls, letters, and even a telegram from individuals whose lives the article had touched. We had grossly underestimated the number of people who are caught in destructive relationships with their bosses and who think that they, themselves, are the cause of their problems. For them, an article that labeled their boss "crazy" was a revelation providing doubts that the strife they had been experiencing was of their own making.

We heard many stories—stories of the ways people found to compensate for the problems created by having a boss who gives no support to their needs to be valued and seen as relevant to the organizational setting in which they were expected to perform. It was in relation to these conversations that we were exposed to accounts of flagrantly devious, clandestine, and malicious political behavior initiated not by the "crazy" bosses but by otherwise rational and positively inclined subordinates who happened to have the misfortune to land in a position that deprived them of context and a chance for success. While many told stories of trying to escape, most had what they saw as darn good reasons for staying where they were and working behind the scenes for their bosses' demise. They also were working diligently to publicize the value of what they produced in an effort to compensate for their apparent lack of context.

We'll spare the specifics because they are not necessary to make our point. Any set of circumstances, such as that described in our metaphor of the "erratic boss," which makes it difficult or impossible to get context, creates the conditions for political conniving among otherwise wonderful people of the caliber of you and us. People who cannot find a niche within the established structure are forced to create their own, and the means they use often serve to politicize the environment in which they and their cohorts work.

3. Too Much Hierarchy

Consistently we have found that organizations with excessive levels of hierarchy are hotbeds of political activity. And when we stopped to think about this the reason was quickly apparent. Too much hierarchy crowds people so that performing an essential function involves variables over which the individual lacks sufficient control; so that a role that capitalizes on the distinctive strengths of an individual usually involves responsibilities and duties that are assigned to someone else; and so that there are too many constraints to performing the activities that make sense in the pursuit of an essential function and distinctive role to which the individual is attached. In short, excessive hierarchy makes it impossible for people to find self-context because there is not a whole job for them to perform.

We have found that most organizations contain at least one extra level of hierarchy. Its existence serves to assure management that all important functions will be performed. And in our experience one extra level does little harm when there's enough real work to keep people busy. Then people at various levels extend above and below themselves to make sure a responsibility is covered, or a project accomplished, without taking anything essential away from others. However, problems resulting in excessive politics arise when there is more than one extra level of hierarchy, for then people's incursions to levels above or below threaten the integrity of the jobs of those whose territory is being entered.

In organizations, people get context from performing an entire job. Whether one's job is that of division manager, section head, or first-level supervisor, as long as the boundaries are clearly delineated and understood, people have the opportunity to succeed. But when the boundaries are not clear and people lack the authority to keep others from overlapping their responsibilities and functions, such as the situations that accompany too much hierarchy, people become fearful. Then they need assurances that cooperation with the other person, and solving the overlap in responsibilities by making it a team effort, will be recognized and valued by the organization. If such assurances are not adequate or forthcoming, people will engage in political jockeying. They attempt to manipulate organization roles and responsibilities so that they can once again perform an entire function. Usually this means stealing parts of someone else's job, not necessarily in an effort to attain more power and prestige, but in an effort to establish the minimal conditions for self-context and thus create the circumstances that are necessary to succeed.

Such personal maneuvering has often gone on at the Pentagon, an organization in which almost everyone has overlapping responsibilities and one that periodically accumulates hierarchy piled on top of hierarchy. At regular intervals reformers are sent in to streamline things, but, typically, a new organization is barely in place before some manager becomes concerned that this or that responsibility is not being covered, or is not receiving sufficient priority, and decides to invent a supplemental group that overlaps an existing unit. Once established, the original unit senses the redundancy, becomes blatantly territorial, and wide-ranging political machinations break out. And one doesn't have to go to the Pentagon to see such dynamics. They can appear in any organization and take place whenever a manager attempts to cope with distrust by inventing a supplemental or slave organization. We've seen a manufacturing department invent its own engineering group that eventually competed with the company's engineering department; we've seen a sales group invent its own marketing unit that eventually caused conflicts both with division and corporate marketing; and we've seen executives hire consultants whose opinions were more like theirs and whose presence supplanted the authority of line managers and other key staff who might disagree with them.

In recent years there have been many expert-led experiments in which hierarchies of people are brought together to examine an entire system with the intent of reevaluating jobs and redesigning them to feature more efficiency and greater effectiveness. While these analyses are almost always conducted as open-ended experiments, with the results neither fixed in advance nor prejudged, all the experiences of which we know have pointed in the same direction. Hierarchies are streamlined to feature fewer jobs with bigger functions. This differs significantly from the conclusions reached when only the upper echelons are involved, for they usually create more jobs with finer breakdowns in function.

While most experiments in job redesign have been directed towards manufacturing operations and what takes place on the shop floor, our own work has involved managers and professionals such as engineers and accountants. Our results are consistent. When viewing the entire system, people always see the problems and inefficiencies that result when their jobs overlap others and they recommend changes that provide larger jobs and less controlled supervision. People instinctively trust and have confidence in the actions of those who had achieved context, and given the opportunity they will attempt to incorporate the conditions that produce context. What's more, engaging in such analyses seems to enlighten people about what others need in the way of context while, at the same time, engendering support for like needs of their own.

4. Insufficient Respect for the Individual

Too many managers talk as if they have a *"magic door"* behind which a line of competent performers stand waiting to take the place of the incompetent person they have just observed. It's as if all one has to do to get rid of one's problems is to open the door and let in the next person in line. We can't begin to tell you how many variations we've heard on this one. Perhaps it's merely a wish that managers utter out loud, perhaps it's merely a cry of frustration, but whatever it is, it's disorienting. The notion that problems can be solved easily by replacing people prevents managers from seeing that others need self-context in order to perform effectively.

Whenever someone important begins to think in "magic door" terms, politics run rampant. And in our experience, whether or not people actually are replaced makes little difference. Making a mistake, failing to produce what one sets out to produce, performing less ably than someone else expects, and not contributing in the proper form become too important. In response people spend long hours figuring out what their bosses expect and attempt to produce it in the proper form while giving only secondary consideration to the appropriateness of what they are doing. They deny their errors and attempt to hide whatever might frustrate someone else's expectations. Power politics become the order of the day as wordsmithing, logrolling, and lobbying become intense.

In the situation we're describing, evaluation is severe and justice occurs in the minds of the evaluators, not in the minds of the judged. An inadequate system of forgiveness exists. In such situations, criticisms become more than just statements of how an individual performed in a given role; they become attacks on an individual's stature. People experience themselves being viewed as objects, as entities that are supposed to accomplish this or that—and not as complete human beings with strengths, needs, and imperfections, human beings who are sometimes strong and sometimes vulnerable and who on any given day are capable of "blowing one." Magic-door thinking strips people of their complexity, deprives them of self-context, and leaves them with little choice but to act political.

Happily there are some organizations where people are treated respectfully and with the proper amount of support and security to insure that they have context and perform at their best. In fact we know of a company, in which one of us spent seven years working as a management consultant, that gets high grades in the dimension of showing respect for people and their needs for context. This is a large consumer products company that has long been included on lists of best managed companies. We liked the respectful way they treated people long before we started thinking about the causes of organizational politics.

At Acme, our fictitious name for the company, people are treated respectfully at every stage of their careers. The emphasis is on succeeding—not in being punished for one's mistakes. No one ever criticizes others in public although they often make tough-minded statements about what a program needs in order to operate more effectively. At Acme, bosses are held responsible for their subordinates' performance and are not given the latitude to blame their inability to produce on the individuals who work for them. But even behind closed doors the poor performers are treated with dignity. Instead of being disgraced, they are given less demanding assignments.

Organizational structure changes frequently at Acme and people are transferred from one function and one department to another without a clear understanding of which job has the higher status. The important thing is to achieve context by becoming a member of a winning team. At Acme the emphasis is always on market competition, rather than competition within the ranks, and when a product wins in the marketplace everybody connected with that product advances.

It's seldom that someone at Acme gets both a promotion and a significant salary increase at the same time. Because of this, people who outlive their usefulness in one role can readily be transferred laterally without a pay change until they find a niche where they can perform effectively. There are "fast-trackers" at Acme and people cheer for them because they are seen as having the ability to pull a project along with everyone on the successful team getting one benefit or another. This produces an excessive reliance on one's team role as the basis for self-context and some people who leave Acme have difficulties putting their needs for context back on more individualistic terms. They take at face value what people in their new organization have promised and don't adequately check to see that what was promised will actually be delivered the way it always is at Acme.

We think that one of the best parts of the Acme spirit is that people seldom gossip disrespectfully about one another. Acme is relatively free of the types of put-downs and contemptuous statements we hear so often in the corridors, closed offices, and cafeterias of other companies. People attempt evenhanded assessments of others even when voicing an out-and-out complaint. They seek to put shortcomings in the context of people's strengths; they attempt to cite what the supporters feel alongside of what the critics say. They attempt to keep their critical comments specific to a particular incident, saying something like, "I don't like the way John did that." They refrain from making criticisms that generalize to all situations or downplay the importance and general ability of the person who is the target of their critique. And when they can't respect the person, they attempt to show respect for that person's job or title.

Perhaps the core of the Acme system is that Acme management never forgets that everyone has a technical job to perform. For all its emphasis on people, Acme's management reserves its biggest rewards for technical contributors, considering marketing and managerial success to be technologies that parallel the scientific and manufacturing disciplines without implying a pecking order. At the upper levels of management, it makes no difference whether one's expertise is in manufacturing, R&D, marketing, or engineering. Candidates from each discipline are considered on the basis of their general business acumen; there are no fixed preferences for one discipline over another. Thus, throughout the company there is the belief that technical skills are necessary in order to be ranked high enough to be considered for management, that general management skills are necessary for promotion, and that anyone in the company, no matter what his or her discipline, can become the company's president.

5. Too Much Job Security

We've consistently seen politics run rampant in situations in which people with context have insufficient incentive to worry about the context needs of those who don't. This often happens in organizations where people are sure that they won't be fired, such as in some echelons of government, where people are protected by civil service or patronage, in some areas of academia, where professors are protected by tenure, in the post office, where no one ever seems to rock the boat, and in pockets within the private sector, often in profitable operations that have yet to experience market adversity.

Without the incentive to consider actively how the current situation hampers others, those who have self-context or who have "secure" jobs resist appeals for change and possible improvement. They act to hold off customers who would like a change in product or service and they act to hold off appeals by people within their organization who lack context and would like to play a more significant role in the organization's accomplishments. And regardless of which side one is on, the situation quickly turns political.

Needing context, needing to renegotiate the organization's roles and functions, and encountering those who appear not to even allow the renegotiating conversation to be raised sends one off thinking about all the circuitous and indirect routes that might provoke a change. People resort to asking themselves "Who do I know at City Hall and how can I position my appeal to get him or her to straighten out this situation?" Conversely people who experience extraordinary and indirect pressures quickly perceive themselves to be in a political role and actively begin to respond appropriately. Now they can further justify their steadfast resistance on the grounds that their integrity depends on holding off those who seek to use "illegitimate" means to get them to change.

We see no need to illustrate this situation. It is familiar to everyone who has ever shaped an appeal to someone else who is not listening with an open mind. When the appeal is important, when one's self-context depends on it, usually the means for getting that person's ear materializes. Sufficient motivation is all that is necessary to trigger a political action.

6. Fixation with the Bottom Line

We want to mention one other situation that predictably triggers a political response. We mention it briefly because so much has already been written about it and we don't want to be redundant. It's the lesson from Japan, the lesson of "Big Auto" and "Big Steel," the lesson of any corporation whose ownership has switched from shareholders taking a long-term perspective to short-term speculators who need an extra dime of quarterly profit in order to keep the price of the company's stock moving up.

When you stop and think about it, it's easy to see why an emphasis on short-term tangible results leads directly to organization politics. How many people do you know who would, of their own volition, choose to define the value of their organizational existence solely on the basis of a short-term tangible indicator? It's a very narrow and, ultimately, self-alienating way to define one's context and value to the organization—even when one succeeds in producing the bottom-line numbers that signal success. And, for the organization, such tactics produce individual success at the price of integration, no matter how clever organization designers are at constructing the bottom-line criteria. Whenever management substitutes bottom-line criteria for the conversations necessary to produce results, in order to squeeze out the slack, people get inventive and devious in pursuing the actions that will give them the context they need to lead personally satisfying and organizationally valued lives at work.

The Most Political Organization We've Ever Seen

We've presented these six situations that frustrate people's needs for self-context as if they are discrete conditions that exist in a pure form. In practice these conditions overlap, and it's seldom that you will find one condition without also encountering the presence of one or more others. In fact we can think of a company in which pieces of each condition exist, and it has to be the most political and least healthy situation we've come across yet. Ironically, this unhealthy company is in the health insurance business. Examining it illustrates how the conditions we've mentioned combine to produce behaviors that are stereotypically political.

For the sake of anonymity we refer to this company as the First Aid Medical Insurance Company. It's a profitable company, not because it operates efficiently, but because its not-for-profit status allows it to pass all operating costs along to its consumers, much as a public utility can, in the form of increased premiums. What's more, feedback time from the marketplace is slow so that the impact of uneconomical decisions today often will not be felt internally for two or more years. It's a company that has benefited greatly from being in the right place at the right time, and its growth has been substantial. And it's a company that is being ruled with an iron hand by a single executive whose political instincts and skills in dealing with diverse and competitive viewpoints have created an aura of invincibility. He knows how to balance the complex interests of such diverse parties as health providers, hospitals, companies that buy insurance plans, claimants, third-party insurers, and a host of legislative and governmental regulators. But internally the organization is a mess.

To begin with, nothing significant happens inside this company without the big boss being involved. He participates in every supervisory and managerial promotion, every change in the organization chart, every modification of the physical facility, and he almost single-handedly makes all the high-level decisions himself. Reporting to him are five vice-presidents and several administrative types. None of these people is especially bright, all are very afraid of him, and each can tell a story of how the big boss hit the ceiling when "so and so" was dumb enough to say "whatever" in a meeting. Each has been that "so and so" and has undergone more than one public scolding.

One would think that the five vice-presidents would band together against the tyranny and harrassment of this erratic boss, but this has not been the case. We're not sure whether it's instinctive genius or sadism that causes the boss periodically to reorganize the company so that masses of people, sometimes several hundred at a time, find themselves reporting to a different vice-president. Three of these vice-presidents are older, without particular ambition, and take these shifts with a grain of salt. The other two are young enough to think about being the boss's replacement when he retires or perhaps accepts a government appointment, which, because he's wealthy and 64 years old, could happen at any time. And when the music in this game of musical chairs stops, they want to be standing in front of a large organization.

Talk about hierarchy, we've never seen so much extra hierarchy as that which exists at First Aid. Very few people seem to have entire jobs, and everyone seems to have enormous amounts of free time, much of which is spent in the company's luxurious dining area conducting private campaigns and collecting the information that will enable them to do a bigger job. People are constantly trying to steal responsibility from those above, below, or along-side of themselves; those who aren't successful in stealing enough responsi-bility to perform an entire job seem to sublimate by gossiping about who has been able to and who is on top of things today.

It's very hard to find context in this company. Because of the extraordi-nary power of the big boss, everyone positions him- or herself in relation to the boss's position. But his position is impossible to predict since most of his viewpoints are dictated at least partially by his constituencies outside the com-pany, about which few people know the details. The best people seem able to do is to avoid winding up on the wrong side of an issue. And the need to avoid being wrong has reached overwhelming proportions. It's gotten to the point where one can't get anyone to agree to anything of substance prior to running a trial balloon past the executive suite. In fact we can't remember the last time we heard anyone give an unequivocal "yes"; the most affirma-tive response we hear is "I wouldn't disagree with that." And instead of say-ing "no," people say "I don't think *Mr. Big* would like that."

Perhaps the most telling symptom of this extraordinarily political environ-ment is the amount of time people spend planning what they are going to say when they get in the room with the higher-level person they want to in-fluence. At First Aid people spend enormous amounts of time rehearsing and attempting to anticipate the reaction they might receive. And while this holds for every level of the hierarchy, it's particularly true for conversations with *Mr. Big.* There are any number of stories about a person who inadvertently said the "wrong" thing or showed a lack of respect in a meeting with *Mr. Big* and how *Mr. Big* didn't even bother to respond, wouldn't dirty his hands, and the next morning the offender's desk was empty. Whether or not these stories are true makes little difference; they reflect what people think is tak-ing place at First Aid.

"Don't surprise your boss" is a sacred slogan at First Aid. One manager described his relationship with his boss this way:

> On the way in they explained to me that he was someone who had long ago re-tired on the job. But I got taken in by his opening words. He told me he was going to take an active interest in my work, so I kept him informed on a daily basis. Then I began to get the message, although I can't even tell you the form in which it came. But eventually I got it: "Keep me clean, don't let me be surprised, make enough contact to give others the impression that we're communicating and in re-turn I'll front for you and give you good ratings." So now we meet three half-hour sessions a month and during that time he keeps me well informed on his golf game.

Job security is a curious commodity at First Aid. Occasionally there is a big scandal, such as the time someone inadvertently made an incorrect entry on the company's large computer and turned up records of an upper-level manager's private business. However, after that manager was fired, he went into business for himself and today is an outside vendor earning more money selling services to First Aid than he earned when he was working full time for the company. But short of scandals First Aid uses a no-layoff policy. And are not planning to return and who

since the demands for most people's performance are modest, many people slip into a low level of self-expectation and begin to wonder how they could survive if they ever left. There's a family atmosphere, and most managers' styles can be described as benevolently paternalistic. People are paid comparable wages whether or not they perform well. Of course, nonperformers spend much of their time conducting campaigns to tell others about how hard and intelligently they are working.

There's not much else to say about First Aid. It's a culture where many people have been knocked around, demoted, and then allowed to continue. It's a culture where personal relationships are very central to one's job success, where numerous people have risen quickly based on the strength of a relationship with a higher-up. And it's a culture where the people who are negatively affected by a managerial decision often receive their bad news in a public meeting where they can be embarrassed. Because of this, the grapevine has grown to new heights of importance. People work hard to get the information that helps them avoid being surprised, and every day there is a new scramble to achieve some semblance of self-context. . . .

Executive Women: Substance Plus Style

Ann M. Morrison, Randall P. White, and Ellen Van Velsor

As individuals, executive women and men seem to be virtually identical psychologically, intellectually and emotionally. But the similarity ends there. Women in the executive ranks, or even middle management in most large corporations, confront two sets of demanding, sometimes contradictory expectations that reflect the dual roles they play as women in business and in society as a whole.

Over the years, many people have argued that the abilities and attitudes of male managers are very different from those of female managers. Historically, the perceived differences have been used to keep women out of management. But now it has become fashionable to say that the differences are beneficial, that women will complement men in the management ranks and bring a healthy balance to business.

The basis for claiming differences between male and female managers—whether used to exclude or encourage women—is suspect at best. Sometimes no data are given to back up such claims, only a few examples and opinions. When data analysis is used to support differences, it is often based on comparing women and men in general or those from other occupational groups or at lower management levels.

The few studies that have looked at women and men in comparable managerial roles have discovered more similarities than differences across sexes, according to a 1986 report by Catalyst, a nonprofit, New York-based organization that helps corporations to foster the career and leadership development of women.

At the Center for Creative Leadership—a nonprofit educational institution established in 1970 to study and enhance leadership—we also found very few personality differences between male and female executives. In connection with our study we searched our data bank of test scores taken from thousands of managers and professionals who have participated in management development programs from 1978 to 1986. The tests measure personality dimensions, intelligence and behavior in problem-solving groups.

The executive women and men scored similarly on most of the measures we examined. And based on behavioral exercises that were conducted and scored by professional staff during our programs, we found that executive women are just as able as executive men to lead, influence and motivate other group members, to analyze problems and to be task-oriented and verbally effective.

Despite these similarities, women are not making the same progress as men are in the executive ranks. Among Fortune-500 companies, only 1.7 percent of the corporate officers are women, according to a 1986 study by Mary Ann Von Glinow, a professor in the school of business at the University of Southern California.

To get a closer look at how women's movement up the corporate ladder compares with men's, we compared female managers from our recent study composed of interviews with 76 women at or near the general management level in Fortune-100 sized companies to male general managers from another study done at the center by Morgan W. McCall Jr., Michael M. Lombardo and Morrison.

We also interviewed 22 "savvy insiders" at 10 of the same companies—16 men and 6 women who are responsible for identifying and selecting executives for top jobs. (The earlier study of male executives also included interviews of savvy insiders.) Both studies looked at the various factors that contribute to success or derailment among executives.

Our criteria for success included reaching one of the top 10 to 20 positions in the corporation and living up to one's full potential in the eyes of the company. Derailment was defined as achieving a very high level in the company but not going as high as the organization had expected. Derailed women may have plateaued, been demoted or fired, accepted early retirement or had their responsibilities reduced.

The savvy insiders were asked to come up with an example of a woman they knew who had made it and an example of one who had derailed. They described the qualities and characteristics that had helped or hurt these women, and we compiled the most frequently mentioned answers into a list of success factors and fatal flaws. The insiders gave us case histories on 19 women who were considered successful and 16 who had derailed.

The insiders in both studies listed roughly the same number of derailment factors for women and men (4 for women on the average, 3.5 for men), but they listed nearly twice as many success factors for women (10.4 on average versus 5.7 for men). This finding may add to the evidence that to progress in today's corporate world, women must outperform men.

The women described to us as successful and as derailed were put through a number of hoops as they progressed up the corporate ladder. They had to show their toughness and independence and at the same time depend on others. It was essential that they contradict the stereotypes that their male bosses and coworkers had about women. They had to be seen as different, "better than women" as a group. But they couldn't go too far and forfeit all traces of femininity because that would make them too alien to their superiors and colleagues. In essence, their mission was to do what wasn't expected of them, while doing enough of what was expected of them as women to gain acceptance.

The hoops held out for women in or aspiring to executive jobs are often paired up, requiring seemingly contradictory types of behavior at the same time. The trick is to pass through only the overlapping portion of each pair of hoops . . . .

This narrow band of acceptable characteristics and actions reflects the multiple expectations of corporate women and the challenge they face of blending very disparate qualities. It is clear that much behavioral territory is off-limits to executive women. Only certain characteristics traditionally accepted as "masculine" and some traditionally thought of as "feminine" are permitted through the narrow band.

The unacceptable area comprises the extremes that would make an executive woman too much like traditional nonprofessional women or too much like women trying too hard to be like men. "Trying to talk and behave like a man can come across as not genuine," one savvy insider said about mistakes some women make.

Certain "male" kinds of behavior are not only allowed but required. Some savvy insiders wanted to see toughness demonstrated by a woman on an executive track because they believe, as a rule, that women aren't tough enough to handle the job. Sometimes people require executive women to be more "masculine" than men in certain ways to be accepted. One executive said that the chief executive officer told her, "You're tougher than most of the men around here. Can't you go find some more of you?"

We have identified four contradictory sets of expectations that women must reconcile to succeed in corporate life.

Take Risks, but Be Consistently Outstanding

The senior executives put great value on risk taking, and for good reasons. Risk often is the name of the game at the top. Top managers are responsible for huge sums of money and thousands of jobs and must make countless decisions about whether to invest or divest, compete or retreat, change or grow, all with only a fuzzy feel for the years ahead when the results of those decisions will become apparent. Taking risks early in one's career is often necessary preparation to be considered for top jobs.

A big element of risk taking is changing jobs and taking on new assignments. One savvy insider felt that this was a critical career turning point for highly promotable women: "Taking a job in a different part of the business broadens your experience base and shows risk-taking ability."

In 14 of 19 success cases described by savvy insiders, a risky job change was mentioned specifically. Such risky job changes included tough transitions from academia to industry; deliberate attempts to broaden one's perspective and knowledge by moving into such areas as finance, employee relations and information services; and the all-important move from a staff position to a line position—a move that usually involved going from having responsibility for analysis, service or support to having clear responsibility for profit and loss, implementation and bottom-line decision making. Some involved a technical area with which the manager was unfamiliar.

Perhaps risk taking means more to executives when exhibited by a woman than by a man, since women are often seen as averse to taking risks. In fact, some see women's reluctance to take risks as a barrier to their moving up. Being too "by the book" and cautious were cited by some of the savvy insiders as weaknesses of women.

To achieve a breadth of experience in the business, women must take more risks than men do. The career moves that the successful women we studied had made—from staff to line positions, moving away from headquarters and so on—had elements of risk that probably would not have existed to the same extent for men. Moving into line positions, for example, involved not only the challenge of new demands but also a more hostile, less tolerant environment. The risk for a woman sometimes involves giving up a promotion in her staff function, where her presence is less threatening, to enter a new part of the business, perhaps at a lower level, where she may be as welcome as the plague and the possibility of promotion may be slim.

Women are also expected to be extremely competent, often even more competent than men in various arenas, such as starting or turning around a department, handling the media, running a business, managing subordinates and customers and chairing a task force.

In general, any candidate for a top job has to be good, but these women were more than good. Some senior executives acknowledged that successful women were at least as good as the best men available for the job.

Because of the visibility of the few women in high management ranks, there is little leeway for mistakes, little allowance for weaknesses. The successful women impressed senior executives with their intelligence and business acumen, their no-nonsense, bottom-line orientation, their strategic perspective and their management prowess. Women who do merely an acceptable job, let alone a less-than-average job, may be pulled off the track.

Women get little compensation for the greater risks they take in advancing their careers. Their performance must be outstanding, whatever the degree of difficulty. If career advancement can be likened to an Olympic diving competition, the dives performed by women would have a higher degree of difficulty than the men's, yet the judges would not follow the customary procedure of factoring the degree of difficulty into their scores.

Be Tough, but Don't Be Macho

Toughness is another characteristic that savvy insiders said they like to see in executive women. They praised the willingness of successful women to make decisions, to call the shots in a fast-moving business and to take a tough stand. The successful women demanded results from their subordinates, fought for a bigger budget or greater visibility for their unit or said what they really thought and did what they needed to do to avoid compromising their personal integrity.

Being cool under pressure was another characteristic of successful women noted by savvy insiders:

"She doesn't fall apart when things get tough."

"She has great cool under pressure. In 50 corporate meetings, I've only seen her lose her cool two times. Most people would lose it one time out of every five. She's very controlled."

Being tougher and not prone to collapse in crises makes these women seem different, which is necessary for them to be considered for high-level jobs. Doing what it takes to show a profit, taking the initiative and defending one's resources are admirable, even necessary actions of a high-potential executive. Even such superficial characteristics as being tall—which was said to help give one woman personal dominance and a commanding presence—are sometimes admired because they suggest that these are tough individuals.

While many men fear that women aren't tough enough to handle big business, the desire for these women to act "like women" still lingers. Toughness, for example, is sometimes qualified or limited to "tough, but not offensive" or "demure, yet tough." And when we look at those who derailed, there is more evidence that being too tough is the kiss of death. One 40-year-old woman with an MBA and an excellent track record was recruited from outside one company some years ago into a job that was a step toward moving her into general management, at a salary of $75,000. Despite her potential, problems developed that made her unacceptable for that critical promotion.

She couldn't adapt to the environment she was in—an "old boy" type of business with older workers who were suspicious and judgmental. She was apparently too willing to be tough and too good at it. Her macho style and her push for perks made her seem too hard and demanding. Some of her business decisions contributed to this image. For example, she got three assignments in a row that took her away from headquarters to assess business units that were not performing up to par. In each case, her conclusion was that the business was a loser and should be closed down. "She got stereo-typed," we were told. "There's 'growth,' 'maintenance' and 'close it.' She was a 'close it' person—take a lot of people out of work and reduce costs. It didn't increase her popularity."

Somewhere in between extremes is a relatively safe zone to which some successful women apparently confine themselves, where they are obviously female and easy to be with but also strong-willed and thick-skinned enough to pass muster. As some insiders told us:

"She's quite feminine, but she doesn't use it or let it get in the way."

"Her uniqueness is that she doesn't differ at all from men. . . . She plays it just like the men do, and she's very comfortable doing it. It's not put on, not contrived. It's very natural."

Be Ambitious, but Don't Expect Equal Treatment

Equal employment opportunity legislation put pressure on corporate execu-tives to find and promote a woman, and the women they chose in their com-panies often turned out to be ones we interviewed. In most cases, that pressure provided these women with the avenue they needed to fulfill their own drive—the chance to take on challenging assignments, to progress higher in their company, even to experience the satisfaction and the trappings of success within the establishment.

Those who were given an opportunity to fill a high-level position were ex-pected to put the job first, family second (if at all). Their strong desire to suc-ceed was a crucial factor that senior executives looked for in designating high-potential women.

"The personal drive and determination to succeed, the willingness to per-sist and work hard to achieve and a total commitment to career as the top priority in life" were some of the necessary qualities one insider shared with us.

The willingness to be mobile and to devote themselves to their company, despite the cultural obligations to marry, have children, run a household and so on, was applauded and noted as a factor in the success of a number of executive women. But their ambition was not so well received when status and benefits were involved; the chance to show their stuff in a nontraditional management role had its price.

According to some we interviewed, being assigned the same responsibili-ties or the same title as men in the company didn't mean that women received equal treatment in other respects. The salary differential is the most obvious example. Salary surveys done over the past several years consistently show that women are still paid considerably less than men at their level, even in management jobs and despite having a Harvard University MBA. Even when salaries are the same, women are given smaller budgets than men in similar jobs. Inclusion in the bonus system, access to high-status conferences and a host of other benefits may also be skewed toward men.

The women who obtained an executive position often felt that they had to make other concessions, in such areas as pay, perks and their rate of advancement. As newly appointed members of the executive club, they were still treated as if they had lower status. The fact that some women derailed at least partly because they made an issue of inequality or simply asked for more pay or perks corroborates the perception that women were tolerated in the club as junior members with fewer privileges than men had. "Wanting too much" was a flaw attributed to half of the derailed women in our study.

Take Responsibility but Follow Others' Advice

Accountability for business performance was emphasized repeatedly by savvy insiders as a necessary factor in executive success. Making difficult decisions, being practical, concentrating on meeting bottom-line goals and even accepting the duties of a supervisory role were all mentioned as aspects of taking responsibility.

Another responsibility mentioned is managing one's own career. It is up to the individual herself to keep her career moving, to get wide experience and exposure to the right people, to get into mainstream positions and to get credit for her accomplishments.

But as with other business behavior, there are two sides to the coin. Senior executives expect women to decide what they want and go for it. On the other hand, if their decisions and wants don't match what the executives want for them, problems often result. Senior executives sometimes seem to expect women to accept whatever advice and opportunities they offer, to do as they are told regarding career moves. For example, proposing an alternative to a promotion offered or trying to negotiate the terms instead of automatically accepting them was considered an affront by some senior executives.

Others that we spoke to regarded taking advice and criticism as a strong, positive factor in the struggle of women to adapt to the workplace:

"She had a tendency to get visibly upset if something was happening that she didn't like and also to be very defensive. I spoke to her about the first problem, and she changed. One of her great assets is the ability to listen and make changes."

Responding to this particular feedback was probably a good decision by this woman. Not all of the advice that female executives encounter is that clear, however. Several of our female executives said that it is important to trust people but only certain people. Some also said they came to understand that others' motives are not the same as your own; when others offer help, it may or may not be to your advantage to accept it or even to believe they are trying to be helpful.

Although the assistance that women received from senior executives in getting new opportunities was vital to their career, these women also realized that they had to choose what was best for themselves and not always depend on others to know what that was. They often had to rock the boat—to turn down high-level staff positions for lower-level line positions, to make an issue of opportunities for career advancement or tuition reimbursement to attend an executive program—to get what they needed instead of what was offered to them.

One interesting finding from our interviews with savvy insiders was that only the men mentioned the willingness to listen to feedback as a success factor for women. Perhaps senior men feel a greater need than senior women to counsel up-and-coming female executives. Or perhaps men see the willingness of women to make changes based on their advice as an indication of women's accepting junior status in the executive club, which may make them easier to be around. Whatever the case, women are left with the tough decisions about what advice to solicit, from whom and what to do about the advice they obtain.

The hoops that executive women confront are not for the faint-hearted. They represent tough battles to be waged throughout a career, battles that get a great deal of corporate attention. Of course, men who choose to pursue the executive ranks are also tested. They succeed and derail for many of the same reasons women do.

And there are groups of men who experience some of the same biases and pressures as women. Hurdles that keep minority managers out of top jobs, according to the *Wall Street Journal* and other sources, are not unlike those that women face—having to work harder and longer than white men to get the same things, being sidetracked into staff jobs and being isolated. Relatives of company leaders also may be isolated, the target of other workers' hostility and suspected of insufficient abilities.

Despite these similarities, the hurdles for women in management seem to be bigger and more numerous. Men typically do not have responsibility for home and family care, so they have some relief from the time, worry and conflicting expectations that are part of such pressure. One black executive interviewed for the *Wall Street Journal* told the reporter, "I always tell young blacks you need a very good wife who can support you."

Women in management experience the special hoops and hoopla that they do because executive women and men have been perceived as more different from each other than they really are. Mounting evidence indicates that, when careers are matched, women are remarkably similar to men in their characteristics, abilities and motives. Yet stereotypical perceptions have led to unrealistic expectations of executive women, and these expectations are part of the environment in which the women must work and live. This environment is qualitatively different from the environment executive men operate in, and this difference may be the crucial—and the only meaningful—one between male and female executives.

The Plateauing Trap, Part 1: Getting Caught

Judith M. Bardwick

Now, and for some time into the future, far fewer people will experience the "success" of promotion. The economic prosperity of the postwar period has proved unsustainable; our economy is experiencing severe withdrawal pains. What this means for today's employees is devastatingly simple: Opportunities for promotion will become relatively scarce, until at least the end of this century.

The fundamental factors that determine overall rates of promotion are impersonal; they have nothing to do with personal competence, and they cannot be changed by any individual. But people don't think about that; they still keep score in terms of how they as individuals fare in the competition. From 1950 to 1975, ambition and performance paid off in promotion. Since not everyone was promoted at the same rate, it was easy to focus on the ability of the individual. Anyone who was smarter, gutsier, luckier, and harder-working kept on receiving promotions. The individual was in the foreground. Relatively few noted that in the background increasing numbers of opportunities were continuously being created. The impersonal factors worked in people's favor then. But not now.

Plateauing creates the most problems in mature organizations, because they are no longer expanding rapidly and thus are not creating the new positions that produce mobility. To make things worse, management opportunities have actually declined in the past two to three years. Faced with increased world competition in the terrible recession that began in 1982, many mature organizations have severely trimmed their ranks of middle management and seem inclined to stay lean. Yet many of these organizations have ignored the plateauing issue because they are afraid it's an indication of their "failure" to continue heady growth.

The current situation demands that we take another look at promotion and organizational structure. Up to now, people have designed their lives around work and articulated their ambitions in terms of promotion. Winning this race is everything; all else is secondary. In the relatively recent past, people started losing in this promotion game when they approached their personal limitations. Now, and into the future, people will stop "winning" long *before* they approach their limits.

Plateauing is the source of widespread tragedy in American business. Its development is wholly logical, and wholly unnecessary. More than anything, people with a history of success at work want to continue being promoted. But the essential fact is that virtually everyone who works in an organization will plateau. The only difference among people is how long they take to reach the level beyond which they will not rise. Because very few are psychologically prepared for the end of the climb, most people experience pain at that point. And if they don't understand what is happening to them, anxiety is added to their depression.

Relatively few managers, professionals, and executives know why promotion has become for them the only organizational response that means success. And only a few fully realize that between now and the year 2015, promotions must become scarcer and the rate of plateauing will increase; people will plateau much earlier in their careers than they have for almost three decades. If they know the facts and understand what is going to happen to them, they can be psychologically prepared. Most need to redefine success but have neither the information nor the perspective that comes from knowing the facts. As a result, promotion continues to be the single most important criterion of success. Unprepared, most people don't understand why they are failing to reach higher levels. In many cases, this is compounded by their organization's failure to be honest about their long-term prospects.

Coming To Terms with Plateauing

Because people have come to regard promotion as the only reward for performance that really counts, only promotion signifies "winning." Psyched up to want only one thing, people are in danger of feeling no longer successful when promotions end. In the extreme, people can feel like failures.

In January 1986, on the editorial page of *The Wall Street Journal*, Robert Goldman described his own experience:

> *I am 42 years old. I work for a large corporation. But I'm no longer moving up. Going in, I knew there could be a price to pay. Too much structure can be confining. But for me, the organizational chart was like a children's playground—a place to climb, swing, and scramble all the way to the top. And that was where I was headed.*
>
> *Year by year, level by level, I made my way up; and if I wasn't laughing all the way, only rarely did I doubt choosing the corporate life. Whatever the reason, I was immediately perceived to be a "star." And though my corporation was too conservative to have a "fast track," I did burn a few cinders as a steady progression of blue memos charted my upward progress. Over the years I gained titles, windows, salary, and perks. Those incentives fueled a fire that was burning very bright indeed. I knew in my bones that I would someday reach the top. Some men might stumble. Others might even fall by the wayside. But not me; never me.*
>
> *Or so I believed right up to the day, right up to the instant, when I learned the fire was out, the star was extinguished, the climb was over. A promotion that should have been mine was handed to someone else. When the blue memo came out,*

I could hardly believe my eyes. How could the corporation make this mistake? Betrayed, vulnerable, I began seeing corporate assassins in the shadows. Predators lurked outside my office—measuring, measuring. Finally I took my fears to a friend on Mahogany Row. "Everyone is happy with your work," I was reassured. "Just keep doing what you're doing." Which was exactly what I did. And when the next promotion came up, and again, the blue memo did not come for me, I finally understood. Somewhere along the line, a test had been given, and I had failed. The corporation would keep me on. I would do my job, and in return, I could expect the average salary increases due the average employee. But there would be no more leapfrog advancements. No more seductive little perks. No more blue memos. I was no longer climbing. I had plateaued out. . . .

It's very depressing for people to realize that their climb is over, that they have gotten as many gains as they ever will. That is especially true for those who gave the bulk of their time and emotional commitment to their work. They feel that the organization has betrayed their trust; it broke its implicit promise to continually reward hard work. Further, breaking that promise implies the organization does not value them as individuals because it has ceased to reward them.

It is certain that when people feel that way, their performance suffers. So does the organization. The problem is particularly acute in organizations that are not straightforward about the normalcy of the end of promotions. Organizations need to be honest about the reality that conditions have changed because you can fool some of the people some of the time, but you cannot fool many of them for long. Organizations that evade the issue create anger as well as feelings of failure in their employees. In that way they assure that productivity will decline. Many of their plateaued people quit working—but stay on the job.

Most of us don't have a developmental perspective about our work. We don't think about the fact that as we climb, the nature of our successes will alter. A developmental perspective lets us see that we have to change what we require from work in order to feel satisfied. From our mid-twenties through our thirties we're in a period of full-out striving, grabbing for long-range opportunity. In the forties the windows of top opportunity open for those few who've won Olympic standing. The rest plateau; those in organizations will have no more major promotions, and self-employed professionals are in danger of becoming burned out because they're too expert in what they do. The fifties are a time of high ambition for a very few; for the majority, they are a period of acceptance.

The Three Kinds of Plateauing

We gain a necessary perspective on what we can do to solve the problems created by plateauing when we look at the different forms that it takes. There are three kinds: *structural, content,* and *life plateauing.* While they are different from one another, they are interrelated.

Structural Plateauing

Structural plateauing refers to the *end of promotions*. It is caused by an organization's hierarchy or structure. All of us know that, as we climb up the familiar pyramid shape of organizations, the number of positions decreases dramatically and the opportunities to move upward decrease proportionately. But even though we know that, we hope we'll beat the odds.

Structural plateauing is not new. What is new is that, today and into the future, people will be structurally plateaued much earlier in their careers than they are prepared for. The phenomenon of structural plateauing is going to generate enormous problems in organizations for the next 15 to 25 years.

Managers, executives, and professionals who work in complex organizations are stimulated to climb the mountain because it is there and because of the intense competition among them. The visibility of the hierarchy and of the competition makes the failure to be promoted painfully obvious. Some people have great difficulty in coming to terms with structural plateauing and getting on with the rest of their lives.

Content Plateauing

People are *content plateaued* when they know their jobs too well. There's not enough to learn. They have become expert in their work, and they are likely to feel profoundly bored.

Marie, who is 41, has been employed as a blood bank technician in a medium-size lab for 11 years. There is no opportunity for her to become a manager; her boss is only 37. Her skills are so specialized that to change her work, she would have to make a major investment in retraining. She says:

> My current job is nice. Comfortable. But not exciting. The pay is excellent, but it is not satisfying. I love work. I love meeting a deadline . . . walking away from a task that I did well. I still enjoy work. What's missing in the job is excitement. Recognition is not enough. The work needs to change. I'm not happy with what I'm doing.

People who are structurally plateaued frequently become content plateaued. In large organizations, structural plateauing is essentially inescapable, but content plateauing is not. The sheer size of the organization creates the possibility for job changes that do not involve promotion, but do involve new tasks and new challenges. In contrast, promotion may be insignificant to people who work in small organizations, those who are self-employed, and professionals who don't want to become managers. For them, structural plateauing is irrelevant, but content plateauing is an ever-constant danger.

Life Plateauing

People are particularly vulnerable to *plateauing in life* when work becomes the most significant sector in their lives—the basis of their identify and self-esteem. This is fine as long as they continue to be successful. But promotions do eventually end, provoking a terrible sense of failure; frequently, too, mastery of the work brings feelings of tedium. When that happens, there is a good chance that they will feel plateaued in life.

> I'm 47 and I don't know what to do. My whole life is boring. All I ever seem to do is meet my responsibilities, and I'm tired of it. Every morning I get up and go to work and come home. When I come home it's the same old routine: I read the paper, eat supper, do some work, watch television, and go to bed; then I get up and go to work again. Work used to be exciting. That's when I put everything into it. But now I've gone as far as I'm going to go. What am I going to do with the rest of my life?

People who feel plateaued in life usually feel trapped; they don't know how to break out of the cycle of despair, and they are afraid to try. If they can accept the fact that they *are* plateaued and at the end of a phase, they are in a position to begin. They have the opportunity to do what they have never done, to experience what they have never felt, to become people they have not yet been. What they stand to gain is the rest of their lives.

A New Approach to Plateauing

The fact is that *everyone* plateaus. The only difference among people is in how they handle it. The first task is always the same; it is true for individuals and it is true for organizations: *The phenomenon of plateauing must be acknowledged and the problems that it causes must be addressed.*

In itself, plateauing is not necessarily bad. In fact, since plateauing in certain aspects of our lives is inevitable, being satisfied with life while being plateaued in some parts of it is necessary for our mental well-being. But plateauing is emotionally depleting when the plateau results in the sense that work or relationships or life has no momentum. People cope and act responsibly, but there is no vitality in what they do.

While *being* plateaued is a fact, *feeling* plateaued is a psychological state. Obviously, people who feel plateaued want to experience their work and their lives differently. But how? The first step in creating psychological change is to gain insight.

When we think about plateauing, we usually focus on structural plateauing, the end of promotions. The reality that promotions will end, and that they will end earlier in our careers, is a wedge that will force us to change our definition of success. Of course we will continue to esteem those who are so exceptional that they rise to the highest levels of responsibility and leadership. But the definition of success has to be broadened to include those who continue to learn and be productive at work and those who continue to mature and change in their lives. Our ideas about success have to alter so that people can feel "successful" during the whole of their lives.

But insight about a problem is only the first step. There has to be real change in how people live and in how organizations respond. Those changes can take place only when the phenomenon of plateauing is addressed and success is redefined. . . . The central goals are these:

- The *organization* must change its culture so that people who are structurally plateaued can continue to earn respect and experience success through mastering new challenges.
- The *manager* must be honest and supportive so that plateaued employees know where they stand and can continue to feel motivated and valued.
- The *individual* must face the issues, give up frustrating old ambitions, and take the initiative in creating new ones.

Plateauing is a natural phenomenon that occurs, in its different forms, in all the phases of our lives. Being plateaued does not, therefore, have to be experienced as a state of failure. Instead, it can be viewed as a period of challenge. Being plateaued can prod us into creating new goals that are significant and achievable. Being plateaued should be a phase, not a permanent state.

●

Airline Field Manager

Agents will work harder for me if they see me out there taking the abuse with them.

Jim Wall

She's a walking, talking whirlwind, in about her mid-thirties, somewhat shorter than average and perhaps a little heavier. Decked out in a professional mustif—an outfit that is sufficiently professional but not a uniform—she darts from one region of her turf to another in one of the nation's busiest airports. She is a field manager for a major airline, and she is currently responsible for her company's ticket counter, security, and sky captains in the airport. That's a lot of responsibility, especially when it's coupled with serving as the airline's number-one flak catcher and occasional overseer of the lost bags, or "bag heaven," operation.

What makes this job, shall we say, "interesting," is that I get pressure from the top and the bottom. Now that's not unusual; you expect that. But I don't have much control over either side. This comes from the top [*she pulls out a computer sheet*]. I'm judged on delays—Do the passengers get there late and delay the plane? For another field manager it's, are the bags late so that the plane is delayed? Somewhere high up in the bureaucracy someone has set up a standard. I have no input into that, but I've got to meet it. And this is the first place it hits. If there's a delay, they call me on the carpet and say, say, "Your loading times are too late. What's wrong? Don't you have proper staffing? What is it?"

Whenever there's a delay, the tower decides who is responsible. I'm judged on my delay. It is a big deal. All airlines do this. Time is money to airlines. There is scheduling of aircraft, and if there's one delay it backs up all the way down the line. The ideal is to have everything on time.

From the top it's "rule by exception." If I don't meet the standard, the pressure comes rolling down. My boss sits down with me and goes through my computerized charts for every month to see how I'm doing, and then gives me feedback. Most of my "upper stress," however, comes from keeping up with my paperwork. I feel that it's more important for me to be out there, especially when things are going bad, than to be back here writing up reports or evaluations or writing letters back to passengers. However, someone in the bureaucracy says, "Fill out the paperwork!"

And the pressure that can come up from below is intense, especially here at the ticket counter. At the counter, the pressure is speed. Here the pressure is to make sure that my passenger lines move as fast as feasible; therefore, I have to get enough staffing so we can handle passengers for that particular time of day. On a full day, that's sixteen positions. The counter handles most customers, but at times I do too. Anyone out there can call me when a customer wants to speak with management. In fact, when it's really bad—I mean a really bad night, weather delays, people missing connections—then I will be out on the counter as a visible member of management. I always try to be up front, visible, when I think I will be needed. You don't hide in this job.

Some of the men, especially the older ones working under me, are MCPs; they just can't handle being supervised by a woman. But I try not to come on with the woman boss image. I try to treat them in a fair manner. I try to let them know my job is to make their job easier, and I'm not there to punish or to make them look bad.

I'll deal with them one-on-one and say something like, "This is what I expect from you, and this is what you can expect from me." A man, say fifty-five years old, sometimes won't respond to that. So my problem is to find out how I'm going to get him motivated. The only thing I can do is say, "You have to spend eight hours a day here. You can spend the eight hours a day being miserable, or you can spend it doing your job, trying to look at this with a different attitude."

When I first took this position, I think that I was pretty successful right away because of my quick reaction to a problem: a baggage belt broke, and we had bags up the yeenee. So I just jumped in there and started throwing bags around. That made them say, "Well, she's not just standing there looking cute. She's in there humping just like we are."

My passenger problems can bring on the major headaches. If we—the company—miss connections, if it's our fault that we've missed connections and if there is no other flight to get the passengers to their destination, then we must put the passengers up in a hotel and get them out on the next flight. One night I stayed until 3:30 in the morning because Las Vegas had a mechanical problem that delayed them, and they still sent the plane here—eight hours late! With connecting passengers on it! Of course, when they got in at 2:30 in the morning, there's nothing going out. So we had to get hotel rooms for all these people. What happened was that Las Vegas shifted *their* problem to us. And when the people got here, they were very tired and bitchy, plus we had to handle them. Not only did the people in Las Vegas screw us; they also were totally uncooperative. I asked them to give me the names of all the people who were connecting—they had the tickets and knew who the passengers were. They wouldn't tell me, so I asked them at least to tell me how many people they had so I would know how many rooms to book. But they wouldn't do that either, so I had to guess. I guessed about 40. So I booked 40 rooms, and it turned out that we needed 50.

As you can see, I have no control over a lot of the problems I face in this position. Other stations shift problems. There are mechanical problems. And if another station doesn't handle it well or chooses not to handle it, I know it's my problem.

Baggage loss is also uncontrollable. I don't lose the bags, but I have to help customers locate them. And people are always so sensitive about their bags. They have to find them *now,* and the contents are always *so* valuable. I work very hard to find a bag, but after a month, if we don't locate the bag we consider that it's gone to "bag heaven," and New York settles with the customer. But in that time we really work hard to find the bag. One nice thing about working baggage is that you get to see the results of your work. When you see a bag that's been missing a long time is found, then there's a good feeling.

I'm under a lot of stress, and to cope with it, I get out on the firing line. I'm visible. I try to ease situations, try to be visible to the agents so that they can come to me. And I release nervous energy. Somebody asked me if I was a workaholic. I'm not, but when I see a counter with lines, I want them down. So whatever I can do to help them, I do. Now I don't just say, "You've got a line out there." I help. When I see there's a line, I walk around behind the counter so people can call on me if there are problems. Then I move out into the lines to see what I can do.

My philosophy of management? I don't want to be a big buddy to people. I'm their boss, not their buddy. Plus I think you should lead by example. When my people ask a question, I come back and give them an answer. If I don't have the answer, then I find it out for them. Whenever there's a problem, I'm always there to deal with it. If an agent calls to say "I've got a passenger I can't deal with," then I'll go right out and deal with him. I know I can handle any problem they have. I can answer any question, and therefore I take pressure off my people. My subordinates have to take the pressure for eight hours; so it's really helpful if I can take it off them once in a while.

When I deal with the problem, say an irate passenger—and the agent's been right—then I'm sure to tell the customer that the agent was correct, and

I tell the agent she was right. If the agent's wrong, I apologize for the agent's behavior and then talk to the agent later.

Sometimes I'm in a position to do something for the customer that the agent can't because I've got more authority. For example, I can handle money adjustments. A lot of times I have to do some things to break the tension. If the agent's having a real hard time I say, "Let's go to the back room and say all the bad dirty words that we want." Then I tell them to go back out there. Or I'll say, "Go back out there and when it gets tough, come back in here and beat on something besides the passenger."

My feeling is that the agents will work harder for me if they see me out there taking the abuse with them. Leadership by example is the way I see it. That's the way I do it. Not everybody does. I do. I was in their place. I know at the end of the day they can be mentally and physically exhausted. If they see me out there in bad times, they know, one, I'm there to help them and two, they know I'm working. If I'm here in the office, they don't know what I'm doing.

But you don't *just* work alongside your people. Sometimes you have to be forceful and step in. Like I say, if there's trouble between the agent and a customer, the agent can call me. And I handle any frictions among my people. For example, there's friction sometimes between the skycaps and the passenger assistants. The assistants are responsible for the wheelchairs and making sure that people in them get to the planes. Sometimes an assistant will tell a skycap to push a passenger to a plane. The skycaps don't like that because they want to be out front or downstairs where they can get tips. The assistant has the authority to tell a skycap to take a passenger, but he also can do it himself. So a lot of times there is friction. Here I step in, rule, and arbitrate. Or if a skycap and a passenger have a problem, I listen and make a decision. Being assertive with people doesn't trouble me; it's just one part of working with people.

I feel one area that the airline is falling down in is training in the airport. Some of our people are not well trained; therefore, they're not sure of themselves. They're unsure of their technological skills. Therefore, they have an overbearing attitude toward passengers and put them down.

Since a competent agent is more effective and courteous, I work very hard to make sure they know their job. But I don't want them just efficient and cold. I want them efficient and courteous. When you're dealing with a large public sector, you're going to have a tendency to be cold. And you tend to be cold to the public when the company is cold to you.

We at this end have to make sure that the company's push for cold efficiency doesn't filter down to us. Sure, I've got to process a lot of people and get them out without delays. But I can't let all that make me a cold supervisor or a cold-fish company representative. I'll be a failure if I'm cold and hard on my people, and they're going to fail if they act that way toward the passengers.

—————————————●—————————————

Assembly Line Supervisor

One year of experience, six times over.

Jim Wall

Day to day, my job is helter-skelter. This fellow asked me last year how much experience I had as a supervisor. When I said six years, he asked me if I actually had six years of experience or if I had one year's experience six times over. That got me thinking about myself and my job.

What do I do? You name it. For one thing, I keep people from coming to work drunk. Like with this fellow Tom Ropes, that upper management traded for gloves. He'd go out and get pickled during lunch. So I caught him coming in and wrote up a reprimand. He kept doing it, so I found the bar where he was going and caught him there. I'd taken my superior so that we had him dead to rights. Of course he went through an appeal procedure, with the union backing him all the way. And the management let him off. They traded him for some gloves.

The workers were issued these gloves to use in some heavy, rough work in the plant, and if they lost them, they had to pay for them. Well, every so often they'd have to turn in the old ones and get new replacements. Since the old gloves many times were in good shape, the workers would want to keep them or would claim to lose them and refuse to pay for the lost gloves, because they were going to be thrown away. So the union backs them on the lost gloves issue, and management struck a bargain: through some horse-trading, Tom Ropes was reinstated, and the workers—the union—agreed not to "lose" but a certain number of gloves per year.

Dealing with the workers can a lot of times prove to be a real challenge. I remember how important it was for us to get 100 percent participation in the payroll savings plan to buy U.S. Savings Bonds. One hundred percent was quite important for a supervisor's future advancement in the company. I worked night and day to get my people to participate and got all of them but two to do so. One of these fellows, I found out, was henpecked, so I went to his wife and sweet-talked her. He came in while I was there, and she told him that I'd explained to her what a good idea it was, and that he *was* now participating in the program.

The other guy was a tougher holdout, but I found that he had this farm that he worked on the side. One day I told him he was the last holdout we had. When he laughed, I asked if he would participate in the program if I agreed to work for him on his farm every Saturday for a year. He laughed again and said, "Sure." I had him.

Reprinted by permission of the publisher, from BOSSES by Jim Wall (Lexington, Mass.: Lexington Books, D. C. Heath and Company, Copyright 1986, Jim Wall).

We make washing machines in this assembly line, so the work is noisy, repetitive, and, worst of all, boring. It comes as no wonder then that workers start pulling stunts. They act like kids. You understand why, but you've got to keep it under control because it can get out of hand. For instance, we have this porcelain dip that the exterior of the machines goes through. Each exterior is dipped; then it is baked; then it has the motor, etc., installed. Well one guy goes up to this unit that has just been dipped and is moving toward the ovens and with his finger writes a four-letter salutation on the side that rhymes with duck. I guess he thought people down the line would see it and get a big laugh out of it. Well, this unit makes it all the way through the line and is delivered to some little old lady in Omaha or somewhere. It comes in a crate; they open it up for her, and there is this nice greeting. Management didn't think that was very funny, so they traced back the serial number, found the production line, and fired the guy.

That's just one example of what we face on a daily basis. Usually the fun and games don't have such negative consequences, so I let them go. For example, "Paul Peters" was an inspector who worked with about thirty other inspectors. He had eyes like that movie star Jack Elam that go off in different directions, and he wore thick glasses, and he didn't have many teeth, so his gums were kind of loose and flopping. And he was real gullible and weird looking—walking around with his hat on sideways, looking at you with these eyes. Oh, he was gullible. He'd believe anything that you told him.

Then there was this other fellow, "Whit Shoe," a real operator, who was a pig farmer. He's a tough, crude-looking guy, but he was real smooth, and he'd come up and could sell you anything. He'd make up stories, and he knew Paul was gullible, so he'd come up to someone who was working near Paul and he'd start telling them a story just loud enough that he knew Paul could hear it. Of course, Paul was a basically nosy sort of person who liked to gossip, so he wanted to pick up these tidbits and go around and tell people about them.

One of these episodes involved me. Whit came up to me while I was standing near Paul and said, "I hear you might be interested in buying a car. If you decide you are interested, I'll get you a deal on one." So he turned around and left. Immediately Paul looked at me. He kind of was looking at me—his eyes were looking in different directions, but one of them was looking at me. And he said, "Don't you ever buy anything from Whit Shoe. He'll skin ye. You know the last time he sold someone a car in here, you know what he did? He found a bunch of Pontiacs they were floating on a barge down the Ohio River. And the barge turned over, and all those Pontiacs were at the bottom of the Ohio River, and a salvage company went down there and pulled them all up and sold them to Whit Shoe at a real low price. So you know what he did? He took them back to Lebanon, cleaned them out as best he could, and then dumped perfume all over them so they would smell okay. And all of these people I know who bought these cars found that after a few months, they all began to smell like fish, and they never could get the fishy smell out."

Then there were the Suki lawnmowers. Paul told me a while back that Whit was going around selling people Suki lawnmowers. And people were buying them, but after a while they found they were falling apart. What he did was to go over to Europe to buy parts, and then he made these Suki mowers in his basement. Paul said that Whit made the engine blocks out of concrete, cheap concrete, and the pistons were made out of old gunshell cases. When he went to Europe, he bought some cannon shell casings and cut them and used them as pistons. So Paul said to me, "If he ever tries to sell you a lawnmower, don't buy it."

He also said to me, "You didn't know old 'Joe Howard,' but Joe died and Whit went over to his widow, masquerading as a preacher, and convinced her to let him give the eulogy. They tell me that Whit Shoe saw the funeral announcement in the paper and got on to that poor widow and got her to agree to let him be the guy who gave the eulogy. So Whit Shoe came in there slick as he could be, all dressed up in a tuxedo and fit to kill and stood up there all holier-than-now and gave the eulogy. Then he bent over the casket to say a few final words, with his back to the audience, and took that diamond ring off Joe's finger!"

You see, Whit would start these stories or go around to someone who worked close to Paul to start them. For example, "Red Coat," a friend of his, would walk up, preplanned, as Paul was looking up into space and say, "Hey, Whit, that lawnmower you sold me is broke again. It's all cracked and it's falling apart. I've only had it a month and I want my money back." Of course, Whit Shoe would yell back, "That's tough luck, buddy, you should have known better when you bought it! You can't abuse a lawnmower that way and expect it to hold together." Then Red Coat would lean down to Paul Peters and say, "The block is made out of concrete, and it cracked right down the middle!" Then he'd bring in a piece of concrete from the road outside to show Paul a piece that had fallen off the engine block.

As a supervisor, I also have to keep workers from stealing stuff. That's tough because they're ingenious. But sometimes the workers do themselves in. We had a big tunnel that went from the factory for about three to four hundred yards underground, under a street to a guardhouselike deal. There we had a lot of gates side by side, like you find going into a football stadium. When the bell rang at 3:30—when we let out of work—all the workers would punch their cards, and thousands of them would push through this tunnel, running up to the guardhouse and the gates. As they went through these gates, the guards would look into anything they were carrying. If they had a lunch box they had to open it, a sack, a briefcase, whatever they had they had to open it. The guards were very careful, and they had to do that because stuff was getting stolen.

So one day these guys were going down there, running like a bat out of Hades, and one of them collapsed as he got out of the tunnel to the gatehouse. And the guards started to do all this heart restarting stuff to save his life, but when they opened up his shirt, he had this copper wire wrapped around his whole body from his waist to his armpits. What had happened was that back up in the factory, he had decided to steal this wire—it was worth a lot of money—so he had taken off his shirt and held his hands over his head while his friend had coiled it around him. Then he lowered his arms, put on his shirt, tucked it in his pants, and put on his coat. Then when the bell rang, he took off running. What had happened was that the guy must have wrapped it too tight for his normal body position, and as he ran through the tunnel he must have hyperventilated [*laughs*]. So he fell down at the guardhouse, and they toted him in.

Communicating

W e have been viewing managing as a difficult balancing act required for coordinating human effort towards achieving the purposes of an organization. Information, perhaps more than anything else, affects coordination. In performing their balancing acts managers depend upon the flow of information. They need to obtain valid information about what things are important and depend upon other people receiving information that directs their attention and effort appropriately. Communication is the word used to refer to the activities for sending and receiving information.

Early in the study of management, communication was seen primarily as flowing up and down the organization's formal hierarchy as diagrammed on the organization chart. It did not take long before people realized that other communication channels existed and were essential. For the actions of people to be coordinated effectively, the people doing the work needed to interact with each other. If only the formal hierarchy was used, the flow of information was too slow.

Perhaps even more important, the hierarchical channel introduced considerable distortion. People at higher levels in the hierarchy often lack the technical expertise to act as effective communication links. The channel has insufficient capacity to process the rich information adequately. Consequently, a great deal of attention has been given to developing new channels to link organizational units—laterally and diagonally across the hierarchy. Management textbooks frequently discuss these steps under the headings of liaison mechanisms and matrix structures.

It also was apparent that there were other problems in the upward and downward flow of information. At first, considerable attention was given to how managers could send information more effectively. Clarity, redundancy, and persuasiveness were stressed as ways to be sure that information was transferred from the people who made the decisions to those who would be charged with implementing them. As we see in "The Manager as

Developer," "Effective Communication Activities of Real Managers," and the poem by Simon Roman on MBAs, such matters are still of great importance in downward communication, but that managing communication along the vertical dimension involves a great deal more.

For the most part, the other articles deal more with upward communication. In the previous section we saw several examples of how the formal hierarchy interferes with the relationships among the members of the organization. Here, additional dimensions of the interference become evident. This interference is most clear when we examine the upward flow of information in an organization.

There are numerous impediments to the flow of valid information upwards. The readings in this section highlight but a few. Intimidation is one of the most important. People who have power intimidate those with less power. The intimidation may stem from a defensive effort of the superior to turn off unwanted information and/or from inhibitions (from real or imagined sources) in the minds of subordinates. Regardless, valid information does not flow. Moreover, upper level managers often deal with the problems of lower level members through numbers and other symbols that reflect the performance and the problems of the lower level participants in highly abstracted form. As a result, the managers simply do not have an accurate picture of what is happening—they lack the context to make appropriate interpretations. Some (see, for example, "More Corporate Chiefs Seek Direct Contact with Staff, Customers") special efforts are required.

In sum, the flow of valid, timely information is an essential ingredient for an effective organization. Achieving it is not easy under the best of circumstances and organizations are far from the best of circumstances. The articles that follow provide insight into the problems and suggest some remedies.

The Manager As Developer

David Bradford and Allan Cohen

. . . The *manager-as-developer* is a leadership model Bradford and Cohen (1984) formulated . . . as a result of working with managers who realized that the more traditional models were no longer fully effective. The manager-developer's basic orientation is to . . . see to it that problems get solved and work gets done in ways that develop subordinates' capacities for and commitment to sharing responsibility for the unit's success. To be effective, the manager-as-developer must accomplish the following three major tasks:

1. Work with direct subordinates as a team to collectively share responsibility for managing the unit.
2. Determine and gain commitment to a common, tangible vision of the department's [overarching] goals and purposes; and
3. Work on the continuous development of individual subordinate skills, especially in the managerial/interpersonal areas needed to be an effective member of the shared responsibility team.

The manager-as-developer, then, seeks to develop in subordinates the willingness and ability to share the responsibility for departmental success. The manager must shape subordinates into a powerful, cooperative, hardworking, dedicated, and responsible team. . . .

An Example of a Successful Developer

. . . Deborah Linke is chief of the repayment staff of one of the offices in the Federal Bureau of Reclamation. . . . The job of her staff [is] to "negotiate, write, and administer all contracts in the geographic area to recover the federal investment in water-resource development," which involved multimillion-dollar dealings with industries, municipalities, and agricultural interests needing water. Her staff's job [is] complex because they [are] dealing with multiple constituencies and each of the various water uses [is] governed by several different set of laws and regulations. Her description of how she built an excellent department serves as a detailed, step-by-step analysis of the developer model.

When I first returned to my job after [a year's assignment in Washington and a leadership] workshop, I held a two-hour staff meeting with my three key subordinates in the office (there were three others scattered through the region in local field offices but the former was my core group). I talked about how I felt I had changed in the nearly 12 months I had been away. . . . [I had] a greater openness to [giving and receiving] feedback . . . and a much greater

From "Effective Behavior in Organizations" by Allan R. Cohen, Stephen L. Fink, Herman Gadon, and Robert D. Willits. Copyright © 1976, 1980, 1984 by Richard D. Irwin. Reprinted by permission of Richard D. Irwin. Also from "Managing for Excellence" by David L. Bradford and Allan R. Cohen, Copyright 1984 John Wiley & Sons. Reprinted by permission of John Wiley & Sons, Inc.

appreciation of and tolerance toward conflict (in the past, I had tended to . . . smooth it over). I shared with them my leadership questionnaire results by handing out copies of the scores [they had given me]. We talked as a group about areas that I could improve on. Out of this discussion came an informal contract that they would call me on behavior that wasn't changing. . . . Naturally, I was apprehensive beforehand . . . but it opened a lot of doors—both ways—and made change much less threatening. It all had a very positive tone.

The discussion of my questionnaire results led . . . into exploring how I could modify my leadership style. I talked a little bit about the . . . Leadership Conference and the concept of Manager-as-Developer. I said that I wanted to make our staff meetings much more important and a place where all of us could share in managing the office. I stated my much greater commitment to their professional development. My intention was to give them a sense of my managerial style so they would know how best to use it.

The concept of an Overarching Goal was introduced, and each of them was given some of the written material on goals from the workshop. . . . I concluded by saying that [I] . . . learned in . . . Washington . . . to appreciate the political process and how it affects our work. More than in the past, I wanted to involve them in political issues as a way to pass on my knowledge.

After this initial session, I decided to wait three or four weeks until our next meeting. My concern was to not overwhelm the staff . . . until they had a chance to get used to my being back as their supervisor and . . . to this new management style which was . . . markedly different . . . from what I had used previously. Also, . . . I felt a critical need to get on top of . . . where we were on a number of projects.

That time was used, however, to follow up on . . . the comments I had made during that initial meeting about appreciating the work they had done in the last year. I realized that words are cheap, so . . . I . . . did the volumes of paperwork that were necessary to get a performance award for the entire team for how they had carried through in my absence (there was no replacement for me for that year; they collectively took over my functions). That award had to be shepherded through Personnel but I saw that they got the award and the visibility for the good job that they had done. I also used that period to do a careful assessment of our workload[,] . . . examining not only what we were already doing but also what we should be doing. On the basis of this analysis, I was eventually able to get my central office professional staff increased from the initial three to our present group of five.

At our second staff meeting, we started to work on drafting an Overarching Goal for our office. Even though I had jotted down a possible goal while at the Leadership Conference, I decided not to share this with my staff at this time, recognizing that what I thought might be appropriate might not be their first choice and that introducing my idea might unduly influence them. What was crucial was that the goal be our goal and not just my goal. I must say that the hardest part was letting the group do the work! . . . We . . . brainstorm[ed] a list of things that we found exciting about our work. I acted as recorder for . . . all the words they came up with. . . .

At this next meeting we picked out the . . . concepts that we felt as a team were most exciting and that we wanted to expand on for our goal. (What was also nice was discovering that many of the same points I had originally found important, they did also.) After much discussion, our final goal was:

"We work with our clients with imagination and an attitude of 'there is a problem, let's solve it.' When we have a good answer, we give it visibility."

The two key words in our discussion were "imagination" and "visibility." I was pleasantly surprised that these two values were extremely important to my subordinates and that they really took great pride in being on the cutting edge and being where they could be seen—no easy feat for government employees. . . . All of them have [the goal] . . . prominently displayed and have referred to it as our activities have progressed. One validation for this new leadership approach is that the goal we collectively developed was a significant improvement over what I had written myself . . . [which] . . . was more stilted, put in "governmentese," and less exciting.

Determining our Overarching Goal was just the first step in building a team where they, and not just I, have influence. Another action was to have each of the subordinates take turns on a rotating basis in chairing our weekly staff meeting. The leader for that week goes through the agenda and sets the priorities; I will buy into those priorities if that is what the group feels is most important. (Sometimes when we are dealing with very delicate issues, I chair the meetings since I still have the best group skills, but those occasions are rare.) The major task issues in the office are decided by this team.

. . . People [now] feel free to raise problems (and not just have a "show-and-tell" of what is going well). . . . Frequently the format is for people to go around and talk about the difficulties encountered and the progress they have made since the previous meeting. Others . . . make suggestions . . . about alternative actions that might have been taken . . . [and] . . . for ways to handle the problems coming up next week. . . . These suggestions usually resolve any problems. But when a person's performance doesn't improve, the group gets increasingly confrontative, so I worry much less about having to be the one who keeps standards high.

We try to do a lot of coaching at these meetings particularly . . . through encouraging consideration of issues from a political perspective. . . . That is probably my strongest suit and one that is very difficult, but important, to impart to others. When I am the only one who is privy to information and can share that, I spend time explaining what has happened in and outside the Department which may affect decisions or policy.

The team is increasingly working on those complex problems that would have been very difficult for any one of us to resolve alone (but which, in my previous style, I would have tried to handle myself). For example, recently a key . . . member . . . brought up a problem she was having. This person has been working on a project for three years and was getting increasingly bored with the work. . . . She was no longer finding it interesting or exciting (although it was still an important project)[,] [yet] the project . . . looked like it might drag on for another two or three years. The group . . . explored various ways the work could be reassigned to alleviate the boredom. On the basis of the discussion, I drew up a suggested work-reassignment list which represented a rather major shift in that person's responsibilities and entailed some of the group members taking on additional tasks. The group . . . went over the list, made some modifications and then accepted the changes. Such a major reshuffling of tasks is usually a sore point, but because it was something they helped design, the change was implemented with very little upheaval.

In terms of dealing one-on-one with my subordinates, I was fortunate in not having any major problems (such as personality clashes or feeling that any of my people were "trouble-makers" or incompetent)[,] . . . The difficulties I did have were with a couple of the people out in the field [who] I . . . had to influence but over whom I had no direct supervisory authority or control. . . . I discovered that part of the problem was mine. Rather than noticing their strengths, I was focusing on their weaknesses. I decided to try a [new] strategy . . . the next time I got upset or angry at their behavior, I would first look at whether . . . the[y] [were] using one of their strengths, but in a way (or a situation) that wasn't appropriate. (Rather than taking the attitude, which I had done in the past, of thinking that the problem behavior was due to their being irresponsible or incompetent.) In most cases, . . . that let me deal with their behavior directly by pointing out (in an authentic way, not for . . . flattering them) their positive strengths and how these were being inappropriately used. Not only was this message heard (and actually led to their changing) but it also made our relationship more open. This has been important to me, because in the past I have felt blocked. In the Government, one doesn't easily have the option of getting rid of people or transferring them to another division.

Even though I didn't have any real relational problems with my staff, . . . it turned out that the change in my management style did lead to even greater openness of communication between us, with each side feeling freer to raise issues that were getting in the way. Not only have I done less pussy-footing with them, but they have also been willing to be more confrontative with me. For example, recently one of my employees told me, "That's certainly a negative way of looking at that—why don't you stop it—it's not doing any of us any good." I could hear and accept that now without getting defensive because I felt the subordinate was saying it with the intention of us working better and this being a better department.

I should add that this informal feedback does not replace the formal systems that are in place. I still do quarterly performance appraisals for each employee; that involves not only feedback to them, but also a chance for feedback from them on how I'm doing with my performance contract.

The improved relationship . . . lets me focus attention on developmental activities [and] . . . to work out an individual development plan with specific goals. I spent a lot of time listening to what their dreams and aspirations were, where they wanted to be in five to ten years and I tried to build the development plan (and my coaching) around those dreams.

I also worked hard to enrich their jobs. I have used such things as new assignments, trips to Washington, and having them represent the department at some of the meetings in other parts of the Agency or with external groups. The last was not easy for me to do but I found that they handled those meetings as well as I would have, if not better[.] . . . For those meetings where I had to be present, a different subordinate would join me each time and afterwards we would talk about how they saw the meetings and how they would have handled it if they had been running it.

This method [also] . . . has been used . . . with . . . others who are not my direct subordinates yet whose cooperation we need to carry out our departmental tasks. This approach, plus recognition of jobs well done, has led to bringing out even more of the positive behaviors we need. Government doesn't offer many opportunities for perks so I have been looking at such things as chances to give talks (especially presentations to other management groups), attending special meetings, travel opportunities and chances to design training for others as rewards and encouragements for further improved performance.

. . . My relationships with my boss and peers . . . have been good. Immediately after my return, I sat down with my boss to talk about how I had changed and what my goals for the office were. I didn't want these changes to be perceived in the wrong way. My boss's style is very different from mine, especially with this new Developer style that I am using. Although he likes people, he is much more interested in the technical problems. This difference has not caused any resistance in him. He respects me for my ability to manage my shop and in how I relate to my subordinates.

With my peers I find this management style to be very helpful. It is possible to "coach" and even "develop" my peers without being condescending. I can say, "Oh, by the way, I noticed that Mary hasn't been getting any field assignments. One of the things that I learned in my stint in Washington is that this could be construed as discrimination and I don't know if you were aware of that." Such off-hand comments are non-threatening, and are getting me a great deal of payoff from my peers and preventing some of the jealousy that might otherwise occur.

Most of these changes were accomplished in the first three to four months after I came back. But for this progress to be truly effective and meaningful, I found that it had to be followed through . . . —it is easy to get sloppy in the press of everyday business. We have done several things to sustain these changes. One is to make sure there is open communication among all of us. . . . I have [used] the Leadership Questionnaire . . . several times . . . to get further feedback on those areas that my subordinates perceived I needed to work on. I have also worked extra hard with feedback one-on-one to each of them to be sure that they know that they are doing productive work of high quality. In our team meetings, I am better about letting conflicts develop and anger be expressed. When we see problems, we plop them out on the table to be directly dealt with. Also, at the end of each session, the leader for that meeting asks the group how they feel the meeting worked, what didn't work, how the team is functioning, and what needs improving. It is now accepted, by the new members as well, that "this is the way we do business." One of the new arrivals came from a department which was quite repressive and is astounded at how open we are in talking about problems and about issues that come up in the office.

I also found that our Overarching Goal helped sustain this new leadership approach. . . . I have mentioned the goal many times with such comments as, "This is an imaginative solution, like our goal suggests," or, "We are getting a lot of visibility for that, which is what we want to be doing," or, "We could be getting more visibility, meet our goal and be more excited if we did this. . . ." Typically we use the goal to formulate how we go about doing our business. Even though many of the contracting decisions are set and cannot be influenced that much, the goal can be used in planning how we go about attacking a problem. We use it as a yardstick as well as a criterion to assess decisions on individual projects and in our group meetings. I also have found that the goal is a good way to integrate our new personnel into the office. When a new employee is hired, I give that person a copy of our goal and say why it is important. The goal thus serves as a standard around which we manage the office. . . .

Has this new leadership style been effective? I think so. One measure is that our office went from last out of seven offices (in terms of responsiveness to changing policy) to being on the top. We have gained a great deal of respect throughout the Agency and are listened to in the head office. There have been many changes in procedures and policies which require a great deal of adaptability on our part. . . . In fact, we are used as an example to the other offices. We have even been asked to develop a training program for others in those areas in which we have been out in front (in our marketing and pricing policies). . . . That training . . . will be done by my subordinates. That entails some risk because most of them have not done any training before, but I am not worried. Based on last year's experience, I have every confidence that by next quarter we will have a top-notch training program that is presented from a unique perspective and given in a very professional manner. . . .

Effective Communication Activities of [Real Managers]

Fred Luthans, Richard M. Hodgetts, and Stuart A. Rosenkrantz

The communication activities of real managers were identified in the study as the observable behaviors associated with exchanging routine information and processing paperwork. These observable behaviors, of course, are not as exotic or sophisticated as the terms and supposed functions presented in the traditional managerial communication literature. Nevertheless, the identified RM communication activities still encompass basically the same processes and dimensions as have been discussed and analyzed over the years. A review of these will lead to a better understanding of how RMs communicate and what they do to improve the effectiveness of communication.

Understanding the Communication Process of RMs

When people communicate, there are four generally recognized steps involved: attention, understanding, acceptance, and action. The literature suggests, and the effective RMs would support, the conclusion that unless all four of these steps are carried out, there is a good chance that the communication will break down.

Attention. Attention is attained when the sender is able to get the receiver to focus on the message and to screen out all disturbances and distractions that can interrupt the necessary concentration. This means overcoming message competition. There are a number of things that can be done to help secure such attention. Two of the most helpful are these:

1. Start off with an attention-getter. For example, one of the RMs told us that when he gave a presentation to the finance committee asking for more funding, he would always present what the main competitor was doing in this area of the business. Because the competitor's funds were usually greater, he could always get the committee's attention.
2. Focus on something that is of primary importance to the receiver. If the receiver is interested in trimming expenses, gear the communiqué to those steps that will help reduce costs. If productivity is a major concern, explain how the plan will lower the cost per unit of production.

Understanding. Understanding requires comprehension on the part of the receiver. The biggest problem here is that while most RMs realize the importance of achieving understanding, they often fail to get it. Why? If they think the receiver does not comprehend their message, they ask the receiver, "Do you understand what I've just said (or written to you)?" Receivers almost always say, "Yes." All the pressure is on the receiver to do so, particularly in the case of downward communication. Few RMs are going to admit to their boss, "I lost you about five seconds into what you were saying." Instead of asking receivers if they understand, senders should ask *what* they understand. This gives receivers a chance to put the message into their own words; and if they are incorrect the sender can say, "No, that's not what I meant to convey. Here's what I'm trying to say." Again, when senders are finished, they should ask receivers to restate the message.

Acceptance. Acceptance occurs when the receiver is willing to go along with the message. Quite often this compliance is automatic; the RM may ask a subordinate to do something and the individual does it. However, sometimes there is resistance which, if not picked up by the sender, results in communication failures. For example, the subordinate may already be overburdened with work and unable to drop everything to find a particular report that has been mislaid. At other times, subordinates may feel that they lack the proper training to carry out the task. For example, the subordinate might say, "I don't know anything about printing files using that word processing program. However, if it can wait until after lunch, Bob will be back and he can take care of it." However, if the RM pushes and says, "There's nothing to it. Get in there and try it, you'll get the hang of it almost immediately," the manager is refusing to acknowledge the subordinate's lack of acceptance. Sometimes this is a good idea because it forces people to train themselves in jobs that they might not voluntarily undertake; at other times, however, the RM is making a mistake by pushing the matter. One manager made this distinction:

> I generally have people respond very quickly to me, but I may not get the results I want. When I tell them something, I emphasize two things: what needs to be done and what type of assistance or support will be provided. Look, if I ask someone to fill out the monthly cost control report and he's never done it before, he's not going to be very receptive to my comments about this being good training. In fact, he thinks he's being dumped on. What I try to do is provide him with previous reports, call in someone who has done these reports before and have this expert brief him on what to do. Then I make myself available to answer questions or get additional assistance if he needs it. People don't mind going the extra mile for you if they think you'll be there for them if they run into trouble.

In dealing with acceptance, the literature suggests and effective RMs would verify the importance of the following:

1. Feedback (both verbal and nonverbal) from the receiver is important. If the individual is given an order or directive and is not allowed to say anything about it, acceptance can only be inferred. If there is a problem, it will not show up until the work is either later or incorrectly done. Communication feedback should not only be tolerated, it should be encouraged.

2. If it is important that the subordinates do what is being asked, the effective RM does not take no for an answer. Effective managers get subordinates the training or assistance needed, and give them moral support and the coaching necessary for the job. However, they also must get subordinates to accept the order by using effective persuasion. Effec-

tive RMs rely on threats or disciplinary punishment only when all else fails.

The Importance of Simple, Repetitive Language

The simpler a message, the more likely it will be understood and acted upon properly. Simplicity takes two forms: direct and complete. Direct means that the messasge gets to the point without providing information that is supplementary, tangential, or simply filler. Complete means that when the message has been relayed, the listener understands everything that the communicator wanted understood.

Simple messages should not be so brief that they leave out salient facts. Repetitiveness is also an important factor when the message contains a series of important facts or analytical or quantitative data that are difficult to digest. By repeating or restating these important facts, the sender increases the likelihood of the message being fully comprehended. The literature suggests, and effective RMs would support, the following guidelines:

1. Do not belabor the point. Determine what is to be said and say it. If the communiqué contains bad news, the effective RM would prepare the other person for it by making introductory remarks that explain the reason for the news. For example, if there is to be a layoff and the individual is to be one of those let go, the effective RM would start off by saying that economic conditions have made the action necessary and that some good people will have to be laid off. Then, after telling the individual that he or she is included in this group, the RM would point out the types of assistance the firm is going to provide or the letter of recommendation that the individual can expect. The remarks would be kept brief and the other person would be given a chance to talk. If nothing else, the individual will probably want to let off steam.

2. Remember that simple words always have greater communication power than sophisticated words. Although there is always the possibility of talking down to listeners, it is far more common for RMs to confuse them by using words that they do not understand than by using words that are below their level of understanding.

3. If a message contains a number of important ideas, it helps to repeat the major points as one goes along or recap them at the end. This may seem trite but it will generally result in improved communication effectiveness. Although this may make RMs feel that they are talking down to their listeners, most of them will welcome repetition of important ideas because it helps them keep track of what is being said. Effective RMs know that every message should be understood. If the subject matter is complex, it should be communicated in manageable portions, giving listeners the opportunity to ask questions or seek clarifi-

cation. Additionally, if RMs recap the message as they go along, listeners will find it much easier to follow the flow of information.

The Importance of Empathizing

Empathy means putting oneself in another person's place. In so doing, effective RMs begin to see things the way their superiors and subordinates do. By empathizing they can begin to know when to be work centered and when to be people centered. They are also capable of answering such questions as: what type of direction does this subordinate need?

The literature suggests that empathy is of particular importance at two stages of the communication process; acceptance and action. When a manager gives an order that a subordinate is reluctant to accept, the effective RM notices the subordinate's hesitancy through such nonverbal cues as facial expressions. For whatever reason, the subordinate may not understand how important the matter is or how significant his or her role will be. Empathy helps the RM determine the best way in which to communicate this importance and helps implement the action stage. The empathetic RM stays alert for signs that the subordinate needs assistance and then sees that this assistance is provided.

The literature emphasizes two major points about empathy with which effective RMs would agree:

1. Empathy is a result of understanding people's needs. Empathy can be improved by allowing subordinates the chance to communicate upward and by interacting with them on a continuous basis. In this way effective RMs begin to obtain improved insights into how their people feel about issues and what can be done to manage them more effectively.

2. There is a big difference between being empathetic and being a push-over. Effective RMs do not lose sight of the fact that their job is to improve performance and obtain objectives. Empathy can help, but it does not mean that the manager should acquiesce to the employees' every need and desire. Effective RMs know that they sometimes must ask their people to do things that are difficult or unpleasant. However, the effective RM's first responsibility is to get things done, not to keep subordinates happy.

Here is a representative example of an RM using empathy:

I try to get to know my people so I know what's important to them. When I have to assign work, I know when to be flexible and when to push hard. Let me give you an example. Last month, the wife of one of our employees had a baby. The fellow was scheduled to go on a trip to the West Coast the following week. He called from the hospital, gave me the news, and asked if he could postpone the trip. It wasn't necessary—when I checked the assignment calendar earlier, I knew that his wife would be having the baby at about the same time he was scheduled to be out of town, so I had a replacement ready to move in. All it took was a little forward planning. Once I know what's important to my people in terms of their career development and personal life, I try to adjust the job to reflect this. The result is usually a win-win situation for my people, me, and—I know this sounds hokey—for the company.

The Importance of Understanding Body Language

Body language is one of the most important forms of nonverbal communication. This "silent" language takes many different forms—from posture to eye movement, to where a person stands in a room in relation to others. Although everybody uses body language, many are unaware that they do. There is considerable literature on guidelines for using nonverbal communication, and effective RMs are aware of the following:

1. Looking people directly in the eye is often, but not always, a sign of honesty. Good liars are able to look people right in the eye with no compunction. If anything, they have come to realize that eye contact is important to convincing their audience.
2. By looking people in the eye it is possible to get some idea of how much stress they are enduring. For example, when right-handed people are trying to deal with an issue on an emotional level, they tend to look to their left. The reverse is true for left-handed people.
3. Touch is an important way of conveying confidence, trust, or friendship. For example, a firm handshake is often regarded as a sign of self-assurance. Touching also is used to convey power relationships. For example, a manager who wants to emphasize an order may grasp the subordinate's arm while issuing the order. An RM who wants to give positive attention to a subordinate may put a hand on his shoulder. These forms of touching reinforce the RM's message.
4. Physical location can also help convey messages. For example, where the RM sits or stands in a room in relation to the subordinate may dictate the style and tenor of the message. When giving commands, RMs can convey greater authority if they stand up and the subordinate remains seated. This enables the RM to look down at the subordinate as the reprimand is delivered. When an RM wants to establish authority in the office, the furniture layout can help convey the necessary power. For example, by placing the desk as far away from the entrance door as possible RMs can increase their perceived authority—distance typically is equated with power. Other ways an RM can enhance authority include: keeping all visitors on the other side of the desk, using the desk as a wall between RMs and visitors; and placing the desk directly in front of a window so that visitors look into the sunlight while RMs have the sun behind their back. On the other hand, if a manager wants to convey a friendly image, he may come out from behind the desk

and sit on the opposite side with visitors. This eliminates the desk as a barrier and quickly establishes a warm, open environment.

5. Even clothing can be used to convey messages. For example, some literature on the topic suggests that the most authoritative pattern for men is the dark, pinstripe suit. This is followed, in order, by the solid, the chalk stripe, and the plaid. For women in business, a conservative, tailored suit carries more authority than a more fashionable suit.

The Importance of Giving and Getting Feedback

Giving and getting feedback is perhaps the primary way for effective RMs to communicate. All of the communication barriers discussed earlier can be overcome with effective feedback. There are a number of ways in which this can be done. One is by soliciting feedback from subordinates. While this can take numerous forms, some of the most effective openers include these:

- "Can you tell me more about . . .?"
- "You've given me some things to think about. I'd welcome any additional ideas you might have along these lines."
- "I think that we're ready to begin impelmentation of this project. What do you think?"

Each of these openers encourages subordinates to expand on their earlier comments or to voice an opinion regarding what to do now. RMs know that effective feedback depends on making the other party feel free to comment and that their input is valued. One of the best ways to ensure this is to keep the tone positive, as one manager attested:

When I'm trying to give or get feedback, I follow one simple rule: make the other guy look good. I emphasize the positive rather than the negative. I never say, "How come things in your unit are all screwed up?" That's not going to get me anywhere. Instead, I review the positive aspects up to this point and ask how I can help the person get back on track if things are not going too well. I approach these matters by making it clear that we're all in this together. You'd be surprised how much people will open up when they find that your objective is to help them rather than catch them doing something wrong.

A second important aspect of feedback is sustaining the flow of information. For example, once the RM has subordinates talking, it is helpful to keep them going. This requires the use of phrases or statements that sustain the action. Some of the most useful are:

- "I understand what you're saying. But tell me, what else do you think we need to do?"
- "Right, right. This all makes a lot of sense. Keep going."
- "What else?"
- "I appreciate what you're saying. It's right in line with the way we've been thinking about approaching this problem. However, how would

you handle the implementation phase of this idea? Whom would you include? How long would it take to get this all carried out? Give me more details on the specifics of your approach."

A third important part of feedback is giving the listeners additional information that elaborates or clarifies what has already been said. Some RMs, fearing overkill, may be reluctant to do this because they think that their people already understand what has been communicated. In other cases, RMs may assume that if subordinates wanted more information they would ask for it. Actually, many subordinates are reluctant to solicit information from their boss for fear of appearing unqualified to do their job. As a result, they remain silent.

To sidestep this reluctance to ask questions, the RM can provide feedback without being asked to do so. The approach of effective RMs was to preface the feedback with an introductory question that allowed the subordinates to say, "No, I already understand that. It's not necessary to go on." A second way was to use an introductory remark that was congratulatory in tone, while at the same time, giving feedback on the matter. Here are some representative examples:

- "I read your report and think that it covers all of the important areas that need to be addressed. However, I'd like to share with you a couple of ideas for expanding it and incorporating more of the cost-related data."
- "I read your report very closely. I like it. What sets it apart from the others I've gone through is . . ."
- "Your progress on this subject has brought you to the point where we need to determine your next step. I'd like to give you my ideas on how we should proceed."

In each of these scenarios, the manager approached the feedback from the standpoint of the receiver. Each comment conveyed something of help or value to the receiver and encouraged him to listen to what is about to be communicated.

The Importance of Developing Effective Listening Skills

Of all the communication activities carried out by RMs, listening may be the most overlooked. Here are listening skills that are suggested in the literature and that effective RMs have developed:

1. Listen to what is being said rather than how it is being said. This means that instead of dismissing the speaker as boring or uninteresting, the effective RM lets the person speak and focuses on the message.
2. Give the speakers a chance to convey their message: hear the person out. It is also important for the listener to assume that the other per-

son has something important to say. In this way, the listener focuses attention more closely.

3. Encourage speakers to stay on the main topic by asking them pertinent questions that redirect them back to the subject.

4. Fight the tendency to tune the speaker out when the presentation becomes overly technical or too difficult to understand. Focus on listening, learning, and remembering.

5. Watch the speaker's approach and see what can be learned. For example, in a formal presentation, did the person effectively use audiovisual equipment? Was the individual able to work in a lot of facts while keeping the presentation lively and interesting? Did the person use an emotional appeal that persuaded people to accept his or her point of view?

6. Evaluate the relevance of what is being said. Are there any new or useful data being communicated that can be of personal value?

7. Listen for intended meanings as well as for expressed ideas. Is the speaker trying to convey any hidden messages? What are they? How do they influence the overall content of the message?

8. Integrate everything the speaker is saying so that it all fits into a logical composite. If any information does not fit into this overall scheme, put it aside and try to integrate it later.

9. Be a responsive listener. Maintain eye contact with speakers and give them positive feedback, such as nods of agreement and bright facial expressions.

10. Accept the challenge of effective listening. Effective RMs recognize that it is important to communication. In most cases, they have taught themselves to do it well—it is not something with which the RM is born.

The Importance of Speaking and Writing Skills

In recent years, we hear more and more that managers, especially younger managers recently out of our educational system, are unable to speak or write well. As managers move up the hierarchy, these basic communication skills increase in importance. The literature suggests the following guidelines in developing these skills and many effective RMs use them:

1. Know your audience. Before speaking or writing to anyone, effective RMs have an idea of what their audience is interested in hearing or learning about, and gear their message to the audience's interests.

2. Have an attention-getting opener. Make the audience want to learn more. If it is a written communique, start with a fact or statistic that the reader may be unaware of and use this to lead into the rest of the message. If it is a formal talk, decide whether a short story or joke is in order. (An after-dinner talk should have one; an in-house presen-

tation to senior level managers should not.) Then briefly relate what the talk is going to be about and begin.

3. Get preliminary feedback on the message. If RMs are giving a talk, they often have a colleague listen and offer suggestions on how they can improve their style. If writing a communiqué, they may have it read over and critiqued by a trusted colleague. RMs use this feedback to improve their overall communication style.

4. Close on a strong point. If giving a talk, effective RMs usually have a story or point for summarizing key points. If it is a report or an extensive memo, this can be done in the last paragraph. If an executive summary of the material is required, they typically put this last paragraph at the front of the paper. An abstract may also be used.

A Final Word

As noted in the earlier empirically based chapters, as well as at the beginning of this chapter, routine communication is a major activity of RMs. In particular, it makes a major contribution to managerial effectiveness. In fact, of the four major activities of RMs uncovered in our research—networking, traditional management functions, human resource management, and routine communication—the communication activity was found to play a more significant role than any of the others for *effective* managers. By contrast, this communication activity did not play as important a role for *successful* RMs. Thus, this chapter on communication primarily concentrated on what effective RMs do. The effective RMs in our study generally do the things suggested in the literature on effective communication; there is a great deal we can learn from them.

Poem on MBAs

Simon Roman

Sir—There may be many American MBA's but their education is seldom impressive. They are often poor communicators, even if their secondary education has been of the literary European variety.

> Far beyond Bermuda, beyond the Tempest's isle,
> The Business Schools all chatter and, Oh, their speech is vile
> They seek to turn out leaders, to make a business go,

Reprinted by permission of *The Economist.*

Administrative experts, the civil GSO,
But yet this type of training full many a mind has blown
And left it almost speechless, no words to call its own.
Untaught in public speaking, mark how man's wit is slow,
Unversed in forceful writing, they wreak industrial woe,
Mewed up in penthouse office, the real world cramps their style.
They read accountants' fiction, from plant they run a mile.
For they have not the diction t'inspire the rank and file.
For all their thoughts are figures, as bottom line they toe,
But math don't cheer the workers, who find such men their foe!

Criticizing Your Boss

Hendrie Weisinger and Norman M. Lobsenz

"Criticize my boss?" "I don't have the right to."
  "I'd get fired."
  "It's his company, not mine."
  Many executives recognize that it's important to encourage criticism from their subordinates. Walking about United Airlines, Ed Carlson solicited criticism, both as a source of information and as a way of conveying respect to middle managers. At ITT, Harold Geneen was well-known for the way he bawled out subordinates, but he also structured the organization to encourage criticism of superiors, including himself. Mr. Geneen felt that criticism of superiors would enable problems to surface more quickly, so they could be nipped in the bud. Konosuke Matsushita built his namesake company with a philosophy stressing criticism as a form of self-discipline necessary to the growth of the individual and the company.
  Unfortunately, not everyone has the good fortune to work in such companies. George Steinbrenner, owner of the New York Yankees, is said to have given manager Billy Martin a contract specifically prohibiting him from criticizing his superiors. And the business sections of newspapers and magazines are filled with examples of criticism of top executives with the source consciously being kept anonymous.
  If you think things could be improved in your company, but aren't quite sure how your boss will respond to criticism, the following guidelines may be helpful:

1. Make sure it is appropriate to criticize your boss. You must have a direct line of communications to him, and his work must affect your job or the job of your subordinates. It is inappropriate to criticize your superior if his decisions or actions have nothing to do with you.

2. Acknowledge that the boss is the boss, that you are not claiming to be right while he or she is wrong. Any criticism that sets up a power struggle will make your superior more intent on defending his position. Phrase your remarks in a *two-sided solution.* Summarize the situation you believe should be changed; present your criticism as a productive alternative. By offering both sides of the situation you are, in effect, acknowledging your superior's view and defusing his need to defend it. The decision—to make a change or not—is left with the boss.

3. Build the validity of your criticism. By offering it as information you want to share for the common good, you maximize its importance. Cite authoritative sources, submit supporting data from objective and reliable sources. While Mr. Geneen welcomed criticism, he did not suffer fools. He demanded that his people have what he called "unshakable facts." Thus, instead of having to accept or reject a "criticism," your superior is in a position of evaluating material you supplied.

4. Ask for your superior's help in resolving the problem you are calling to his attention. By doing so you will not be "criticizing" your superior, but seeming to criticize yourself by taking responsibility for the "problem." You are making your superior your ally. For example, if your boss is chronically late in providing you with data you need to function effectively, you can say, "I'm having trouble running my department when I don't have the necessary data on time. Can you give me some suggestions for improving this situation?" If your criticism is valid, chances are your superior will "solve the problem"—and resolve the criticism—by meeting his or her deadlines more promptly.

There also may be ways to determine how receptive your superior is to criticism. If he interacts with you outside of structured meetings, and if he is flexible enough to make changes in organizational policy from time to time, he probably tends to see criticism as a source of information rather than as an emotional attack. If your boss keeps to himself and seldom encourages change, criticism will probably not be acceptable, despite its constructive intent, and you will likely be seen as a complainer.

What about those impossible bosses—the ones with short tempers, the ones who "never listen"? Can or should you attempt to offer criticism to them? Only if you can be clever and creative. Gear your strategy to this fundamental question: "How can I communicate this information so that my superior perceives it as being useful?"

●

More Corporate Chiefs Seek Direct Contact with Staff, Customers

One Executive Interviews Employees at Breakfast; Others Try Spot-Checks

Handpicking Boss's Potatoes

Thomas F. O'Boyle and Carol Hymowitz

WASHINGTON—J. Willard Marriott Jr., the chief executive officer of Marriott Corp., is wandering around the basement of his flagship hotel here. Randomly yanking a dinner plate out of a storage cabinet, he spots a splotch of dried food. "You really ought to soak some of these dishes," he reminds the hotel manager.

In Cupertino, Calif., James G. Treybig (pronounced try-big), the chief executive of Tandem Computers Inc., is peering into a computer terminal scanning the complaints and suggestions that he has solicited from managers and production workers.

And halfway across the world in Taiwan, Joseph A. Baute, the chief executive of Markem Corp., listens to a customer's complaint that orders of Markem's labeling machines aren't arriving on time. Within minutes, Mr. Baute is telephoning company headquarters in New Hampshire rearranging deliveries.

Firsthand Knowledge

These executives are among a small but growing number of corporate chiefs who are determined to know firsthand exactly what is happening to their companies and who are willing to go out of their way to find out. As a result, they are breaking with management practices in vogue since the 1950s that emphasized an aloof, rigid financial analysis rather than direct contact.

Many chief executives are content to remain in headquarters suites, insulated from the day-to-day workings of their corporate kingdoms. Their information is gleaned from committee reports and financial statements, or it is passed on by layers of lower managers, who often filter out the bad news.

"The No. 1 managerial productivity problem in America is, quite simply, managers who are out of touch with their people and customers," asserts

Thomas J. Peters, a management consultant and co-author of "In Search of Excellence." "The alternative doesn't come from computer printouts," he says. "It comes from wandering around, directly sampling employees' environments."

Many executives say they do that. But all too often, their visits to company facilities are mere formalities that yield little insight or new information. "It's easy for them to delude themselves into thinking they know what's going on, but it's a tremendous misconception," says Ralph Kilmann, a University of Pittsburgh business-school professor. Mr. Kilmann recalls an executive who described visits to several plants in which he waved to employees but never got out of his limousine.

Promotes Loyalty

The chief executives who reject this isolation often head new high-technology and service companies, rather than more mature—and more traditional—manufacturing concerns. Some have built their companies from scratch. They see management informed by firsthand knowledge as critical to forging a corporate environment that promotes employee and customer loyalty.

The executives have distinct styles of intelligence gathering. John Sculley, the president and chief executive of Apple Computer Inc., listens to customer complaints on Apple's toll-free 800 number, and insists that other top executives do the same. John B. McCoy, the president of Banc One Corp. in Columbus, Ohio, reads "exit" interviews with employees who leave the company.

Richard G. Rogers, the president of Syntex Corp., a pharmaceutical maker, eats breakfast each morning at 7:30 in the employee cafeteria in Palo Alto, Calif. Over coffee and toast, he queries employees, and in exchange he is often asked to give career counseling and advice.

Of course, this direct approach can't replace financial analysis and other standard management tools. There is also a risk that executives who spend too much time gathering minute details may miss the broader picture. Then, too, actually obtaining reliable information can be difficult because employees, fearing retaliation, may withhold or distort facts.

False Data

Sometimes information gathering can border on spying. A chief executive at a publishing company used to read the messages that employees had left in the company's computer system. A chief executive at a large Midwestern manufacturing concern acknowledges that during a strike he got information from certain managers who were friendly to the union and used those managers to transmit false information he knew would frighten the strikers. The false information involved the suggestion that the company planned to contract out work to nonunion employees.

Nevertheless, experts say, management based on direct knowledge offers benefits that outweigh being aloof and out of touch. The advantages were aparent at Marriott Corp., where the practice is a family tradition begun by J. Willard Sr., Mr. Marriott's father. With his wife, Alice, the senior Mr. Marriott visited his Hot Shoppes restaurants constantly, ordering meals, talking to customers, and employees, even rummaging through garbage cans to check for waste.

Now the Marriott empire is a lot bigger. The younger Mr. Marriott, now 52 years old, estimates he logged 200,000 miles last year visiting more than 100 of the chain's 141 hotels and resorts.

Often he checks out his hotels at odd hours: midnight in the kitchen, for instance, or 5 a.m. in the laundry room. "When you start trying to anticipate what he'll find, you get better as a manager," says John Dixon, the general manager of the new JW Marriott hotel here.

On a recent visit, Mr. Marriott found plenty. Seconds after entering the atrium-style lobby, his eyes darted left to a pink marble pillar. On a visit to the hotel a few weeks before, Mr. Marriott had noticed an unwaxed strip about half an inch wide circling the pillar's base. "I see you cleared up that problem. Looks good," he said approvingly, shaking Mr. Dixon's hand.

A few minutes later, Mr. Marriott was in the kitchen. Looking like a man running for office, he greeted about a dozen employees with firm pumps of the hand, a broad smile, and a "Hi, how ya doin'?" He addressed a few of the old-timers by their first names and embraced one.

Then he grimaced as he discovered a batch of hash browns left over from breakfast two hours earlier, a violation of one of the strict written rules that dictate food portions and preparations. "This is a penny business," says Wes Merhige, the general manager of the Santa Clara, Calif., Marriott, "and Bill knows how to keep track of the pennies."

Before his two-hour tour ended, Mr. Marriott peeked in on the front desk, the laundry ("good, no wrinkles"), the loading dock, the exercise spa, storage lockers ("what's hidden in here?") and about half a dozen rooms and suites. At the employee cafeteria, he swept through the room shaking hands with at least 50 startled workers.

In fact, Mr. Marriott is so involved in every detail of his business that he selects the color of the carpeting for hotel lobbies. Some managers argue that this style can usurp decision making from lower levels and cause resentment. But Marriott Hotels' occupancy rate is 10% above the industry average, and Mr. Marriott believes his involvement has given the company an advantage. "The edge in this business is people," he says. "I'm trying to communicate that I care and that the role they play in the organization is an extremely vital one."

While Mr. Marriott queries employees, Mr. Baute, the plain-spoken 57-year-old chief executive of Markem Corp., calls on customers, especially those with complaints. "I don't like to make honey-and-roses calls," he says. "I like to go where I can make a difference." Besides, he adds, "if you only want to hear the good news, you miss most of what's happening."

During a recent trip to the Far East, Mr. Baute visited a customer in Tokyo who was having difficulty using one of Markem's printing machines. After a quick call to a company engineer, Mr. Baute was able to show the customer how to adjust the machine.

Sometimes a customer's complaints aren't justified. "I've had people tell me that we didn't send them what they wanted only to find out later that they didn't order correctly," he says, noting that "you have to be careful to check out the information you collect."

Nevertheless, Mr. Baute, who spends 25% of his time visiting customers, believes his emphasis on service has helped Markem enlarge its market and win back a few disgruntled buyers since he took over as chief executive four years ago. Revenue at the closely held company last year approached $100 million.

Customer Complaints

At Markem's Keene, N.H., headquarters, Mr. Baute answers his own office phone. He also insists that the company's 1,200 managers and workers listen to tapes of customers from more than a dozen industries, describing their diverse needs. "It's not Joe the chairman talking, it's the person paying the bills," he says. "There's a lot more credibility when employees hear complaints directly from the customer."

Not all direct contact yields reliable information. As chief executive of Frito-Lay Inc., Michael H. Jordan used to marvel at the quality of the potato chips he sampled at the company's Dallas plant. Then he discovered that plant supervisors hand-picked potatoes in preparation for his visits and made sure he sampled only perfectly shaped chips. From then on, Mr. Jordan sampled potato chips that he purchased off supermarket shelves.

Embarrassing Questions

In another attempt to get the facts, Mr. Jordan, who is now the executive vice president of parent PepsiCo Inc., installed a computer terminal at his desk to monitor business. The computer provided him with data on everything from inventories and sales to marketing. "I wanted some raw facts that hadn't been scrubbed by layers of management," he explains.

To uncover the truth, executives also have to overcome human obstacles. Workers may feel intimidated and awkward talking openly to the top boss. "When I first started visiting plants, managers were apprehensive," says Markem's Mr. Baute. "They thought workers might ask embarrassing questions, like why didn't they get raises." But as it turned out, "employees were afraid. We had to work like the dickens to convince them there would be no retribution" if they spoke honestly.

Quentin C. McKenna, the chief executive of Kennametal Inc., a Latrobe, Pa., cutting-tool maker, always travels alone when visiting one of the company's 43 manufacturing and sales sites. It's an approach he adopted three years ago in an effort to raise employee productivity and involvement. His visits are announced—a surprise call once caused "panic" among workers, he says. But by traveling without an entourage of public-relations staff and other corporate lieutenants, he believes he can communicate more easily.

One of his techniques: randomly inviting half a dozen employees to lunch or dinner when he visits their plant. Some employees think the invitation is a prank, and a few even decline. But those who do accept usually provide Mr. McKenna with valuable information. He learned of a union organizing drive at one plant, and at another he discovered that an expensive piece of new equipment wasn't operating.

Rapid Growth

Maintaining contact with employees requires an enormous commitment, executives at many high-growth companies have discovered. At People Express Airlines, for example, Donald C. Burr, the chief executive and founder, acknowledges that "people can get lost quickly when you have very rapid growth." In just four years, the airline, now the nation's 12th-largest carrier, has expanded to 4,000 employees from 250.

Mr. Burr, who requires all employees to do a variety of jobs, used to share tasks, too, from taking reservations to checking baggage. "We'd all put in 12-hour days and share pizza at the end," recalls Gail Taylor-May, a customer-service manager at People's Pittsburgh terminal and one of its first employees. Today, she says, there are newer employees who wouldn't know top executives if they saw them.

Mr. Burr still lectures at orientation sessions for new employees, and, to create more of a community feeling, he is reorganizing the company into smaller operating units. But, he laments, "I can't afford to spend all my time traveling around the system. I have to rely on other people's eyes and ears."

Checks Facts

Other companies, such as Tandem Computers, use technology to link the chief executive with employees. Every morning Mr. Treybig of Tandem switches on his computer terminal and reads at least two dozen new messages from virtually every department and rank in the company. One recent messasge came from an employee in Austin, Texas, who complained that co-workers who had worked for his supervisor at another company were being favored for promotions. When Mr. Treybig checked out the complaint, he found that it was false—and wrote the employee directly to quell his concerns.

Another communications technique is the "beer busts" Tandem holds every Friday afternoon at each of the computer maker's 132 offices world-wide. The intention, says Mr. Treybig, who founded the company in 1974, is to create an informal environment where employees, including himself, can exchange ideas. "People feel intimidated to walk into your office," he says. But over beer and popcorn, "employees are more willing to talk openly."

Mr. Treybig believes that the "beer busts" and electronic mail have helped give Tandem a turnover rate that is half that of competing high-technology companies in Silicon Valley; three-quarters of the 32 original employees are still with Tandem today.

One employee, recalling how he has seen a sweating Mr. Treybig in shorts walking through the company lobby after his daily jog, says, "It makes me comfortable to know that the president is one of the guys. This is a human company."

The Manager: Master and Servant of Power

Fernando Bartolomé and André Laurent

Most managers are action oriented. As a result, many are not inclined to be introspective about how they relate to others on the job. They don't fully realize, for example, how power differences can disturb interpersonal relations at work and, consequently, undermine organizational effectiveness.

Let's look at three typical problems:

Brian Dolan and John Miller, both senior engineers in an electronics company, had worked well as colleagues in their company's R&D department. Their relationship was friendly and informal. Each felt free to drop in unannounced on the other to discuss technical problems or swap company gossip.

Then Brian was promoted to director of R&D, and shortly thereafter he called John and asked him to come to his office to discuss installation plans for the company's new computer-aided design system. The call puzzled and angered John. Brian was only two doors away. Why didn't he just drop by? After all, they were good friends. Why did he have to play the boss? When John went to Brian's office, it was all he could do to hide his irritation. Brian greeted him warmly, but John was reserved during their discussion.

Why, Brian wondered on the trip home that evening, had John acted so oddly? Was it because he had been promoted and not John? That had to be it. John was jealous. John, on the other hand, didn't understand how Brian's new position could make him insensitive to how John might react.

Mary Scarpa, divisional director for a specialty steel fabricator, asked Roger Harrison, a middle manager, for his opinion on a major capital investment decision she was about to make. Roger had serious reservations about the assumptions underlying her cash flow projections. He wanted to level with her, but he also worried that honest criticism would upset her. He knew Mary could be very touchy. Although she had asked for candid feedback, Roger wasn't sure she really meant it; he sensed she really wanted reinforcement. Feeling caught in a bind, Roger conveniently "forgot" her request.

Annoyed by Roger's behavior, Mary complained to a colleague at another company about problems with her subordinates, saying they just wouldn't stick their necks out. They were afraid to give honest opinions because they were insecure, she said. On his part, Roger was insensitive to the reasons why bosses may find it risky to have subordinates challenge their judgment, even when they ask for it.

Dick Rapp, vice president of production for a household appliance manufacturer, told his subordinates that his priority was quality control and cost containment. He wanted defect and scrap rates brought down. He wanted the division to be results driven, not rule driven. "If you have to bend a rule to get the job done, do it," Rapp would say.

His employees took him at his word at first and assumed that any improvement in efficiency would be welcome. But they quickly learned otherwise. Dick Rapp cared as much about style and form as he did about substance. How memos were worded and typed, for example, seemed to concern him as much as what they said. He also chewed out several plant supervisors for approving ad hoc scheduling and other changes and not going through the chain of command.

Understandably, this behavior frustrated Dick's subordinates. They faced conflicting expectations, and they had to take time away from important tasks to meet what they considered frivolous demands. No one tried to understand, though, why bosses prefer to have things done their way and how this may be their means of heightening their feelings of being in control and reducing uncertainty. And nobody dared to explore these issues with Dick, nor could he see that he was sending mixed messages and burying people in the very red tape he wanted them to cut through.

How did these situations develop? Did Brian Dolan subconsciously need to pull rank on subordinates? Did Mary Scarpa relish putting her employees in a double bind? Did Dick Rapp enjoy tripping up his people? Were the subordinates rebellious people, unwilling to accept authority and take direction?

Such problems occur with surprising frequency in work situations. Usually they arise not because superiors are inherently insensitive or power hungry or because subordinates are naturally rebellious but because people don't understand how strongly hierarchical position affects behavior in organizations. Workplace conflicts are often attributed to personality differences, but the root of the problem is usually structural. The organization's power hierarchy can distort mutual expectations.

Power in the Organization

Unevenness of power in the organization subtly influences how managers and subordinates relate to each other. Mary couldn't understand Roger's reticence. But if she had reflected on her own experiences as a subordinate, she might have realized that she too had been cautious at times about giving honest feedback to superiors. Had Brian been able to put himself in John's shoes and think of a new R&D director officiously summoning *him,* he might have better understood John's behavior.

Dick was a results-driven manager who said he cared about quality, not style. Today he works for superiors whose preference for ritualistic, by-the-book action frustrates him. Yet he can't see that he's doing the same thing. He doesn't relate his own experience as a subordinate to the feelings and behavior of the people working for him.

Brian, Mary, and Dick all had trouble putting themselves in their subordinates' shoes. In subordinate roles, on the other hand, John and Roger couldn't see how it might feel to be a boss. This lack of sensitivity on both sides can have ripple effects throughout the organization. Managers who believe they are on the receiving end of unreasonable or unfair actions from their bosses, for example, may act similarly toward those below them in the organizational pyramid. And the pattern may repeat itself down the chain of command. Or relations with peers may suffer. A troubled relationship at one level can affect many other relationships.

When superiors can't see how their behavior affects their subordinates, their authority may also deteriorate. Most bosses know instinctively that their power depends more on employees' compliance than on threats or sanctions. When managers create no-win situations for people, as Mary did, or make confusing demands on workers, as did Dick, subordinates may respond by losing enthusiasm or withdrawing commitment. If workers think they've been put in impossible situations or if a superior's exaggerated need for power makes them feel inferior, they may give the company their worst rather than their best. The response could mean just going through the motions of the job or even sabotaging organizational goals.

True, managers have power. They can call on official sanctions for punishing uncooperative subordinates. But such blatant use of their clout is rarely able to restore effective working relationships. It is a weak rather than a strong pillar of authority.

There are other consequences arising from this asymmetry in power relations and role perceptions, as we can see when we look at managers as subordinates. If the danger for superiors is being insufficiently sensitive about their subordinates' potential reactions, the danger for subordinates tends to be excessive concern about superiors' potential reactions. Managers who worry excessively about offending their bosses are much less likely to defend subordinates when higher-ups deal unfairly with them.

But if a manager doesn't defend subordinates, he or she will lose their respect. When subordinates sense that the boss won't defend them against unfairness, their morale will plummet and they will withdraw commitment to the job. A vicious circle results. As their performance deteriorates, their superior's position weakens further. The boss will receive fewer rewards and resources to dispense to subordinates, thus further undermining his or her effectiveness as distinct from merely titular authority.

It's ironic that so many managers are insensitive to this problem because almost all managers occupy a dual position in the organization. They have subordinates who report to them, and they report to superiors. Being both masters and servants of power, they should be able to understand the perspectives of the two groups of people who play the most important roles in their professional lives—namely, their superiors and subordinates.

To probe this duality of the manager's role and the sharp differences in expectations that power differences create, we recently collected questionnaires from 105 executives of major companies. We divided the people into two similar groups, matched according to age, management position, and other characteristics. We asked one group of managers to describe the expectations they had for their superiors, the second, to describe expectations for subordinates. In addition, we had conversations with a number of the executives we surveyed.

. . . The expectations of the two groups differed sharply. Of the managers we asked to take the superior role, 78% said they are primarily concerned about subordinates' performance. A majority also said they expect subordinates to be loyal and honest. A typical comment was "I expect effective performance and loyalty even when difficult or unpleasant duties have to be performed."

The superiors we talked to view loyalty, honesty, and performance as linked. They also see honest communication and a willingness to follow orders as necessary to get the job done. But at the same time, they don't see the potential conflict that lies in demanding loyalty and desiring honesty and frankness from subordinates. Many seem unaware of the extent to which they confuse loyalty with agreement and obedience. They also seem to underestimate the difficulty subordinates have in being honest about their own problems or weaknesses with people who have so much influence on their careers.

What happens when the shoe is on the other foot?

When managers take the subordinate position, they expect leadership and good communication from their superiors. A director of finance we talked to said, "I expect my superior to give me clear messages about what he expects from me." A vice president of engineering commented, "The boss should establish his requirements absolutely clearly."

Why do subordinates want clear communication and decisive leadership from their superiors? One reason is that they need reassurance that their bosses are competent. Clear communication is a good measure of competence. Subordinates also want to minimize uncertainty in their environment. Clear communication reduces guesswork. But decisiveness and clarity of communication alone aren't enough. Our interviews revealed that subordinates also want consistency.

Managers in both interview groups gave initiative and autonomy much lower ratings than we had expected. Fewer than a third of the people who took the superior role said they expect initiative from subordinates. Only 37% of those in the subordinate position said it is important for their superiors to grant them autonomy. This is odd when one considers how strongly management experts today endorse job autonomy and broad participation in decision making.

Subordinates don't want superiors to be constantly peering over their shoulders. Instead, they want enough leeway to do the jobs as they see fit. "The boss shouldn't interfere in details," a sales manager said, and "My manager should give me enough space to do my job," said an administrative officer.

Subordinates also want fair performance appraisals, support, and encouragement. Another sales manager said, "My superior should show fairness, objectivity, honesty, and a willingness to give feedback without my having to ask for it." A division manager answered, "I expect help, encouragement, and coaching, and the opportunity to learn from my mistakes." And an R&D director reported, "I expect support in conflict situations."

Managers as Superiors

As bosses, managers are not only often unaware of how they misuse their power in relation to subordinates, but they are also frequently unaware of the contradictory messages they send and their motives for doing so. For example, they may tell subordinates that they expect them to be candid and to feel free to offer criticism. Yet at the same time, they communicate disapproval of candid feedback through subtle and sometimes not so subtle cues.

Managers may even confuse excessive deference (pleasing behavior) with the normal level of compliance that they feel they have a legitimate right to expect. They may not see the ways in which they signal to subordinates demands for excessively deferential behavior—and they are also often unaware of the deep resentment that these demands produce.

In the superior role, most managers say that they are more concerned about their subordinates' performance than with obedience for its own sake or with workers doing things the boss's way. Despite the overt message they send, however—"good performance is what really counts in my department"—many managers communicate subtly to subordinates that obedience and deference are just as important, if not more so. This is usually subconscious on the managers' part.

Most executives have trouble learning about the expectations their subordinates have of them simply because they are rarely forthright about how they'd like *their* bosses to behave. Actually, most subordinates work hard to adapt their behavior to what they think the boss expects. Although the chief's actions may be very frustrating to them, few will express openly their dislike of the behavior or try to persuade the boss to change—even when invited to criticize.

This reticence can lead to surprising angry outbursts when smoldering resentment suddenly surfaces. The superior ends up wondering, "Why didn't you come to me earlier with this problem?" Bosses will often deny blame and claim they've always had an open-door policy. Many apparently assume that such a policy alone is sufficient to guarantee a fully open relationship and to minimize the effects of power.

Managers as Subordinates

As subordinates, managers develop an exaggerated concern over pleasing their bosses because they believe they have very little power to change the superior's behavior. Whatever the boss's rhetoric may be, they are convinced they know the real score. As a result, they spend much time scrutinizing the boss's behavior for cues that indicate approval or disapproval.

As one manager put it, "I suppose it's true: I study [my manager's] likes, dislikes, and other personal tastes; his objectives and motivations and the time pressure he may be under." One division head said of his superior, "I take into account how his thinking differs from mine, what things he is likely to view in a different way."

Managers as superiors know how much they depend on their subordinates' performance and, therefore, how much real power, as opposed to formal power, their subordinates have over them. But when bosses are subordinates, they often forget this reality of organizational life. They forget that the boss's performance depends heavily on how committed the subordinates are to their jobs and on the quality of their work. Consequently, the subordinates often seem to focus too much on accommodating their superiors' stylistic preferences and not enough on performance per se. They don't always recognize that they possess real power that they can use with their bosses to negotiate and obtain satisfaction for their legitimate needs and demands. They seem unable to transfer their experiences as bosses to their behavior as subordinates.

Because subordinates perceive themselves as being too weak to alter their superiors' behavior, managers in the subordinate role are extremely concerned with whether they have a natural match ("good chemistry") with their bosses. When relating to subordinates, on the other hand, managers don't seem concerned about compatibility. They assume that their subordinates can easily learn to conform to their expectations and that this reshaping of behavior will not harm the organization. In reality, however, having to adapt like this is likely to keep subordinates from making a full contribution. In most cases, inhibiting people this way creates resentment.

Consequences of Power

When managers fail to understand how deeply the unequal distribution of power can hurt interpersonal relations and productivity, serious problems can arise from the organization. The most important and pervasive negative effect of the hierarchical structure can be summarized in the saying, "Trust flees authority." Good ideas often remain unexpressed because subordinates believe they will be punished for disagreeing with their superiors or showing too much competence. Honest feedback about the superior's managerial style is withheld because subordinates are afraid they'll be blackballed when decisions on promotions are made.

Reducing the upward flow of ideas and feedback can have many adverse consequences. Take, for example, the many MBO programs that run into difficulty. An honest contract between superiors and subordinates, based on a fair exchange of contributions and rewards between the individuals and the organization, should be at the core of an MBO program. This is only possible, however, if subordinates feel that they will not be punished for defending their interests or balking at unreasonable demands from the top. Unfair MBO agreements may work in the short term, but they will usually fail in the long haul.

When managers are dissatisfied with the contracts they have with their bosses, unfair contracts may follow at each level down the ladder. Such a pattern can damage management's credibility as well as the whole organization's authority.

What Can Managers Do?
Nobody is to blame for these distortions of hierarchical power. The problem is inherent in organizational life because authority differences are both inevitable and also functional to a degree. The problem cannot be avoided, but it can be controlled if managers strive to link their two roles as masters and servants of power.

When they are in the superior role, they should ask themselves, "How would I feel if my boss behaved this way or demanded this of me?" For example, Brian in our first case might have stopped to think, "I need to talk to John, but if I summon him, he may think I'm trying to remind him that I got the promotion and he didn't. And why, after all, am I doing this? Can't I get the information just as well by phone? Come to think of it, I remember the time I got angry when *my* boss asked me to come running on a moment's notice."

Managers can also ask whether the tasks they assign to subordinates are truly critical to the job—as distinct from ritualistic demands motivated by an unconscious desire to show people that "rank has its privileges" or to reassure themselves that they can make people do what they want them to do. "Power: use it or lose it," as another saying goes.

The burden for getting relationships back on a healthy basis falls mainly to bosses because they have more power and because it would be unrealistic to expect subordinates to take the initiative and complain about their bosses' unreasonable or unfair conduct. Even if superiors encourage honest feedback, people rarely believe that they mean it. So, generally they won't risk testing the boss's sincerity.

When they are the superior, managers need to ask themselves, "What can I do to increase my employees' trust, or at least decrease their mistrust? What signals may indicate problems?" Managers need to learn to monitor subordinates' subtle cues. It helps to understand that it's easier for subordinates to learn about bosses' reactions and desires because superiors are more likely to express their feelings openly. By the same token, it's more difficult for bosses to find out their subordinates' real feelings; they're likely to express them indirectly and with caution.

Directly questioning subordinates rarely works when you're trying to find out what's wrong. Managers must look for subtle cues. Eventually, they can create the necessary atmosphere of trust for solving problems, but they can't do it instantly. It will come only from consistently demonstrating fairness and honesty toward the people working for them.

In the subordinate role, on the other hand, managers may find that they can more easily manage their relationships with superiors by just asking them what they want. This approach should work with competent and insightful superiors. But for some people, asking questions may not be enough; observing behavior is often equally important. Once again, the managerial subordinate should take advantage of his or her own experience as a boss and ask, "What do I care most about when I'm in the superior role?" Managers who can answer this question insightfully and realistically should be able to move ahead in the important process of understanding and managing their own superiors.

The Younger Boss: Green over Gray Needn't Lead to a Clash

Marilyn Machlowitz

Authority has long been associated with age. So executives and professionals who supervise people older then themselves face a special kind of management challenge.

A youthful college president attended his first meeting of a prestigious educational association. His counterparts mistook him for a waiter.

An international lawyer looked so young that opposing counsel assumed she was a secretary. They handed her some critical documents to photocopy.

It's usually best for the young executive not to make much of a fuss about such embarrassing incidents. Sometimes it is even possible to turn them to one's advantage: The lawyer wished she had been given more sensitive documents to copy.

But aside from being mistaken for a "gofer," the young manager must learn how to assert his authority when he doesn't fully look the part. Since authority has also been associated with sex, young woman bosses operate against a double whammy. Such expressions as "fair-haired boy" have few feminine equivalents.

Some young bosses try to appear older. Clothes do the trick for some, while the "boy wonder" beard works for others. These can be a disservice, however, if they only emphasize the person's youth because of the contrast to his countenance.

Others flaunt their youth, mentioning it before anyone else can as a sort of preemptive strike. Youth offers some protection in that even ordinary performance may be judged extraordinary for someone who is a mere 22. But this defense calls into question one's legitimacy as a decision maker and supervisor.

Perhaps the greatest danger is an inconsistency that confuses subordinates. As the young person inexperienced at exercising authority experiments, he may overdo it on occasion and then back off to compensate. Unsure of how to behave, he may unwittingly reduce his legitimate authority by trying to be overly chummy or by retreating to the role of a precocious child.

A second problem for young bosses is finding peers. Contemporaries may be several levels lower and counterparts may be 20 years older. Peer support is helpful both personally and professionally, and the young high achiever makes a mistake if he places a high value on seeming self-sufficient and has trouble seeking assistance. At the same time, some senior people may feel threatened by the younger person's rate of progress and be reluctant to assist anyone who seems to be advancing very well as it is.

In such circumstances, it often helps to seek superiors, sponsors or friends who have enjoyed similar fast starts. Such people probably won't feel any need to show you a thing or two to put you in your place, and may extend themselves. Alair Townsend held responsible positions while still in her 20s. Now older and budget director for New York City, she is said to have organized lunch-time seminars for bright young people on her staff to keep them involved, interested and informed.

The mere presence of a young new boss creates ripples throughout a department. These seem to occur in the following sequence. The first is psychological: Your older subordinates' pride is hurt. The second is political: They feel you may be blocking their paths. The third is practical: They worry that your knowledge and values may be a generation apart from theirs.

These reactions are understandable, and there may not be much you can do about them initially. It's important to recognize, however, that any animosity isn't directed at you personally. So don't be defensive.

At the same time, don't come on like Gangbusters. Don't hide your expertise, but don't boast about it either or others will try to knock you off the pedestal. When Michael Weisman became an associate producer at NBC Sports at 24, he says, he made a point not to "come in and start pushing people around. I came in very humble and was very appreciative of whatever they could add."

Don't behave as though you're just passing through. It can rile your staff to think that the position that might be the capstone of their careers is just a stepping stone for you.

Extend yourself to others, especially if you come in from outside. When Donna Shalala became president of Hunter College in her 30s, she reportedly went to meet faculty members in their own offices, instead of asking them to come to hers. Be tactful. Don't refer to those who've labored long and hard for your company by such derogatory terms as "lifers" or "old-timers."

Don't assume that problems have to develop. Such situations may be hard, but they need not be horrid. T. George Harris, editor-in-chief of American Health magazine, is 26 years older than his publisher and boss, Owen Lipstein. Mr. Harris explains: "Time and time again, there are things I want to try out that most publishers would say 'No' to, but we work them out." His conclusion? "Owen is the best publisher I've ever worked with."

Listen to Your Whistleblower

Michael Brody

Smart managers find out about nasty problems before the story shows up on the 11 O'Clock News. One increasingly popular way to do that: Set up a hot line to the top, answered by someone called an ombudsman, and encourage employees to use it.

The phone rings at home late one evening. At first your caller will not give his name. After you have assured him three times that your office *is* confidential, you are asked to an early morning breakfast in the crowded anonymity of a restaurant downtown. Over breakfast a very nervous research manager from your company describes a serious problem brought to him by two of his engineers.

The manager wants first to tell you about his loyalty to the company, his 100% commitment to his boss, the hours of hard work he put in to try to prevent this from happening. Then comes the problem: The two young engineers began last week to do thorough tests of new equipment the company is producing for the Defense Department. The tests indicate some production problems. Even worse, there may be serious design flaws. The equipment may not be safe to use.

Worse yet, the first shipments went out a week ago. The manager admits that very little of the testing required by the contract ever got done. He has been working around the clock; so have his people. But critical deadlines slipped away, and no one at the top was willing to wait for adequate testing. His immediate superior insisted on shipping the equipment to meet the contract deadline.

It's a possible disaster in the making for the company. And now it's your baby. How will your top management respond?

In too many bureaucracies, corporate or otherwise, the boss's attitude to disturbing whispers from below approximates that of the witch in the film *The Wiz:* "Don't bring me *no* bad news." Then the bad news gets out, and the company's reputation takes a pounding. Just ask Manville Corp. or Morton-Thickol. The lesson: If bad news isn't dealt with in-house, public whistleblowing by employees can generate disastrous headlines, *60 Minutes* specials, inquiries by state and federal regulatory agencies, congressional investigations, and multimillion-dollar class-action lawsuits. Sadly, this is true even if the whistle-blower turns out to have been wrong, as Karen Silkwood was in accusing Kerr-McGee Corp. of covering up defective welds in nuclear fuel rods.

Making sure that bad news gets passed up the chain of command is a topic receiving a lot of attention in executive suites these days. Many companies have long had "open door" policies. IBM, for example, guarantees the right of any employee to appeal a supervisor's decision without fear of retaliation. But in the past few years, dozens of other major companies have set up formal "ombudsman" systems, in which a senior executive operating outside the normal chain of command is permanently available at the end of a hot line to deal with employee grievances and alarms on a confidential basis.

The name "ombudsman," off-putting enough in the original Swedish—the word was coined as the name for a civil servant who investigates citizen complaints about government bureaucracy—is even worse in its sensitized form, ombudsperson. But after kicking around for years, the idea appears to be catching on in the U.S. The four-year-old Corporate Ombudsman Association (from whose training materials the whistleblowing scenario above is borrowed) already includes many members of the FORTUNE 500, from Anheuser-Busch to Control Data to Upjohn. In the discreet spirit of her trade, the association's president, professor Mary Rowe of MIT, will not release the membership list. Dozens of other companies, ranging from McDonald's to Martin Marietta, have ombudsmen but aren't in the association.

Companies untouched by scandal have set up such hot lines as a healthy preventative. Others have introduced the system only after public embarrassments. The latter group includes some big defense contractors. General Electric, after disclosures of fraudulent billing in its defense electronics business just over a year ago, pulled executive John Peterson out of the company's internal financial controls operation and put him in charge of an ombudsman office.

Most defense firms insist that the new systems are part of an overall interest in improving internal communications and business ethics, not just a response to scandal. At McDonnell Douglas, for example, both McDonnell

Aircraft in St. Louis and Douglas Aircraft in Long Beach, California, have set up ombudsman programs in the past year. In a report for other interested companies, the St. Louis operation takes pains to characterize its system as far broader than just a hot line for "snitching" on waste, fraud, and abuse. Ombudsmen Virgil Marti in St. Louis and Gene Dubil in Long Beach have found that most of their cases concern corporate housekeeping matters: conflicts with supervisors, arguments over promotions and transfers, claims of discrimination, misunderstandings over benefits. Most such problems can be sorted out by a direct call to the department head involved, without invoking higher authority. Only a few calls have raised questions as to the safety of a product design or the billings on a defense contract.

A single important phone call, of course, could convince a chief executive that his ombudsman is his own best friend. Nationwide the grapevine among ombudsmen buzzes with rumors of potential front-page scandals they have averted, from the dumping of hazardous wastes to airline disasters. As might be expected, though, companies are loath to talk about scandals that no one else ever heard of because the company's system caught them in time.

The sort of engineering disputes that could trigger public outcry about defective products are obviously among the most sensitive subjects. At Douglas, ombudsman Gene Dubil, the former head of engineering for the company, says that he has received only one safety-related complaint from an engineer in the past six months. Dubil told the man that it didn't sound to him like a safety problem, but that the employee, if he chose, could jump ranks to take it up with the vice president for engineering. At Martin Marietta, corporate ombudsman Winant Sidle, a retired general, says he has faced only one engineering-related alarm to date, raised by a young engineer new to the plant. When investigated, it proved to be a false alarm.

Companies that put these systems in place some time back say they are worth the modest cost even if they don't uncover corporate scandals. The sheer number of calls logged—over 3,000 so far this year at General Dynamics, for example—suggests that workers like and trust ombudsmen. By monitoring the complaints, companies can pin-point plants, programs, or managers causing serious morale problems. At AT&T's Bell Labs, ombudsman Martha Maselko says that the costs of recruiting and training a skilled engineer are so high that simply keeping three employees a year from quitting is enough to cover the $200,000-a-year cost of her office.

The savings in legal costs may be substantial as well, and not just from avoiding lawsuits alleging discrimination or sexual harassment. Increasing protection for whistleblowers is a hot trend both in the courts and in the legislatures. Courts in roughly half the states have cut back the employer's traditional right to hire and fire at will, ruling that employees cannot be discharged for refusing to violate state laws or for revealing violations of those laws. Five states—California, Michigan, New York, Connecticut, and Maine—have passed statutes codifying such rights.

The U.S. Senate has passed and sent to the House legislation sponsored by Senator Charles Grassley (R-Iowa) that would strengthen the rights of employees under the False Claims Act, a law that dates from the Civil War. That act already allows a whistleblower fired by a government contractor to sue his boss in the federal courts for defrauding the government. Grassley's bill would impose triple damages and a criminal penalty of up to $1 million if the case is proved; the whistleblower could collect his attorney's fees and up to 30% of the funds recovered. Two major suits are already pending against defense contractors under the existing act: one against TRW Inc. over what is alleged to be falsified billing on defense contracts; the other against FMC Corp., filed by an engineer dismissed after he claimed that the company had falsified test results for the controversial Bradley armored troop carrier.

Not everyone is a fan of the ombudsman system. Former Du Pont chairman Irving Shapiro thinks an extensive personal grapevine is a top executive's best protection against nasty surprises; his own version of management by wandering around, he notes, was "doing a lot of business in the men's room." In a company where everyone knows the boss wants to hear about things, Shapiro suggests, if the engineers down below are arguing with their superiors over the safety of some product, "there will be someone along the line who will get on the phone and call the boss and say, 'We've got a problem you'd better know about.' "

But in corporations that have not traditionally fostered upward communication, traditional methods may not suffice. A companywide 800 number to an executive with clout can go a long way to encouraging troubled employees to speak up—before they speak out.

6

Controlling

While the previous sections have had a number of specific themes, a few ideas have been common to all of them. One such theme is that organizations are composed of individuals who have needs and interests that are, at least in part, unique to themselves. A second common theme is that organizations are superimposed on less formal relationships among people and that the formal systems that organizations employ create other new patterns of relationships and new sets of interests. Third, we have suggested that the major function of managing is to achieve coordination among the activities of individuals and groups that have these diverse interests.

In the sections on organizing, influencing, and communicating, we have seen a number of ways that managers work to achieve such coordination. A fundamental question is: How does controlling differ from these other activities? In an important way, it does not—controlling entails a set of activities designed to achieve coordination. On the other hand, controlling has a quite different connotation than do words such as influencing and communicating; controlling implies greater inequalities of power and less mutuality than do the others. For instance, Webster's dictionary defines the verb "control" as "To have under command; to regulate; to check; to restrain; to direct."[1] In contrast, "to influence" is defined as "To act on the mind, to sway, to bias; to induce."[2] Guided by the word "control" and the connotations it evokes, managers' efforts to coordinate often lead them to mechanistic approaches that are detached from the organic system they are attempting to improve. The reality of the matter is that they need a balance of the two.

As several of the articles in this section (for example, Mrs. Fields' "Secret Ingredient") reveal, control devices, even mechanistic ones, contribute much to the effectiveness of organizations—without them, the organization balkanizes. It must be stressed that the key is fit. Regardless of the type of control device, it must be related to the requirements of the business and not become an end in itself. Also, it must be understood by the people in the system and consistent with the human system embodied in the organization. If it is not, the results can be disastrous. All of us can cite many examples where a control system itself interferes with the organization achieving its ends. When employees become concerned with looking good as judged by standards that are only partially related to the goals of the organization something is wrong with the control system.

The articles also show the integral relationships between the attitudes and values of human beings and the technologies used in controlling. Sophisticated technology can be extremely helpful or it can create colossal new problems, depending on how it is related to the organic nature of the organization. In fact, as "A 'Virus' Gives Business a Chill" suggests, sophisticated control systems are extremely vulnerable to human error and deliberate sabotage.

Other articles demonstrate the need for control. "The Evolution of Corporation Man," for example, reveals that organizations themselves help to create a mind set in people that leads to waste—"It's the corporation's money." The demand for "Accountants Who Specialize in Detecting Fraud" shows that fraud directed against the company is a major concern.

Several of the articles indicate how important it is to understand the relationship between the control activities and the human beings who run and are subject to them. The control system is one of the most direct ways that organizations use to imprint their goals on human beings. Among other things, the control system affects people's expectations. If the expectations are too high or too low, the organization is heading for problems. When viewed in this way, we see that controlling is very much like influencing—it is less concerned with commanding people than with influencing their minds.

Obviously, managers must find ways to balance the controlling and influencing roles played by control systems. In our opinion, control systems often do too much of the former and too little of the latter. You may not agree, but we suggest keeping this thought in mind as you read the section.

References

1. *Webster's Dictionary* (Larchmont, N.Y.: Book Essentials Publications, 1981), p. 86.
2. *Ibid.*, p. 193.

Mrs. Fields' Secret Ingredient

*The real recipe behind the phenomenal
growth of Mrs. Fields Cookies cannot
be found in the dough*

Tom Richman

Part of the late Buckminster Fuller's genius was his capacity to transform a technology from the merely new to the truly useful by creating a new form to take advantage of its characteristics. Fuller's geodesic designs, for instance, endowed plastic with practical value as a building material. His structures, if not always eye-appealing, still achieved elegance—as mathematicians use the word to connote simplicity—of function. Once, reacting to someone's suggestion that a new technology be applied to an old process in a particularly awkward way, Fuller said dismissively, "That would be like putting an outboard motor on a skyscraper."

Introducing microcomputers with spreadsheet and word-processing software to a company originally designed around paper technology amounts to the same thing. If the form of the company doesn't change, the computer, like the outboard, is just a doodad. Faster long division and speedier typing don't move a company into the information age.

But Randy Fields has created something entirely new—*a* shape if not *the* shape, of business organizations to come. It gives top management a dimension of personal control over dispersed operations that small companies otherwise find impossible to achieve. It projects a founder's vision into parts of a company that have long ago outgrown his or her ability to reach in person.

In the structure that Fields is building, computers don't just speed up old administrative management processes. They alter the process. Management, in the Fields organizational paradigm, becomes less administration and more inspiration. The management hierarchy of the company *feels* almost flat.

What's the successful computer-age business going to look like in the not-very-distant future? Something like Randy Fields's concept—which is, in a word, neat.

What makes it neat, right out of the oven, is where he's doing it. Randy Fields, age 40, is married to Debbi Fields, who turns 31 this month, and together they run Mrs. Fields Cookies, of Park City, Utah (see "A Tale of Two Companies," INC., July 1984). They project that by year end, their business will comprise nearly 500 company-owned stores in 37 states selling what Debbi calls a "feel-good feeling." That sounds a little hokey. A lot of her cookie talk does. "Good enough never is," she likes to remind the people around her.

But there's nothing hokey about the 18.5% that Mrs. Fields Inc. earned on cookie sales of $87 million last year, up from $72.6 million a year earlier.

Won't the cookie craze pass? people often ask Debbi. "I think that's very doubtful . . . I mean," she says, "if (they are) fresh, warm, and wonderful and make you feel good, are you going to stop buying cookies?"

Maybe not, but the trick for her and her husband is to see that people keep buying them from Mrs. Fields, not David's Cookies, Blue Chip Cookies, The Original Great Chocolate Chip Cookie, or the dozens of regional and local competitors. Keeping the cookies consistently fresh, warm, and wonderful at nearly 500 retail cookie stores spread over the United States and five other countries can't be simple or easy. Worse, keeping smiles on the faces of the nearly 4,500, mostly young, store employees—not to mention keeping them productive and honest—is a bigger chore than most companies would dare to take on alone.

Most don't; they franchise, which is one way to bring responsibility and accountability down to the store level in a far-flung, multi-store organization. For this, the franchisor trades off revenues and profits that would otherwise be his and a large measure of flexibility. Because its terms are defined by contract, the relationship between franchisor and franchisee is more static than dynamic, difficult to alter as the market and the business change.

Mrs. Fields Cookies, despite its size, has not franchised—persuasive evidence in itself that the Fieldses have built something unusual. Randy Fields believes that no other U.S. food retailer with so many outlets has dared to retain this degree of direct, day-to-day control of its stores. And Mrs. Fields Cookies does it with a headquarters staff of just 115 people. That's approximately one staffer to every five stores—piddling compared with other companies with far fewer stores to manage. When the company bought La Petite Boulangerie from PepsiCo earlier this year, for instance, the soft-drink giant had 53 headquarters staff people to administer the French bakery/sandwich shop chain's 119 stores. Randy needed just four weeks to cut the number to 3 people.

On paper, Mrs. Fields Cookies *looks* almost conventional. In action, however, because of the way information flows between levels, it *feels* almost flat.

On paper, between Richard Lui running the Pier 39 Mrs. Fields in San Francisco and Debbi herself in Park City, there are several apparently traditional layers of hierarchy: an area sales manager, a district sales manager, a regional director of operations, a vice-president of operations. In practice, though, Debbi is as handy to Lui—and to every other store manager—as the telephone and personal computer in the back room of his store.

On a typical morning at Pier 39, Lui unlocks the store, calls up the Day Planner program on his Tandy computer, plugs in today's sales projection (based on year-earlier sales adjusted for growth), and answers a couple of questions the program puts to him. What day of the week is it? What type of day: normal day, sale day, school day, holiday, other?

Say, for instance, it's Tuesday, a school day. The computer goes back to the Pier 39 store's hour-by-hour, product-by-product performance on the last three school-day Tuesdays. Based on what you did then, the Day Planner tells him, here's what you'll have to do today, hour by hour, product by product, to meet your sales projection. It tells him how many customers he'll need each hour and how much he'll have to sell them. It tells him how many batches of cookie dough he'll have to mix and when to mix them to meet the demand and to minimize leftovers. He could make these estimates himself if he wanted to take the time. The computer makes them for him.

Each hour, as the day progresses, Lui keeps the computer informed of his progress. Currently he enters the numbers manually, but new cash registers that automatically feed hourly data to the computer, eliminating the manual update, are already in some stores. The computer in turn revises the hourly projections and makes suggestions. The customer count is OK, it might observe, but your average check is down. Are your crew members doing enough suggestive selling? If, on the other hand, the computer indicates that the customer count is down, that may suggest the manager will want to do some sampling—chum for customers up and down the pier with a tray of free cookie pieces or try something else, whatever he likes, to lure people into the store. Sometimes, if sales are just slightly down, the machine's revised projections will actually exceed the original on the assumption that greater selling effort will more than compensate for the small deficit. On the other hand, the program isn't blind to reality. It recognizes a bad day and diminishes its hourly sales projections and baking estimates accordingly.

Hourly sales goals?

Well, when Debbi was running *her* store, *she* set hourly sales goals. Her managers should, too, she thinks. Rather than enforce the practice through dicta, Randy has embedded the notion in the software that each store manager relies on. Do managers find the machine's suggestions intrusive? Not Lui. "It's a tool for me," he says.

Several times a week, Lui talks with Debbi. Well, he doesn't exactly talk *with* her, but he hears from her. He makes a daily phone call to Park City to check his computerized PhoneMail messages, and as often as not there's something from Mrs. Fields herself. If she's upset about some problem, Lui hears her sounding upset. If it's something she's breathlessly exuberant about, which is more often the case, he gets an earful of that, too. Whether the news is good or bad, how much better to hear it from the boss herself than to get a memo in the mail next week.

By the same token, if Lui has something to say to Debbi, he uses the computer. It's right there, handy. He calls up the FormMail program, types his message, and the next morning, it's on Debbi's desk. She promises an answer, from her or her staff, within 48 hours. On the morning I spent with her, among the dozen or so messages she got was one from the crew at a Berkeley, Calif., store making their case for higher wages there and another from the manager of a store in Brookline, Mass., which has been struggling recently. We've finally gotten ourselves squared away, was the gist of the note, so please come visit. (Last year Debbi logged around 350,000 commercial air miles visiting stores.)

Here are some other things Lui's computer can do for him.

Help him schedule crew. He plugs his daily sales projection for two weeks hence into a scheduling program that incorporates as its standards the times Debbi herself takes to perform the mixing, dropping, and baking chores. The program gives him back its best guess of how many people with which skill levels he'll need during which hours. A process that done manually consumed almost an hour now takes just a fraction of that time.

Help him interview crew applicants. He calls up his interview program, seats the applicant at the keyboard, and has him or her answer a series of questions. Based on the answers given by past hirees, the machine suggests to Lui which candidates will succeed or fail. It's still his choice. And any applicant, before a hire, will still get an audition—something to see how he or she performs in public. Maybe Lui will send the hopeful out on a sampling mission.

Help with personnel administration. Say he hires the applicant. He informs the machine, which generates a personnel folder and a payroll entry in Park City, and a few months later comes back to remind Lui that he hasn't submitted the initial evaluation (also by computer), which is now slightly past due. It administers the written part of the skills test and updates the records with the results. The entire Mrs. Fields personnel manual will soon be on the computer so that 500 store managers won't forget to delete old pages and insert revised ones every time a change is made.

Help with maintenance. A mixer isn't working, so the manager punches up the repair program on the computer. It asks him some questions, such as: is the plug in the wall? If the questions don't prompt a fix, the computer sends a repair request to Park City telling the staff there which machine is broken, its maintenance history, and which vendor to call. It sends a copy of the work order back to the store. When the work gets done, the store signs off by computer, and the vendor's bill gets paid.

That's a lot of technology applied to something as basic as a cookie store, but Randy had two objectives in mind.

He wanted to keep his wife in frequent, personal, two-way contact with hundreds of managers whose stores she couldn't possibly visit often enough. "The people who work in the stores," says Debbi, "are my customers. Staying in touch with them is the most important thing I can do."

It's no accident, even if Lui isn't consciously aware of why he does what he does, that he runs his store just about the same way that Debbi ran her first one 10 years ago. Even when she isn't there, she's there—in the standards built into his scheduling program, in the hourly goals, in the sampling and suggestive selling, on the phone. The technology has "leveraged," to use Randy's term, Debbi's ability to project her influence into more stores than she could ever reach effectively without it.

Second, Randy wanted to keep store managers managing, not sweating the paperwork. "In retailing," he says, "the goal is to keep people close to people. Whatever gets in the way of that—administration, telephones, ordering, and so on—is the enemy." If an administrative chore can be automated, it should be.

Store managers benefit from a continuing exchange of information. Of course, Park City learns what every store is doing daily—from sales to staffing to training to hires to repairs—and how it uses that information we'll get to in a minute. From the store manager's perspective, however, the important thing is that the information they provide keeps coming back to them, reorganized to make it useful. The hour-by-hour sales projections and projected customer counts that managers use to pace their days reflect their own experiences. Soon, for instance, the computer will take their weekly inventory reports and sales projections and generate supply orders that managers will only have to confirm or correct—more administrative time saved. With their little computers in the back room, store managers give, but they also receive.

What technology can do for operations it can also do for administration.

"We're all driven by Randy's philosophy that he wants the organization to be as flat as possible," says Paul Quinn, the company's director of management information systems (MIS).

"There are a few things," says controller Lynn Quilter, "that Randy dislikes about growth. . . . He hates the thought of drowning in people so that he can't walk in and know exactly what each person does. . . . The second thing that drives him nuts is paper."

"The objective," says Randy, "is to leverage people—to get them to act when we have 1,000 stores the same way they acted when we had 30."

He has this theory that large organizations, organizations with lots of people, are, per se, inferior to small ones. Good people join a growing business because it offers them an opportunity to be creative. As the company grows, these people find they're tied up managing the latest hires. Creativity suffers. Entropy sets in. Randy uses technology to keep entropy at bay.

He began by automating rote clerical chores and by minimizing data-entry effort. Machines can sort and file faster than people, and sorting and filing is deadly dull work, anyway. Lately he's pushed the organization toward automated exception reporting for the same reason. Machines can compare actual results with expected results and flag the anomalies, which are all management really cares about anyway. And within a few years, Randy expects to go much further in his battle against bureaucracy by developing artificial-intelligence aids to the running of the business.

Understand that it's not equipment advances—state-of-the-art hardware—

that's pushing Mrs. Field's Cookies toward management frontiers. The machines the company uses are strictly off the shelf: an IBM minicomputer connected to inexpensive personal computers. It is, instead, Randy's ability to create an elegant, functional software architecture. He has, of course, had an advantage that the leader of an older, more established company would not have. Because Mrs. Fields is still a young enough company, he doesn't have to shape his automated management system to a preexisting structure. Every new idea doesn't confront the opposition of some bureaucratic fiefdom's survival instinct. Rather, the people part and the technology part of the Fields organization are developing simultaneously, each shaped by the same philosophy.

You see this congruence at corporate headquarters and in the company's operational management organization.

Between Debbi as chief executive officer and the individual store managers is what seems on paper to be a conventional reporting structure with several layers of management. But there's an additional box on the organization chart. It's not another management layer. It transcends layers, changing the way information flows between them and even changing the functions of the layers.

The box consists of a group of seven so-called store controllers, working in Park City from the daily store reports and weekly inventory reports. They ride herd on the numbers. If a store's sales are dramatically off, the store controller covering that geographical region will be the first to know it. If there's a discrepancy between the inventory report, the daily report of batches of cookies baked, and the sales report, the controller will be the first to find it. (It is possible for a smart thief to steal judiciously for about a week from a Mrs. Fields store.) "We're a check on operations," says store controller Wendy Phelps, but she's far more than just a check. She's the other half of a manager's head.

Since she's on top of the numbers, the area, district, and regional managers don't have to be—not to the same degree, at any rate. "We want managers to be with people, not with problems," says Debbi. It's hard, Randy says, to find managers who are good with both people and numbers. People people, he thinks, should be in the field, with numbers people backing them up—but not second-guessing them. Here's where the company takes a meaningful twist.

Problems aren't reported up the organization just so solutions can flow back down. Instead, store controllers work at levels as low as they can. They go to the store manager if he's the one to fix a discrepancy, a missing report, for instance. Forget chain of command. "I'm very efficiency minded," says Randy.

So the technology gives the company an almost real-time look at the minutiae of its operations, and the organizational structure—putting function ahead of conventional protocol—keeps it from choking on this abundance of data.

Some managers would have problems with a system that operates without their daily intervention. They wouldn't be comfortable, and they wouldn't stay at Mrs. Fields. Those who do stay can manage people instead of paper.

If administrative bureaucracies can grow out of control, so can technology bureaucracies. A couple of principles, ruthlessly adhered to, keep both simple at Mrs. Fields.

The first is that if a machine can do it, a machine *should* do it. "People," says Randy, "should do only that which people can do. It's demeaning for people to do what machines can do. . . . Can machines manage people? No. Machines have no feelie-touchies, none of that chemistry that flows between two people."

The other rule, the one that keeps the technological monster itself in check, is that the company will have but one data base. Everything—cookie sales, payroll records, suppliers' invoices, inventory reports, utility charges—goes into the same data base. And whatever anybody needs to know has to come out of it.

Don't enforce this rule, and, says Randy, "the next thing you know you have 48 different programs that can't talk to each other." Technology grown rampant.

Having a single data base means, first, that nobody has to waste time filing triplicate forms or answering the same questions twice. "We capture the data just once," says controller Quilter.

Second, it means that the system itself can do most of the rote work that people used to do. Take orders for chocolate, for instance. The computer gets the weekly inventory report. It already knows the sales projection. So let the computer order the chocolate chips. Give the store manager a copy of the order on his screen so he can correct any errors, but why take his time to generate the order when he's got better things to do—like teaching someone to sell. Or, take it further. The machine generates the order. The supplier delivers the chips to the store and bills the corporate office. A clerk in the office now has to compare the order, the invoice, and what the store says it got. Do they all match? Yes. She tells the computer to write a check. The more stores you have, the more clerks it takes. Why not let the computer do the matching? In fact, if everything fits, why get people involved at all? Let people handle the exceptions. Now, the clerk, says MIS director Quinn, instead of a processor becomes a mini-controller, someone who uses his brain.

The ordering process doesn't happen that way yet at Mrs. Fields, although it probably will soon as Randy continues to press for more exception reporting. You can see where he's going with this concept.

"Eventually," he says, "even the anomolies become normal." The exceptions themselves, and a person's response to them, assume a pattern. Why not, says Randy, have the computer watch the person for a while? "Then the machine can say, 'I have found an anomaly. I've been watching you, and I think this is what you would do. Shall I do it for you, yes or no. If yes, I'll do it, follow up, and so on. If no, what do you want me to do?' " It would work for the low-level function—administering accounts payable, for instance. And it would work at higher levels as well. "If," Randy says, "I can ask the computer now where are we making the most money and where are we making the least and then make a decision about where not to build new stores, why shouldn't that sort of thing be on automatic pilot too? 'Based on performance,' it will say, 'we shouldn't be building any more stores in East Jibip. Want me to tell (real-estate manager) Mike (Murphy)?' We're six months away from being able to do that."

The ability to look at the company, which is what the data base really is, at a level of abstraction appropriate to the looker, is the third advantage of a single data base—even if it never moves into artificial-intelligence functions. It means that Debbi Fields and Richard Lui are both looking at the same world, but in ways that are meaningful to each of them.

The hurdle to be overcome before you can use technology to its best advantage—and that isn't equivalent to just hanging an outboard motor on a skyscraper, as Buckminster Fuller said—isn't technical in the hardware sense. Randy buys only what he calls plain vanilla hardware. And it isn't financial. For all its relative sophistication in computer systems, Mrs. Fields spends just 0.49% of sales on data processing, much of which is returned in higher productivity.

Much more important, Randy says, is having a consistent vision of what you want to *accomplish* with the technology. Which functions do you want to control? What do you want your organization chart to look like? In what ways do you want to leverage the CEO's vision? "Imagination. We imagine what it is we want," says Randy. "We aren't constrained by the limits of what technology can do. We just say, 'What does your day look like? What would you *like* it to look like?' " He adds, "If you don't have your paradigm in mind, you have no way of knowing whether each little step is taking you closer to or further from your goal."

For instance, he inaugurated the daily store report with the opening of store number two in 1978. The important thing was the creation of the report—which is the fundamental data-gathering activity in the company—not its transmission mode. That can change, and has. First transmission was by Fax, then by telephone touch tone, and only recently by computer modem.

Having a consistent vision means, Randy says, that he could have described as far back as 1978, when he first began to create it, the system that exists today. But he doesn't mean the machines or how they're wired together. "MIS in this company," he says, "has always had to serve two masters. First, control. Rapid growth without control equals disaster. We needed to keep improving control over our stores. And second, information that leads to control also leads to better decision making. To the extent that the information is then provided to the store and field-management level, the decisions that are made there are better, and they are more easily made.

"That has been our consistent vision."

Skips and Dots

Earl Shorris

Did we not love mankind, so meekly acknowledging their feebleness, lovingly lightening their burden and permitting their weak nature even sin with our sanction?

The Grand Inquisitor

The amounts were intolerable. It was not a question of three-martini lunches or theater tickets, the man was spending over fifty thousand a year, more than the travel and entertainment budget for the entire regional office. And of course he had receipts for everything but coatroom tips. One issue that might be brought up was whether any of the expenses were legitimate: he entertained only federal officials, senators, and congressmen, and they did virtually no direct business with the government through his division.

On the other hand, the man had been assistant to the under-secretary of the Navy during a previous administration. He knew his way around Washington, and the office products division sold everything from paper clips to file cabinets to the government. But the man was assigned to him, and his division sold machinery to manufacturers and parts suppliers.

Fifty-one thousand dollars! He stared at the print-out, awed by the numbers. No other salesman in the division, perhaps in the entire company, spent one tenth of that amount. The man was exactly as the comptroller described him, The Thief of Sans Souci.

The comptroller had other news, as well. He had flagged the print-out of the T&E costs for the region at 173 per cent of budget. There would be trouble. Profit for the division was adversely affected, production for the region was down. A management review was indicated. The comptroller had advised him to get started on his written report to the senior vice-president in charge of marketing.

It was nearly seven o'clock. He had been sitting at his desk with the Dictaphone in his hand for nearly an hour. The office was empty, but for him and the cleaning women who passed through the halls with their carts and dustrags. He stared at the square microphone in his hand, then moved his gaze over to the print-out, and back to the microphone. He was afraid to speak.

Why had he not spoken to the man? The expense accounts passed across his desk, he initialed them, every one. Hadn't he realized what was happening? Why did he permit a man to spend three, four, even six hundred dollars for dinner night after night? Was he out of his mind? Was he getting some sort of kickback? Something was very wrong, perhaps illegal, certainly illegal.

He could hear their questions, he imagined their conclusions, for they were the same conclusions he would reach, given the evidence. He did not know what would happen to him if he did not explain, and he did not know what would happen to him if he did explain.

Fifteen months ago, when the man had first been moved into the Washington regional office, with responsibility for several major accounts in the Baltimore industrial area, he had spoken with him about the rules for expenses. And the man had replied, Yes, I understand that those rules apply in ordinary situations, but my situation is not quite ordinary. You see, I have a dotted line reporting relationship with the vice-chairman. Government relations reports to him, but I don't report to him through them; I'm doing something directly for him. By the way, the sort of thing I'm doing doesn't come cheap. I'll be turning in some very large expense accounts. It's Washington, you know. You can't impress a U.S. Congressman or even his administrative assistant with a bowl of chili and a handful of crackers.

We set sales goals, you know. No matter what you do for the vice-chairman, you'll have to meet your sales goals.

That may be impossible, the new man said.

In this division we meet sales goals or I'll know the reason why.

You'll have to take that up with the vice-chairman.

If the vice-chairman's so interested in you, why aren't you on his staff? He could put you in public relations or finance or government relations. What the hell are you doing here?

The new man smiled indulgently. I guess he wants to be careful about his lobbying costs.

Well, maybe I ought to have something in writing from him on this.

The new man laughed aloud.

Now he wished he had let his naïveté save him. Now he had either to put the whole story in writing in a report that could be subpoenaed or take the blame himself. Should he have known how to handle the situation? Should he have fired the man? What if the man had been lying, if he didn't have any dotted line relationship to the vice-chairman? Should he have known how to bury the expenses? Should he have brought the whole situation to light a year ago?

He turned the Dictaphone on, but he said nothing. The vice-chairman could destroy him. He turned the Dictaphone off. He did not know what to say. He had never been so afraid.

Dotted line and skip-level reporting relationships are so common in business and government organizations that anyone who doesn't have at least one such relationship considers himself marked for failure. These reporting relationships comprise the second structure of organizations, the onion's layers described by Hannah Arendt as the more significant structure of a totalitarian organization.

By superimposing the onion structure upon the pyramid of efficient organization, the leader creates a nest of spies and informers. No man in the organization can ever be secure in anything he says or does. Dread fills him up. He fears the role of originator, knowing that safety lies in immobility. His life becomes a cautious stutter.

It is a curious aspect of totalitarianism, for it limits growth and inhibits innovation. In this respect totalitarian organizations are like the tribal organizations of neolithic man: locked in the circle of stasis. Were the organization to have achieved its impossible goal of totality, the immobilizing tension between the two structures would serve to maintain the status quo; but in the drive for growth the tension of the dual structures produces a contradiction that cannot be other than the seed of destruction of the organization.

A 'Virus' Gives Business a Chill

'Bug' in Software Can Destroy Data

John Markoff

For the first time in the United States, a software "virus," a type of computer program that can secretly spread from computer to computer and potentially destroy stored data, has infected a major commercial personal computer software product.

The incident earlier this month, illustrates a growing hazard for software publishers who must insure that their programs are not inadvertently or intentionally contaminated.

Several major publishers expressed concern about the incident involving the Aldus Corporation of Seattle and acknowledged that they, too, were vulnerable to the deliberately planted programs. They said they were working to minimize the possibility that their software products could be corrupted.

Deliberately Planted

In recent months computer security experts have noted the emergence of vandals and mischief makers who deliberately plant the destructive programs in computer systems. But the latest incident illustrates the increased risk that the rogue programs pose for the nation's businesses that use personal computers. Increasingly, the experts say, companies will have to monitor the software their employees place on personal computers used in the workplace.

Software viruses are so named because they parallel in the computer world the behavior of biological viruses. They are programs, or a set of instructions to the computer, that are deliberately planted on a floppy disk meant to be used with the computer or introduced when the computer is communicating over telephone lines or data networks with other computers.

The programs have the ability to secretly copy themselves into the computer's master software, or operating system, that controls the computer and to be passed to additional floppy disks inserted in the computer. Someone who carried a tainted floppy disk from one computer could pass it to another.

Depending upon the intent of the program, it might do something as benign as print a message on the computer's screen or something as evil as systematically destroy data in the computer's memory.

The latest incident involves a program secretly introduced into Macintosh computer software in December by a group of programmers in Montreal associated with MacMag, a computer hobbyist magazine. It turned up earlier this month in Freehand, a graphics illustration program written for the Macintosh and recently introduced by Aldus. Freehand is expected to become an important tool in computer graphics and desktop publishing activities.

. . . Freehand is normally harmless, programmed to read a Macintosh's internal clock and print a message on Macintosh screens on March 2, the first anniversary of the Macintosh II's introduction. The program then destroyed itself.

The message said: "Richard Brandow, publisher of MacMag magazine, and its entire staff would like to take this opportunity to convey their universal message of peace to all Macintosh users around the world."

But computer security experts said the program could easily have been more sinister, erasing computer files, subtly altering data or even causing the computer to crash.

Aldus officials were not certain how the unauthorized program entered their software, but said the program may have been inadvertently passed to Aldus by Marc Canter, president of Macromind Inc. of Chicago, a contractor that supplies training disks for the Seattle company.

Work Destroyed

Mr. Canter said he discovered the virus program on March 2 when he turned his Macintosh on and the virus program, reading the computer's internal clock, was activated. He said the virus displayed its message and in his case was not harmless—it destroyed his computer's operating system file and work he was preparing.

Other Macintosh owners who had installed the Aldus program or had been contaminated with the rogue program from other sources presumably saw the same message when they turned on their computers on March 2. If they

Message that appeared on Macintosh screen on March 2.

Richard Brandow, Publisher of MacMag, and its entire staff
would like to take this opportunity to convey their
Universal Message of Peace
to all macintosh users around the world.

did not operate their computer that day, the message did not appear later and no damage was done.

Mr. Canter said he believed he had brought the program home on a floppy disk he had obtained at a Canadian computer user group meeting in Montreal. He was given a new computer game for the Macintosh and believes the rogue program was embedded within the game.

Back home, he apparently played the game and passed the program to his Macintosh.

'It's a Real Loss'

Mr. Canter said that the incident had damaged his business relationship with Aldus. "I just don't believe someone would write a program like this unless it's for a mischievous purpose," he said. "For the average user it's a real loss. As a whole to this industry, it's an unbelievably damaging thing."

The MacMag magazine programmers said the program had been spread both by diskette and over on-line information services such as Compuserve.

Mr. Brandow said the program had been placed on several Macintosh computers in the magazine's office for several days in December. He denied that MacMag had intentionally distributed the program. He said the program was written as an experiment to see how far the virus would travel and to illustrate the widespread practice of software piracy. The program ultimately infected several hundred thousand Macintosh computers, Mr. Brandow said.

"We've prevented software piracy, we've made people aware of it," he . . . distributed as part of a three-day production run of the program, manufactured in early February. The company said the number of copies of the program in customers' hands was in the "low thousands." Aldus said it was not planning a product recall but intended to offer customers the option of exchanging their infected diskettes.

The company said it has changed its software production procedures as a result of the incident. "It's like when your home is burglarized," said Kerri McConnell, an Aldus product manager. "You buy an alarm system. We're doing more failsafe checking and we're putting in more safeguards."

Other software publishers said they were taking steps to prevent a similar occurrence.

'Sterilizing' Programs

"We're cognizant that we have a weak point," said Jeffery Harbers, director of application development at the Microsoft Corporation in Redmond, Wash. He said the company was "sterilizing" the software development programs it uses. "However, the thing that happened to Aldus could have happened to us," he said.

The threat of viruses is likely to alter the way companies develop software in the future. "I can see spending more of our development time trying to counterattack terrorism," he said.

Publishers said the task of defending against viruses as well as eliminating more traditional software "bugs" has become a highly complex process because source code—instructions written by programmers—for advanced personal computer applications can frequently grow to more than 400,000 lines of code.

No Guarantees

"We've separated the software development process from quality assurance and testing," said Roy Folk, an executive vice president at the Ashton-Tate Company in Torrance, Calif., "but would I guarantee that there is no way that somebody could beat us? I wouldn't say that."

Aldus said that it was consulting its attorneys about possible legal action. Computer crime experts said the unauthorized programs may violate a number of state and Federal laws, including wire fraud and computer crime statutes.

The programs raise issues of civil law as well. "There's a warning out there for people to be very careful about the code they transfer to other people," said Susan Nycum, a Palo Alto, Calif., lawyer who specializes in computer law. "Due diligence has to go to levels that people historically haven't worried about."

How a Rogue Program Spreads

 1. A programmer creates a program that can secretly bind to another program or a computer operating system and copy itself.

2. The program is placed on a floppy diskette or hidden in a program sent to an electronic information service, or electronic 'bulletin board', where information is exchanged by computer over telephone lines.

3. When an unknowing user inserts the floppy diskette in a computer or retrieves data containing the rogue program from another computer via telephone, a new computer is infected.

4. Once inside the new computer, the program copies itself onto a new floppy diskette or the computer's hard disk.

5. Later, the program is activated according to instructions originally embedded within it by the programmer. It might be set off on a certain date or after making a certain number of copies of itself. The instructions can be as benign as displaying a message or as destructive as the erasure of all the data stored in the computer.

The Evolution of Corporation Man

Antony Jay

O N E of the most important discoveries of my working life was made between 8:30 a.m. and 6:00 p.m. on Thursday, April 9th, 1964.

On Wednesday, April 8th, I left the British Broadcasting Corporation, which I had joined more or less straight from university and military service nine years earlier. At BBC I had been a trainee, a production assistant, a producer, a program editor, a head of department. But at 8:30 a.m. on April 9th I was just me, sitting at my desk at home with a number of writing assignments which I had prudently contracted before giving in my notice. The discovery I had made by 6:00 p.m., to express it the way it appeared at the time, was the enormous amount of work that could be done in a day. Nine years in a great corporation had obliterated the memory of how much time there was if you had no telephone calls, correspondence, minutes, routine meetings, departmental meetings, budget reviews, requests for authorization, annual interviews, policy documents, appointments with visitors, and all the rest of that endless succession of events and non-events that compose the manager's day, and his year, and his life. . . .

But it is not only time that evaporates in large corporations. Money evaporates as well. Just before I left, I went into a stationery shop to buy typing paper, carbons, paper clips, and so on. I actually paid money over the counter for them. Real money, the sort that gets you into theaters and out of restaurants, and buys groceries and furniture and presents for the children. Previously, all stationery was bought for me with corporation money, which bore no relation to human money. It was a purely notional currency that appeared on forms and memos, but never passed through pockets or wallets. Indeed, the budget for a single edition of a weekly program might be more than the producer's annual salary. Dealing with such large sums, it was only worth a very limited effort to save a thousand dollars of corporation money on a fifty-thousand-dollar program budget, even if there were any incentive to do so. By contrast, a thousand dollars of human money could take a year's hard and conscious saving to accumulate. Equally, you could save five dollars by shooting twelve seconds' less film, and five dollars was the difference between a glass of beer and a bottle of wine for supper. But it was impossible to make the connection: corporation money, like corporation time, was simply something that was there. It had to be used up somehow, and each of us was allocated separate quantities of it to achieve various objectives. There was a certain professional pride about keeping to your own budget, but a great deal of corporation money was not on your own budget: carpets, curtains, offices, and any number of other central facilities. These we wheedled and cajoled and argued and fought for without any compunction at all, and if we finished up with more research assistants or film units or studio time than we needed we would not have dreamed of handing any back: we could always use them in some way.

An illuminating manifestation of this attitude toward money appeared when I was discussing with a top executive a proposal which might earn a considerable profit. He was not very interested (it would have meant more work for him) and more or less terminated the discussion by saying, "You realize that even if it made a million dollars a year, that's still only one percent of our gross revenue?" So it was; but it was also a million dollars, which if offered to him privately, in human money instead of corporation money, would have been worth almost any effort or sacrifice. But for all the relationship he felt between it and the money in his wallet, he might as well have been playing Monopoly. But the classic case was the one hundred pounds that the BBC advanced to the comedy writers Frank Muir and Denis Norden for a program that was ultimately canceled. Some time later they received a request from the BBC to send it back, and they replied, "We regret we have no machinery for returning money." This apparently was a completely satisfactory answer, and they never heard about the one hundred pounds again. No individual human would accept such a reason for surrendering one hundred pounds of his own money—but obviously the rules for corporation money are totally different.

Even while I was a member of the BBC I wondered if this attitude to time and money was unique or unusual among corporations. After leaving, I worked with quite a number of big organizations, and realized that in fact the BBC was rather good. (I ought in fairness to point out that the present BBC, after an almost complete change of top management and a going-over from McKinsey's, bears little relationship to the corporation I knew: but even the old BBC would have shuddered at some of the examples of corporate behavior I have since collected.) My favorite instance happened to a friend who was also a free-lance writer. He had worked out a series of comedy commercials for a detergent firm, and the agency was so delighted they fixed up a day-long conference with him and the client at a London hotel. A dozen of them met in a room with pads and pencils and blotters at each place. Around the walls were waiters and waitresses manning three tables, one with urns full of coffee and milk, another groaning under bottles of every conceivable drink, the third piled high with plates of cold ham and chicken and tongue, salads, trifles and cakes, ready for the marathon session. The clients opened the proceedings by saying they thought comedy diminished the dignity of cleanliness. The agency men turned and stared at my friend. He agreed that it might well be so—he was a writer, not a market researcher. They thereupon agreed it was better not to risk it, and the meeting was over. They all trooped out into the London street, but my friend is convinced that he was the only one who was haunted for the rest of the day by the thought of the empty room, spread with a vast banquet which no one was going to eat. But then I suppose it was corporation food.

Accountants Who Specialize in Detecting Fraud Find Themselves in Great Demand

Daniel Akst and Lee Berton

Douglas Carmichael normally deals with numbers. But when he discusses one particular facet of his work, he sounds more like a man who deals with murder.

"When the death of a company (occurs) under mysterious circumstances, forensic accountants are essential," he says. "Other accountants may look at the charts. But forensic accountants actually dig into the body."

So-called forensic accountants—investigators who specialize in uncovering fraud in the ledgers of businesses—are finding their talents much in demand these days. Huge fraud cases—like the one involving ZZZZ Best Co. in California—and an increase in the number of malpractice suits against mainstream accounting firms have brought Mr. Carmichael, an accounting professor at City University of New York-Baruch College, and his fellow investigators into the limelight.

"Forensic accounting is big business," says James Loebbecke, an accounting professor at the University of Utah.

Looking for Fraud

Ideally, a company's regular accountants are supposed to guard against financial finagling. Indeed, the Auditing Standards Board of the American Institute of Certified Public Accountants recently adopted rules that specifically require auditors to look for fraud.

But critics say accountants often muzzle themselves; they are too dependent on the big audit fees that come from the clients they are supposed to police. And when fraud is suspected or a big accounting firm is sued for malpractice, other accounting firms are usually reluctant to assist prosecutors. The reason: Opposing a big firm can jeopardize business opportunities.

That's when forensic accountants are called in. Such individuals are often retirees or professors or are found in small accounting firms. But their work goes far beyond routine auditing.

In a standard audit, accountants test samples of inventory, receivables and payables. They ask banks to confirm the amount of cash in a company's account and send form letters to outside firms that have contracts with the company being audited. The idea is to make sure the other company exists and the contract is real.

But a firm like John Murphy & Associates Inc. in Santa Ana, Calif., goes much further. Digging into the affairs of a hypothetical Jones Corp., for example, Murphy accountants and investigators in many cases will examine each and every document. If there is a contract between Jones Corp. and an equally hypothetical Smith Corp., Murphy will find out who owns Smith. And then the questions begin. Is that person related to someone inside Jones? Is there collusion? Kickbacks?

Last May, the Murphy firm was hired to unravel the tangled affairs of ZZZZ Best, the Reseda, Calif., carpet-cleaning company. Murphy's efforts in that case illustrate the difference between a routine audit and the sleuthing done by forensic accountants to uncover fraud.

Now bankrupt, ZZZZ Best left lenders and shareholders with as much as $70 million in losses, prosecutors say. Its founder, Barry J. Minkow, is in prison, awaiting trial on charges of fraud, money laundering and racketeering.

The Murphy firm was hired after ZZZZ Best board members unaligned with Mr. Minkow became aware of credit-card abuses within the company. The president of the Murphy firm, John Murphy, assigned accountants and conventional investigators to the case.

The investigators first prepared a written profile of every key person involved with the company, including corporate officers, employees and vendors. The investigators relied heavily on vast computer data bases, which are available commercially and can be tapped using a personal computer. Those data bases allowed Mr. Murphy's team to track, among other things, licenses, property records, civil and criminal court cases and liens.

Mr. Murphy says the background work enabled his investigators to learn that several individuals involved with ZZZZ Best had a shady past. He further determined that two key figures in the case owned a separate business, and that one of them lied about it on his 1985 federal income-tax return. The individual who falsified his taxes, Mr. Murphy alleges, teamed up with a third ZZZZ Best figure to try and defraud a major insurance company.

The accountants then began their work in earnest, scrutinizing ZZZZ Best ledgers, contracts, and bank statements. Company checks—there were thousands—were particularly suspect, says William A. Davey, a Murphy accountant, because they tended to be written by hand, in large round numbers, and were often payable to cash.

To facilitate the investigation, the information from every check was entered into a computer equipped with special software. That made it easy to see who received what: Checks made out to different people or firms but paid into the same account could be discovered, and the amounts matched to other documentation, says Drew Maconachy, an accountant on Mr. Murphy's team.

Mr. Maconachy and his associates also analyzed the flow of funds in and out of ZZZZ Best and to two other companies: Interstate Appraisal Services, which gave ZZZZ Best the lucrative building refurbishing jobs that accounted for nearly 90% of its business, and Marbil Management Co., a contractor that was supposedly working on jobs for ZZZZ Best.

The investigative accountants paid close attention to the timing of deposits and withdrawals and soon became convinced there wasn't much in the way of genuine sales at ZZZZ Best. Says Mr. Murphy: "I felt what we had was a monstrous check kite. It was a cash race track."

A Circular Cash Flow?

Murphy accountants say the amounts, dates, and destinations of various checks and deposits indicated that the same money—obtained from ZZZZ Best investors and lenders—was going around and around: from ZZZZ Best to Marbil, back to Interstate, and apparently back yet again to ZZZZ Best.

The purpose of all this movement was to make ZZZZ Best look like a legitimate business, investigators say. Based on that appearance, the company persuaded Drexel Burnham Lambert last year to raise a reported $40 million for it. But the financing fell through last May.

Perhaps the most unsettling discovery made by Mr. Murphy's team was that ZZZZ Best's major source of revenue—its building-refurbishing contracts—appeared to be bogus.

Purportedly, ZZZZ Best had major contracts to refurbish buildings that had been damaged by fire. So Murphy investigators visited supposed refurbishing jobs in Sacramento, San Diego, Santa Barbara, and Dallas. They also contacted local fire and police departments. Their conclusions: There were no fires and no jobs.

Ernst & Whinney, ZZZZ Best's regular auditor, resigned last June after it suspected that one of the company's major contracts was nonexistent. The firm is now one of about 50 defendants being sued by disgruntled shareholders for alleged violations of federal securities and state law. Ernst & Whinney denies wrongdoing and says there isn't any basis for the suit.

Petty Paranoia

Craig M. Mooney
Defense Research Board, Department of National Defence, Ontario, Canada

Since eating a gumdrop, 11 year old Charlotte Sexton hasn't been to Westerville Hawthorne School's Sixth Grade for four days. It seems Charlotte defied a regulation banning eating on buses. Until her parents reassure the driver she will eat no more, Charlotte is not allowed to board the bus. Ray Morris, Westerville

School Superintendent, said the regulation has been in effect at least 17 years. Its purpose is to prevent children from throwing orange peels, apple cores and candy wrappers at each other on the bus, stirring up trouble.

AP News Item, 24 Nov. 1959,
Columbus, Ohio

A couple of years ago, in a moment of bitterness, I coined the name *petty paranoia* to describe a form of minor madness that afflicts many clerks and officials. The occasion was the failure of my watch and my subsequent attempts to ascertain the time by telephone—the only means available to me. To all my pleas the operator coldly and mechanically repeated that they did not give out that information. As a result, I missed a train.

Since then I have intermittently studied this affliction to confirm my hunch that it is an authentic lunacy, and that I have hit upon the right name for it. Further reassurance has come from many friends who, in relating their own frustrating experiences at the hands of institutional robots, have found *petty paranoia* a most felicitous term.

Although it has remained for a psychologist to make the final identification, others have come close to naming it. The philosopher, Henri Bergson, referred to it as "professional automatism." The economist, Thorstein Veblen, called it "trained incapacity." The educationist, John Dewey, spoke of it as an "occupational psychosis." The sociologist, Kenneth Burke, remarked that "people may be unfitted by being fit in an unfit fitness." Harold D. Lasswell, another sociologist, observed that "the human animal distinguishes himself by his infinite capacity for making ends of his means." The irate citizen has frequently referred to it less elegantly as "damned foolishness."

London, Oct. 25 (Reuters).

A Manchester decorator hurled a chair through a window of the Canadian Government's citizenship and immigration offices in London Saturday after a ship sailed for Canada without him.

"I did this because it seemed the only way I could draw attention to this case," Albert Hartwell, 41, said in court.

He said he had applied to emigrate to Canada, filled in the necessary forms, had a medical examination, was accepted, and paid $168 for passage on a ship sailing Saturday.

Five days ago he got a letter saying his wife had to be medically examined.

He said this must have been a mistake as his wife was not travelling with him. He wrote back noting the mistake but received a telegram telling him to bring his wife from Manchester to London. On Friday he was told at the immigration office he could not sail because his wife had not been examined.

The shipping office said he would have to apply for later passage. He went back to the immigration office and explained that having sold his home and left his job he had only enough British money to get through Saturday.

The magistrate said Hartwell seemed to have broken the window in a fit of temper.

He was freed on a charge of willful damage but ordered to pay two pounds, the cost of replacing the window.

Frankfurt, April 9 (Reuters).

Mrs. Lisa Lehr, a German woman, cannot join her husband in the U.S. because she chopped down a tree on government land in 1946, the United States army newspaper Stars and Stripes reports. American consular officials said her action legally constituted "moral turpitude" and automatically barred her from getting a visa.

Winnipeg, Aug. 20 (Toronto Star, Aug. 21).

Dr. Dennis Harmar over-parked at a meter here May 10 and returned to his practice at Swan River where he mailed a $3 cheque to cover the fine. The day after he mailed the cheque a summons arrived. He disregarded it because the cheque was sent in.

A month later he got a letter saying his $3 cheque was inadequate because a summons had been issued and the bill was now $5.30. He consulted his lawyer, and mailed a cheque for $5.30 to Winnipeg, then left on a vacation.

He returned to Swan River Sunday and found another letter from city police court demanding another 15 cents to cover exchange on the cheque. The same letter announced that a warrant had been issued and was in the hands of the RCMP at Swan River.

The next day two RCMP plainclothesmen arrived. The doctor said they hit him hard on the shoulder and tore his heel and pants because he resisted arrest.

He was driven 311 miles to Winnipeg and jailed at Rupert Ave. police headquarters Wednesday night. An hour and a half later his lawyer arrived, he paid a deposit on the $2 fine and over $72 to cover costs.

The court upheld the fine and costs on Thursday and a court official told magistrate M. H. Garton: "We feel we have given Dr. Hamar every opportunity to pay his traffic ticket."

Deputy Attorney-General O. M. Kay suggested the doctor might apply to have the costs remitted. He said the court had followed correct procedure. RCMP are investigating the means of arrest.

On the more humorous side was the case, well publicized a couple of years ago, of the Irishman, Michael Patrick O'Brien, who was kept on the ferry-boat between Macao and Hong Kong for eleven months because he didn't have a passport and nobody at either end would give him one.

Harmless and hilarious was the incident related a while ago in Maclean's Magazine "of the civil servant at Deep River, Ont., in atomic-energy land who thought he had learned all about government red tape until he mailed some superannuation forms to Ottawa. Many days later, back they came. No, there was nothing wrong with the way they were filled out, and the official departmental stamp showed they'd been received in good time. But, explained an accompanying letter, a new regulation said such forms could not be received by the superannuation office unless they had been registered at the post office to ensure delivery. Would he please mail them back and this time would he please register them?"

The newspapers like to feature these stories. They publish them straight, since no comment is needed. Our sympathy is immediate since we too have been similarly entangled. A couple of my personal experiences will bring some of your own favorites to mind.

An unknown cartage firm was bringing me my furniture out of storage from another city. I was to have a certified cheque for fifty-five dollars ready for the driver of the van when the furniture was delivered. Off I went to the bank to get the certified cheque. The clerk verified that I had ample money on deposit and then said I had forgotten to fill in the name of the payee. I said I didn't know it but that I would fill it in when I met the driver of the van. The clerk looked shocked and said no, that wouldn't do; they couldn't certify a cheque unless they knew to whom it was being paid. I asked him what I should do under the circumstances. He said I should phone and find out. I said I didn't know the name or I would. He said then they couldn't certify the cheque. I said all right, but tell me, as a matter of curiosity, why you can't certify the cheque. He said it was the bank rules. I asked what was the reason for such a rule. He flushed and said he didn't want to discuss the matter any more.

I had a most remarkable experience on a train. I work for a firm in Toronto and, at the time, I was living in Brampton, some thirty miles away. My firm was sending me to Ottawa for a week and had provided me with one round-trip set of tickets between Brampton and Toronto, and another between Toronto and Ottawa. I got on the train at Brampton at ten-thirty at night and when the conductor came along I gave him the little streamer of tickets for the Brampton-Toronto trip. He studied them for a while and then shook his head and returned them to me. No good, he said, you'll have to pay your fare. Astonished, I scrutinized the tickets carefully. There were three of them hooked together. One was stamped Brampton-to-Toronto, another Toronto-to-Brampton. I asked him what was wrong with the tickets. He said they were the wrong tickets. I checked them again. Was this the correct railway line? Yes. Was this train going to Toronto? Yes, yes! What was the matter then? He pointed to the bottom one with a trembling finger. It read Toronto-to-Brampton. Wrong ticket, he said. I pointed to the ticket above which read Brampton-to-Toronto. There it is, I said. But that's Brampton-to-Toronto, he said. I know, I said, that's just what I'm doing, going from Brampton to Toronto. He became angry at this and roared that the tickets were no good and was I going to pay my fare? When I replied mildly that I wasn't because these looked perfectly good to me, he stamped off in a rage. I called him back and asked him to explain what the trouble was. He took a deep breath and then rattled off the information that he couldn't tear off the tickets from the top (Brampton-to-Toronto portion); that would make all the rest void. Tickets had to be torn off from the bottom. Round-trip tickets for people starting out *for* Brampton *from* Toronto were hooked together in reverse order to that for round-trip tickets for people starting out *for* Toronto *from* Brampton. According to my tickets (which had been purchased in Toronto) I was supposed to be going *to* Brampton (and return), not *from* Brampton (and return). I thanked him for this lucid explanation, and then remarked that I still couldn't see what difference this really made. At this the conductor lost all patience. Was I going to pay my fare? No! He jumped up and viciously ripped off the *top* ticket (Brampton-to-Toronto), tossed the remainder in my lap and strode away waving his arms and shouting void! void! When, at the end of the week, I returned to Brampton and tendered the remainder of my tickets to the new conductor, he punched and pocketed them automatically and passed on his way.

There is an element of the farcical or a touch of the waking nightmare in these experiences, depending on whether you are onlooker or victim. One is suddenly on the other side of the looking glass where reason is unreason and sanity is insanity. Here in this limbo of ludicrous logic, along with the Hartwells, Harmars, and Lehrs, are adults unborn for the want of a birth-certificate; corpses exonerated by the crimes for which they were hung; heirs disinherited being legally dead; babies bastardized by annulled marriages; and numberless other victims of human ministers who tailor all without exception to their Procrustean beds of rules and procedures.

What strikes us in these bizarre instances is the monstrous irrelevance of the official rulings and actions. The real points, surely, were to get Hartwell on his way to Canada, to reunite Mr. and Mrs. Lehr, to rescue O'Brien from that abominable ferry-boat. But to such imperative realities the afflicted officials are complacently and implacably blind. They deny the validity of any plea made on grounds of sense or compassion. And to any questioning of their technical *fiats* they react with hostile and vindictive defensiveness.

We have the picture of a psychosis. We are looking at behavior that is insane on at least three counts. It is obsessive. It is inappropriate. It is paranoid. What saves those who exhibit it from certification as lunatics is that they are legitimate madmen; they have an occupational warrant and are, therefore, mad within their rights. This may sound extreme. But how do you deem a man mad except by his behavior? Although to himself the lunatic may seem sensible we do not account him sane simply because he is convinced of the reasonableness of his motives and actions. Instead, we judge him mad for the want of good sense, propriety, and flexibility in his behavior as a social member. To himself the afflicted clerk or official seems sensible. It is true that there is always his side of the story. But this does not exonerate him. A respectable citizen is picked out of the gutter on a Saturday night and nonchalantly thrown into the cells to sober up. He dies there and the Monday morning investigation reveals that he was not drunk but in a coma—from a heart attack, or epilepsy, or malaria, or concussion, or diabetes. The police side of the story hardly matters—the man is dead. A woman in labor pleads for bed and attention in the admitting office of a hospital; the defence of the officials that before she can be admitted she must fill out biographical forms and prove financial responsibility is nonsense. There is only one side here and that is the imminent and irreversible fact of childbirth. Paramount human needs cannot be annulled by technical *fiats*.

Really what else is there to say of agents who exhibit this senseless, stereotyped, and vicious kind of institutional behavior other than that they are suffering from a real and particular kind of madness? It deserves to be recognized and named. And the proper name for it would seem to be petty paranoia.

Petit, in medicine, describes an affliction that is not severe. The corrupt English version, petty, means much the same but carries an extra touch implying spitefulness or meanness. *Paranoia* comes out of the text-books on mental disease. Dr. Menninger *(The Human Mind)* speaks of it as "a slowly progressing tendency to regard the whole world in the light of a system of delusions . . ." Dr. Strecker *(Fundamentals of Psychiatry)* remarks that "the evolution of the delusional system is an amazingly gradual and painstaking process, requiring many years to reach full flowering." Lichtenstein and Small *(A Handbook of Psychiatry)* state: "If certain premises are granted, the superstructure of false beliefs is built by a perfectly logical and understandable series of steps. The thinking processes are formally correct and contact with reality is not usually disrupted. Paranoiacs are quite reasonable and show normal intellectual functioning in all subjects except those allied to the particular delusional system. It is as though the delusional topic were enclosed in a logic-tight compartment walled off from the rest of the personality." Put *petty* in front of this and you have in *petty paranoia* the apt term for what was wrong with the immigration officials, the police, the conductor, and all the rest who behave like them.

In speculating about the origins of the disease we must go beyond the usual "red tape" explanation. It doesn't lie simply in rules and regulations; these are necessary if there is to be any efficiency in running a complicated society. It doesn't lie simply in clerks and officials; we must have these dutiful and reliable agents if organized systems are to operate at all smoothly. It doesn't lie simply in customers and clients because, in the last analysis, it is for them and by them that the whole machinery exists.

We must suppose that *petty paranoia,* like many other kinds of madness, is serviceable. People who develop it do so because they need it. It resolves some kind of conflict for them. The conflict is usually engendered by competing demands or values. We might look, therefore, at the working lives of institutional or professional agents to see if we can find indigenous elements of personal conflict.

Institutional pressures may be a major predisposing factor. Any large institution—railroad, bank, post office, hospital, labor union, police force—necessarily develops internal values bearing on its own stability and well-being. It is, essentially, a social organization. Rooted in its equipments, buildings, history and traditions, it represents a way of life for all the people in it, and to operate it and maintain it become, for these people, ends in themselves—often more important for them than the efficient and sensible performance of the public service which, in crass utilitarian theory, is the sole reason for the existence of the institution.

Thus, for example, internal operating efficiency may be valued more highly by an institution than efficient public service. Here, as sociologist Robert K. Merton, in an article called *Bureaucratic Structure and Personality,* remarked,

"The bureaucratic structure exerts a constant pressure upon the official to be methodical, prudent, disciplined. If the bureaucracy is to operate successfully it must attain a high degree of conformity with prescribed patterns of action. . . . Formalism, even ritualism, ensues with an unchallenged insistence upon punctilious adherence to formalized procedures. This may be exaggerated to the point where primary concern with conformity to the rules interferes with the achievement of the purpose of the organization, in which case we have . . . the bureaucratic virtuoso who never forgets a single rule binding his action and hence is unable to assist many of his clients."

When these peremptory institutional goals and roles get internalized in the individual agents and become for them genuine and paramount, it is not surprising to find them, in their public dealings, acting on *inverted* premises. They no longer see themselves as existing to serve the client; they see the client as existing to serve them.

Further, the institutional nature of the agent's work can contribute to his involutional outlook. It is what the sociologists speak of as routine-versus-crisis. Your problem, your need—such are crises for you; but they are routine for the agent who specifically and continuously deals with them. Whatever your crisis—wanting change for a fifty dollar bill, or seeking a writ of habeas corpus—you want specialized, individual treatment, and you want it promptly. But so does everyone else in the same fix, and your problem is an old one to the agent. Although you, singly, may but once in a lifetime meet the customs inspector, the magistrate, the surgeon, the hangman, it is you as a host who comprise their daily clientele. The agent develops a mundane routine which he prefers to run off with the least trouble and inconvenience to himself. He has become professionally hardened, detached, impersonal. If his job is especially unpleasant, unpopular, or harrowing, this natural hardening process will be further encouraged by his need for the self-protection afforded by a rigorously correct mode of thinking and acting. If his job is especially menial, trivial, or boring, he may remove himself from it, in a sense, by self-abnegating automatism and indifference, or try to invest it and himself with importance by unnecessary complication of his duties, elaboration of procedures, and coyness or pomposity in his public dealings.

The end result is naturally an agent who sees himself, his work, and his "proper" responsibilities quite differently than his client sees them. His conception of professional virtue stems from considerations of institutional good and occupational convenience. The client's conception is grounded on considerations of public good and personal service. The agent is most concerned for meticulous observance of the institutional rules not only on his part but on the client's part; but the client couldn't care less—he wants his money-order, information, connection, without rigmarole and he wants it fast. The doctor and the lawyer are most respectful of "professional ethics" and expect their clients to be no less respectful; but their clients don't give a hang for such niceties—they simply want their damages or their medical treatment. The elements of conflict are obvious. The more righteous and intractable the agent, the more frequently and severely will he be criticized by an impatient public. And since it is the public that does pay and must somehow be served, he can never be completely indifferent to the people who face him from the other side of the counter. He is caught in the middle. He must not unduly offend the all-important public, nor must he exceed his authority in trying to please it. This dilemma may well contribute to that defensive animosity which is the hall-mark of *petty paranoia.*

We know that the disease is not inevitable. It cannot be condoned as simply an occupational disease. We have all met exceptional agents in stations, stores, hospitals, and other busy public places who genuinely want to help their clients and, when they cannot, will sensibly and courteously explain the rules by which they or their clients have to be governed. Many, indeed, can laugh heartily with their clients at those unavoidable bureaucratic restrictions that are patently nonsensical. They do not have to make a virtue of their professional necessities. Clearly, although encouraged by many institutional factors, *petty paranoia* is rooted in intellectual and temperamental deficiencies.

While various correctives might be applied at organizational and managerial levels to minimize the growth of *petty paranoia,* it is doubtful if anything but radical psychotherapy would help the individual suffering from it. Simple admonitory approaches would be worse than useless. As with paranoia generally, the first difficulty is almost insurmountable—to persuade the victim that he is afflicted and in need of treatment. While the present outlook is not promising, still, as with any disease, in accurately describing and naming it we have taken a major step forward. And at the very least we can confront it with its proper name hereafter, whenever we encounter it.

———————●———————

Inside Heaven's Gate

How a $44 Million
Obsession Killed a
Movie Studio

Charles Champlin

Given the profligate disregard for money that characterizes the making of Michael Cimino's Heaven's Gate from birth to death, it's a small irony of precision that at the moment of the film's disastrous premiere in New York on Tuesday, Nov. 18, 1980, United Artists knew that its production had cost exactly $35,190,718.

That was slightly more than three times the original budget of $11.6 million. When the film was finally written off as an irrecoverable loss, the figure, now including promotional costs, had grown to $44 million.

It was not the costliest film, nor even the costliest failed film, in Hollywood history, but it remains the most *conspicuous* failed film in the annals of American movie making.

It cost the jobs of virtually every United Artists executive who had had anything to do with it, including the author of **Final Cut,** Steven Bach, who was at the end UA's senior vice-president in charge of worldwide production. The failure of the film was approximate cause of the sale of UA by Transamerica to Kirk Kerkorian of MGM, so that Heaven's Gate can be said to have killed UA.

Part of the problem with Heaven's Gate was that its timing was all too perfect. As the press reported the escalating costs born of Cimino's spare-no-expense zeal for visual perfection, and as the hostilities between Cimino and UA became common knowledge, the movie seemed to be the pre-eminent symbol of all that ailed the whole industry, especially the surrender of the studios of their traditional strict controls over production.

How had it all been allowed to happen? Not simply the cost overruns, which a box office smash would have reduced to matters of minor embarrassment and a vow to be stricter next time, but a film so unfocused and unsympathetic that critics generally hated it and, more damagingly, audiences could not be persuaded to go see it.

Bach, the senior UA executive most directly involved with the project from the start, writes with great skill and a novelist's gift for scenes, details, feelings and dialogue. What is perhaps even more remarkable is Bach's balance, his ability to see and report where and why Heaven's Gate went wrong, absolving no one, himself included.

While **Final Cut** is centrally about Heaven's Gate, it's also about the whole context of decision making (other projects, other film makers), travel, corporate anxieties and infighting, of which Heaven's Gate was the noisiest part.

In the end, the process, the system, seems to become a force all its own, dictating a course (often on the basis of dubious conventional wisdom). The project thereafter gathers speed and inexorability, like a cannonball careening down a toboggan chute, impossible to stop or deflect even if you sense there will be a splintering crash at the bottom.

The conventional wisdom said that Cimino was hot. The rumbles on The Deer Hunter were good, although it had not yet won him his two Oscars. But he was a catch, at a moment when UA under its new management needed to look clouty, like a force to conjure with in the industry.

One of the several lessons from the debacle is that there is still no substitute for a finished script that everyone has read and agreed upon, and a budget that bears a close and relatively unalterable relationship to that script. But the script, which Cimino had been working on for years and was originally called The Johnson County War, was far from set when UA and Cimino made their deal. From the beginning, the *real* film and the final nature of the characters were actually going to be what Cimino vaguely promised they would be.

At that, Bach has no doubt that Cimino always intended, and fought, to make an epic, a masterpiece.

Yet Bach's portrait of Cimino during production—and indeed right through the opening of the shortened version of the film, is poisonous, a picture of a cold and arrogant man who refused to hear about the skyrocketing costs and refused to see visiting UA executives, and whose perfectionist demands approached mania. (Before he was through, Cimino printed 1.3 million feet of film, enough for a movie 220 hours long.)

Bach discusses the several options UA considered as the costs soared like a pinball machine gone haywire. These included suspending production, abandoning the production or firing Cimino and bringing in another director (assuming one could be found who would take over so personal a project). Each solution would have been dearly expensive (though cheaper in the long run than that $44-million write-off).

But, more expensive corporately, each option would have been an admission of grievous administrative incompetence, a loss of face unacceptable to the UA brass and to the conglomerate owners at Transamerica in San Franciso. UA did finally talk tough, forcing Cimino to shoot the film's Prologue (at Oxford, substituting for Harvard) for $2 million instead of the $10 million he sought. It is some of the best stuff in Heaven's Gate, although it characteristically goes on a good deal too long.

There were still the desperate, lingering hopes that Cimino had brought it off; that, as Bach said before one of the screenings, "maybe the cow would fly."

It catastrophically didn't, in either Cimino's long version or in a much-reduced version that played briefly.

But Bach says, "The weaknesses and foolishness of an entire industry had been focused and exposed by Heaven's Gate and United Artists."

He gives the film a penetrating and regretful obituary: "Not only the film-maker but the film, too, was 'out of control.' . . . Characters and story were sacrificed to the film-maker's love of visual effect and production for their own sakes. The 'look' of the thing subsumed the sense of the thing and implied a callous or uncaring quality about characters for whom the audience was asked to care more than the film seemed to. . . .

"Whether those characters were well or ill conceived, they seemed sabotaged by their creator's negligence of them as he pursued the 'larger, richer, deeper' things that surrounded them, obscuring them, making them seem smaller, poorer, more shallow. The larger failure of Heaven's Gate is not that the 'golden string' finally stretched an irrecoverable $44 million . . . but that it failed to engage audiences on the most basic and elemental human levels of sympathy and compassion, and this failure is finally cardinal."

Making It Right the First Time

Christopher Knowlton

In 1979, Tennant Co. received two pieces of life-threatening news. Word arrived at Minneapolis headquarters that a potentially fatal defect had appeared in the motorized factory floor sweepers that it was exporting to Japan. The sweepers were chronically dripping oil. The second piece of news was Toyota's announcement that it was bringing out a competing product. In an all-out effort to save its 40% North American market share, Tennant, the world's biggest manufacturer of floor maintenance equipment, embarked on an ambitious, by-the-book quality improvement program that over the next few years upgraded its sweepers and scrubbers from good to great. Today the company has 60% of the North American market and 40% of the world market; sales grew from $98 million in 1979 to $167 million last year.

President Roger Hale started the process of upgrading the company's goods by consulting the quality expert Philip Crosby. Arguing that the product had to be made right the first time, Crosby recommended that the company eliminate its rework area, where 18 of the most experienced mechanics fixed mistakes made during the assembly process. The repercussions of Crosby's reform were enormous: Workers had to make fewer blunders and catch those they did make. In order to eliminate errors, management and workers, brainstorming in small groups, developed scores of new assembly procedures that changed the shape of assembly lines and rerouted the delivery of parts. Employees were taught statistical process control, a method of monitoring defects and setting goals to reduce them.

The group that looked into the oil leaks discovered that the company's engineers had ignored the latest hydraulics technology, and a number of the assembly workers had been improperly trained to put together the hose joints. Worse, 16 different suppliers were delivering fittings and hoses made to varying specificiations. As a result, the parts didn't go together properly. Once the workers had been retrained and the number of suppliers reduced, leaks—which averaged two per machine in 1979—occurred in fewer than one of every 18 machines by 1986. Says Roger Hale proudly: "The leadership on the quality program has come from the factory floor."

Tennant succeeded in protecting its leading market share and enhancing its reputation within the industry. Better yet, says Robert Maples, a security analyst with Piper Jaffray, "improved product quality is largely credited with forestalling Toyota's expansion into the U.S. market." Morale has soared. Murals of paddling loons, grouse, and jumping bass adorn what were once bare factory walls. The floors shine, and the workers gladly show off their handiwork to visitors while chatting knowledgeably about quality control. Employees award each other teddy bears—known as Koala T. Bears—for taking the initiative in problem solving and achieving quality goals.

Every 18 months, to keep things in sharp focus, the company celebrates Zero Defect Day with a magic show and other live entertainment. At the end of the all-day fete, the workers renew their pledge to do their work correctly. "It sounds corny," says Maples, "but the corniness works."

Taking Control in a New Job

George Tamke

I want to describe, in some detail, what I do when entering a new job. Throughout my career, when changing jobs, I have always moved into an organization that had very visible problems (cost, quality, schedule and/or people-related difficulties). As a consequence, whether pressured directly or not, I have always felt under a time crunch to get the ball moving in the right direction. For this reason, I have invariably jumped in with both feet to try to understand what is going on around me.

In my last two jobs I was responsible for a functional entity: manufacturing and production control. In each job, I was at the fourth level of management, with three layers of management reporting to me. The two organizations were comprised of lower-level employees, compared with those in areas like engineering, marketing, new products, etc. It is also important to note that in each of those jobs, I was new to the location and as a consequence did not know any of the employees personally. From a size standpoint, the organizations consisted of 300–500 people, with approximately 50 managers (36 first level, 10 second level, and 4 third level).

Obtaining Technical Control of the Organization

One of the very first things that I do, after my arrival has been announced to the organization, is to hold a staff meeting with all of the people who will report directly to me. Working from an agenda prepared prior to the meeting, I discuss the following points:

1. My background, specifically covering the organizations and the locations that I have worked in.

This case was prepared by George Tamke under the supervision of David Bradford, Lecturer in Organizational Behavior, Stanford Graduate School of Business. This case was prepared as a basis for class discussion and not to indicate either correct or incorrect handling of administrative problems.

2. My administrative style. For example,
   a) Weekly status report due to me by 9:00 a.m. Monday, covering the following items:
      —accomplishments
      —problems/concerns
      —planned activity for the coming week
   b) As reports, letters, etc., get distributed from my office, a number of them will have questions/comments addressed to specific individuals. Unless otherwise noted, I would expect a response within two days, recognizing that a valid response may require more time.
   c) I expect all appraisals to be completed on time and objectives to be in place for all employees.
   d) I want to review all management appraisals before they are given.
3. Please get on my calendar within the next five days and be prepared to discuss with me the following topics:
   —workload versus people on board versus approved budget plan
   —product cost posture by product by operation (actual versus targets)
   —quality performance by product
   —expense budget posture (actuals versus target)
   —major project commitments with status
   —latest opinion survey results with action plan highlights
   —planned promotion activity
   —appraisal distribution
   —absenteeism and overtime trends
   —major objectives for the next 12 months
   —personnel problems
4. My view of my job.
   Basically it is one of helping my managers get their job done. If they feel that I am being overbearing on a particular issue or with my specific requests, I would hope that they would bring it up so we could discuss it. Also if they don't understand why I'm asking for a certain work product or don't agree with my appraisal on a problem, I would also hope that they would mention it.

   My main intent, from a technical standpoint, is to get the information needed to understand the decisions that will be made in my organization. Unless I am aware of the numbers, the plans, and the problems that my organization is living with, I feel very uncomfortable in the leadership role. I think this is caused by my almost complete dependency on the people working for me, when I do not yet know the producers from the parasites. Also, the fact that the only reason I am there is because the organization is in trouble does not make me feel comfortable in this position. Therefore, I always attempt to get myself up to speed as quickly as possible. Apart from the selfish reason of trying to become less dependent (initially, until I know whom I can trust) another gain from this meeting is that an hour after the staff meeting is over, the grapevine will have heard about all of the "demands that new guy has made" and as a result, all of the managers will be on their toes—not really knowing what to expect, but recognizing that "he is serious."

As the individual review meetings take place, I usually find that there is a general attempt to satisfy my requests, but not sufficient thought given to the issues. The managers quickly find themselves with many more questions than answers, and more work to do. Word gets out, and the quality of the presentations improves, as does the level of anticipation within the management ranks.

Obtaining People Control of the Organization

The key point that I try to stress from day one is "tough but fair" and I attempt to do that by my actions, rather than by what I say. There are some tools/techniques that I use:

1. Past Opinion Survey Review
One of the areas that I probe into very deeply, very quickly is the temperature of the water among the workers. I use the results from an annual company-wide survey to measure employee attitudes about work conditions and their supervision. Each supervisor receives a summary of responses from his/her subordinates and from this develops an Opinion Survey Action plan aimed at correcting any problems. By examining the supervisor's action plan I begin to get a feel as to the level of thought that was put into the plan. By asking how frequently the managers review the status of their plan with their people, I get a feeling for the level of commitment that is felt on the manager's part. The purpose of this review is really twofold; I quickly become familiar with how the people feel about their jobs, their manager, etc., and—as important, if not more important—it sends out another signal to the managers that I am really serious about this area.

The reason I feel very strongly about this is that, in my view, if people are basically happy with what they are doing and how they are being treated, a lot of the other problems (cost, quality, schedule) tend to go away. In addition, I also feel that an individual's morale basically revolves around his/her view of the immediate manager and what kind of a job that person is doing. This is an area that my management team will be spending a lot of time working on, and I like to get the seed planted in their minds early that I think this is an important area.

2. Shadow Program
Beginning with my first week on the job, I have each third-line manager spend a full week with me. This activity entails going to the meetings I go to, reading the mail I read, discussing issues as they come up, etc. This allows me to get to know each manager and also allows them to get to know me

personally—to see how I react, how I think, and hopefully to relieve some of the anxieties/tensions that may have built up since my arrival.

3. Meeting with Each First-Line and Second-Line Manager Individually

Over the course of the first few weeks, I schedule a one-hour meeting with each manager, to give me an overview of their departments or project covering their mission, their department morale, and what they consider to be their biggest accomplishment and/or biggest problem. With the first-line managers, this meeting ends with a tour of departments where I meet the employees. More times than not, questions come up which are not answered to my satisfaction and which require follow-up on the part of the manager. Again the results are twofold; I get to know each manager and his/her views of their department, and they get to tell me about something which should be very familiar to them. They recognize that this is a very time-consuming process on my part, and I think they appreciate the fact that I am willing to take the time.

4. Employee Breakfast Meetings

Once I have been around to all of the departments and have met all of the people, I schedule a breakfast meeting a few times a week with 15 non-management people at a time. The purpose of the meeting is to discuss whatever issues they may have on their minds, to give them my views of what we are, and where we are headed, etc. The only topics which I cut off are those which deal with specific individuals. Those types of problems I cover with the individuals who brought them up outside of the group meeting.

I think as a result of these and similar techniques, I begin to get people control of the organization. I meet all of the people, and they meet me. I stress to my management team the importance of good people management and try to show it with the resource that is most valuable to me—my time. Early on, I consciously try to find ways to show how I feel about certain things, by doing and saying rather than by just saying.

My Relationship with My Peers

In addition to working downward in my organization, I also sit down and discuss with my peers their views of my organization, and the problems that they or their people have in dealing with it. I like to do this near the start of the sequence of things so that I am not clouded by my own views. Later on, this also helps me determine in my own mind whose views I agree with and/or respect, and whose views leave me cold. This data becomes very useful to me.

Depending upon the way the meetings evolve, I also think it gets our relationship off on the right foot. I am asking for their opinion on something, and this tends to make them feel good. I also take copious notes during these meetings, which further supports their good feelings. From my perspective, I form impressions of them on the basis of how prepared they are, and who feels basically secure or insecure in their own job. This allows me also to determine my peer power structure.

My Relationships with My Superiors

This is an area that I don't spend a lot of time thinking about because I have made sure, before accepting the job, that my new boss understands my level of aspirations and the type of relationship that I hope we will have. I emphasize the fact that I would like to know at any time if he isn't pleased with my work or the way that I do my job; I don't like surprises in this area. Once this has been established, I do not remember having to bring it up again. I find that there is a degree of mutual respect that exists and tends to carry over as the relationship develops.

Once I have taken the job, I find that my other activities (interactions with subordinates and peers) dovetail nicely with meetings with my boss. I quickly appear to understand the numbers and to have drawn some conclusions about past problems. In addition, as a result of having walked through the significant problems with my subordinates I either understand and agree with the action being taken, or I have initiated additional work. I am able to discuss what we plan to do and report any status to date. The peer conversations also have a way of getting back to the boss, and when coupled with the other things going on, appear to choke off the normal additional requests that tend to come from the boss to the new organization member. I think these requests are in part the boss's attempt to make sure the right things are being looked at. If his curiosity can be satisfied early in the process, I believe the probability of significant future requests is also greatly diminished. For this to work effectively, another requirement is to keep him properly informed on the major things that are going on and what is being done about them, so that he is able to field any questions that his boss may have about your operation.

I think that this is a necessary ingredient to getting effective control of your organization. Without it, the priorities you have set will be continuously jockeyed around to satisfy your boss's requests. The result on your managers would be catastrophic, leading them to wonder (rightly so) who is running your organization.

I have tried to explain and characterize the management style that I use when I enter a new job. I work hard and long trying to get a quick, effective grasp on my new area of responsibility. I get to know the people as quickly as possible and continually emphasize to my management team the importance of being an effective people manager.

In the early stages, I would say my decision-making style is predominantly participatory in that I actively solicit comments and input from my managers, and tend to ride with their decisions. As I become more knowledgeable, although I still solicit comments and inputs to the same degree, I tend to play the devil's advocate much more, push harder and, depending upon the situation, it would not be above me to be downright autocratic.

I emphasize to my managers and my people that I consider helping them to get their job done one of my main responsibilities. If they have a problem, and they think I might be able to help, I urge them to come in and see me. I try to be open and honest with my managers and share with them any information I have that is work related. I also emphasize the importance of good two-way communication and how I really use the data they provide me. This point becomes crucial because I can very easily lose my credibility if they provide me with "bum data." To the degree that it is practicable, I try to establish the same openness and honesty in my dealings with my peers and my boss. I find it much easier to tell everybody the truth, than to selectively "curb the truth" and try to remember what I have told to whom.

7

Managing Human Resources

I f, as we have been suggesting, organizations are formally designed systems superimposed on less formal relationships among humans and the primary function of managing is the coordination of human effort, it goes without saying that managing human resources is a central concern of managers. Clearly this expectation is confirmed. (Managers often see the human resources issues as the ones they feel are most important and the ones that they wish they had given more attention to learning about when they were students.) Managers want to find ways to help people perform what the organization is attempting to accomplish in a cost effective manner.

Most management textbooks devote a great deal of attention to summarizing knowledge that managers can use towards this end. We will make no attempt to repeat these efforts here. Instead, we want to complement them by exploring a few matters that illustrate some of the tensions that often exist in meshing the needs of the organization and the characteristics of human beings, but are seldom given much attention in conventional textbooks on human resources. The topics we chose are only a small sample of these tensions.

Although, until now we have been most concerned with the fact that organizations are superimposed on human beings, it is also true that human beings instill their interests in the organization. Whereas earlier, particularly in our discussions of influencing and communicating, we tended to see the impact that personal inclinations make as positive for coordinating human effort, here the articles treat a number of ways in which this impact might have dysfunctional consequences for the operation of the formal systems of the organization. We also see additional examples of how the demands of the organization can be dysfunctional for the individual.

As we see it, human society is currently evolving ways of organizing cooperative relationships that will reduce the impact of these tensions. It seems likely that progress along this path will mean that organizations as

well as individuals will change. For example, compare a typical factory today with one typical of the late 19th or early 20th century. Things we take
for granted today such as toilets, drinking fountains, ventilation, and numerous safety measures were simply absent then. Similarly, working hours and
even the design of jobs themselves have been altered (to some degree) to
be more consistent with a number of human needs and preferences. On the
other hand, people have become much more prepared to work in organizations as we know them. They have the basic educational skills that organizations require and the personal and social discipline that suits them far better
for bureaucratic organizations than was true a century ago. Whether these
developments are evaluated positively or negatively depends on the set of
values one selects for building criteria. Our only point is that both individuals
and organizations appear to have accommodated to each other and we expect more of this in the future. There are still many sources of tension—
many of which are manifested around topics associated with managing the
human resource.

Central concerns of human resource management often include: selection, training and development, appraisal, compensation, and termination.
While these functions often seem relatively simple to perform, the articles
in this section reveal that they are not. "Behind the Mask . . ." demonstrates
the political dimensions of employee appraisal. In "Suddenness" we are made
aware of the human consequences performing these functions can have. The
final article introduces other consequences performing these functions have
for both the people who do them and who are affected by them. In exploring them we see new elements of the human drama that organizations spawn
for managers, as they try to balance their organizational missions with what
they and others judge as right.

Behind the Mask: The Politics of Employee Appraisal

Clinton O. Longenecker
The University of Toledo

Henry P. Sims, Jr.
George Mason University and The Pennsylvania State University

Dennis A. Gioia
The Pennsylvania State University

There is really no getting around the fact that whenever I evaluate one of my people, I stop and think about the impact—the ramifications of my decisions on my relationship with the guy and his future here. I'd be stupid not to. Call it being politically minded, or using managerial discretion, or fine tuning the guy's ratings, but in the end I've got to live with him, and I'm not going to rate a guy without thinking about the fallout. There are a lot of games played in the rating process and whether we [managers] admit it or not we are all guilty of playing them at our discretion.

According to management books and manuals, employee appraisal is an objective, rational and, we hope, accurate process. The idea that executives might deliberately distort and manipulate appraisals for political purposes seems unspeakable. Yet we found extensive evidence to indicate that, behind a mask of objectivity and rationality, executives engage in such manipulation in an intentional and systematic manner. In performance appraisal, it appears that some of the Machiavellian spirit still lives.

Our original goal was to conduct a scholarly investigation of the cognitive processes executives typically use in appraising subordinates. We held in-depth interviews with 60 upper-level executives who had extensive experience in formally evaluating their subordinates on a periodic basis. During these interviews, we heard many frank admissions of deliberate manipulation of formal appraisals for political purposes. In this article we'll discuss the "why and the how" of such politically motivated manipulation.

On the Appraisal Process

Almost every executive has dreaded performance appraisals at some time or other. They hate to give them and they hate to receive them. Yet, like them or not, every executive recognizes that appraisals are a fact of organizational life. In terms of time, a formal appraisal of a subordinate takes perhaps three

"Behind the Mask: The Politics of Employee Appraisal" by Clinton O. Longenecker, Henry P. Sims, Jr., and Dennis A. Gioia, from the Academy of Management EXECUTIVE, 1987, Vol. 1, No. 3, pp. 183–93. Reprinted by permission of the publisher and the authors.

or four hours out of the working year; in terms of impact on the lives of executives and their employees, appraisals have significance that reaches far beyond the few hours it takes to conduct them.

Because of the important role appraisals play in individual careers and corporate performance, a great deal of attention has been given to trying to understand the process. Special attention has been directed toward the issue of accuracy in appraisals.[1] Academicians in particular have expended (some might say wasted) substantial energy trying to design the perfect instrument that would yield an accurate appraisal. That effort now appears to be a hopeless, even impossible, task.

More recently, a flurry of activity has centered on the arcane mental processes of the manager who gives the appraisal. It is an intriguing approach because it involves a kind of vicarious attempt to climb inside an executive's head to see how he or she works. Predictably, however, this approach has confirmed the elusiveness of deciphering managerial thought processes. Moreover, it has not yet resulted in appraisals that are any more accurate than existing appraisals.[2]

Even more recently, some effort has been directed toward demonstrating that appraisal is, in addition to everything else, a highly emotional process as well. When emotional variability gets dragged into the process, any hope of obtaining objectivity and accuracy in appraisal waltzes right out the office door.[3]

Taken together, all these approaches apparently lead to the depressing conclusion that accuracy in appraisals might be an unattainable objective.[4] More realistically, perhaps accuracy is simply a wrong goal to pursue. Even if we have a perfect understanding of instruments and mental and emotional processes, would that result in accurate appraisals? Our research indicates that it would not. All of these avenues to understanding appraisal tend to ignore an important point: Appraisals take place in an organizational environment that is anything but completely rational, straightforward, or dispassionate. In this environment, accuracy does not seem to matter to managers quite so much as discretion, effectiveness or, more importantly, survival. Earlier research has either missed or glossed over the fact that executives giving appraisals have ulterior motives and purposes that supercede the mundane concern with rating accuracy.

On Politics in Performance Appraisal

Any realistic discussion of performance appraisal must recognize that organizations are political entities and that few, if any, important decisions are made without key parties acting to protect their own interests.[5] As such, executives are political actors in an organization, and they often attempt to control their destinies and gain influence through internal political actions.

Thus, it is likely that political considerations influence executives when they appraise subordinates.[6] *Politics* in this sense refers to deliberate attempts by individuals to enhance or protect their self-interests when conflicting courses of action are possible. Political action therefore represents a source of bias or inaccuracy in employee appraisal. To understand the appraisal process thoroughly, thus, we must recognize and account for the political aspects of the process.

Politics in Appraisal: Findings from the Study

The political perspective emerged as a surprisingly important and pervasive issue affecting the way executives appraise their employees. Conclusions derived from our interviews are summarized in Exhibits 1 through 4. Because a strong attempt was made to allow executives to speak for themselves in describing the politics of performance appraisals, direct quotations from the interviews have been included in our analysis, where appropriate. Our findings are discussed below.

Politics as a Reality of Organizational Life

The most fundamental survey finding was an open recognition and admission that politics were a reality in the appraisal process. In fact, executives admitted that political considerations *nearly always* were part of their evaluation process. One vice-president summarized the view these executives shared regarding the politics of appraisal:

> *As a manager, I will use the review process to do what is best for my people and the division. . . .I've got a lot of leeway—call it discretion—to use this process in that manner. . . .I've used it to get my people better raises in lean years, to kick a guy in the pants if he really needed it, to pick up a guy when he was down or even to tell him that he was no longer welcome here. It is a tool that the manager should use to help him do what it takes to get the job done. I believe most of us here at ---- operate this way regarding appraisals. . . .Accurately describing an employee's performance is really not as important as generating ratings that keep things cooking.*

Executives suggested several reasons why politics were so pervasive and why accuracy was not their primary concern. First, executives realized that they must live with subordinates in a day-to-day relationship. Second, they were also very cognizant of the permanence of the written document:

> *The mere fact that you have to write out your assessment and create a permanent record will cause people not to be as honest or as accurate as they should be. . . .We soften the language because our ratings go in the guy's file downstairs [the Personnel Department] and it will follow him around his whole career.*

Perhaps the most widespread reason why executives considered political action in the appraisal process was that the formal appraisal was linked to compensation, career, and advancement in the organization. The issue of money was continually cited as a major cause of intentional distortions in ratings.

I know that it sounds funny, but the fact that the process is ultimately tied to money influences the ratings a person receives. . . . Whenever a decision involves money things can get very emotional and ticklish.

Although the logic of tying pay to the outcome of performance ratings is sound, pay linkages increase the likelihood that ratings will be manipulated. Both managers and the organization as a whole are guilty of using the rating process as an opportunity to reach salary objectives regarding employee compensation that have little, if any, relationship to pay for performance. A director of research and development very candidly described the predicament from the rater's perspective:

Since the pay raise my people get is tied to the ratings I give them, there is a strong incentive to inflate ratings at times to maximize their pay increases to help keep them happy and motivated, especially in lean years when the merit ceiling is low. . . . Conversely, you can also send a very strong message to a nonperformer that low ratings will hit him in the wallet. . . . There is no doubt that a lot of us manipulate ratings at times to deal with the money issue.

At times, an organization uses the appraisal process as an instrument to control merit increase expenditures. The manipulative process can be summarized as follows:

This thing [the appraisal process] can really turn into an interesting game when the HR [Human Resources] people come out with a blanket statement like, "Money for raises is tight this year and since superior performers get 7% to 10% raises there will be no superior performers this year." Talk about making things rough for us [raters]! . . . They try and force you to make the ratings fit the merit allowances instead of vice versa.

Influences on Political Culture

Executives made it clear that if an organization was political, the appraisal process would reflect these politics:

Some organizations are more aggressive and political than others, so it just makes sense that those things carry over into the rating process as well. . . . The organization's climate will determine, to a great extent, how successful any rating system will be, and it follows that if any organization is very political, the rating system will be political. . . .

Exhibit 1 Politics as a Reality of Organizational Life

- Political considerations were nearly always part of executive evaluative processes.
- Politics played a role in the evaluation process because:
  - —executives took into consideration the daily interpersonal dynamics between them and their subordinates;
  - —the formal appraisal process results in a permanent written document;
  - —the formal appraisal can have considerable impact on the subordinate's career and advancement.

Several factors were identified by the executives as having a strong influence on the political culture in which the performance appraisal process operates. Perhaps the strongest was the extent to which the formal appraisal process was "taken seriously" by the organization. A plant manager in this study describes what it means for an organization to "take the process seriously:"

> At some places the PA [performance appraisal] process is a joke—just a bureaucratic thing that the manager does to keep the IR [industrial relations] people off his back. At the last couple of places I've worked, the formal review process is taken really seriously; they train you how to conduct a good interview, how to handle problems, how to coach and counsel. . . . You see the things [appraisals] reviewed by your boss, and he's serious about reviewing your performance in a thorough manner. . . . I guess the biggest thing is that people are led to believe that it is a management tool that works; it's got to start at the top!

This quote suggests another important factor that turns the appraisal process into a political process: the extent to which higher level executives in the same company use political factors in rating subordinates. A "modeling" effect seems to take place, with managers telling themselves, "If it's okay for the guys upstairs to do it, then we can do it, too."

According to one executive we interviewed,

> I've learned how not to conduct the review from the bosses . . . but you do learn from your boss how much slack or what you can get away with in rating your people. . . . It seems that if the manager's boss takes it [the appraisal] seriously, the subordinate [manager] is more likely to follow. If the boss plays games with the review, it seems like the subordinate [manager] is more likely to do so.

The economic health and growth potential of the organization appeared as important factors influencing the organization's culture and, consequently, the appraisal event. Similarly, the executive's own personal belief system—his or her perception of the value of the appraisal process—also seemed to have an impact. Generally, executives who honestly believed the process contributed to the motivation of their subordinates were less likely to allow political factors to affect the appraisal. Conversely, executives who saw the appraisal as a useless bureaucratic exercise were more likely to manipulate the appraisal.

Moreover, if executives believed the appraisals would be seriously scrutinized, reviewed, and evaluated by their superiors, then the influence of political factors was likely to be reduced.

> If somebody is carefully reviewing the marks you give your people, then the game playing is reduced . . . [but] as you rise in the organization, your boss has less direct knowledge of your people and is less likely to question your judgment, so the door is open for more discretion.

The degree of open communication and trust between executives and subordinates seemed to have some influence on the impact of political factors. The more open the communication, the less likely that politics would play a role:

> If the manager and employee have a trusting and open relationship and shoot straight with each other, then the manager is less likely to play games with ratings.

Exhibit 2 Factors Influencing the Political Culture of the Organization

- The economic health and growth potential of the organization
- The extent to which top management supported and, more importantly, did or did not practice political tactics when appraising their own subordinates
- The extent to which executives sincerely believed that appraisal was a necessary and worthwhile management practice or just a bureaucratic exercise
- The extent to which executives believed that their written assessment of their subordinates would be evaluated and scrutinized by their superiors
- The extent to which an organization was willing to train and coach its managers to use and maintain the performance appraisal system
- The degree to which the appraisal process was openly discussed among both executives and subordinates
- The extent to which executives believed the appraisal process became more political at higher levels of the organizational hierarchy

---

Last, but not least, the appraiser's level in the organization's hierarchy also seemed to have an influence. Executives generally believed the appraisal process became more political and subjective as one moved up the organizational ladder:

> *The higher you rise in this organization the more weird things get with regard to how they evaluate you. . . .The process becomes more political and less objective and it seems like the rating process focuses on who you are as opposed to what you've actually accomplished. . . .As the stakes get higher, things get more and more political.*

Inflating the Appraisal

Although academicians have been preoccupied with the goal of accuracy in appraisal, executives reported that accuracy was not their primary concern. Rather, they were much more interested in whether their ratings would be effective in maintaining or increasing the subordinate's future level of performance. In fact, many reported they would deliberately misstate the reported performance level if they felt performance could be improved as a result:

> *When I rate my people it doesn't take place in a vacuum . . . so you have to ask yourself what the purpose of the process is. . . .I use this thing to my advantage and I know my people and what it takes to keep them going and that is what this is all about.*

Overall, executives reported that deliberate distortions of the appraisal tended to be biased in the subordinate's favor:

> *Let's just say that there are a lot of factors that tug at you and play on your mind that cause you to tend to soften the ratings you give. It may not have a great impact all the time but when you know a "5" will piss a man off and "6" will make him happy. . . .You tell me which one you'd choose. . . .Plus, you don't want to be the*

bad guy, the bearer of gloom. It seems like ratings are almost always a little in-flated at a minimum because of people aspects in the evaluation process.

Typically, executives tended to inflate the overall rating rather than the in-dividual appraisal items. Interestingly, although the overall rating was gener-ally the last item on the appraisal form, this overall rating was determined first; then the executive went back and completed the individual items.

Most of us try to be fairly accurate in assessing the individual's performance in differ-ent categories. . . .If you are going to pump up a person's ratings, for whatever rea-son, it's done on the subordinate's overall evaluation category. That's all they really care about, anyway. . . .The problem is these things have to match up, so if you know what the guy's overall rating is in the first place it will probably color the rest of the appraisal.

Of course, this backward procedure is usually contrary to the recommended procedure and is also inconsistent with the typical assumptions about how decisions are supposed to be made "objectively." Executives articulated several reasons as justification for consciously inflating subordinate ratings. The most frequently given reason was to maximize the merit increases that a subor-dinate would be eligible to receive. This reason was more likely to be given by executives in organizations that closely linked the numerical score on the formal appraisal and the subsequent merit raise.

Sometimes executives wanted to protect or encourage a subordinate whose performance was temporarily suffering because of personal problems. In a similar vein, executives would sometimes inflate a rating simply because they felt sorry for a subordinate. They wanted to avoid short-term "punishment" in the hope that the subordinate would recover and perform once again at an acceptable level.

It may sound kind of funny to say this, but sometimes there is a tendency to give subordinates ratings a little higher than they deserve because you feel sorry for them. . . .I just had a guy go through a divorce and I'm not going to kick him when he's down, even if his performance drops off. . . .If anything, you might use the re-view to help pick him up and get him back on his feet.

If the appraisal was reviewed by people outside the department, executives sometimes inflated ratings to avoid "hanging dirty laundry out in public." Clearly, many executives preferred to keep knowledge of problems contained within the department.

There are two reviews at times, the written one and the spoken one. The spoken review is the real one, especially if there are things of a sensitive nature. . . .I gener-ally don't put those things down on paper in the review for the whole world to read because it is generally none of their damn business. . . .I could make all of us look bad or worse than we really are.

Executives also admitted to inflating a rating to avoid a confrontation with a subordinate with whom the executive had recently had difficulties. They took this action mainly to avert an unpleasant incident or sometimes to avoid a confrontation that they believed would not lead to an effective outcome.

On occasion, an executive might inflate the rating because the subordinate's performance had improved during the latter part of the performance period, even though the overall performance did not merit such a rating. Again, the motivation for this higher-than-deserved rating was a desire to encourage the subordinate toward better performance in the next period:

> *Many of us have trouble rating for the entire year. If one of my people has a stellar three months prior to the review . . . you don't want to do anything that impedes that person's momentum and progress.*

Executives also recognized effort, even though the effort might not pay off in actual performance:

> *If a man broke his back trying to do the best job humanly possible, his ratings will generally reflect this if his boss understands people. Take two people with the same performance, but one tried much harder—their ratings will show it in my department. Low ratings might trample that person's desire to put forth effort in the future.*

Last, although not frequently reported, a few executives admitted to giving a higher rating to a problem employee to get the employee promoted "up and out" of the department. Although executives only occasionally admitted to this, the "up and out" rating process was almost universally discussed as something *other* managers actually do. One plant manager candidly remarked:

> *I've seen it happen, especially when you get a young guy in here who thinks he's only going to be here a short while before he gets promoted. People like that become a real pain in the ass. . . . If you want to get rid of them quick, a year and a half of good ratings should do it. . . . A lot of people inflate ratings of people they can't stand, or who think they are God's gift to the department, just to get rid of them. Amen.*

Of course, this practice helps an executive avoid dealing with performance problems and passes the problem along to someone else. Mainly, this tactic was employed when an executive felt unable or unwilling to deal with a performance problem or, especially, when the source of the problem seemed to be based on "personality" or "style" conflicts.

Deflating the Appraisal
For the most part, executives indicated that they were very hesitant to deflate a subordinate's rating because such a tactic would lead to subsequent problems:

> *I won't say I've never given a subordinate lower rates than he or she deserves because there's time and place for that type of thing, but let's just say I hesitate to do that sort of thing unless I'm very sure of what the outcome will be and that it won't backfire.*

Exhibit 3 Inflating the Appraisal

- Executives inflated the appraisal to provide ratings that would effectively maintain or increase the subordinate's level of performance (the primary concern was not the accuracy of the ratings).
- Inflated ratings occur primarily on the overall performance rating, as opposed to the individual appraisal items
- Executive justification for inflating the appraisal:
  —to maximize the merit increases a subordinate would be eligible to receive, especially when the merit ceiling was considered low;
  to protect or encourage a subordinate whose performance was suffering because of personal problems (feeling sorry for a subordinate also resulted in an inflated appraisal);
  —to avoid hanging dirty laundry out in public if the performance appraisal would be reviewed by people outside the organization;
  —to avoid creating a written record of poor performance that would become a permanent part of a subordinate's personnel file;
- to avoid a confrontation with a subordinate with whom the manager had recently had difficulties;
- to give a break to a subordinate who had improved during the latter part of the performance period;
- to promote a subordinate "up and out" when the subordinate was performing poorly or did not fit in the department.

Nevertheless, negative distortions did occur. Executives gave several reasons for using this tactic. First, an overly negative rating was sometimes used to jolt a subordinate to rise to his or her expected performance level:

I've used the appraisal to shock an employee. . . .If you've tried to coach a guy to get him back on track and it doesn't work, a low rating will more often than not slap him in the face and tell him you mean business. . . .I've dropped a few ratings way down to accomplish this because the alternative outcome could be termination down the road, which isn't pretty.

Also, a deliberately deflated rating was sometimes used to teach a rebellious subordinate a lesson:

Occasionally an employee comes along who needs to be reminded who the boss is, and the appraisal is a real tangible and appropriate place for such a reminder. . . .

Deflated ratings were also used as part of a termination procedure. First, a strongly negative rating could be used to send an indirect message to a subordinate that he or she should consider quitting:

If a person has had a questionable period of performance, a strong written appraisal can really send the message that they aren't welcome any longer and should think about leaving. . . .The written review sends a clear message if the person has any doubt.

Exhibit 4 Deflating the Appraisal

* Executives indicated that they were very hesitant consciously to deflate a subordinate's ratings because of potential problems associated with such a tactic.
* Nevertheless, they sometimes deflated appraisals:
  —to shock a subordinate back on to a higher performance track;
  —to teach a rebellious subordinate a lesson about who is in charge;
  —to send a message to a subordinate that he or she should consider leaving the organization;
  —to build a strongly documented record of poor performance that could speed up the termination process.

Second, once the decision has been made that the situation was unsalvage-able, negative ratings could then be used to build a strongly documented case against the marginal or poor performer:

> *You'll find that once a manager has made up his or her mind that an employee isn't going to make it, the review [the written document] will take on an overly nega-tive tone. . . .Managers are attempting to protect themselves. . . .The appraisal pro-cess becomes downwardly biased because they [the managers] fear that discussing and documenting any positives of the employee's performance might be used against them at a later point in time.*

Of course, this tactic has recently become more common because of lawsuits challenging the traditional "employment at will" concept. The courts have clearly stated that terminations must not be frivolous; they must be justified by economic constraints or documentation of poor performance. In these cases managers will use the process to protect themselves from litigation associated with an unlawful termination lawsuit.[7]

Summary

Our research clearly showed that executives believed there was usually a justifi-able reason for generating appraisal ratings that were less than accurate. Over-all, they felt it was within their managerial discretion to do so. Thus our findings strongly suggest that the formal appraisal process is indeed a political pro-cess, and that few ratings are determined without some political considera-tion. Although research on rater "error" has traditionally suggested that raters can and do inflate ratings (leniency errors) and deflate ratings (stringency er-rors), researchers have typically not accounted for the realities of the appraisal context to explain why these errors occur.

In the minds of the managers we interviewed, these thoughts and behaviors are not errors but, rather, discretionary actions that help them manage peo-ple more effectively. Executives considered many factors beyond the subor-dinate's actual performance in their ratings. Thus, organizational politics was a major factor in the intentional manipulation of subordinate ratings.

Our findings provide support for the following political realities of organiza-tional life: (1) executives in large organizations are political actors who attempt to avoid unnecessary conflict; (2) they attempt to use the organization's bureaucractic processes to their own advantage; and (3) they try to minimize the extent to which administrative responsibilities create barriers between them and their subordinates.

We also conclude that the organizational culture in which the appraisal event occurs significantly influenced the extent to which political activity would both develop and operate. Of course, organizationwide patterns are also strongly influenced by the support and practice of top management. Indeed, we know that lower-level managers tend to emulate high-status executives, and the way they use the appraisal process is no exception. Thus, if top managers prepare ratings poorly or deliberately distort them, this behavior will tend to cascade down the organization.

Given these findings, what informative observations or constructive recommendations might we make to minimize, or at least manage, the detrimental effects of politics in employee appraisal? In fact, we have several for both the individual manager and the organization as a whole.

The Individual Manager

1. Quite frankly, our data suggest there are times in organizational life when political necessity supercedes the usually desirable goals of accuracy and honesty in appraisal. The executives interviewed suggested several compelling reasons for exercising managerial discretion contrary to traditional appraisal research recommendations. Clearly, there are times when individual employees and the organization as a whole can benefit as a consequence. The caveat, of course, is that the occasions when politics and discretion necessarily intrude on the appraissal process should be chosen judiciously. The overall effect on the organization should be given due consideration.

2. Performance appraisal is perhaps most usefully viewed as a high-potential vehicle for motivating and rewarding employees, rather than as a mandatory, bureaucratic exercise used only for judgmental or manipulative purposes. Ideally, it should be treated as an opportunity to communicate formally with employees about their performance, their strengths and weaknesses, and their developmental possibilities.

3. Executives should bear in mind that appraisal-related actions, like many other organizational activities, serve as guides for subordinates. Employees who must conduct appraisals often learn appraisal attitudes and behaviors from their bosses. Thus if appraisals are to be effective, high-ranking executives must treat the process as significant so that political manipulation is discouraged.

4. In addition, openness and trust between managers and subordinates seems to be associated with a lower level of detrimental political activity. Cultivating understanding seems to reduce the perceived need for resorting to interpersonal politics.

5. Finally, inflating or deflating appraisal ratings for political ends might serve temporarily to help executives avoid a problem with certain employees or to accomplish some specific purpose. However, such intentional manipulation may eventually come back to haunt the perpetrating executive and, ultimately, the organization as a whole. This is especially likely if the company comes to accept political manipulation of appraisals as part of the norm.

The Organization as a Whole

1. The appraisal process should operate in a supportive organizational culture. Effective appraisal systems are characterized by the support of top managers (who conduct appraisals themselves), training, open discussions of the appraisal process on an annual basis (perhaps a quality circle approach to appraisals), and rewarding the efforts of managers who do top-notch appraisals.
2. Systematic, regular, and formal appraisals should start at the top of the organization. We found that top executives want formal appraisals and rarely get them. If appraisals are not done at the top, the message sent to the rest of the organization is, "They aren't very important and thus shouldn't be taken seriously." As a result, the door to more political activity is opened wider.
3. Further, although training on *how* to do effective appraisals is important, managers also need to be trained on *why* they need to be done. Understanding the rationale for appraisals is important in building the perception that the appraisal process is an effective managerial tool and not merely a required bureaucratic procedure.
4. Open discussion of the political aspects of the appraisal process (and their legal ramifications) should be included in appraisal training programs. Although managers made it clear that political manipulation of rating is commonplace, political issues were *never* openly discussed in either training programs or in management development efforts.
5. When money is tied to the rating process, politically oriented ratings tend to increase. This creates a dilemma: A "pay for performance" management philosophy depends on the "objective" measurement of performance. Yet the realities of politics in the measurement process often mean that measurement will not be objective. Should we therefore divorce appraisal ratings from salary decisions? We think not. Pay for performance is still a good concept in our view, even in light of our findings. Attention to the recommendations we present in this section should minimize the impact of manipulative politics in appraisal ratings.
6. In addition, the number of people who have access to the written appraisal should be minimized. The more people who have access to the appraisal, the greater the temptation for the rater to "impression manage" it. Remember, the fact that the appraisal is written down of-

ten means that it is less than completely accurate, simply because it is publicly available.

7. The findings of this study have legal implications as well. Organizations are more susceptible to litigation involving charges of unlawful discharge or discrimination than ever before. Accurate, valid appraisals can help an organization defend itself; inaccurate, invalid appraisals can put the organization at risk. Of course, the relatively recent practice of extensive documentation of poor performance has been in part a response to the modern legal climate. Paradoxically, that climate has arguably *increased* the role of politics in formal appraisal, as organizations try to maintain legal grounds for termination decisions. Still, the often politically motivated practice of building a case for dismissal via documentation of poor performance has come under closer scrutiny as trends in employee appraisal are given closer examination. The best advice here is to stress honesty in appraisal as a "default option" policy. Credible and consistent appraisal practices are the best defense against litigation. Thus some counseling in the legal ramifications of appraisal should become part of executive training.

Conclusion

Perhaps the most interesting finding from our study (because it debunks a popular mythology) is that accuracy is *not* the primary concern of the practicing executive in appraising subordinates. The main concern is how best to use the appraisal process to motivate and reward subordinates. Hence, managerial discretion and effectiveness, not accuracy, are the real watchwords. Managers made it clear that they would not allow excessively accurate ratings to cause problems for themselves, and that they attempted to use the appraisal process to their own advantage.

The astute manager recognizes that politics in employee appraisal will never be entirely squelched. More candidly, most of us also recognize that there is some place for politics in the appraisal process to facilitate necessary executive discretion. The goal, then, is not to arbitrarily and ruthlessly try to eliminate politics but, instead, to effectively manage the role politics plays in employee appraisal.

Endnotes

1. For an extensive discussion of this point, see F. J. Landy and J. L. Farr's "Performance Rating," *Psychological Bulletin,* 1980, *87,* 72–107. This issue is further developed in Landy and Farr's book, *The Measurement of Work Performance,* New York: Academic Press, 1983. It is clear that the psychometric aspects of the appraisal process are only one part of understanding and improving appraisals.

2. DeNisi, Cafferty, and Meglino have recently discussed the key issues and complications associated with understanding the psychology of managerial decision making in the appraisal process in their recent article, "A Cognitive View of the Performance Appraisal Process: A Model and Research Prospective," *Organiza-*

tional Behavior and Human Performance, 1984, *33,* 360–396. For a discussion of further cognitive complications in the appraisal process as a result of unconscious information processing, refer to D.A. Gioia and P.P. Poole, "Scripts in Organizational Behavior," *Academy of Management Review,* 1984, *9,* 449–459.

3. For an exploration of some of the emotional and affective factors that might bear on appraisal processes, see O. S. Park, H. Sims, Jr., and S. J. Motowidlo's "Affect in Organizations: How Feelings and Emotions Influence Managerial Judgment," in H. P. Sims and D. A. Gioia and Associates (Eds.) *The Thinking Organization.*

4. Jack Feldman suggests in his article, "Beyond Attribution Theory: Cognitive Processes in Performance Evaluation," *Journal of Applied Psychology,* 1981, *66,* 127–148, that raters have certain cognitive flaws in information processing that make complete objectivity and validity in rating unobtainable. Also see W. C. Borman's "Explaining the Upper Limits of Reliability and Validity in Performance Ratings," *Journal of Applied Psychology,* 1987, *63,* 135–144.

5. Jeffrey Pfeffer, in his book *Power in Organizations,* Marshfield, MA: Pittman Publishing Co., 1981, makes a strong case that political gamesmanship and the use of power in organizations surround almost every important decision in organizational life. The implications of the appraisal process (e.g., pay raises, promotions, terminations) make the appraisal of performance an important decision-making enterprise.

6. Bernardin and Beatty in their book *Performance Appraisal: Assessing Human Behavior at Work,* Boston, MA: Kent, 1984, suggest that extraneous variables that are not performance related have an effect on the rater's decision processes and that this influence is in fact a primary source of bias and inaccuracy in performance ratings.

7. For an in-depth treatment of the legal issues concerning performance appraisal, see P. S. Greenlaw and J. P. Kohl's *Personnel Management,* New York: Harper & Row, 1986, 171–173. See also W. F. Cascio and H. J. Bernardin's "Implications of Performance Litigation for Personnel Decisions," *Personnel Psychology,* Summer 1981, 217.

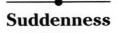

Suddenness

Earl Shorris

. . .Today, people are more persuaded than ever that they have perfect freedom, yet they have brought their freedom to us and laid it humbly at our feet.

The Grand Inquisitor

The one thing he knew about the management of the company was that they valued him. They had told him so, he had told her so. Whenever he felt unhappy with his job, whenever they felt the pinch of inflation at home, she reminded him of how he was valued by the company. It saw them through a bank loan to consolidate and stretch out their other loans. It saw them through their children attending public schools instead of the country day school they had planned on. It saw them through the fleabites and itchings of their lives.

They were not unhappy. She said he watched too much television on weekends. He wondered aloud if it was healthy for her to watch television in the afternoons. A week before their fifteenth wedding anniversary he bought a sex manual, but he had second thoughts about it—she might consider it a criticism of her performance in bed—and he left the manual on the seat of the bus.

On Sundays they went to church. She collected money for the United Fund, he did his best to hire minorities and women in his section, they despised Richard Nixon after Watergate. The evening of the day the car broke down he said to her that life was not easy for decent middle-class people anymore.

But we haven't lost our values, she answered.

His hair was thinning, she had developed a varicose vein in her left leg. One night while they were in bed, he said, Time is passing.

It's not so bad, she said.

I don't know, honey, I think the Joneses have passed us by.

You have a good job, and it'll get better. You provide for us.

He kissed her. She wiped the moisturizing ointment from her hands before she touched him.

He was not an easy man to work for. Mistakes irritated him; he did not hesitate to point them out to those who erred. He believed people were happier when they did their best, and he told them so. Everyone was equal in his eyes: male and female, black and white. No one escaped criticism for an error, even if it came in the form of a long coffee break or an unexcused morning lateness. Some people said he was grumpy, an old woman rather than a middle-aged man. Neither was he an easy man to supervise: his ways were set, he knew what was best for the company, and he did not hesitate to say so. He did not deviate from the rules: there were no shortcuts, he abhorred cheating in any form, the thought of stealing a paper clip or a moment was odious to him. When he refused to reconsider scrapping a thousand gross of journey crosses because an indeterminate number had been forged with one side three hundredths of an inch too short, the vice-president congratulated him, taking responsibility for the error as his own.

His dismissal was the greatest surprise of his life. What did I do? he asked.

You didn't *do* anything, the vice-president said. You're simply not promotable in the job. God almighty, you must know that by now, man.

I like my job. I do it well. You told me I do it well. You told me how valuable I am to the company.

It's policy. We don't want any first line managers who can't be promoted. It's policy. I can't do anything about it.

But I haven't done anything. I don't steal, not even a paper clip, not even a piece of notepaper. I never let down on quality. I gave it all I had.

You can't argue your way back into the job. Make it easy on yourself. The vice-president offered his hand. While they shook hands, the vice-president took an envelope from his pocket. He said it was a check for fifteen weeks' severance and four weeks' vacation pay.

When he left the vice-president's office, he went to the men's room to wash his face with cold water, especially his eyes, which were burning and itching, as if he'd been touched by some industrial pollutant. He looked at himself in the mirror above the sink. It was an honest face. The thinning hair, the eyeglasses, the fold of flesh above his shirt collar, the beard so bluegray and steely on his white skin, the manly pores of the skin on his nose, everything about him was forthright, decent. He was an ordinary, hardworking American, veteran, taxpayer, husband, father, Rockefeller Republican, and he had been fired!

He cleaned out his desk and took the pictures off the wall behind him, sorting out what was his from what was theirs. He had three tins of aspirin. Was that wasteful, he wondered, or had the headaches been so bad?

Everything fit into his attaché case, the present his wife and children had given him the Christmas after his promotion. The case was scarred, one lock was broken, and he had put a piece of adhesive tape on the handle where the leather had come loose. The tape was gray now. He paused to consider it for a moment, the time was all there on the piece of tape, every morning, every evening, all the work he had taken home to do on the kitchen table. He slammed the case shut, closed the one lock that still worked, and left his office. He said good-by to no one. He had been a severe man, an honest man, who gave no quarter. That had been his value to the company. Even now, he wasted no one's time in farewells.

On the way home he tried to make a plan, knowing that a man couldn't go about looking for a job in a haphazard manner. Discipline was important. He would get up at the same time, he would shower and shave and catch the same train he always caught. He knew all the failings of weak men: he would not spend time in bars, he would not go to the ball game in the afternoon.

She kept coming to mind, more than the job hunting, more than the children. What would she do? What would she say? She would cry, she would think of the bills, she would hug the children. When they went to bed, she would not put ointment on her hands, saying they could no longer afford it. Late at night, after he had gone to sleep, she would permit herself to cry; he would know by the redness around her eyes in the morning.

At the station there was a woman selling orange and gold and rusty brown autumn flowers. He bought a bunch from her. They were only a dollar and they would look so good, so cheery on the dining room table. They were just right for the green vase.

He opened the front door and called out to her, Hi, honey! It was like every other evening. He smelled the food cooking in the kitchen, a chicken roasting; he hoped she had basted it with orange juice.

She came hurrying out of the kitchen, through the dining room, wiping her hands on her apron. Her hair was so neat, the same bangs she had always worn, the gray not spoiling it at all; her face was so sweet, made sweeter by the weight she had gained in the past few years. He held the flowers out to her.

It's an occasion, she said. She blushed, running the last few steps, embracing him, dancing him half a turn. It's an occasion! She leaned her head back to watch his face.

You know how valuable they say I am.

Juridical man has dignity and entertains feelings of autonomy because he knows himself as a legal person, more than an animal or a thing, a person capable of beginnings, a person who must be considered in the special category of humanity. Juridical man exists in his own eyes and in the eyes of others, he leaves a mark in the world, he can engage in politics. In societies based on law, he expects to have certain rights: no one can do violence to him without breaking the law.

Totalitarian organizations seek to destroy the concept of juridical man in their search for total power. Things submit to domination more easily than legal persons. Things do not begin; there is no thing new under the sun. To do violence to a thing breaks no laws, even the murder of a thing does not call for punishment. When all persons are reduced to things, law has no meaning, all is permitted, without limit.

Night and Fog was the Nazi code name for the order that people who were considered security risks were to disappear without a trace. It implied that enemies of the organization were not legal persons. Stalin chose first to destroy those who opposed him and then to destroy those who agreed with him in order to rid the Soviet Union of the notion of juridical man. His method included concentration camps, assassinations, and the sudden dismissal of people who had performed well in their jobs.

Corporations, by turn paternalistic and cruel, teach their employees not to consider themselves juridical persons, with rights, living under the rule of law in human fashion. The sudden and apparently unprovoked dismissal of a few people or even of one person makes the rest docile. It teaches that the will of the organization is greater than the will of law or even of reason: the will of the organization is incontestable.

Men who live in such circumstances are not free, for there can be freedom only when law limits power. A man can be either a juridical person or a slave, he may have recourse against power or he may not. When men have no legal existence, when power may be exercised against them without the restraint of law, the social contract has been abrogated, human society has been replaced by the organization of things, all human values have been lost. The man who believes himself to be a creature utterly without rights belongs to a mass of disconnected atoms, no one of which has any unique value. That man obeys. He considers it his happiness.

The Case of the Mismanaged Ms.

Sally Seymour

It started out as one of those rare quiet mornings when I could count on having the office to myself. The Mets had won the World Series the night before, and most of the people in the office had celebrated late into the night at a bar across the street. I'm a fan too, but they all like to go to one of those bars where the waitresses dress like slave girls and the few women customers have to run a mine field of leers when they go to a ladies' room labeled "Heifers." Instead, I watched the game at home with my husband and escaped a hangover.

So I was feeling pretty good, if a little smug, when Ruth Linsky, a sales manager here at Triton, stormed past my secretary and burst into my office. Before I could say good morning, she demanded to know what business it was of the company who she slept with and why. I didn't know what she was talking about, but I could tell it was serious. In fact, she was practically on the verge of tears, but I knew she wasn't the type to fly off the handle.

Ruth had been with the company for three years, and we all respected her as a sensible and intelligent woman. She had been top in her class at business school and we recruited her hard when she graduated, but she didn't join us for a couple of years. She's since proved to be one of our best people in sales, and I didn't want to lose her. She fumed around the room for a while, not making much sense, until I talked her into sitting down.

"I've had it with this place and the way it treats women!" she shouted.

I allowed her to let off some more steam for a minute or two, and then I tried to calm her down. "Look, Ruth," I said, "I can see you're upset, but I need to know exactly what's going on before I can help you."

"I'm not just upset, Barbara," she said, "I'm damned mad. I came over to Triton because I thought I'd get more chances to advance here, and I just found out that I was passed over for director of the marketing division and Dick Simon got it instead. You know that I've had three outstanding years at the company, and my performance reviews have been excellent. Besides, I was led to believe that I had a pretty good shot at the job."

"What do you mean, 'led to believe'?"

"Steve heard through the grapevine that they were looking for a new marketing director, and he suggested I put in my name," she said. "He knows my work from when we worked together over at Forge Techtronics, and he said he'd write a letter in support. I wouldn't have even known they were looking for someone if Steve hadn't tipped me off."

Steve Baines is vice president of manufacturing. He's certainly a respected senior person in the company and he pulls some weight, but he doesn't have sole control of the marketing position. The hierarchy doesn't work that way, and I tried to get Ruth to see that. "Okay, so Steve wrote a letter for you, but he's only one of five or six VPs who have input in executive hiring decisions. Of course it helps to have his support, but lots of other factors need to be considered as well."

"Come off it, Barbara," Ruth snapped. "You know as well as I do there's only one thing that really matters around here and that's whether you're one of the boys. I've got a meeting this afternoon with my lawyer, and I'm going to file a sexual discrimination suit, a sexual harassment suit, and whatever other kind of suit she can come up with. I've had it with this old-boy crap. The only reason I'm here is that, as human resources director, you should know what's going on around here."

So the stakes were even higher than I had thought; not only did it look like we might lose Ruth, but we also might have a lawsuit on our hands. And to top it off, with the discrimination issue Ruth might be trying to get back at us for promoting Dick. I felt strongly about the importance of this legal remedy, but I also knew that using it frivolously would only undermine women's credibility in legitimate cases.

"Ruth," I said, "I don't doubt your perceptions, but you're going to need some awfully strong evidence to back them up."

"You want evidence? Here's your evidence. Number one: 20% of the employees in this company are women. Not one is on the board of directors, and not one holds an executive-level position. You and I are the only two in mid-level positions. Number two: there's no way for women to move into the mid-level positions because they never know when they're available. When a vacancy comes up, the VPs—all men, of course—decide among themselves who should fill it. And then, over and over again I hear that some guy who hasn't worked half as hard as most of the women at his level has been given the plum. Number three: there are plenty of subtle and sometimes not-so-subtle messages around here that women are less than equal."

"Ruth, those are still pretty vague accusations," I interrupted. "You're going to have to come up with something more specific than feelings and suppositions."

"Don't worry, Barbara. Just keep listening and maybe you'll learn something about how this company you think so highly of operates. From the day Ed Coulter took over as vice president of marketing and became my boss, he's treated me differently from the male sales managers. Instead of saying good morning, he always has some comment about my looks—my dress is nice, or my hair looks pretty, or the color of my blouse brings out my eyes. I don't want to hear that stuff. Besides, he never comments on a guy's eyes. And then there's that calendar the sales reps have in their back office. Every time I go in there for a sales meeting, I feel like I've walked into a locker room."

So far, this all seemed pretty harmless to me, but I didn't want Ruth to feel I wasn't sympathetic. "To tell the truth, Ruth, I'm not so sure all women here find compliments like that insulting, but maybe you can give me other examples of discriminatory treatment."

"You bet I can. It's not just in the office that these things happen. It's even worse in the field. Last month Ed and I and Bill, Tom, and Jack went out to Dryden Industries for a big project meeting. I'll admit I was a little nervous because there were some heavy hitters in the room, so I kept my mouth shut most of the morning. But I was a team member and I wanted to contribute.

"So when Ed stumbled at one point, I spoke up. Well, it was like I had committed a sacrilege in church. The Dryden guys just stared at me in surprise, and then they seemed actually angry. They ignored me completely. Later that afternoon, when I asked Ed why I had gotten that reaction, he chuckled a little and explained that since we hadn't been introduced by our specific titles, the Dryden guys had assumed I was a research assistant or a secretary. They thought I was being presumptuous. But when Ed explained who I was, they admitted that I had made an important point.

"But that wasn't all," she went on. "The next day, when we explained to them that I would be interviewing some of the factory foremen for a needs assessment, one of the executives requested that someone else do it because apparently there's a superstition about women on the factory floor bringing bad luck. Have you ever heard of anything so stupid? But that's not the worst of it. Ed actually went along with it. After I'd pulled his bacon out of the fire the day before. And when I nailed him for it, he had the gall to say 'Honey, whatever the client wants, the client gets.'

"Well, we got the contract, and that night we all went out to dinner and everything was hurray for our team. But then, when I figured we'd all go back to the hotel for a nightcap, Ed and the guys just kind of drifted off."

"Drifted off?" I asked.

"Yeah. To a bar. They wanted to watch some basketball game."

"And you weren't invited?"

"I wasn't invited and I wasn't disinvited," she said. "They acted like they didn't know what to say."

By this point Ruth had cooled down quite a bit, and although she still seemed angry, she was forthright in presenting her case. But now her manner changed. She became so agitated that she got up from her chair to stare out the window. After a few minutes, she sort of nodded her head, as if she had come to some private, difficult decision, and then crossed the room to sit down again. Looking at her lap and twisting a paper clip around in her hands, she spoke so softly that I had to lean forward to hear her.

"Barbara," she began, "what I'm going to tell you is, I hope, in confidence. It's not easy for me to talk about this because it's very personal and private, but I trust you and I want you to understand my position. So here goes. When Steve Baines and I were both at Forge, we had a brief affair. I was discreet about it; it never interfered with business, and we ended it shortly after we both came to work here. But we're still very close friends, and occasionally we have dinner or a drink together. But it's always as friends. I think Ed found out about it somehow. The day after I notified the head office that I wanted to be considered for the director position, Ed called me into his office and gave me a rambling lecture about how we have to behave like ladies and gentlemen these days because of lawsuits on sexual harassment.

"At the time, I assumed he was referring somehow to one of our junior sales reps who had gotten drunk at the Christmas party and made a fool of himself with a couple of secretaries; but later I began to think that the cryptic comment was meant for me. What's more, I think Ed used that rumor about my relationship with Steve to block my promotion. And that, Barbara, is pure, sexist, double-standard hypocrisy because I can name you at least five guys at various levels in this company who have had affairs with colleagues and clients, and Ed is at the top of the list."

I couldn't deny the truth of Ruth's last statement, but that wasn't the point, or not yet. First I had to find out which, if any, of her accusations were true. I told her I needed some time and asked if she could give me a week before calling in a lawyer. She said no way. Having taken the first step, she was anxious to take the next, especially since she didn't believe things would change at Triton anyway. We dickered back and forth, but all I could get from her was a promise to hold off for 24 hours. Not much of a concession, but it was better than nothing.

Needless to say, I had a lot to think about and not very much time to do it in. It was curious that this complaint should come shortly after our organization had taken steps to comply with affirmative action policies by issuing a companywide memo stating that we would continue to recruit, employ, train, and promote individuals without regard to race, color, religion, sex, age, national origin, physical or mental handicap, or status as a disabled veteran or veteran of the Vietnam era. And we did this to prevent any problems in the future, not because we'd had trouble in the past. In fact, in my five years as HRM director, I'd never had a sexual discrimination or harassment complaint.

But now I was beginning to wonder whether there had never been grounds for complaint or whether the women here felt it was useless or even dangerous to complain. If it was the latter, how had I contributed to allowing that feeling to exist? And this thought led me to an even more uncomfortable one: Had I been coopted into ignoring injustices in a system that, after all, did pretty well by me? Was I afraid to slap the hand that buttered my bread?

Questioning one's own motives may be enlightening, but it's also time consuming, and I had more pressing matters to deal with before I could indulge in what would likely be a painful self-analysis. I asked my secretary fo find George Drake, CEO of Triton, and get him on the phone. In the meantime, I wrote down as much as I could remember of what Ruth had just told me. When George finally called, I told him I knew his schedule was full but we had an emergency of sorts on our hands and I needed an hour of his time this morning. I also asked that Ed Coulter be called into the meeting. George told me I had the hour.

When I got to George's office, Ed and George were already waiting. They were undoubtedly curious about why I had called this meeting, but as I've seen people do in similar situations, they covered their anxiety with chitchat about ball games and hangovers. I was too impatient for these rituals, so I cut the conversation short and told them that we were going to have a serious lawsuit on our hands in a matter of days if we didn't act very quickly. That got their attention, so I proceeded to tell Ruth's story. When I began, George and Ed seemed more surprised than anything else, but as I built up Ruth's case their surprise turned to concern. When I finished, we all sat in silence for I don't know how long and then George asked Ed for comments.

"Well, George," Ed said, "I don't know what to say. Ruth certainly was a strong contender for the position, and her qualifications nearly equaled Dick's, but it finally came down to the fact that Dick had the seniority and a little more experience in the industrial sector. When you've got two almost equally qualified candidates, you've got to distinguish them somehow. The decision came down to the wire, which in this case was six months seniority and a few more visits to factory sites."

"Were those the only criteria that made a difference in the decision?" George wanted to know.

"Well, not exactly. You know as well as I do that we base hiring decisions on a lot of things. On one hand, we look at what's on paper: years at the company, education, experience, recommendations. But we also rely on intuition, our feel for the situation. Sometimes, you don't know exactly why, but you just feel better about some people than others, and I've learned that those gut reactions are pretty reliable. The other VPs and I all felt good about Dick. There's something about him—he's got the feel of a winner. You know? He's confident—not arrogant—but solid and really sharp. Bruce had him out to the club a couple of times, and I played squash with him all last winter. We got to know him and we liked what we saw; he's a family man, kids in school here, could use the extra money, and is looking to stick around for a while. None of these things mean a lot by themselves, of course, but together they add up.

"Don't get me wrong. I like Ruth too. She's very ambitious and one of our best. On the other hand, I can't say that I or any of the VPs know her as well as we know Dick. Of course, that's not exactly Ruth's fault, but there it is."

I had to be careful with the question I wanted Ed to respond to next because Ruth had asked for my confidence about the affair. I worded it this way:

"Ed, did any part of your decision take into account Ruth's relationship with anyone else at the company?"

The question visibly disturbed Ed. He walked across the room and bummed a cigarette from me—he had quit last week—before answering: "Okay, I didn't want to go into this, but since you brought it up. . . .There's a rumor—well it's stronger than a rumor—that Ruth is more than professionally involved with Steve Baines—I mean she's having an, ah, sexual affair with him. Now before you tell me that's none of my business, let me tell you about some homework I did on this stuff. Of course it's real tricky. It turns out there are at least two court cases that found sexual discrimination where an employer involved in a sexual relationship with an employee promoted that person over more qualified candidates.

"So here's what that leaves us with: we've got Steve pushing his girlfriend for the job. You saw the letter he wrote. And we've got Dick with seniority. So if we go with Ruth, what's to keep Dick from charging Steve and the company on two counts of sexual discrimination: sexual favoritism because Ruth is Steve's honey and reverse discrimination because we pass over a better qualified man just to get a woman into an executive position. So we're damned if we do and damned if we don't. We've got lawsuits if we don't advance Dick, and, so you tell me, lawsuits if we don't advance Ruth!"

We let that sink in for a few seconds. Then George spoke up: "What evidence do you have, Ed, that Steve and Ruth are having an affair?" he asked.

"Look, I didn't hire some guy to follow them around with a camera, if that's what you mean," Ed said. "But come on, I wasn't born yesterday; you can't keep that kind of hanky-panky a secret forever. Look at the way she dresses; she obviously enjoys men looking at her, especially Steve. In fact, I saw them having drinks together at Dino's the other night and believe me, they didn't look like they were talking business. All that on top of the rumors, you put two and two together."

Well, that did it for me. I'd been trying to play the objective observer and let Ed and George do all the talking, but Ed's last comment, along with some budding guilt about my own blindness to certain things at Triton that Ruth had pointed out, drove me out in the open. "Come off it, Ed," I said. "That's not evidence, that's gossip."

Now Ed turned on me: "Look," he shouted, "I didn't want to talk about this, but now that you've brought it up, I'll tell you something else. Even if we didn't have to worry about this sexual discrimination business, I still wouldn't back Ruth for the director's job." He calmed down a bit. "No offense, Barbara, but I just don't think women work out as well as men in certain positions. Human resources is one thing. It's real soft, person-to-person stuff. But factories are still a man's world. And I'm not talking about what I want it to be like. I'm talking facts of life.

"You see what happens when we send a woman out on some jobs, especially in the factories. To be any good in marketing you have to know how to relate to your client; that means getting to know him, going out drinking with him, talking sports, hunting, whatever he's interested in. A lot of our clients feel uncomfortable around a woman in business. They know how to relate to their wives, mothers, and girlfriends, but when a woman comes to the office and wants to talk a deal on industrial drills—well, they don't know what to do.

"And then there's the plain fact that you can't depend on a woman the way you can on a guy. She'll get married and her husband will get transferred, or she'll have a baby and want time off and not be able to go on the road as much. I know, Barbara, you probably think I'm a pig, or whatever women's libbers call guys like me these days. But from where I'm sitting, it just made good business sense to choose Dick over Ruth."

"Ed, I don't believe it," I said. "The next thing you'll tell me is that women ought to stay at home, barefoot and pregnant." There was a long silence after that—my guess was that I had hit on exactly what Ed thought. At least he didn't deny it. Ed stared at the rug, and George frowned at his coffee cup. I tried to steer the conversation back to the subject at hand, but it dwindled into another silence. George took a few notes and then told Ed he could go back to work. I assumed I was excused too, but as I started to leave, George called me back.

"Barbara, I'm going to need your help thinking through this mess," he said. "Of course we've got to figure out how we can avoid a lawsuit before the day is out, but I also want to talk about what we can do to avoid more lawsuits in the future. While Ed was talking I took some notes, and I've got maybe four or five points I think we ought to hash out. I'm not saying we're going to come up with all the answers today, but it'll be a start. You ready?"

"Shoot."

"Okay, let's do the big one first," he began. "What should I have done or not done to avoid this situation? I mean, I was just patting myself on the back for being so proactive when I sent out that memo letting everyone know the company policy on discrimination. I wrote it not thinking we had any problem at Triton. But just in case we did, I figured that memo would take care of it."

"Well, it looks like it's not enough just to have a corporate policy if the people in the ranks aren't on board. Obviously it didn't have much of an effect on Ed."

"So what am I supposed to do? Fire Ed?"

Being asked for my honest opinion by my CEO was a new experience for me and I appreciated it, but I wasn't going to touch that last question with a ten-foot pole. Instead I went on to another aspect: "And even if you get your managers behind you, your policy won't work if the people it's supposed to help don't buy it. Ruth was the first woman to complain around here. Are the others afraid to speak up? Or do they feel like Ed about a woman's place, or have husbands who do? Maybe they lack confidence even to try for better jobs, that is, if they knew about them."

"Okay," he said, "I'll admit that our system of having the VPs make recommendations, our 'old-boy network,' as Ruth called it, does seem to end up excluding women, even though the exclusion isn't intentional. And it's not obvious discrimination, like Ed's claim that Ruth is unqualified for a position because she is a woman. But wouldn't open job posting take away our right to manage as we see fit? Maybe we should concentrate instead on getting more women into the social network, make it an old boys' and old girls' club?"

"To tell you the truth, George, I don't much want to play squash with you," I replied, "but maybe we're getting off the subject. The immediate question seems to be how we're going to get more women into executive positions here, or, more specifically, do we give Ruth the director of marketing position that we just gave Dick?"

"On that score, at least, it seems to me that Ed has a strong argument," George said. "Dick is more qualified. You can't get around that."

I had wanted to challenge Ed on this point when he brought it up earlier, but I wasn't quite sure of myself then. Now that George was asking me for advice and seemed to be taking what I had to say seriously, I began to think that I might have something valuable to offer. So I charged right in. "George, maybe we're cutting too fine a line with this qualifications business. I know a lot of people think affirmative action means promoting the unqualified over the qualified to achieve balance. I think that argument is hogwash at best and a wily diversion tactic at worst. To my mind, Ruth and Dick are equally qualified, or equal enough. And wouldn't it make good business sense to get a diverse set of perspectives—women's, men's, blacks', whites'—in our executive group?"

"But isn't that reverse discrimination—not promoting Dick because he's a man? How would a judge respond to that? That's a question for a lawyer."

George leaned forward. "Let's talk about my last point, the one I think we've both been avoiding. What about this affair between Ruth and Steve? Boy, this is one reason why women in the work force are such trouble—no, just joking, Barbara, sorry about that. Look, I don't like lawsuits any more than anyone else, but I'd do anything to avoid this one. We'd be a laughing stock if it got out that Triton promoted unqualified people because they slept with the boss. I don't know how I'd explain that one to my wife."

"Look, George," I said, "in the first place, Dick's superior qualifications are debatable; in the second place, we have no proof that Ruth and Steve are involved in that way; and in the third place, what if they were once involved but no longer are? Does a past relationship condemn them for life? Isn't there a statute of limitations on that kind of thing, or are we going to make her put a scarlet letter on her briefcase? I thought these discrimination laws were supposed to protect women, but now it looks like a woman can be denied a promotion because someone thinks she's a floozy."

"Wait a second, Barbara. Don't make me look like such a prig," George said. "I realize that when men and women work together sexual issues are bound to crop up. I just don't know what I'm supposed to do about it, if anything. In some cases a woman may welcome a guy coming on to her, but what if it's her boss? And then there's that subtle stuff Ruth brought up—the calendar, dirty jokes, the male employees excluding women by going to bars to watch TV—and other women. And Ruth's treatment at that factory—how can we control our clients? I'm not sure these are things you can set policy on, but I am sure that I can't ignore them any longer."

And there we were. All the issues were on the table, and we had about 21 hours to make our decisions and act on them. . . .

8

Managing Hazards

Throughout the book we have encountered numerous examples of the tensions generated by the imperfect meshing of the characteristics of formal organizations and the characteristics of individuals. When students of management first confronted these tensions, their inclination was often to try to separate the two. Specifically, they sought to eliminate the impact of the personal factors from the organization. As Joseph Massie observed, the early writers encouraged managers to ignore personal problems and characteristics.[1] Management was viewed primarily as planning and formalizing relationships. Supervisors were urged to model rationality and objectivity and avoid feelings and emotions. Adequate planning and the development of rules and procedures could make the organization into an efficient machine, buffered from the idiosyncrasies of human beings.

It soon became apparent that human beings—both the workers and the managers—brought their human emotions, needs, and individual differences with them into the organization. Separation was impossible—the *mutual* influence of human beings and organizations are simply too deep. The initial tendency, however, to separate the two lives on, albeit to a lesser degree.

Even though it is widely recognized that the influence is mutual, the study of management has centered mainly on the influence of individuals on the organization. Managers are taught how to recruit, select, train, supervise, motivate, and communicate with individuals so that their efforts become coordinated to achieve the organization's goals. Although the approaches are much more informed by knowledge of human behavior than were the approaches described earlier, they are still concerned with protecting the organization from the problems that humans can introduce. In this section we are concerned with both directions, but we are more concerned with the consequences that organizations have for individuals both in and outside of the workplace. These articles center on the effects that organizations can have on individuals. Since we deal here mainly with what we judge to be the negative consequences, we use the word "hazards."

The hazards stem from several sets of sources. Some hazards are simply the result of pathological behavior (see, for example, "Violence of Workplace . . ."). It is often easy to assume that the people we deal with are "normal" despite certain "idiosyncrasies" that some might have. Yet, there are enough reports of seriously disturbed individuals reacting violently to events at work to remind us that management can not isolate the organization from all facets of human behavior. Similarly, humans are physically and sexually attracted to each other (see, for example, "Sexual Attraction at Work . . .") and bring these characteristics to work as well. People also have certain indulgences—they smoke and they overeat. As several of the articles show, these behaviors have consequences for the organization, as well as for the individuals themselves.

It is also important to recognize a number of hazards that the organization presents for the individual. Smoking, being overweight, being attractive, and being attracted can all interfere with people obtaining their goals in the organization. Even though some of these things are, at most, remotely related to performance of one's tasks, they can have a major impact on the evaluation of people's performance. (As we have already seen, performance appraisals are far from objective.)

Finally, being part of an organization changes people directly. Psychologists tell us that when individuals are rewarded for particular behaviors, they tend to repeat them. Modern organizations reward people for using their time efficiently, for working intensely, and for devoting themselves to the organization's purposes. Just as organizations have problems buffering themselves from the personal characteristics of employees, the employees have difficulty separating themselves from the organization. Not only do they "take their work home with them" but they carry the behaviors that they are rewarded for at work into their personal lives (see, for example, "To Love or to Work . . ."). They approach their leisure time, for instance, just as they are taught to approach their work time. As Schaef and Fassel (see, "Hooked on Work") note, people can become addicted to the organization and to work. These traits have consequences for their families as well as for society at large.

The articles in this section touch on a few of the ways that organizations and people influence each other. Again, separation is impossible and we are at an early point in the history and of our understanding of this dynamic process. Is there any way to achieve a balance?

Reference

1. J. L. Massie, Management theory. In J. G. March, ed., *Handbook of organizations* (Chicago: Rand McNally, 1965) pp. 387–422.

If I Had My Life to Live Over

Nadine Stair, 85-years-old
Louisville, Kentucky

I'd dare to make more mistakes next time.
I'd relax. I would limber up. I would be sillier
than I have been this trip. I would take fewer
things seriously. I would take more chances.
I would take more trips. I would climb more
mountains and swim more rivers. I would eat
more ice cream and less beans. I would perhaps
have more actual troubles, but I'd have fewer
imaginary ones.

You see, I'm one of those people who live
sensibly and sanely hour after hour, day after
day. Oh, I've had my moments and if I had it
to do over again, I'd have more of them. In fact,
I'd try to have nothing else. Just moments, one
after another, instead of living so many years
ahead of each day. I've been one of those persons
who never goes anywhere without a thermometer, a
hot water bottle, a raincoat, and a parachute.
If I had to do it again, I would travel lighter
than I have.

If I had my life to live over, I would start
barefoot earlier in the Spring and stay that way
later in the Fall. I would go to more dances.
I would ride more merry-go-rounds. I would
pick more daisies.

From the AHP Newsletter, July 1975. Reprinted by permission of the Association for Humanistic Psychology.

Violence of Workplace: Unseen Signs, Unexpected Explosions

Glenn Collins

When a shooting spree erupts in the workplace, workers everywhere are suddenly uneasy. The latent rage in an office or factory, a confined environment where self-esteem and financial worth are on the line, takes on new meaning.

"The workplace is a relatively inhibiting place for violence," said Dr. Edwin I. Megargee, a professor of psychology at Florida State University who is an expert on the causes of homicide and other violent behavior. Psychologists and social scientists say stress in the business environment and the family can lead to such incidents.

One barometer of such stress is employee assistance programs, which deal with threats from workers made desperate by converging problems at work and at home. Counselors are trained to take the threats seriously.

Dr. Robert Schrank, a sociologist who has taught at the Massachusetts Institute of Technology and is a consultant on worker motivation for the World Bank, the Champion Paper Company and Exxon, said: "Employees see the workplace as their family, their community, their life. For some, losing a job can hurt worse than being rejected by a lover or a mate."

The Latest Eruption

Both types of rejection seem to have been involved in the shootings Tuesday in Sunnyvale, Calif. Richard W. Farley, 39 years old, a computer programmer, was dismissed two years ago by ESL Inc., a subsidiary of TRW Inc., for harassing a female colleague. After seven people were killed, the police said, he told the police he meant only to "shoot out" computers. Laura Black, 26, who had spurned him, was wounded.

The prospect of dismissal was involved in August 1986 in the case of a Postal Service worker, Patrick Henry Sherrill, who shot 20 people, killing 14, in an Edmond, Okla., post office.

Last December a former employee of a convenience store in Russellville, Ark., went on a shooting spree that left 2 of his former supervisors dead and 4 former co-workers injured. Weeks earlier a dismissed airline worker apparently shot his former supervisor on a Pacific Southwest Airlines jet, causing a crash that killed 43 people.

Threats are Not Uncommon

Federal crime categories do not include homicide in the workplace, but encountering threats is not uncommon in workplace counseling. "We get something like this at least every couple of weeks," said Dr. Victor Klodin, a psychologist who is mental health consultant for the Control Data Corporation of Minneapolis, which counsels more than 150 other companies.

"Someone loses a job, gets angry and starts talking about getting even," he said. "Other employees feel there is the potential for violence and let us know."

In one instance, he said, workers called a corporation's security office about a manager who had been laid off. The man had spoken of "taking care of the people at headquarters" to "teach them about work force reduction."

"Security suggested he get in touch with us," said Dr. Klodin. "Until we talked with him, I don't think he realized how on edge he was." The manager got psychological and job counseling and found new work.

Of those workers who have been violent, "some are psychopaths or sociopaths who have not developed inhibitions against violence," Dr. Margergee said.

Voices That Told Him to Kill

Dr. Carol Dubnicki, a psychologist who advises corporations for Hay Management Consultants in San Francisco, recalled:

"A clerk in a shopping center who had been a good worker for years began hallucinating and hearing voices saying his supervisor wanted to fire him. The employee told others at work that he was going to kill the supervisor. A co-worker came to me and told me the man was carrying a gun. I got the man to come to my office, and the first thing I said was, 'I'm nervous with you being in this room. People say you can be very violent and they say you're carrying a weapon.'

"He reassured me that he wasn't. In fact, as we talked, I realized that he was only angry and hostile on this one issue—the voices telling him that his supervisor wanted to fire him. We got the employee into treatment, and on medication."

The man was eventually able to return to work.

Dr. Harry Levinson, clinical professor of psychology at the Harvard Medical School, recalled a sales trainee at a pharmaceutical company who had been told by his supervisor that he would never make a salesman. In the supervisor's office the trainee began talking about suicide.

"I happened to be in the office next door, consulting with another manager," said Dr. Levinson. "The supervisor came in and said, 'What do I do? he's going to kill himself!'" Dr. Levinson and the manager got the trainee home. With family support and counseling, the crisis passed, and the trainee worked in the company in a nonsales job.

Consultants said violence also may involve an old grudge. "The classic example of that is the Mad Bomber case," said Dr. Megargee. George P. Metesky conducted a 16-year vendetta against Consolidated Edison in New York City in the 1940's and 1950's. He had been hurt in an accident while working for Con Edison in 1931. He later planted explosives on the utility's property and public places. Thirty-seven explosions were attributed to him before his arrest in 1957.

"When you delve into these violent cases, often you find that there were warning signs," said Dr. Dubnicki. "The cheerful, reliable worker may suddenly have become highly irritable or late for work, or the highly verbal employee suddenly becomes withdrawn and morose."

Employee assistance programs seek to increase worker awareness of warning signals, which may reflect problems like chemical dependency or marital distress. "The E.A.P.'s can provide a safety net for troubled employees just by establishing a presence in a company," said Tom Delaney, executive director of the Association of Labor-Management Administrators and Consultants on Alcoholism in Arlington, Va. About 10,000 business organizations have employee assistance programs.

Dr. Klodin said: "The sensational cases are the ones that get in the newspapers, but what we see more of are people who take out their feelings against themselves by drinking, or who go home and are hostile to their wives or physically abusive to their kids. The cost of this kind of violence is much greater than in the relatively rare incidents where the guy actually goes to the post office and shoots the other workers."

On Corporate Ladder, Beauty Can Hurt

Georgia Dullea

The notion that beauty is only skin deep has been buried many times in the last decade by psychological studies that confirm a pervasive bias in favor of good-looking men and women. Not only are they more socially desirable, they are also expected to have better jobs, better marriages and happier lives, the studies found.

The expectation that good looks and success go together is so strongly documented that researchers were surprised recently by an apparent flaw in the "beauty is best" principle: beauty can backfire on women as they climb the corporate ladder, according to studies by Madeline Heilman, the latest of which appears in the current issue of The Journal of Applied Psychology.

"My research runs counter to the assumption that people who are good-looking are always better off," Dr. Heilman, a New York University psychologist, said in an interview. "In managerial jobs or jobs thought to require male characteristics, good looks are an advantage for men but not for women."

Similar Effect in Politics

Similar findings emerged from a study on the effect of physical appearance on political elections. When the only thing known about a candidate is the way he or she looks, voters of both sexes tend to choose attractive men and unattractive women, according to this study, published recently in the journal Woman and Politics.

Ann O'M. Bowman, a University of South Carolina political scientist who headed the study, concluded: "Attractive women labor under an impediment in running for public office. Their own good looks, which have purportedly paid dividends in childhood and adolescence in both educational and social spheres, have become a hindrance."

Why would beauty hinder women who aspire to positions of influence and power? One theory holds that attractive women are perceived as more feminine, and attractive men as more masculine. If beauty is sex-typed, the theory goes, an attractive woman in a job traditionally held by a man seems incongruous, giving rise to doubts about her competency.

Dr. Heilman's studies, begun five years ago, trace a pattern of bias against attractive women in the executive ranks. This bias is seen when the women apply for the jobs, when their job performances are evaluated and even after they have been promoted to better jobs.

In her latest experiment, conducted with a doctoral student, Melanie Stopeck, 113 working men and women in New York were given a detailed résumé of a corporate executive. Attached was an identification card with a photograph.

The résumés were essentially the same, but the photos varied. Half showed men who were either attractive or unattractive, and half showed unattractive or attractive women.

Participants in the experiment were asked to indicate the importance of factors such as hard work, ability, luck and politics in the executives' success. They were also asked to characterize the executives by selecting from various adjectives.

The attractive men and unattractive women were rated best. Both were seen, for example, as having more integrity than their counterparts. Moreover, less capability was attributed to attractive women. "Simply put," the study said, "they were most often believed to have gotten where they were for reasons other than their skill and/or talent."

Such attitudes, the study concluded, are bound to undermine the credibility, effectiveness and leadership abilities of women who happen to be good-looking.

Dr. Heilman said she is often asked whether corporate women should strive to appear unattractive. "Absolutely not," she said. "That would be a ridiculous conclusion to draw from my research. But women should be aware that, to the extent that being attractive is associated with ultrafemininity, there may be problems."

Nor are mannish clothes the answer, in her view. "It's important for women to succeed as women," Dr. Heilman said. "I really don't like this business of wearing only gray suits and not being yourself. You end up doing a disservice to yourself and your company."

There is agreement from others with a professional interest in the role that appearance plays in judgments about people.

"The outfit that wins the day for women, even in conservative places, is the androgynous one that has a mixture of masculine and feminine cues," said Thomas Cash, a psychologist at Old Dominion University in Norfolk, Va., who has studied sex-role stereotyping in grooming.

"A woman in a man's clothes elicits suspicion and distrust," Dr. Cash said. "Also, to the extent that the mannish suit has become a uniform, it says nothing distinctive about her, and others may feel they're being manipulated."

The beauty backlash is seen in the classroom as well as the office. In a study by Dr. Cash and others, college freshmen were asked to rate essays said to have been written by other freshmen. Accompanying the essays were photos of attractive and unattractive men and women.

Some essays dealt with such stereotypically masculine topics as "How to Buy a Used Motorcycle," and others with such feminine ones as "How to Make a Quilt." Over all, the quality of the writing was rather poor, Dr. Cash said.

Good looks paid off in higher marks for men, whether the topic was stereotypically male or female. Marks were also high for attractive women who wrote on feminine topics. On masculine topics, the attractive women scored lower than unattractive women.

"There was the phenomenon again—a poor rating for an attractive woman in a masculine context," Dr. Cash said.

The phenomenon appears as well in political campaigns, as Ann O'M. Bowman found in a study on looks and votes. Her peers in political science tend to ignore appearance in survey research on elections, she said, "probably because they feel this would trivialize the process."

The Importance of 'Image Creation'

"What we find is a deep gulf between the scholarly political scientist and the more practical political strategist," she said. "Any book on campaign management has a chapter on image creation."

In Dr. Bowman's study 125 college students, both men and women, were asked to rank hypothetical candidates for local, state and Congressional office solely on the basis of photographs.

Among male candidates, students of both sexes gave the highest rankings to attractive men. The opposite was true for female candidates, with unattractive women ranked higher. Though the pattern held for all types of offices, attractive women inexplicably did slightly better in Congressional races.

In this and other studies on beauty, the researchers say the message is clear: attractive women are seen as having all the qualities needed for success except the ones that would allow them to step out of the roles traditionally assigned them.

The Wall Street Journal, March 8, 1988.

Overweight Job Seekers

Overweight job seekers can expect to spend five more weeks than their trim rivals in the quest for work, say outplacement specialists Madeleine and Robert Swain. Tall candidates, they figure, have a four-week edge over short people.

●
———————

Sexual Attraction at Work: Managing the Heart

Duncan Spelman, Marcy Crary, Kathy E. Kram, James G. Clawson

Male-female attraction in the workplace—the subject seems to hit a sensitive nerve in almost everyone. Think how quickly the national media picked up on the story of Mary Cunningham and William Agee at Bendix. Front-page articles appeared day after day in virtually all the major newspapers, bringing Cunningham and Agee instant fame—some would say notoriety—and elevated the story of their affair to near-mythic status. Across the country, countless people might not be able to say what the Bendix Corporation does—but chances are they'll know Mary Cunningham's name.

Similarly, an article by Eliza Collins entitled "Managers and Lovers," published in the *Harvard Business Review,* prompted a number of emotional letters—some signed, some anonymous—from readers who for one reason or another were upset by her discussion of love relationships in the office. Moving romance from somewhere out there into the workplace dramatically changes the way people think. Love, we are told, is blind—but not in the office. Everyone loves a lover—but not in the office.

You will probably not find yourself or your relationships the center of attention that Mary Cunningham and her relationship with William Agee were. Yet the special feelings you may have for a co-worker of the opposite sex could complicate your professional and private life just as significantly as it did Cunningham's. Sometimes you will be able to manage such feelings easily; they will be only a pleasant addition to life on the job. But probably not always. For example, put yourself in Sue Bredbeck's place in the following situation.

The Case of Sue Bredbeck and Doug O'Connor

Sue had been employed at the Prospect Company for eighteen months when she met Doug O'Connor at a friend's party. Doug also worked for Prospect, as the team leader of a new product development team. The two of them hit it off immediately, dividing their conversation between talk about work and discussion of common interests in skiing, science fiction, and alumni activities at the local university of which they both were graduates.

Over the next couple of months the relationship between Sue and Doug developed, although it was not romantic. They went to lunch together fairly regularly, joined mutual friends for ski weekends, and attended basketball games at their alma mater, but never really had a serious date.

After Sue had known Doug for about six months, she raised the possibility of joining his project team. She was working in a much less exciting part of the company and had been looking for an opportunity to become involved in a position that would be more interesting and would allow her to showcase her abilities. After lengthy discussions of Sue's background and career goals, the team's work, and Doug's needs, Sue and Doug agreed it would make sense for both Sue and the team if she joined Doug's group.

Sue's initial experiences with the team were both exciting and confounding. The work itself was very stimulating, but she was disturbed about the cool reception she received from the men and women on the team. Doug had described them as an extremely close-knit group that enjoyed an easygoing, friendly, productive approach to their work—and drinks together after work on a fairly regular basis. But Sue's experience with the team members seemed quite formal to her, and she was not invited to any after-work social gatherings.

Doug, too, was concerned. During one of their frequent lunches together he mentioned to Sue that he had noticed a tension in team meetings that had not existed before. The familiar banter was absent, and communications seemed to be flowing less freely.

Once they had voiced their shared concerns, Sue and Doug spent many hours trying to diagnose the sources of the problem. Following one such conversation over dinner after work on Friday, the discussion became more personal and ended with both Sue and Doug expressing a desire for their relationship to become "more than friendship." They agreed to go away for a romantic weekend together.

Over the next few weeks life on the project team became both better and worse for Sue and Doug. After a brief period in which they had some difficulty concentrating on their work because of the intensity of their new relationship, they soon found themselves working together extremely well. Their joint efforts were exciting and very productive. But the other members of the team were increasingly cool toward Doug and cold toward Sue. The once smoothly functioning team was in trouble.

One day Doug's boss pulled him aside and told him he had heard through the grapevine about problems in the project team because of a romance. He told Doug to identify the people involved and put a stop to it before things got out of hand. Now Doug was unsure how to handle the situation. The effectiveness of his team had been disrupted, and his boss was unhappy about a mystery romance of which Doug himself was a part. Yet Doug's relationship with Sue was a source of both personal and professional satisfaction.

Sue, concerned about her relationships with her co-workers, decided to pay a visit to Karen Boyer in the Human Resources Department. During her orientation to the company, Sue had been particularly impressed with Karen's presentation on the unique challenges faced by women at Prospect. Karen suggested to Sue that the team members might feel threatened by her relationship with Doug, even if there was no real reason for them to worry. Karen also asked Sue if she had considered fully the potential consequences of the relationship. Sue left with misgivings about her decision to become involved with Doug. She focused especially on what would happen if the relationship soured. She also worried about whether people would assume she was trying to "sleep her way to the top."

To Love or to Work: Must We Choose?

Joan R. Kofodimos

Larry Grant was a model of competence and effectiveness, a manager whose work life at Chemco consisted of success after success. But is there enough time for him to be a husband and father as well? Is time really the issue?

[The events of the story presented here, though taken from a variety of sources, are not fiction; they exemplify the experiences of real managers struggling to find a balance between their work and private lives.—Ed.]

Larry Grant sat in his office two hours after everyone else had gone home, smoking his fortieth cigarette of the day. He was staring at a printout of next year's production goals for his division. He was deeply absorbed by the problem of what to do about the low figures for Xylac, their flagship antihypertensive drug. The patent that his company, Chemco, had held on the drug for five years had expired and several aggressive competitors had entered the field. The separate strands of three possible strategies for keeping Xylac the leader in the field were weaving together in his head when the telephone rang, shattering his concentration.

"Larry." It was Gloria, his wife. "Have you forgotten about dinner?" Tonight was the occasion for one of the major events of the Philadelphia social season, and Gloria was naturally as excited as an ingenue.

"Sorry," Larry said. "You can go without me, can't you?"

"I should have known." Gloria's voice fell. "Sweetheart, it doesn't look good for me to keep going to these things by myself."

"Sorry, honey, I've got to finish this."

Gloria retorted, "I'm sorry, too." There was a click as she hung up.

Larry put the phone down and turned back to the printout. Within minutes he was once again immersed in the intricacies of formulating a competitive strategy for Xylac.

Larry had always felt uncomfortable and shy at the social events his wife so much enjoyed, although at work his shyness vanished and he was comfortable and confident, the Larry Grant respected and admired by almost all of his coworkers. To these coworkers, Larry seemed to lead a charmed life. Only forty-one, he was Executive Vice President in charge of the Pharmaceuticals Division. His technical skills, native intelligence, and easygoing demeanor impressed top management and sped his ascent ever since he joined the company as a financial analyst fresh from his MBA at Wharton.

Back in those Wharton days, Gloria had dazzled Larry. She was a Main Line debutante attending Bryn Mawr College, and her upper-crust background was so different from that of his own family, which was solidly middle class. It wasn't that Larry was ashamed of his background—his father was a self-made man who had started out washing cars and ended up owning a successful car dealership in Trenton, New Jersey—it was just that Larry wanted more for himself. Though his parents had become affluent, they were always frugal and lived modestly. They had instilled in Larry the values of hard work and integrity, and he intended to make the most of himself. Marrying Gloria had been a first step on that road, or so he had thought.

Half an hour after Gloria's call, Larry was still buried in thought about the Xylac problem. There was a knock at the door, and Ed Brentano peeked in.

Ed was a chemist in the development lab. Though he was several levels below Larry, the two were good friends. They were often the only two left working after hours. (Ed, a bachelor, was sometimes rumored to spend entire nights in the lab, napping as he waited for time to lapse on his experiments.) Many evenings Ed and Larry ran into each other in the halls or at the coffee machine and ended up talking about developments in the lab or business trends. Larry loved these discussions. He sensed a kindred spirit in Ed. It felt good to talk to someone with intelligence, who understood the complexities of Larry's job. In Ed Larry also admired a certain maverick quality, a slight contempt for the accepted rules of worklife. This was probably because Larry himself did not always act on his own rebellious impulses.

"Hey Larry!" Ed called out, coming into Larry's office with several scraps of paper in his hand. "I'm glad you're still here. Got a minute? Take a look at this."

Larry's eyes lit up. He needed a break from what he was doing. He looked at the slips of paper Ed had tossed on his desk.

"Are these on the most recent compound?"

"Exactly!"

"But the tolerance is so high!"

"Right! And you know what that means, don't you?" Ed had tutored Larry in basic research chemistry.

"Yeah. It means a broader application."

"That may be an understatement! Of course, this has to be confirmed by independent tests."

Larry shook his head in wonder. "Think of all the implications, if this is true!"

And the two of them took off with speculations about the possibilities. Before Larry knew it over an hour had passed. It was nine o'clock. Reluctantly, he told Ed he had to get home. Sometimes he wished he didn't have family obligations. Sometimes he wished he could stay up all night working when he felt like it.

In his youth, Larry had always worked hard; his achievements had always been of utmost importance to him. He enjoyed the feeling of accomplishment, as well as the praise and rewards he got from his parents and teachers for doing well. Larry's achievements were also important to his parents, who had held great expectations for him. He was the first in his family to go to college, and he felt very special because of it. So he worked even harder in college and graduate school than he ever had before. He liked the strangely thrilling, almost romantic feeling of aloneness in the darkened dorm or in the corner of the library late at night.

When Larry got home, he found his daughter Karen, age twelve, in the den watching a movie on the VCR.

"Have you done your homework?"

"Yeah," Karen replied, her eyes glued to the screen.

"Where's your brother?"

"In his room."

That kid! Larry thought to himself. Matthew, age sixteen, had recently taken to locking himself in his room and listening to music. Larry knew that kids Matthew's age were prone to rebellion, but the boy really was beginning to concern Larry. It had gotten to the point where his grades—always high before and a source of pride to Larry—had begun to slip.

Gloria had been the first to notice a problem. Larry had been working on performance appraisals in his study one Sunday (he claimed that was the only way to get them done) when Gloria came in and announced, "I'm concerned that Matthew's been hanging around with a fast crowd. Do you know what time he got in last night? Two o'clock in the morning. I can't talk to him. I think you need to."

Larry had been annoyed at the intrusion. "He's a teenage kid, Gloria. Teenagers do things like that." At the time he had assumed she was making a big deal out of nothing. But lately Larry had noticed Matthew bringing home some unsavory-looking friends, and he was becoming hostile and unresponsive to Larry's attempts to talk to him. He was always off somewhere, and he was neglecting his household duties.

Tonight, for example, was the night to take out the trash—Matthew's job—and it was still in the garage. Larry went up to Matthew's room and knocked. No answer. He tried the knob—the door was locked. He banged louder. Finally Matthew opened the door. A pair of earphones closed out the world.

"Take those things off!" Larry yelled.

"What?" Matthew replied as he pulled the headphones down around his neck.

"I thought I told you not to lock your door. And didn't your mother ask you to take out the trash? You're not too old to be grounded, young man."

"Yeah, right. Just because I don't want to work all the time like you do!" And he slammed the door.

Larry stared at the closed door for a moment, then turned and walked away. The kid was getting out of hand. But this wasn't the time to do anything about it. Larry prided himself on his ability to put problems out of his mind when there was nothing he could do about them. It was a reaction that served him well at work, and he saw no reason why it couldn't work equally well at home.

Larry went to the kitchen and made himself a sandwich. He sat at the kitchen table and read the *Wall Street Journal* as he ate. Soon Matthew appeared, looking sheepish.

"I took out the trash, Dad. I'm sorry I yelled at you. I was wondering if— there's a basketball game at school tomorrow night. Could I have the car?"

Larry thought: So, the kid is willing to work a deal, is he? An apology and good behavior in return for the car. "You want the car on a week night?" he asked.

Matthew shifted his feet. "C'mon Dad, everyone is going!"

"So ride with someone else."

"Aw, you know the guys are counting on me to drive. C'mon."

"I can't have you talking to me with such disrespect, Matthew."

"I know, Dad. I said I was sorry."

Larry felt a twinge of guilt. Maybe it was wrong to hold it over the kid's head like that. But he had to get some control. "OK, but you be home by eleven," he said.

"Thanks, Dad!" Matthew ran out.

Finally feeling tired, Larry went off to bed. Gloria had not returned from the benefit. Probably still "mingling," strengthening her social contacts. He wondered if anyone at work was there? And what they thought of her being there alone? He brushed those thoughts away—he'd never cared what they thought. He did what he thought was right and he figured that those with enough sense respected him for it. Those were Larry's last thoughts as he dropped off to sleep.

Larry had always prided himself on his independent attitude. He knew he was intelligent and insightful about business, and he preferred to operate by his own lights. Yet he was also aware of organizational realities. He had been lucky to have a mentor in his early days, a vice president of finance, who had seen Larry's aptitude and motivation and advised him that the route to the most comprehensive understanding of the industry—and to the top of Chemco—was through broad exposure to all functions and aspects of the business. He convinced Larry to spend a couple of years in production, at a plant. Gloria, just getting into the swing of things as a Philadelphia wife, chafed at the prospect of moving to Oklahoma. But Larry assured her that it was only for a couple of years and then they could move back to the city and he would have a much bigger and better job. Gloria acquiesced and they moved, just after she gave birth to Matthew.

Then, to his surprise, Larry found that he was fascinated by production and by life at the plant. So instead of moving back to Philadelphia, they embarked on a series of moves, "From one hick town to another," as Gloria would remark to others. In each new town, Gloria joined the "right" clubs and committees—the Junior Leagues, the Historical Preservation Societies, the Friends of the Hospitals, the Theatre Centers, the Arts Guilds. Though being a "big fish in a small pond," as she put it, was fun at first, the novelty soon wore off. Having grown up in a world of high culture and finishing schools, she had little in common with small-town people.

When she had first met Larry, he was like nobody she had ever known. He was such a go-getter, so ambitious and intelligent he was bound to be a success. And he was certainly attractive in an all-American kind of way. Sure, he was a bit rough around the edges, but that would go away with time and her help. So she was shocked to discover that he actually liked the quiet small-town lifestyle. She had tried her best to initiate him into the excitement of social life, to no avail. So she bided her time and finally, a year ago, they had moved back to Philadelphia. In a wish to bring in some innovative new ideas to recharge a stagnant area, top management had chosen Larry to take over the Pharmaceuticals Division.

The next morning Larry woke up to find Gloria asleep next to him. As he got out of bed she opened her eyes.

"You missed a fabulous party. Everyone was asking about you. I told them you were sick."

Every response Larry could think of was bound to start an argument, so he said nothing except, "The new compound Ed's been working on turns out to have an amazingly high tolerance. This could really cut back on some of our development times . . ."

"Mm-hmm," said Gloria, distractedly inspecting her manicure.

Why do I even try to talk to her about work things, thought Larry to himself. "Matthew's taking the car to a basketball game tonight," he said.

"What? With all the tricks he's been pulling lately you reward him with the car? I told you, I don't like the looks of his friends. Who knows what he's been getting into."

Any doubts or concerns Larry might have had were swept away by Gloria's reaction. "You're too protective—stop worrying. He can take care of himself. Didn't you ever do crazy things when you were in high school?" Of course, he knew she hadn't. In fact, neither had he.

As a teenager, Larry had been every mother's dream. Captain of the football team, vice-president of the Student Council, active in his church's youth group. Most of his friends were from church and Student Council, and their relationships revolved around the activities of those groups. Everyone looked up to Larry, and he enjoyed his stature among his peers.

Larry was gratified by his accomplishments in and of themselves, but he was also responding to what he knew was his parents' desire for him to accomplish great things. They didn't say this in so many words, it was just obvious in everything they did for him, in the way they made over him when he did well and were so disappointed when he would occasionally not do his best.

Though on the surface Larry's choice of Gloria as a wife flew in the face of his parents' middle class values, the similarities ran deeper than the differences. Gloria, like Larry's mother, was a traditional wife and mother who, though she was more socially ambitious than Larry's mother, shared the value placed on family and stability. She was also like Larry's mother in her rational and pragmatic attitude toward life. Gloria had no patience with "overblown" emotions. This was comfortable for Larry. He and his parents had never shared personal feelings. His parents had rarely expressed anger and had disapproved when Larry got angry or upset. Very occasionally as an adult Larry would lose his temper, as he had with Matthew and as he sometimes did with members of his staff, but he tried to avoid this. He saw himself as a calm and steady person and he liked for others to see him this way too.

For this reason, rather than get into an argument with Gloria that morning, Larry lit a cigarette and left the bedroom to her. He got dressed quickly and took coffee and a micro-waved pastry in the car with him. He had a meeting scheduled first thing with Sally O'Brien. Sally was a financial analyst on Larry's staff. In fact, she held the same job Larry had held when he first joined Chemco, and she was a brand new and very bright MBA just as Larry had been. Larry thought of himself as a mentor to her. Her obvious admiration and respect for him was flattering. More than that, though, he really liked her. They had good conversations about business. They seemed to share many likes, dislikes, and interests. On the few occasions they had traveled together for business, Larry had had a great time. But of course, he told himself, their relationship was strictly business. They never talked about their lives outside of work. He had once met her husband, a banker, at an office party. Gloria had met Sally there, too. After the party, Larry had asked Gloria if she'd liked Sally. "Who? The mousy one?" Oh well, Gloria didn't have to like her. He liked her, and that was all that mattered.

The purpose of the meeting was for Sally to present to Larry a financial report she had prepared at his request.

"Larry, I have to tell you. I don't know why no one has ever thought of breaking the figures down this way before. Sometimes you just amaze me."

Larry scanned the top sheet of paper and smiled. She had done a good job. "Why don't you just summarize the main points to me."

Sally went through the report, highlighting the key points.

"What would your recommendations for action be, Sally, based on this report?" This was an unorthodox question to ask of Sally in light of her inexperience and junior status. But Larry liked to challenge his sharp young people with ideas. She looked taken aback but rose to the occasion, as Larry had known she would.

Sally's answer led her and Larry into a long and enjoyable brainstorming session on possible changes in the company's financial reporting procedures. Finally she glimpsed the clock on Larry's wall.

"Oh! I wish we could keep talking but I have another meeting. I just want to say, I really appreciate how you give me the chance to be involved in these problems. Most people around here can't be bothered with my opinions. It really makes my job a whole lot more enjoyable to feel like I can contribute."

Larry was a little embarrassed. He stood up. "Good! This will get you more acquainted with the workings of the division. Why don't you put those recommendations in writing for me, and copy your boss too?"

Sally was unable to suppress the grin that appeared on her face as she left Larry's office. Larry gave himself a moment to bask in the admiration she had for him and the gratification he got being helpful to her.

That afternoon, Larry was scheduled to give a presentation to the Executive Committee. It was just a status report, but he had spent many hours preparing it. Presentations always made him anxious, even though he had devoted a great deal of attention to honing his speaking skills. He suspected that he still took more time preparing—or overpreparing—than he needed to, but it made him feel better to do so. Today, as usual, he was armed to the hilt with charts and overheads. All the top brass were there, including his own boss. With a flush of excitement, he gave his presentation, touching on the past year of the division, new product opportunities, current development activities, problems the division was facing, and ideas for their solution. The executives were impressed.

"That was very well put together."

"Sounds like Pharmaceuticals is finally coming around."

"I like that new way of breaking down the financials."

"Larry, can you come to next month's meeting and give us an expanded picture of new products with some ideas on how you might get together with other divisions?"

Larry beamed as he left the conference room. He would never admit it to anyone, and he didn't know exactly why, but the praise and esteem he got from the Executive Committee pleased him more than it did coming from anyone else. It gave him feelings of security and warmth and happiness. God knows, he thought, I get enough positive feedback from most people around here, and from most of the things that I do, that I don't need to rely on praise from my bosses. And I certainly don't cowtow to them. When I disagree, I say so! Larry was aware, however, that when he disagreed it was with good reason, and his bosses respected him even more because of it.

As he drove home that evening, Larry thought about the presentation he had been asked to do for next month. The part about getting together with his peers in other divsions didn't excite him. He didn't think too highly of most of the other division heads and didn't like spending much time with them. Most, in Larry's opinion, had been in their jobs too long. They insisted on sticking with their outmoded ideas even though they had become a detriment to Chemco's productivity. This bothered Larry and made him more than a little angry at times.

Larry was getting home at 7:30, a reasonable hour for a change. He looked forward to a restful evening. He poured himself a drink and went to his study to watch the news. Gloria and the kids were probably somewhere in the house. No, he remembered, Matthew was going to the basketball game. They probably had eaten dinner already, without Larry. He didn't mind eating alone after the buzz of his day at work, though. A little TV, a little dinner, maybe another drink would relax him just fine.

A couple of hours later, Larry was awakened from a snooze in his easy chair by Gloria. Her face was white. "The police just called. Matthew wrecked the car and was arrested for drunk driving. And they found some kind of barbiturate in his blood in addition to the alcohol. He wasn't at the basketball game at all—he was on the other side of town. At a party in the woods."

Waiting at the police station later, Larry felt floods of emotion wash over him. Frustration and anger. Anger toward Matthew. What had happened—he had been such a good kid before! Now he'd really screwed up, and totaled the car to boot. Anger toward Gloria. Taking care of the kids was her job. She had never been able to discipline them. Plus, she was so busy with her damn society parties that the kids probably got the short end of the stick. But, he remembered, Gloria had tried to get him to help her deal with Matthew. Larry wondered, have I done anything wrong myself? No, I've tried to discipline Matthew—just last night, for example, I've been trying to be a good father, when there's time.

It turned out that part of Matthew's penalty required the family to see a counselor assigned by Juvenile Court. The counselor they got was a young man named Carl. He asked many questions about the family's lifestyle and activities, then he said, "Sometimes when a teen engages in this kind of behavior it has to do with problems in family relationships. Can any of you recall any evidence of such problems?"

"There's nothing wrong with our family life. He just got in with a bad crowd," Larry responded, feeling defensive.

"What kinds of things do you do together—any recreation, sports, or hobbies?"

"Well, I haven't had much time lately."

"Can you tell me more about that?"

"My work load has gotten heavier lately, since we came back to Philadelphia. You know, moving into a new job, trying to make some changes in the organization . . ."

"Has it ever occurred to you that Matthew may be missing spending time with his father? Missing having a relationship with his father?"

Gloria added, "I think he's right. You're never around—the kids hardly know you, except for the once in a while when you come in and yell at them. And you know, it might not be a bad thing for all of us if you were around a little more."

Later at home, Larry asked Gloria about her statement.

"Well, the two of us haven't seen much of each other either. Remember when we used to do things together—day trips; dinners, movies?"

Larry thought about this and slowly it all began to come together. He really hadn't had much to do with his family at all lately. He'd been so caught up in his work. Even when he was at home with his family, he was usually thinking about work. He really did love all of them. It was just that he didn't seem to have much in common with any of them any more. The kids were into their kid things. Gloria was into her social things. He was into his work. Maybe it was his fault. Maybe he needed to spend more time with them. That was it! He made a vow to himself to try to balance the time and energy he spent working with more time and energy with his family. Enthusiastically, he told Gloria and the kids about it. They seemed pleased. This would be the ticket to turning things around in the family, Larry assured himself.

Larry began to make a point of coming home and having dinner with the family. It seemed strained at first. He would ask the kids, "What did you do today?" They would respond, "Nothing," or "Same old thing," or "Went to school." He would say, "How was school today?" They would say, "Fine" or "Boring." It was bound to get better, he told himself, after everyone got used to having him around.

Matthew was stuck in the house a lot since Larry had grounded him after the drunk-driving incident. Larry hadn't said much to Matthew about that incident—he didn't know what to say. He tried to draw Matthew into conversations about what he was doing in school, but the boy was sullen and Larry sensed resentment. Larry would suggest they go to a baseball game together, or fishing, but Matthew was never interested. He would try to get the boy to help with the home chores Larry was once more getting involved in—

painting the shutters, cleaning out the garage—but Matthew would just stand around. Larry would inevitably end up yelling at him, and Matthew would react by retreating into angry silence. Larry was frustrated—he was trying to do what he should do, and what the family claimed they wanted him to do, spend more time with them, but the family didn't seem to appreciate his efforts.

He spent more time with Gloria in the evenings. Sometimes they ate dinner with the kids and watched TV. Other times they went out, to what Larry called "Gloria's things"—but these evenings out were a strain on Larry, who became even more convinced that her friends were shallow and pretentious. He said nothing, however. In an attempt to preserve the apparent harmony with Gloria, he tried to act as if he were having a good time, though he always breathed a secret sigh of relief when the evening was over and he could retreat to his study or his bed.

One night Larry and Gloria went to a party at a neighbor's house. Larry had taken to having a few drinks at these events—it helped to loosen him up and relieve some of the strain. He had had a few too many on this evening when he was accosted by the hostess, a woman whom he particularly disliked. She was a prominent hostess in town, but Larry thought she was loud and arrogant.

She grabbed Larry by the arm and said, "Darling, you don't have to be so stuffy! You've barely said two words to anyone all evening. Why don't you loosen up and have a good time? Gloria's told me about those dull engineers you spend all your time with. You should consider yourself lucky to have this chance to get away from all that!" And she laughed.

Larry felt fury rising up inside him. What right did this woman have to foist her warped values on him? Before he could stop himself, the words came out. "You know what I really think? Not a single person in here is fit to wipe the shoes of those engineers. They're good, hard-working people and you all are full of crap!"

The woman gasped. "Well! I never—Gloria!" she called. "Larry is not enjoying our company and would like to go home!" She walked away in a huff.

"What's this all about?" asked Gloria as she walked up to Larry.

"Never mind, let's just leave."

"But wait, I was just talking to someone . . ."

Larry guided Gloria out of the house.

As they drove home, Larry told her what had happened.

"How could you? Those are all very important, very powerful people. I'm so embarrassed! We'll never be invited anywhere again!"

"That would be most delightful," Larry replied sarcastically. "I've always thought I hated these people and now I know why."

"But I thought you were finally beginning to enjoy yourself, finally beginning to see that there is more to life than just the office."

"I have never had a good time. God knows I've tried. But I hate every minute of it and I've had enough."

"Fine," she replied. "Ruin my life while you're at it."

They finished the drive home in silence. They did not speak to each other the rest of the evening.

The next morning at breakfast, Larry announced to the whole family, "I think we all need to take a vacation together. Get away, relax, have a good time. I'll arrange my schedule at work so I can get away for a couple of weeks."

Gloria was delighted. "Great! We'll go to the Caribbean! How about St. Thomas? Great beaches, great shopping . . ."

Larry held up his hands. "Hold on, now. I think we should do something interesting. We've always said we wanted to take the kids out West. See the Grand Canyon, Mount Rushmore, that kind of thing. While we're at it, we can visit your aunt and uncle in Chicago, and my brother Pete in Denver."

The discussion continued, both Larry and Gloria trying to stay reasonable and controlled, but both stubbornly holding onto their own ideas about the kind of vacation they wanted. Larry managed to clear up to weeks of his schedule. A couple of months later, the family went on vacation—on a car trip, to visit relatives and see the sights out West.

Six months after the vacation, Gloria asked Larry for a divorce.

What happened? Larry had been taking steps to balance his time and improve his family life—or so he thought. His view of the problem was that his investment of time and energy between work and home was out of balance, that he was too focused on his work and too inattentive to his family. When he tried to turn more time and attention to his family, somehow it fell flat.

He felt betrayed by Gloria. He had tried to correct the emerging problems in the only way he knew. When he asked her why she wanted to end the marriage, she replied, "You're not the same person I married. You weren't there for us—even when you were in the house, you weren't there."

What led her to feel this way, and what Larry didn't understand, was that underneath the patterns of his behavior, underneath his focus on work and his inattention to his family, lay deep-rooted reasons why he had structured his life in the way that he had. His focus on work satisfied his need to feel competent and to appear competent in the eyes of others. And his inattention to family helped him to avoid intimacy and emotion, a side of experience that was unfamiliar and threatening to him.

Larry's need to be competent had been evident ever since his childhood—his parents had subtly pressed him to achieve and rewarded him when he did so. His youthful lifestyle revolved around structured activities oriented toward achievement, and the esteem and stature he gained from his leadership roles in these activities served as added rewards. In his role as a competent achiever, Larry could play the part of strong, rational, unemotional—all the qualities he came to see as "good."

In contrast, Larry had never learned to be intimate—he had never shared personal feelings with his parents, never learned to understand or express his emotions. This was reflected in his personal relationships as an adult, both at work and at home. The relationships with coworkers that he enjoyed so much were focused on task accomplishment. Even with his family, all he could do was try to engage his wife and children in activities. This was partly because task-forced interaction was all that he had known. It also may have been that becoming intimate, expressing emotion and vulnerability, represented a threat to the strong and competent person that Larry wanted to be.

Thus, when Larry tried to bring balance into his life by allocating his time and energy more evenly, he missed the boat because he was still focusing on competence and goal-orientation, and still avoiding intimacy and emotional expression.

This is not just a story about Larry Grant, but about many managers and others who have become successful in their careers by focusing on work rather than family, and on achievement rather than intimacy. The question is: Do we have to choose one or the other? Can we have achievement and intimacy, work and love? Possibly. But first we must be honest with ourselves, we must face the issue squarely. Here are some suggestions for beginning to work toward a more balanced life:

1. Become aware of what you truly value. Be honest with yourself about the importance of work to your self-esteem. How does it compare with the esteem you get from being a spouse and parent?
2. If you value your relationships as parent and spouse, consider the nature of those relationships, not just the amount of time you devote to them. Do you share *yourself* as well as your time? Do you know your family as unique people with hopes and fears, dreams and desires, and not just as your wife, your son, your daughter?
3. Recognize that the rewards of intimacy and sharing are different from the rewards of work. You may get from your work a sense of achievement and competence that draws you toward it; you may seek the same sorts of rewards in other areas of your life. But relationships don't have to be goal-directed. They can provide other kinds of rewards that are just as satisfying in different ways, rewards such as love, a sense of belonging, giving and receiving support, sharing sorrow and joy.
4. Recognize that expressing emotion and vulnerability with your family does not take away from your strength and competence at work. Though expressing vulnerability may not be functional in most work situations, it is essential in developing close relationships. Similarly, though cultivating strength and competence is useful at work, these attributes are not the cornerstone of intimate relationships.
5. Look for opposites within. Perhaps the real secret to balancing work and personal life is to find within yourself the counterweight to whatever qualities you have worked so hard to make preeminent. If you have striven to take charge, be a follower; if you have worked to be strong, look for the weakling; if you have driven yourself to achieve, look for the laggard. In becoming aware of the weaknesses we have

worked so hard to banish and forget, we may find a truer self who can work and who can love.

Hooked on Work

Anne Wilson Schaef and Diane Fassel

As we began recognizing the addictive process in organizations, we started to share our observations with those who attended our workshops and training groups. Frequently a discernible hush would fall over the group, and as we described the characteristics of addicts and co-dependents in the work place, people's eyes would light up, heads would nod, and looks of recognition would cross their faces. By the end of our discussion, people would be saying, "You've described where I work. I feel as if you've been in there with me."

For years we had observed, studied, worked with, and experienced personally the effects of addiction on individuals and on families. We initially believed the organization was just another context in which addictive behavior occurred. Then, about a year ago, we began to realize we were seeing something in addition to the organization as a setting for addictive behavior. We were also seeing that in many instances the organization itself was the addictive substance. This realization provided an entirely new perspective on the addictive organization and resulted in our moving to another level of understanding of both addictions and organizations.

Anything can be addictive when it becomes so central to a person that life feels impossible without it. We recognized that for many the work place, the job, and the organization were the central focuses of their lives. Because the organization was so primary in their lives, and because they were totally preoccupied with it, they began to lose touch with other aspects of their lives and gradually gave up what they knew, felt, and believed.

One of the major ways the organization functions as an addictive substance is through the promise it makes and holds out to every employee. The purpose of such a promise in the addictive system is to take people out of the here and now. This process moves the person from what he knows and encourages him to look outside the self for answers, security, and a sense of worth.

The organization holds lots of promises. It promises that you will get ahead. It promises power, money, and influence. It promises that you will be a nice guy or gal if you perform in certain ways. If you live up to what the company promotes, you may even be liked and "belong."

Almost all the promises of the organization are linked to the promises of the society. They are the same: power, influence, and money—the good life as defined by popular culture and advertising. This is seductive.

The promise of the good life keeps us actively focused on the future in the belief that even if things are not so good now, they will get better. The future orientation of the promise in the organization prevents us from looking at the present, functioning in the system, and seeing the system for exactly what it is: addictive. People often feel mired in organizations. Rather than acknowledging their feelings, they find it easier to look forward to the weekend, a vacation, or retirement. By continuing to present us with the promise, the organization remains central in our lives, in control of our present, "hooking" us into an addictive relationship with the organization, the promiser.

Some organizations promise things people long for in their families and have never gotten, like recognition, approval, social skills, and caring. "We are one big happy family here," a software executive said of his company. "We socialize on Friday nights. We play ball together. We know each other's spouses. We help each other out." "Oh," we responded, "and what do you do when someone doesn't want to socialize or gets out of line?" "They don't stay around long," said the executive.

This was an organization where the best-adjusted employees were the ones who had come from dysfunctional homes and were willing to let the company become their families. Those who had no family came to believe that family consisted of the types of activities promoted in the organization. They let this model feed back into their primary families. Those who did not feel so comfortable being taken in by the wide arm of the corporation, whose spouses and children resisted company picnics and wearing company T-shirts, always felt uneasy, usually did not readily move up in the company, or left.

Those who looked to the company and believed it was a family were hooked by a very seductive promise indeed. For what kind of a family can the organization possibly be?

It is the kind of family where membership is dependent on playing by rather rigidly defined rules and behaving according to established norms. Acceptance in the corporate family is won by learning the right thing to do and doing it (just as it is in the addictive family). The main thing learned about family from the promise of the organization is that membership is conditional upon not being yourself, upon not following your own path. The other lesson learned is to keep attuned outside yourself, to be constantly vigilant about what you need to do to stay in the company's good graces and win approval.

Another area where we see the organization's promise operating is in its mission and goals. All organizations have a mission; it is their public statement for why they exist. Presumably all employees are oriented toward the accomplishment of the mission. Companies with unclear missions often flounder helplessly because they have no sense of why they exist or the meaning of their work.

Although we have worked with numerous types of organizations, we find those in the helping professions—hospitals, schools, agencies, churches, and community organizations—have the most difficulty with the promise of the mission. The reason many people are attracted to the helping professions is that they identify with, and sincerely believe in, the stated goals of the organizations they join, as well as with the professions with which they are identified. Often, however, what they are committed to and what they experience are quite different.

Let us use as an example a group of nurses with whom we once worked in a large metropolitan hospital. At one point, it became clear that the nurses were confused and angry about their work. Since this confusion and anger appeared to relate to the discrepancy between what they thought they should be doing and what they were actually doing, we asked them what the stated goals of the hospital were. The goals they listed were concerned with promoting health and wellness, being responsive to the needs of the people, providing high-quality health care, and developing new forms of healing. The nurses all felt comfortable with these goals. We then asked them to list the unstated goals of the hospital. These goals turned out to be saving the city money, being the vehicle for the political advancement of hospital administrators, upholding the reputation of the hospital, and increasing federal funding.

Inevitably, the accomplishment of the unstated goals was how they spent most of their time. They had joined the hospital to support the stated goals, yet in reality they spent most of their time working toward the unstated goals. They were confused, frustrated, and angry, because they had been promised something that was a con. The power of the promise is that it seems possible—just possible enough to keep people hooked.

Addicts are consummate con artists. Initially their deceptive statements look good to others; unfortunately, they usually end up conning themselves as well. They come to believe their own lies. The promise of the mission has similar qualities. The very fact of *having* goals frequently can be enough to con employees into believing that everything is all right with the organization. The mission is like a household god. As long as it is in its shrine, the organization is protected, even if what the organization is doing is at odds with the stated mission.

When organizations function as the addictive substance, it is in their interest to keep promoting the vision of the mission, because as long as the employees are hooked by it, they rarely turn their awareness to the discrepancies. They choose to stay numb in order to stay in the organization. The mission is a powerful source of identification for workers. It is a type of philosophical orientation that appeals to their values. Through the mission they find a link between themselves and the organization.

In addition to the mission, there are other, more concrete processes by which employees stay hooked into the company. These are the processes by which the organization keeps itself central in the lives of its employees. Loyalty and the benefits of loyalty are other paths to the organization's becoming an addictive agent, or "fix."

There is nothing inherently wrong with being loyal to an organization, nor with being a dedicated employee. In fact, this kind of orientation is essential for a good working relationship. Loyalty to the organization becomes a fix, however, when individuals become preoccupied with maintaining the organization. When loyalty to the organization becomes a substitute for living one's own life, then the company has become the substance of choice. The organization itself has ways of enhancing its centrality in workers' lives. It does this primarily through such means as benefits, bonuses, and tenure.

We are not opposed to benefits and retirement packages for workers. We believe that benefits are important and necessary and that too few workers have adequate benefits. The issue is not benefits per se but the way the organization uses them to stay central in the lives of workers and to prevent workers from moving on and doing what they need to do. When the benefits become a controlling factor in a person's life, the organization becomes the addictive agent. It is when the organization is willing to take advantage of the worker's dependence and not be competitive with other work places for the worker's loyalty and creativity that the organization functions as the addictive agent.

Many of the people we interviewed are completely burned out at their work. They may be sick or aging or simply unable to be creative in their field any longer. Most want to be doing something else. When we challenge them to explore other opportunities, they respond that they cannot afford it. We should not miss the real message here: They also cannot afford to take the risk of being fully alive.

Benefits encourage dependency. In cases where workers lose all benefits when they leave a company, the company is burdened with people who are often counterproductive because they do not want to be in the organization but are afraid to leave. In order to stay, they have to become not dead and not alive—zombies. The organization has become the addictive agent.

As with any addictive substance, the organization's benefits and bonuses become the controlling factor in the lives of employees. Getting one's fix becomes primary. We have an acquaintance who works in the highly competitive photocopier field as a sales representative. His company offers substantial rewards in the form of bonuses, parties, and eventually vacations. Our friend laughingly says that he sometimes finds himself selling customers products he knows they do not need in order to meet personal and team quotas.

We know that addicts will stop at nothing to get a fix. Their behavior also becomes increasingly more self-centered and personally immoral. This kind of incentive program encourages similar behavior. The rewards become primary, and the individual's ethics begin to recede into the background. This is what it means to be out of touch with one's personal morality and one's spirituality. It is what Alcoholics Anonymous (AA) means by moral deterioration. The organization becomes the source of moral deterioration as it makes itself indispensable to its employees through the structure of benefits, bonuses, and tenure.

We want now to consider a prime example of the way an organization can become the addictive substance in one's life. Work, of course, is the primary link one has with an organization. The fatal form of work in addictive organizations is workaholism.

To understand workaholism, one must penetrate an almost impenetrable wall of denial. Thousands of articles have been written on the related subject of stress and burnout. Their focus is primarily the reduction of stress by exercise, diet, and lifestyle change. In a computerized search through several university libraries, we could find only five books specifically on workaholism, and only two of these offered a serious treatment of the issue. We were incredulous. How could a topic that is clearly part of the popular culture be the subject of so little inquiry? And why were so many inquiries directed at treating the symptoms and not addressing the underlying disease process itself?

We began to see more and more evidence that society actually supports and promotes workaholism. Many of the magazines for career women, like *Working Woman* and *Savvy,* appear to tout the profile of the workaholic woman. Articles on women who had made their first million before the age of thirty describe superbeings who founded companies, jog or swim daily, put in sixty hours at the office, have a family and children, bring work home in the evenings and work weekends. The message is, Work like this and you will get ahead.

Interviews in such magazines have women saying to themselves, "I am a workaholic and I love it." What other addictions can you say this about? Imagine a well-dressed executive saying in an interview, "I am an active alcoholic and I love it."

Only a system that deliberately chooses to be blind to the effects of this disease and that thoroughly accepts its denial can promote workaholism as a condition to be emulated.

Despite this widespread acceptance, workaholism adversely affects personal relationships, both at home and on the job. The workaholic becomes addicted to the process of work, using it as a fix in order to get ahead, be successful, avoid feeling, and ultimately avoid living. It is a progressive disease that may result in death if not treated. The side effects of the stress of workaholism, in fact, may be even more severe than the physical effects of alcoholism.

Work is a very tricky addiction, however. When workaholics are most "into" their disease, they feel most alive, even though it may be killing them. In our interviews with workaholics, we have found that the fix may not be the work itself but the adrenaline high that accompanies the work. Many workaholics describe the surge of energy they get from their work. They identify this surge with feeling alive. They do not get the same surge on a family vacation or a night out with friends. In fact they experience a total letdown and depression when they are not at work or thinking about work.

For people who are not work-addicted, pauses between projects are a time to savor success, to rest, and to spend time with loved ones. For the work-aholic, the prospect of these pauses is terrifying, for they are experienced not as a time of release and quiet but as a time of being deprived of the fix of the addictive substance and of functioning in an arena that cannot be controlled by the work process.

Researchers working on stress have said that stress is life-threatening because the body was not built to withstand a constant rush of adrenaline. Adrenaline is the substance that allows us to perform normally impossible physical feats in times of severe crisis. Stress researchers say that modern life tricks the body into believing there is a constant crisis, with the result that we are producing tremendous amounts of adrenaline every day.

Stress research provides us with an interesting perspective on workaholism. Many workaholics have taken the recommendations of stress researchers to exercise daily and eat right. This "healthiness" results in their being able to work even harder and thus maintain their addiction. Compare this to the alcoholic who will do anything to protect his supply. The insidious thing is that workaholics' stress-reduction activities appear to be promoting health, when in actuality these activities allow workaholics to prolong their addiction. Stress reduction actually supports the addiction, and serves as a con for themselves and others.

Work addiction is also extremely destructive to families and personal relationships. When we listen to stories adults tell of growing up in families with a workaholic parent, they sound identical to those of members of active alcoholic families. Said one woman of her experience:

> *Everything revolved around my father's work. If we got too playful and made noise, we would be quieted because Daddy was either working or sleeping. When work went poorly, he was moody, angry, and destructive. When it went well, he was jolly. We were constantly watching him to see what kind of day he had had so that we could act accordingly. We rarely saw him. Sometimes he stayed in the city overnight, or on big projects he would be gone for weeks at a time. Work was the overriding excuse for everything; family celebrations, plans, and vacations all bowed to the demands of work. We could never count on anything. My father married his work and it had the excitement of a mistress. I don't think my mother or our family were ever second place in my father's life; I believe for him we didn't exist at all. I grew up spending inordinate amounts of time thinking about my father yet never really knowing him. I hate him for this and I miss him deeply.*

It should be noted that making a lot of money is not the purpose of work-aholism. It is the actual process of working that is the fix, not the outcome. Like any addiction, work takes over one's life; it becomes primary, resulting in a loss of perspective on other realities. This is because the addictive process becomes its own reality. It is a closed system. . . .

Our interviews with workaholics and our experience with them in organizations has led us to the conclusion that the addictive organization needs workaholism and consequently rewards workaholic behavior. Workaholism clearly has many payoffs for the organization. Certainly the most obvious is a core of workers who are totally dedicated to the company. We have also concluded that workaholism is the most socially acceptable addiction because it is so socially productive. Many people have responded to our description of workaholism with statements like, "It is not the same as alcoholics who destroy themselves and their loved ones; workaholics are productive members of society."

We have to recognize that, for some organizations and for some people, destroying your life and loved ones is acceptable if you produce something useful for society. And that, of course, is what a workaholic does. It is also interesting to see another process of the addictive system at work. In the addictive system, if one can find anything at all wrong with a person or an idea, that person or idea can be completely dismissed. The opposite is also true: If one good thing can be found about workaholism, then the whole process is "good."

Since we have worked with many church organizations, it is difficult for us to miss the role of the church in the promotion of workaholism. The good Christian as presented by the church, is one who works hard. The good martyr is the typical co-dependent who works selflessly for others and never attends to his own needs. Workaholism may be the designer drug for the church as well as for the corporation.

We believe that the denial about workaholism is so pervasive because underneath this addiction is an attachment no one is willing to face. It is the attachment to an economically based system, capitalism, and to the social structure that undergirds this system. We believe that the Protestant work ethic and Christian theology support both.

Ironically, workaholism has also contributed to the loss of spiritual values in the organization and in society. We heard many workaholics describe their immersion in their work as a kind of altered state, similar to what one might experience through drugs. We soon realized that this work-induced state was the adrenaline high, and that it acts as a mood-altering drug, removing one from the reality of the present and creating a feeling of transcendence. It is a delusion keeping the person in the addictive process and longing for more. Sadly, the feeling of transcendence results in a loss of spirituality while feeding the illusion that it is something akin to spirituality.

The addictive organization promotes workaholism. It loves it as the "cleanest" of addictions. Unlike drug- or alcohol-addicted people, workaholics rarely miss a day (they just drop dead). Like good co-dependents and adult children of alcoholics, workaholics can be counted on to go the extra mile; they rarely let you down.

What we have charted here—the promise of the organization, the mission, the benefits, the support for workaholism—are the ways the organization positions itself centrally in the lives of employees and becomes the addictive agent. To break this habit, the organization must be willing to look at itself and all of its processes. A close scrutiny is unlikely without the support of top management. Intervention teams can develop descriptions of the company procedures that have addictive implications. They can show how the organization models addictive patterns and identify the attitudes that feed into these patterns. But without cooperation from the whole system, a change is not possible. Actually, we find that wholehearted cooperation is not always necessary, but the willingness to at least look at the data about addictiveness at all levels in the organization is.

Organizations that are willing to look at themselves as the addictive substance are facing the prospect of multilevel, long-term change. They must examine all of their organizational structures, especially those that engender loyalty. They may even need to examine what loyalty means to them. Their reward structure of benefits and bonuses should be reviewed. They also need to look at the ways they promote workaholism, not just through rewards but also through the entire culture of the company.

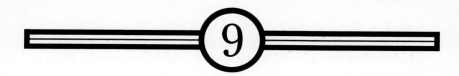

Managing Ethically

All members of a society experience pressures to behave ethically—
that is, to do what is right and not what is wrong. These pressures
come from at least two sources. First, one's actions are evaluated by other
people who will reward and punish the individual according to how they
judge the person's actions *vis-à-vis* their criteria for what is right and wrong.
Second, individuals have their own internal standards of what is ethical behavior. These standards are developed through one's life experiences which
include attempts by parents and institutions to establish ethical behavior and
by the numerous cases in which the judgments of others have been directed
at the individual. These experiences seem to produce an internal standard
of what is right and wrong. This internal standard (called by various names
such as the superego by Freud, or the impartial spectator by Adam Smith,
or the conscience in common parlance) serves to pressure a person to behave in accordance with its dictates.

We begin with the assumption that no universal agreement on the content of the standard exists. First, substantial differences between cultures
exist. Second, contradictions among the standards within societies are also
prevalent. One set of contradictions that is of particular interest in American business stems from tensions between the pursuit of self-interest and
the achievement of some social good. Our long-standing acceptance of the
invisible hand, operating through free markets to channel individual self-
interests into actions that promote the common good, is a major ethical force
underlying the free-enterprise system. At one extreme, this belief can serve
to justify the view that "greed is enough"; other ethical principles are simply unnecessary for managers. On the other hand, many people argue that
considerable constraint must be exercised on human self-interest if anything
approaching ethical behavior is to be achieved. This debate, seldom far from
the surface in discussions of business ethics (at least in the United States),
is central to this section's articles.

Even though the content of the internal standards varies widely among social systems, the particular standards that exist within a system play an important part in helping human beings to establish and sustain cooperation. People whose actions are guided by common standards find it easier to predict what each other will do. Moreover, to the degree that these standards inhibit acting on impulses to harm others and introduce more altruistic inclinations, they increase the level of trust in a social system. Knowing what to expect of other people, particularly knowing that they are unlikely to harm others, makes it easier to begin doing business with them or to cooperate in some other way. In short, ethical behavior is very important for achieving management's central task—coordination of human effort.

When organizations are superimposed on human relationships, new dimensions are added to knowing what is right and wrong and doing what is appropriate. For example, as we saw in the last section, as organizations become especially central to people, they face strong temptations to do what they perceive to be good for the organization even when it means they act inconsistently with the standards of ethical behavior.

Organizations appear to have a negative effect on ethical actions in at least five ways. First, they may operate in ways that lead people to perceive that they are rewarded for such behavior. (Recall the example given by Schaef and Fassel in the previous section of people selling goods that they know the customer does not need.) Second, organizations provide ways to help individuals justify behavior that they may consider to be wrong in some other context. (For example, members of an organization sometimes come to believe that all of their competitors behave in unethical ways and if they fail to follow suit, their organization will fail.) Third, organizations add new variables which seem to make it difficult to do what one feels personally is right. James Gordon's discussion in "Manager" provides an excellent example of such complicating factors as well as showing how an organization's climate can help people to do what they think is right.

In this context, it is important to note that the ambiguous nature of the ethical issues managers face makes the organization's climate especially powerful. Toffler points out in "Ethical Situations at Work," that the ethical dilemmas that confront managers seldom have a "right answer." Given such ambiguity, some very subtle elements within organizations have major consequences on what people do. Faced with ambiguity, individuals search for cues about what to do and are extremely susceptible to social influence. Actions by key organizational members are apt to have great impact under such conditions. Such actions can not only affect what one perceives as right or wrong, but can be a source of ideas for rationalizing a given course of action.

The fourth negative effect of organizations on ethical behavior stems from a discontinuity between one's intentions and the consequences of one's actions—a discontinuity that is far greater than in less complex and more personal settings. This contrast can be illustrated by comparing a small group (such as a small nuclear family) with a large organization. In the former, each person is well-known to the others and has frequent face-to-face contact with the others. As a result, each can observe and discuss the consequences of various actions on each other and explain or alter these to achieve the intended effects. Although even in a family many times one's intentions produce unintended consequences that are very difficult to change, a person has a far better chance to adjust his or her actions to produce the intended consequences. In a large complex organization, however, any action can have so many consequences that the results one intends are difficult to monitor. So many other people and events are affected that one's intentions are often unrelated to the consequences of one's actions. In some ways organizations are very blunt instruments.

Finally, organizations create situations that require attention to issues in ways that more personal relationships seldom do. Policies must be set that govern the behavior of people in their organizational roles. The organization comes to have special obligations that in some sense impose greater constraints on their members than do other institutions. The example of dealing with AIDS in this section is but one such example. (The "Case of the Mismanaged Ms." in the section on Managing Human Resources is another.) Organizations spawn dilemmas that other contexts do not. As the scope of business grows, more complications arise. Of special relevance today is the fact that the business arena is now a global one. In such a world, the cultural relativity of the personal standards one has learned and the organizational standards that organizations in any given nation have evolved become evident. Ambiguity increases dramatically.

Most of the articles in this section develop some of these and other complications. Several of them also reveal a less pessimistic side of things— organizations can help people do what they believe is right. The final article about the response of Kodak to an ethical dilemma shows that while organizations can do a great deal of harm, many modern organizations control massive resources that their managers could use to help make things "right." On the other hand, this sort of ethical behavior can be very expensive and what is right remains uncertain. Many conflicting points of view exist about whether this is the "right" way for managers, as agents of the stockholders, to spend corporate resources. The complexity of the matter is increased by the fact, as noted in the article, that even such a significant step can be seen as unethical from some perspectives. To repeat Toffler, the ethical dilemmas managers face simply have no right answer.

Somewhat paradoxically, the lack of clarity can provide a second way for managers to resolve some of their ethical dilemmas as they attempt to balance competing demands. The lack of an external norm can give the manager some latitude—the manager's own personal standards are not in direct competition with any prescription. Once managers realize this, they can act on their own personal standards of right and wrong. Stated boldly, under such conditions, a manager's personal standards are all he or she has to go by. As the title of the article by Sir Adrian Cadbury puts it, "Ethical Managers Make Their Own Rules."

Ethical Situations at Work

Barbara Ley Toffler

The word "ethical" will appear repeatedly throughout the book. According to the definition found in *Webster's Seventh New Collegiate Dictionary,* it means "relating to what is good or bad, and [having to do] with moral duty and obligation." ("Moral" is defined as "relating to principles of right and wrong.") And in fact, "ethical" has become a label we attach to situations which produce some sense that a wrong might be or has been done. Attaching labels frequently implies that we assume not only that we know what we mean, but that others mean the same thing when they use the label. This is often not the case. When managers in this study were asked for a definition of the word ethical, they exhibited different understanding of this common label:

"Ethics are eternal verities of right and wrong."

"They [ethics] are really rules—rules of behavior."

"Integrity is what it means; it has to start from within [the individual]."

"The most appropriate meaning of ethical is: conforming to the standards of a given profession or group. So any group can set its own ethical standards and then live by them or not."

These statements represent the four categories of personal definitions offered: basic truths, rules of behavior, the integrated unity of an individual's character, and institutional (or cultural) codes. Although the common thread of these definitions is that "ethical" has something to do with right and wrong, good and evil, virtue and vice, there is no agreement on the substance of right and wrong, its source, or on the universality of application.

"Ethical" derives from the Greek word "ethos," which means both "character" and "sentiment of the community"—what we might call culture. The dual meaning reflects the four categories presented above; it also reflects the definition of ethical with which I undertook this project. For me, ethical has to do with a general conception of right and wrong in the attitudes and actions of individuals and the communities (institutions) of which they are a part. I did not, however, give my definition to the participants. The definition each offered held for his or her interviews. That these people were not working from a common definition of ethics is compatible with the approach this book takes; connotatively, they and I were all talking about the same thing. Our definitions were not completely congruent but were more in the nature of circles of meaning that overlapped at various points. How managers defined ethics certainly affected how they perceived and handled problems. Such differences, however, did not impede our understanding of each other.

This approach seems to accept that there can be different notions of right and wrong. However, this book is built on a basic assumption that there are principles such as honesty, promise-keeping, doing no harm, which are held by most people, at least in the Western world. This assumption allows us to make statements like "that's unethical" about a given action, with which most of the general public would agree.

One final comment on the use of "ethical." There are two common uses of this word: one to refer to a problem that implies a right versus wrong solution, for example, when we talk about facing an ethical dilemma; and two, to refer to a "right" choice or action ("she did the ethical thing")—or obversely ("she behaved unethically"). As in ordinary discourse, the word will be used in both ways in the interviews and comments that follow them. In each case I believe the meaning is self-evident.

Ethically questionable situations in business most frequently cited by the public are either practices involving outright illegal activities such as the application of personal expenses to contract budgets, the stealing of company products, or practices which compromise a recognized corporate code or policy like gift-giving, or practices that result in physical harm to a person or group like producing a gas tank vulnerable to rear-end collisions or dumping of toxic wastes into a local river. These common examples suggest that situations concerning ethics in businesses are those dealing with the breaking of laws and rules or with the causing of physical harm, and are situations in which the individuals involved are offered a clear choice between doing right and doing wrong. The data from the managers in this study, however, suggest that ethical concerns in business are more pervasive and complex than is generally recognized. In fact, *ethical concerns are part of the routine practices of management;* they are characterized less frequently by legal issues than by *concerns about relationships and responsibility;* and while they deal with right-and-wrong decisions, they *frequently involve factors that make the right and wrong less than patently clear.* . . .

These findings support the notion that ethical concerns in business are part of the routine practices of management. They are not problems set apart from the rest of management. Ethics is intertwined with personnel, finance, production, and every other part of business management activity.

Elements of Ethical Situations

After identifying ethical situations they had faced, managers were asked why they called those problems ethical. Four elements emerged from the interviews as key to why managers identified particular problems as having an ethical dimension: people, competing claims, intervention, and determining responsibility. While these elements can and often should be talked about in relation to each other, they are sufficiently different to be described individually.

Element	Components
PEOPLE	Relationship
	Commitment
	Proximity
	Harm
	Inevitability of causing
	Response of the harmed
COMPETING CLAIMS	Between two or more personal values
	Between personal value(s) and
	value(s) of others
COMPETING CLAIMS	Between means and ends
(continued)	Between two or more individuals or
	groups to whom one has an obligation
INTERVENTION	With value agreement
	With value conflict
DETERMINING RESPONSIBILITY	

People

"Having to do with people" sounds both trite and general: general because it really doesn't tell us specifically what "having to do with people" entails, and trite because it seems the matter of pop music and media advertising. (Of course, frequently, the reason things become trite is because they express a general truth.) But as managers talked about their concerns in dealing with people and why they felt that "people" contributed to a situation's being called ethical, two aspects emerged.

The first is *relationship.* As managers expressed their concerns about people, it became evident that they did not really mean nameless, faceless people but specific individuals, known to them, who knew them, and with whom they had some kind of contract—formal or informal, written or psychological, role-determined or personally determined. In other words, individuals with whom they had a relationship. The notion of relationship has several parts. One is commitment: an explicit or implicit set of obligations that allows the parties to the relationship to hold trustworthy expectations about what the other will do. Managers make commitments to their subordinates, their bosses, their coworkers, to suppliers and customers. They depend on reciprocal commitments from those people to get their own jobs done.

A second part of relationship is proximity: a degree of nearness that makes the commitment felt. Although proximity is usually thought of in spatial terms, psychological proximity is also a characteristic of relationships. We all have relationships with people, family members for instance, with whom we are not necessarily physically proximate. But some of what maintains the relationship is a proximity by verbal contact (phone calls) or written communication (letters and cards). So, too, do managers describe the proximity that contributes to the ethical quality of relationships, whether the proximity be adjacent offices, a daily or weekly phone call, or a monthly report. What seems to be at the heart of the proximity concern is, first, that it affects the managers' sense of responsibility ("if I am near to a situation, I may have, or be thought to have, the capacity to do something about it"), and second, managers will get direct and reasonably immediate feedback on the effects of their actions. Feedback is important. Most people would agree that the pain of making and implementing difficult decisions of any kind is increased by the anticipation of direct feedback from the affected parties. One CEO said that he was more keenly aware of an ethical dimension in dealing with the plateaued career of a senior vice-president than in making policy decisions about the company's involvement in South Africa. The reason he offered for this difference was that he would have to face the reaction of his vice-president, with whom he had a relationship, whereas there was no immediacy of contact with South Africa and those affected by the decision.*

The second element is *harm.* Harm as an ethical dimension is more frequently triggered by managers' concern for people than by the need to adhere to a principle that says "Do no harm." For managers, causing harm can mean a number of different things. It can mean doing something that threatens the life or physical well-being of another person; but it can also mean causing emotional or psychological distress, or even simply doing something that will be less satisfying to another person than what that person would have desired.

Although there are some situations in which decisions resulting in the potential for life-threatening or physical harm are posed for managers, more frequently they find themselves in positions in which the possible harm is of a lesser nature. In these cases there are two critical factors that appear to affect the labeling of a situation as ethical. One is the *inevitability* of causing some harm. The possibility of managers wending their way through the many needs and demands placed on them without causing some discomfort somewhere is close to impossible. Similarly, many of the necessary actions managers are required to take must, by their very nature, cause harm. Telling an employee that he or she is unlikely to be promoted is one such action which managers frequently cite as an ethical situation because it causes harm (unhappiness, loss of self-esteem, etc.). But, if you look beneath this genuine concern, the second factor appears: the response of the person harmed. Managers wish to cause no harm out of a fear of being disliked. As one interviewee put it, "One of the biggest problems in management is cowardice. It's very difficult to sit down with someone and really criticize him—fairly and honestly criticize him. You want to be liked."

---

*It is interesting to note that whenever an intuitively "ethical" example was needed, interviewees almost always mentioned doing business in South Africa—and these interviews took place in 1983.

Competing Claims

Competing claims—being "pulled in two or more directions"—was frequently cited as an identifying feature of ethical situations. Competing claims appear in a variety of guises: conflict between two or more personally held values, conflict between personal value(s) and the value(s) held by another person or the organization, conflicts between basic principles and the need to achieve a desired outcome (a means/end conflict), and conflict between two or more individuals or groups to whom one has an obligation.

Conflict between two personally held values can be exemplified by the painful dilemma of a manager concerned about a troubled employee. On the one hand, his concern about caring, about the importance of helping others, may propel the manager to investigate the difficulty by asking questions or calling the spouse or taking some other action. On the other hand, if the manager also believes in respecting others' privacy, which may compel him to take a hands-off approach, the manager may find himself torn between competing personal values.

Suppose, then, the manager decides his values of caring predominate and he very carefully and respectfully asks the troubled employee what the problem is. If the employee holds privacy as critical and responds, "Mind your own business," the manager is dealing with an interpersonal value conflict. To carry it one step further: suppose the company has a policy saying that every alcoholic employee must attend the company alcoholism program or be terminated. If the manager thinks his employee's problem is, in fact, alcohol, but he has no evidence and cannot get any without invasion of privacy, and if, as well, the manager has questions as to the appropriateness of such a policy, there is now a conflict among the manager, the subordinate, and the company.

The conflict between a basic principle and a desired outcome can be exemplified by the manager who considers lying to a subordinate about why she was not promoted to allow the subordinate to save face, a common example of compromising a principle to achieve a "good" result.

The final area of the conflict of competing claims has to do with obligations to two or more stakeholders. Whether trying to get the best deal for the company while being "fair" to all suppliers, or adjusting policy for a needy employee while rejecting the demands of other employees, in balancing work and family commitments, the pull of multiple obligations signals "ethical" to managers.

Intervention

Many managers consider a situation ethical if their decisions and actions result in their intervening in the lives of others, or if they perceive their own lives are being affected by others' intervention. In many cases, the kinds of decisions and actions they refer to are things like making personnel decisions about subordinates, canceling contracts with suppliers, and speeding up production at the behest of a boss. These kinds of activities are part of their normal managerial roles and support the notion that when managers talk about the ethics of intervening in others' lives, they are saying there is a core ethical dimension to their professional work.

The notion of intervention has to do with an emotionally charged word—control. When managers talk of intervening in others' lives, they are really talking about who is in control, who makes the choice about what is done. Most people want control, at least of the things that matter most to them. And most people have a fear of or frustration with situations which are beyond their power to manage. Thus the notion of intervention or control works in two ways. Managers see situations in which they intervene in people's lives as ethical. They also see as ethical, situations in which they are rendered impotent by other people or by their organizations.

Intervention can have two substantive forms: when there is agreement about what ought to be done and when there is conflict. Intervention with agreement occurs, for example, when, as the parent of a teenage driver, we insist on an early curfew because of drunk drivers on the road. Both parent and teen agree that the danger is real, but both recognize the parental intervention as controlling the behavior of the youngster who would prefer "to make my own decisions about what to do." That situation is substantively different from an intervention accompanied by a conflict. The parent who sets limits on a teenager based on the parent's assessment that the teen's friends, who the teen thinks are great, are a bunch of bums, is both imposing beliefs and controlling behavior.

Determining Responsibility

The final "marker" of an ethical situation interviewees identified concerns responsibility, a subject treated in depth later in this section. For the moment, however, a few points can be made.

The question of whether or not a manager has a responsibility in a situation is critical from two perspectives: Should she do something? Should she *not* do something? First of all, if a manager does have a responsibility and fails to act, she is committing a breach of obligation. The manager also may be allowing circumstances to occur which may produce harmful or other negative results for other people and/or the organization. The manager who has the capacity to prevent an injury on a faulty machine, but who says "It's not my job," might be considered by many people to be acting in an ethically questionable fashion. However, many managers would ask, "How *does* that manager know if she has a responsibility or not?" Similarly, the manager who leaps into the fray inappropriately where she has no responsibility can slow down production, intervene in others' lives, and affect a number of outcomes in detrimental ways. Repeatedly the question, "How do I know *when* I have the responsibility to act?" signals an ethical concern for many managers.

That managers do experience as ethical those problems having to do with people, with competing values, with intervention, and with determining responsibility, further supports the assertion that ethical concerns are present in a high proportion of routine and not-so-routine managerial activities. And it challenges the notion that business ethics is primarily concerned with the breaking of laws and rules and the causing of physical harm. . . .

Ethical Managers Make Their Own Rules

Sir Adrian Cadbury

In 1900 Queen Victoria sent a decorative tin with a bar of chocolate inside to all of her soldiers who were serving in South Africa. These tins still turn up today, often complete with their contents, a tribute to the collecting instinct. At the time, the order faced my grandfather with an ethical dilemma. He owned and ran the second-largest chocolate company in Britain, so he was trying harder and the order meant additional work for the factory. Yet he was deeply and publicly opposed to the Anglo-Boer War. He resolved the dilemma by accepting the order, but carrying it out at cost. He therefore made no profit out of what he saw as an unjust war, his employees benefited from the additional work, the soldiers received their royal present, and I am still sent the tins.

My grandfather was able to resolve the conflict between the decision best for his business and his personal code of ethics because he and his family owned the firm which bore their name. Certainly his dilemma would have been more acute if he had had to take into account the interests of outside shareholders, many of whom would no doubt have been in favor both of the war and of profiting from it. But even so, not all my grandfather's ethical dilemmas could be as straightforwardly resolved.

So strongly did my grandfather feel about the South African War that he acquired and financed the only British newspaper which opposed it. He was also against gambling, however, and so he tried to run the paper without any references to horse racing. The effect on the newspaper's circulation was such that he had to choose between his ethical beliefs. He decided, in the end, that it was more important that the paper's voice be heard as widely as possible than that gambling should thereby receive some mild encouragement. The decision was doubtless a relief to those working on the paper and to its readers.

The way my grandfather settled these two clashes of principle brings out some practical points about ethics and business decisions. In the first place, the possibility that ethical and commercial considerations will conflict has always faced those who run companies. It is not a new problem. The difference now is that a more widespread and critical interest is being taken in our decisions and in the ethical judgments which lie behind them.

Secondly, as the newspaper example demonstrates, ethical signposts do not always point in the same direction. My grandfather had to choose between opposing a war and condoning gambling. The rule that it is best to tell the truth often runs up against the rule that we should not hurt people's feelings unnecessarily. There is no simple, universal formula for solving ethical problems. We have to choose from our own codes of conduct whichever rules are appropriate to the case in hand; the outcome of those choices makes us who we are.

Lastly, while it is hard enough to resolve dilemmas when our personal rules of conduct conflict, the real difficulties arise when we have to make decisions which affect the interests of others. We can work out what weighting to give to our own rules through trial and error. But business decisions require us to do the same for others by allocating weights to all the conflicting interests which may be involved. Frequently, for example, we must balance the interests of employees against those of shareholders. But even that sounds more straightforward than it really is, because there may well be differing views among the shareholders, and the interests of past, present, and future employees are unlikely to be identical.

Eliminating ethical considerations from business decisions would simplify the management task, and Milton Friedman has urged something of the kind in arguing that the interaction between business and society should be left to the political process. "Few trends could so thoroughly undermine the very foundation of our free society," he writes in *Capitalism and Freedom,* "as the acceptance by corporate officials of a social responsibility other than to make as much money for their shareholders as possible."

But the simplicity of this approach is deceptive. Business is part of the social system and we cannot isolate the economic elements of major decisions from their social consequences. So there are no simple rules. Those who make business decisions have to assess the economic and social consequences of their actions as best as they can and come to their conclusions on limited information and in a limited time.

We Judge Companies—and Managers—by Their Actions, Not Their Pious Statements of Intent

As will already be apparent, I use the word ethics to mean the guidelines or rules of conduct by which we aim to live. It is, of course, foolhardy to write about ethics at all, because you lay yourself open to the charge of taking up a position of moral superiority, of failing to practice what you preach, or both. I am not in a position to preach nor am I promoting a specific code of conduct. I believe, however, that it is useful to all of us who are responsible for business decisions to acknowledge the part which ethics plays in those decisions and to encourage discussion of how best to combine commercial and ethical judgments. Most business decisions involve some degree of ethical judgment; few can be taken solely on the basis of arithmetic.

While we refer to a company as having a set of standards, that is a convenient shorthand. The people who make up the company are responsible for its conduct and it is their collective actions which determine the company's standards. The ethical standards of a company are judged by its actions, not by pious statements of intent put out in its name. This does not mean that those who head companies should not set down what they believe their companies stand for—hard though that is to do. The character of a company is a matter of importance to those in it, to those who do business with it, and to those who are considering joining it.

What matters most, however, is where we stand as individual managers and how we behave when faced with decisions which require us to combine ethical and commercial judgments. In approaching such decisions, I believe it is helpful to go through two steps. The first is to determine, as precisely as we can, what our personal rules of conduct are. This does not mean drawing up a list of virtuous notions, which will probably end up as a watered-down version of the Scriptures without their literary merit. It does mean looking back at decisions we have made and working out from there what our rules actually are. The aim is to avoid confusing ourselves and everyone else by declaring one set of principles and acting on another. Our ethics are expressed in our actions, which is why they are usually clearer to others than to ourselves.

Once we know where we stand personally we can move on to the second step, which is to think through who else will be affected by the decision and how we should weight their interest in it. Some interests will be represented by well-organized groups; others will have no one to put their case. If a factory manager is negotiating a wage claim with employee representatives, their remit is to look after the interests of those who are already employed. Yet the effect of the wage settlement on the factory's costs may well determine whether new employees are likely to be taken on. So the manager cannot ignore the interest of potential employees in the outcome of the negotiation, even though that interest is not represented at the bargaining table.

Black and White Alternatives Are a Regrettable Sign of the Times

The rise of organized interest groups makes it doubly important that managers consider the arguments of everyone with a legitimate interest in a decision's outcome. Interest groups seek publicity to promote their causes and they have the advantage of being single-minded: they are against building an airport on a certain site, for example, but take no responsibility for finding a better alternative. This narrow focus gives pressure groups a debating advantage against management, which cannot evade the responsibility for taking decisions in the same way.

In *The Hard Problems of Management,* Mark Pastin has perceptively referred to this phenomenon as the ethical superiority of the uninvolved, and there is a good deal of it about. Pressure groups are skilled at seizing the high moral ground and arguing that our judgment as managers is at best biased and at worst influenced solely by private gain because we have a direct commercial interest in the outcome of our decisions. But as managers we are also responsible for arriving at business decisions which take account of all the interests concerned; the uninvolved are not.

At times the campaign to persuade companies to divest themselves of their South African subsidiaries has exemplified this kind of ethical high-handedness. Apartheid is abhorrent politically, socially, and morally. Those who argue that they can exert some influence on the direction of change by staying put believe this as sincerely as those who favor divestment. Yet many anti-apartheid campaigners reject the proposition that both sides have the same end in view. From their perspective it is self-evident that the only ethical course of action is for companies to wash their hands of the problems of South Africa by selling out.

Managers cannot be so self-assured. In deciding what weight to give to the arguments for and against divestment, we must consider who has what at stake in the outcome of the decision. The employees of a South African subsidiary have the most direct stake, as the decision affects their future; they are also the group whose voice is least likely to be heard outside South Africa. The shareholders have at stake any loss on divestment, against which must be balanced any gain in the value of their shares through severing the South African connection. The divestment lobby is the one group for whom the decision is costless either way.

What is clear even from this limited analysis is that there is no general answer to the question of whether companies should sell their South African subsidiaries or not. Pressure to reduce complicated issues to straightforward alternatives, one of which is right and the other wrong, is a regrettable sign of the times. But boards are rarely presented with two clearly opposed alternatives. Companies faced with the same issues will therefore properly come to different conclusions and their decisions may alter over time.

A less contentious divestment decision faced my own company when we decided to sell our foods division. Because the division was mainly a U.K. business with regional brands, it did not fit the company's strategy, which called for concentrating resources behind our confectionery and soft drinks brands internationally. But it was an attractive business in its own right and the decision to sell prompted both a management bid and external offers.

Employees working in the division strongly supported the management bid and made their views felt. In this instance, they were the best organized interest group and they had more information available to them to back their case than any of the other parties involved. What they had at stake was also very clear.

From the shareholder's point of view, the premium over asset value offered by the various bidders was a key aspect of the decision. They also had an interest in seeing the deal completed without regulatory delays and without diverting too much management attention from the ongoing business. In addition, the way in which the successful bidder would guard the brand name had to be considered, since the division would take with it products carrying the parent company's name.

In weighing the advantages and disadvantages of the various offers, the board considered all the groups, consumers among them, who would be affected by the sale. But our main task was to reconcile the interests of the employees and of the shareholders. (The more, of course, we can encourage employees to become shareholders, the closer together the interests of these two stakeholders will be brought.) The division's management upped its bid in the face of outside competition, and after due deliberation we decided to sell to the management team, believing that this choice best balanced the diverse interests at stake.

Actions Are Unethical if They Won't Stand Scrutiny

Companies whose activities are international face an additional complication in taking their decisions. They aim to work to the same standards of business conduct wherever they are and to behave as good corporate citizens of the countries in which they trade. But the two aims are not always compatible: promotion on merit may be the rule of the company and promotion by seniority the custom of the country. In addition, while the financial arithmetic on which companies base their decisions is generally accepted, what is considered ethical varies among cultures.

If what would be considered corruption in the company's home territory is an accepted business practice elsewhere, how are local managers expected to act? Companies could do business only in countries in which they feel ethically at home, provided always that their shareholders take the same view. But this approach could prove unduly restrictive, and there is also a certain arrogance in dismissing foreign codes of conduct without considering why they may be different. If companies find, for example, that they have to pay customs officers in another country just to do their job, it may be that the state is simply transferring its responsibilities to the private sector as an alternative to using taxation less efficiently to the same end.

Nevertheless, this example brings us to one of the most common ethical issues companies face—how far to go in buying business? What payments are legitimate for companies to make to win orders and the reverse side of that coin, when do gifts to employees become bribes? I use two rules of thumb to test whether a payment is acceptable from the company's point of view: Is the payment on the face of the invoice? Would it embarrass the recipient to have the gift mentioned in the company newspaper?

The first test ensures that all payments, however unusual they may seem, are recorded and go through the books. The second is aimed at distinguishing bribes from gifts, a definition which depends on the size of the gift and the influence it is likely to have on the recipient. The value of a case of whiskey to me would be limited, because I only take it as medicine. We know ourselves whether a gift is acceptable or not and we know that others will know if they are aware of the nature of the gift.

As for payment on the face of the invoice, I have found it a useful general rule precisely because codes of conduct do vary round the world. It has legitimized some otherwise unlikely company payments, to the police in one country, for example, and to the official planning authorities in another, but all went through the books and were audited. Listing a payment on the face of the invoice may not be a sufficient ethical test, but it is a necessary one; payments outside the company's system are corrupt and corrupting.

The logic behind these rules of thumb is that openness and ethics go together and that actions are unethical if they will not stand scrutiny. Openness in arriving at decisions reflects the same logic. It gives those with an interest in a particular decision the chance to make their views known and opens to argument the basis on which the decision is finally taken. This in turn enables the decision makers to learn from experience and to improve their powers of judgment.

Openness is also, I believe, the best way to disarm outside suspicion of companies' motives and actions. Disclosure is not a panacea for improving the relations between business and society, but the willingess to operate an open system is the foundation of those relations. Business needs to be open to the views of society and open in return about its own activities; this is essential for the establishment of trust.

For the same reasons, as managers we need to be candid when making decisions about other people. Dr. Johnson reminds us that when it comes to lapidary inscriptions, "no man is upon oath." But what should be disclosed in references, in fairness to those looking for work and to those who are considering employing them?

The simplest rule would seem to be that we should write the kind of reference we would wish to read. Yet "do as you would be done by" says nothing about ethics. The actions which result from applying it could be ethical or unethical, depending on the standards of the initiator. The rule could be adapted to help managers determine their ethical standards, however, by reframing it as a question: If you did business with yourself, how ethical would you think you were?

Anonymous letters accusing an employee of doing something discreditable create another context in which candor is the wisest course. Such letters cannot by definition be answered, but they convey a message to those who receive them, however warped or unfair the message may be. I normally destroy these letters, but tell the person concerned what has been said. This conveys the disregard I attach to nameless allegation, but preserves the rule of openness. From a practical point of view, it serves as a warning if there is anything in the allegations; from an ethical point of view, the degree to which my judgment of the person may now be prejudiced is known between us.

Shelving Hard Decisions Is the Least Ethical Course

The last aspect of ethics in business decisions I want to discuss concerns our responsibility for the level of employment; what can or should companies do about the provision of jobs? This issue is of immediate concern to European managers because unemployment is higher in Europe than it is in the United States and the net number of new jobs created has been much lower. It comes to the fore whenever companies face decisions which require a trade-off between increasing efficiency and reducing numbers employed.

If you believe, as I do, that the primary purpose of a company is to satisfy the needs of its customers and to do so profitably, the creation of jobs cannot be the company's goal as well. Satisfying customers requires companies to compete in the marketplace, and so we cannot opt out of introducing new technology, for example, to preserve jobs. To do so would be to deny consumers the benefits of progress, to shortchange the shareholders, and in the longer run to put the jobs of everyone in the company at risk. What destroys jobs certainly and permanently is the failure to be competitive.

Experience says that the introduction of new technology creates more jobs than it eliminates, in ways which cannot be forecast. It may do so, however, only after a time lag and those displaced may not through lack of skills, be able to take advantage of the new opportunities when they arise. Nevertheless, the company's prime responsibility to everyone who has a stake in it is to retain its competitive edge, even if this means a loss of jobs in the short run.

Where companies do have a social responsibility, however, is in how we manage that situation, how we smooth the path of technological change. Companies are responsible for the timing of such changes and we are in a position to involve those who will be affected by the way in which those changes are introduced. We also have a vital resource in our capacity to provide training, so that continuing employees can take advantage of change and those who may lose their jobs can more readily find new ones.

In the United Kingdom, an organization called Business in the Community has been established to encourage the formation of new enterprises. Companies have backed it with cash and with secondments. The secondment of able managers to worthwhile institutions is a particularly effective expression of concern, because the ability to manage is such a scarce resource. Through Business in the Community we can create jobs collectively, even if we cannot do so individually, and it is clearly in our interest to improve the economic and social climate in this way.

Throughout, I have been writing about the responsibilities of those who head companies and my emphasis has been on taking decisions, because that is what directors and managers are appointed to do. What concerns me is that too often the public pressures which are put on companies in the name of ethics encourage their boards to put off decisions or to wash their hands of problems. There may well be commercial reasons for those choices, but there are rarely ethical ones. The ethical bases on which decisions are arrived at will vary among companies, but shelving those decisions is likely to be the least ethical course.

The company which takes drastic action in order to survive is more likely to be criticized publicly than the one which fails to grasp the nettle and gradually but inexorably declines. There is always a temptation to postpone difficult decisions, but it is not in society's interests that hard choices should be evaded because of public clamor or the possibility of legal action. Companies need to be encouraged to take the decisions which face them; the responsibility for providing that encouragement rests with society as a whole.

Society sets the ethical framework within which those who run companies have to work out their own codes of conduct. Responsibility for decisions, therefore, runs both ways. Business has to take account of its responsibilities to society in coming to its decisions, but society has to accept its responsibilities for setting the standards against which those decisions are made.

———————————•———————————

James Gordon, Manager

Barbara Ley Toffler

I am corporate administration manager, although I'm an engineer by background and have only been in the administrative world for three years. The responsibility of our group is to come up with a set of procedures and systems support for our function. Basically, we develop the systems to improve productivity and quality of the personnel work. We train 150 people out in our facilities who are the main interface with employees on administrative issues.

Part of the strength of this company is that it isn't really a company in a sense. It's very decentralized, very fragmented; I believe individuals can use that fragmentation to build for themselves the environment they want. So if you're really looking for a lot of structure, you can find it here. There are some organizations, a finance organization for one, that is very structured. There's no two ways to add numbers together; you do it a certain way. You can also find yourself in a complete lack of structure. I positioned myself in a place where our organization is typically unstructured, although my job has structure to it and I can use both pieces to satisfy myself. And I can be an entrepreneur. I've got a million-dollar budget here. I can run that pretty much the way I want.

The company is many things to many people, so a lot of people feel satisfied with it. I just saw the results of the survey that was done in one of the company's groups. Ninety-five percent of the people that work in that group said they would recommend this place to a friend as a good place to work. I think that pretty much wraps it up. I enjoy our success, I enjoy being part of the company. I enjoyed it even before we became well known, but I'm convinced that in 10 years we'll be as well known as the biggest in the business right now. There's an ego thing for me when I tell people I work here. I feel like I'm part of a winner.

When I joined the company, they handed me the company's philosophy. It was the first time that I said to myself, "I think they're serious." With every other company in which I've worked, they said, "Here are the golden rules for the company." Then when I would begin working for that company, I would realize it was all bullshit, that the profit motive was probably the thing that drove most people, and that individuals would get chewed up because it was best for the system. Our philosophy here says that it's not enough to tell customers the truth; it's your responsibility to make sure that whomever you're talking to understands the truth. And that was written at a time when we had problems with customers because we couldn't deliver enough product; demand was so high. But it was the first time I'd ever seen that articulated in such a way. I sit on a policy committee for the company, and time and time again I've seen things that looked like they would be terrific for the company voted down because they would be bad for the individual. I have seen people being taken care of by the company, far beyond anything that was the law or that the company's policy would dictate, because of a feeling about the individual. I have seen individuals in the company who don't have any formal power change the company because they had the right ideas. I think that's all on purpose and by design.

On the other side of that coin, there are things that happen that are not on purpose and aren't by design, which are as nasty as things that go on in other organizations. But they happen for a different reason. I see them happening in other organizations because an individual decides, "I'm going to get that bastard," and the structure allows it to happen. In this company, because we're so unstructured, because we're so decentralized, and because we are typically comprised of very bright, very strong people, there are no support structures for those individuals who are hired in and need the support. If you're sensing some confusion where people are concerned, you're right. This company, because of the lack of structure, ends up chewing up a lot of people. But it is not by design. It's a function of the culture, and any attempts to try to create structure are going to be countercultural and will destroy a lot of things I like about the place.

What I am trying to do is balance the part that says "This is the best place I've ever worked for, they care about the individual and they really are committed to that," against the fact that if you went out and took some measurements, you'd find some individuals who were in pain, who don't know who the hell their boss is or how to do their jobs or what their goals are. For people who care about what they're doing, that's going to be painful. In other organizations, you see people in pain and it's controllable by one or two individuals who are causing that pain. In this company, I see people in pain, but it's a result of the fact that the system is not structured in a way to help the individual. So an employee in trouble may not have anywhere to go other than to work the system. And some people don't do that very well. We don't do a very good job of telling people that, either. We just sort of assume everybody knows.

When I think about ethics, I think there are certain things that somehow get programmed into us early on in life around what's good and bad. And goodness for me, in that context, without intellectualizing at all, is just a gut feeling. Goodness for me is helping your fellow man, and not doing anything to damage others, and spending extra time helping people that are in trouble, and so on. Bad is doing anything that would harm other people. Somewhere in the back of my mind there's a tape that plays that. Intellectually, that's different for me than what's right and wrong. A lot of what's the right thing to do and what's the wrong thing to do, I think is, for me, situational. But there's the whole piece around what's good and bad that has to do with basic values. I think of all of this as a matrix that looks like this:

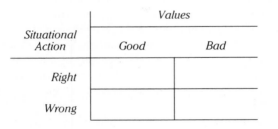

Situational Action	Values	
	Good	Bad
Right		
Wrong		

Let me give you some examples. The good thing to do and the organizationally right thing to do is fair and equal treatment for folks. The good thing to do but the wrong thing to do in an organizational setting is being too honest, thereby undermining organizational effectiveness. So, for example, good things say you'll always tell the truth and you're always straightforward with people, but organizationally that can get you into a whole bunch of hot water and undermine your effectiveness. So from an organizational point of view, that's often the wrong thing to do. A bad thing to do is to tell white lies; goodness says you never lie. But sometimes that is the right thing to do, for instance, to help someone save face. That's doing bad for the right reason. And bad and wrong is, say, deliberately causing personal pain. This matrix sort of puts things in perspective for me in terms of being able to articulate the constant tugging inside me. I spent eight years in a Catholic grammar school, four years in a Catholic youth organization as an officer, four years in a Catholic fraternity in college. I've had that whole Judeo-Christian good-bad stuff drummed into my head. And yet I know damn well that I operate oftentimes in this matrix.

I have been in organizations where the right thing to do from the organization's perspective felt awful to me, and the reason it did is because I think I felt it was not only the wrong thing to do, but that my definition of goodness and badness was so strong around the issue that I said, "Not only is that bad, that's also wrong." And so even though I've been in some situations where I've been able to say the bad thing to do was really the right thing to do, I've also been in situations in other organizations where the bad thing to do has also been what I thought was the wrong thing to do. And then I've been faced with a dilemma around the organization telling me "You gotta do it," and I believe it was bad and it was wrong. That's when dilemmas have really felt awful to me. The interesting thing about this company is that there are very few organizational imperatives around what to do. So I feel much freer to be consistent with this matrix. Generally speaking, when I do the bad thing, it's for the right reason organizationally, and it feels good in here (points to his stomach), yeah. I have not been put into a position in the three years I've been with the company where I've ever had to do what I consider to be the bad and the wrong thing. I've had to do the bad and right, but that bad, as I said, is not an intellectual bad for me, it's a gut-feel value programmed in very early on by a bunch of nuns and a bunch of other folks, my parents and whomever, who probably didn't always live by those either.

Here is an interesting example. We've got a woman who works in our department, Mary, and she has had virtually every disaster that can happen to a person happen during the past two years: death of both parents, major physical problems, incredible personal problems with a sibling and other relatives. She got very sick. OK. The good thing to do is to take care of your fellow man. There is some question in my mind about whether the company policies would say what I did was right or wrong, from an organizational point of view. I chose to do what I think our chairman would agree was the right thing.

A little bit of background on this woman: she's a local person; she grew up in the community in which we are headquartered, went to high school there, and has always dreamed of working for this company. There's a whole piece around community relations that subtly entered my head around her and I said, "Part of me wants to treat her well because she's a local person working for us." The other thing I noticed was that she works in a place where you start at eight, you take your coffee break, you take your lunch break, and you take your coffee break in the afternoon, and the rest of the time you're just out straight; you get driven by the phones. Two women, Mary and Sue, handle on the order of 3500 phone calls a month. And they love it. When we were getting ready to move over here, Sue came in to me and she said, "Mary and I have talked, and we're not going to be able to pack those files for the move and answer the phones at the same time. Would you mind if we came in on Saturday? We don't care about the pay, but would you care

if we did that?" I'm saying, "Holy . . .!" I mean, where do you find these people? Well, that's what Mary is all about, too. She is really dedicated. So I say,
"The hell with the company policy. I'm going to treat her well." So, essentially, I paid her for a lot of the time she was out. I didn't want to take away
all of her sick time. She was beginning to chew into her vacation time. There
she was, someone whose life involves getting up in the morning, taking care
of her relatives, working here, going home, taking care of her relatives, and
also going to school. She was going to community college to pick up some
credits. And I'm saying, "I'm not going to pile any more crap on that lady."
Now, I don't know if that's the right or the wrong thing to do from the company's point of view, but I think our chairman would probably support the
concept of disregarding sick time, short-term disability, and long-term disability. That, to me, was a fairly easy dilemma to work myself out of. It certainly was the good thing to do. There was a little bit of question about the
right thing to do from an organizational point of view, but again, this company has convinced me that the right thing in that case was to disregard company policy and to use my own judgment around what I did with her.

Actually, the only dilemma piece was that the company policy states she
should have used up her sick time, vacation time, and then gone on short-
term disability. So I said, "I'm probably taking a risk here." The other nice
thing was, I went in to my boss and said, "Look, I've got a person in my
group . . . ," and I told him her background, and I said, "I'm not asking for
you to do anything other than to understand that I'm going to treat her well,
because I think she deserves it. She's given loyalty and hard work and dedication to this department and to the company; she's a local person; I just think
there's a whole bunch of things that we need to do for her."

Q. What was the risk?

*Part of the risk was other people in the department knowing that I'd done it,
and saying, "Hey, you did it for her. I want to take next week off, because I think
I just need some R&R time." Another part of the risk was somebody poking around
and finding out I was paying her as if she were here when she wasn't. But I really
feel as if no one in the company would challenge what I did because it was the
right thing to do. When I say I feel that, I feel that now. But when I was going through
the decision making on it, I still had some question as to whether somebody would
force the company policy on me (which in itself is fairly liberal, it treats people
fairly well).*

But this company, quite frankly, does treat people differently, depending on
their situation, and in spite of all company policy. And I see the only risk
being one of doing it in some kind of discriminatory fashion, where you're
doing it just for white males, for example. Then I think you're really opening
yourself up for a risk. But as I've said before, the company has really made
me feel like I'm owning my own business here; I'm an entrepreneur. And
if I owned my own business and could afford it, I probably would've done
exactly the same thing. So there was a piece of me that said, "Look, I'm run-

ning a business here, and what I want to do is to treat that person well, because her loyalty has been such, and the amount of work she's put in is such that I don't think the policy applies to her." If it ever ended up in a one-on-one conversation between the chairman and me, which it never would, I've got a feeling he'd probably support me. I think the nice part about being here is I don't have a whole lot of dilemmas that are placed on me by the organization because I think, first of all, it is very moral and ethical in the way it positions itself, and second of all, it's so decentralized that there isn't that kind of pressure that says "The right thing for the company to do, you jerk, is this. Now you go off and do it."

So the ethical question was: here is a person who I would like to be able to help during a very trying part of her life, but I know that some of the things I'm doing are against company policy and procedure, which, by the way, I helped write. Is that really the right thing to do? Should I really be going that extra mile, or should I say to myself, "Policy was written because we know some people are going to get themselves sick and need time off. She'll get 80% of her salary for a while and then two-thirds of her salary. Sorry, that's just the way life is sometimes." So I went through that whole thought process of "Do I really want to go against company policy around how I treat people? What if everybody did that? Then the policy would be worth garbage, and the company would be spending all kinds of money." So I put all the stuff aside and I said, "Well, let me look at her as an individual. I can't justify not helping her out." Now, she is on short-term disability. There came a point when we had to say, "OK, we've done everything we know how, and now we're going to try to preserve her vacation time for her, which we did. But I probably gave her seven or eight days that should have been vacation or sick time or something. So I'm not talking about huge amounts of money. But there came a point at which I said, "OK, she is going to be out for an extended period of time. (She had an operation.) Now it's time for short-term disability to come into play."

It sent a message to the other people in the department. I've heard a little bit of feedback that said people really appreciated what I did for her. The message says (a) Jim's a humane manager, and (b) he must work for a fairly humane company to allow him to get away with that. I think most people know it wasn't something I hid, and I didn't have to get devious to make that happen. I just made a decision that that's the way it should be. So there were all kinds of payoffs to the company, because there are 16 other people out there who all say this really is a neat place to work—look what they did for Mary. And they don't even try to personalize it and say, "Son of a bitch, what are they going to do for me now?" or "Why would they do that for her and not for me?" They all understand she's a unique case. In fact, we had one individual who has been out. She went through a real attitudinal thing for whatever reason, things going on at home. Then she hurt her back. She wanted to take some extra time around a funeral, and from everything I could tell, it really wasn't a close relative. And she was told "No, you've been out X number of days." I have two people between myself and that individual, and they came to me and said "We're going to get tough with Ellen about coming in. We just want you to know we're doing it. We think it's the proper thing to do." And I supported it. And never once did she come back and say—that's where the danger was—"Well, look what you've done for Mary and you're not willing to give me. . . ." I believe she knew there was a difference between just being in a lousy mood and being in bed.

Look at the matrix. When I'm in the bad and the right box, the thought process I find myself using is sort of incremental rationalization which means that each step makes sense within the context of doing the right thing from a situational point of view. And I'm fairly comfortable about overriding the bads as long as I can incrementally justify each step as being the right thing to do. Now it feels different when I do it in the Mary case. In the case where it's good but it may be wrong, my decisions tend to be binary. They tend to be: that's what I'm going to do. I mean, I'll do some talking about it ahead of time, but there's very little rationalizing. With Mary I made a decision that I was going to do something and I didn't have to incrementally rationalize it, I just said, "BOOM. I believe that this is the right thing to do. I know I'm taking some risk personally here, but screw it. BOOM! I'm going to do it." Combined with the piece that said if she had been another employee who gives me 40 hours and goes home and does not have her dedication to the company and dedication to the job, then I could very easily say, "It's a situation defined by the policy and what I can do for you is this. Thank you very much." So there was a rightness that had to do with the quality of the person. It was an organizational rightness, I felt, that had some fringes that were kind of frayed because the policy kept nipping away at me and I had to sort of balance that stuff. But it wasn't incremental for me. It was "Consider all that stuff and then BOOM."

The hardest box in the matrix to be in is the bad-wrong. It's a bad thing to do, and I think it's the wrong thing to do organizationally, and somebody says you have to do it. And I've been in those situations a couple of times. That's a tough one for me to deal with because I generally end up folding and doing it because you can't win. I guess you do have a choice. The choice is to leave. Or to start laying the groundwork for leaving the organization. You can't do too many of those. By the way, lest you get the wrong idea, the matrix came directly as a result of your asking me to think about ethics. One of the things you should know about me is that I don't generally have a very structured way of sitting down and processing my own feelings and thoughts. The matrix came out of my attempt to sit down and take a generic question around ethical dilemmas. I started just playing around with "Well, what is ethics?" And that's how it came up. What I was trying to structure was situations where a dilemma occurs for me. I have a friend who did his divorce that way. It was mind-boggling. He did pros and cons and guess what? He had two pros and 57 cons and said, "It's time to leave." This guy's an MIT grad and very bright. The thing to know about me is I don't have the structure I probably should have around some of these questions. I tend to go with my gut more often than not.

When there are competing claims, what I think happens is that somehow I process all of those claims, give a certain weight to each, and then end up in one of these boxes, saying, "Yeah, overall, after I weigh everything together, the right thing to do is going to mean taking a couple of bad steps or whatever. Understanding that some people are going to be hurt by that, and some people are going to benefit by that, but the overall right thing to do is this." Then the question is, is the right really my new set of values? Is that my real set of values or is the good and the bad my real set of values? It's hard; I haven't thought about it a lot. And it's hard because you can probably argue that my real set of values is the right and wrong, and that the good and bad are just sort of childhood underpinnings, sort of a base which I don't subscribe to all that strongly. Sometimes it feels that a lot of things I was taught were bad, I find myself being able to rationalize in terms of what's right. I mean, if I went out and told the truth to everyone in my department, there would be very few people standing up. And I'm sure they could do the same to me. So I guess my values really are that the right thing to do is to protect that shell, and organizations tend to encourage that. This company less than others. We tend to encourage people to be honest about what they're thinking. The first couple of times I made presentations here, I said, "I'm either failing or I'm doing real good. I can't figure out which." Oh, the stuff that gets stirred up: "I don't agree with that." "That's bullshit." And I found that people are doing that because they were really wired into what you were saying, instead of sort of sitting there. It takes some time to get used to that.

There's a tremendous amount of consistency between the way I view myself as an individual and the way I feel the company views itself and wants me to act. And so I've yet to really confront an issue and have to worry about inconsistency between what I believe is right to do and what the company believes is the right thing to do. And they don't define "right" all that well. They say, "You're sitting closest to it, you do the right thing." "Right" means not doing a dumb thing just because the policy book says to do it that way, or because you've got a memo saying to do it that way. So I guess I'm very fortunate to feel that consistency, that congruency, and it's nice because it's congruent with the rest of my life. I don't have to set up one set of behaviors and values here, and silence all the ethical questions, and just go out and do what's best for the organization. And I don't have to do that at home. I don't have to make decisions at home that are in conflict with what the company wants. It's a nice balance for me.

Postscript

One year after I interviewed James Gordon, he had to make the difficult decision to fire Mary. He had continued to bend the rules for her until it came to a point where, for a number of personal reasons on her part, she was unable to fulfill the requirements of her job. He explains the decision in terms of incrementally doing the "right" thing until it gets to a point where the next step no longer is justifiable from a "good" or a "right" perspective.

Comments

In Jim Gordon's matrix, we see reflected a theme relevant to most of the dilemmas discussed in these pages: How do I balance basic beliefs and values with being effective and responsible in a complex and ambiguous world. We need to recognize that for all the pain represented by his model, Jim, in his present organization, has it easier than some. The reason is that the matrix is based on the assumption that Jim—or whoever is using it—*can* act as he chooses and is not subject to a "do it" command from above. Jim mentions that when he says the "awful" situation to find yourself in is to be in the bad/wrong box on an action which your superior insists you do.

As Jim talks about his dilemma with Mary, it is clear he felt *he* could decide what to do and his decision either would be supported by the company or, if not, would not involve great personal risk for him. According to his matrix, Jim was in the good/wrong box—it is good to help a person in need, but it is wrong to compromise an organizational policy. Jim says that in a good/wrong situation he just does what he feels is right, BOOM, regardless of the risks or other circumstances. Certainly that seems to be the case in the Mary situation.

Jim believed he *could* get the job done, but there was an organizational value system in place as well. Jim felt he could adjust the disability policy because (1) the company does believe in treating people differently, in spite of policy, as long as the different treatment is not discriminatory, (2) the role of policy in the company is not clear, and (3) if he went one-on-one with the chairman, Jim believed the chairman would back him up.

The supportive corporate environment allowed Jim to resolve his dilemma with some useful devices. First, he was able to focus almost solely on a single stakeholder, Mary; so the key question became "What is best for her?" With the company behind him, he did not feel pulled in too many directions at once. Second, he did not have to hide his action or engage in other covert activities. He told his boss and allowed his decision to become public knowledge in the company, which mitigated any sense of "wrong" and reinforced for him the doing of good.

Jim's situation raises a critical concern about the role of policy in organizations. Policy is written to express corporate values in a particular area and to set the guidelines for actions relating to that area. But the general nature of a policy cannot take into account all of the possible configurations of events—the exceptions—that must occur in any organization. The question is: How do you deal with the exceptions? Rigid policy that demands absolute adherence can be dysfunctional and even ethically harmful to a company by compromising both the integrity and competence of managers within it. On the other hand, policy that can be ignored or distorted or interpreted in a variety of ways can lead to similar outcomes by creating a too anarchic environment. In Jim's and his company's case, the line between blind compliance to, and manipulation of a policy was trod with finesse. The outcome supported Mary, the company, the other employees, and Jim. As Jim points out, however, his actions might have set a precedent which could have eroded the respect for policies, rules, and procedures in the organization.

●

Is Greed America's New Creed?

A Reply by Amitai Etzioni

Every week, it seems a new insider trading scandal dominates the headlines of the business press.

Young Wall Street traders with a six-or-seven figure income seem oblivious to the law in their pursuit of the yuppie dream of "having it all."

Is the new generation of business leaders less ethical than its predecessors? Has greed become the chief motivating force in today's business world? Are American business schools adequately preparing their students for ethical business practice? . . .

Cult of Greed

Amitai Etzioni, *professor at The George Washington University, director of the Center for Policy Research and the author of* Capital Corruption, *replied:*

The focus on the inside traders is temporary and unfortunate. They are but one segment of the community currently held up to public criticism—and punishment. Soon—quite possibly by the time these lines are published—the rarely sated public taste for censure, confessions, and judgment will turn to some other sector. Whether it is going to be TV preachers, the Marines, rabbis, professors, or politicians matters little. The sad fact is that this sector, too, will be found riddled with corruption.

The deeper point is that currently our society is not very moral. There is a cult of greed; an unwillingness to be seriously concerned with the rules of the game; a preoccupation with winning whatever way. There is a fascination with rotten apples but not patience to understand the cracks in the barrel and how they might be sealed.

Until we stop hopping around from one headline crisis to another, a corruption of criticism, there is precious little hope that we shall come to terms with what afflicts us. Indeed, as our headlines and minds are filled with the tidbits of the latest Irangate, Godgate, Greedgate or whatever is next, we shall remain distracted from a study and treatment of the body society as a whole. Seen in this way, the present examination is itself pitched on the wrong level.

●

Corporations Urge Peers to Adopt Humane Policies for AIDS Victims

Marilyn Chase

Many U.S. companies have been deaf to health officials' exhortations about the AIDS epidemic. But there is one voice they may heed: that of their peers.

With that hope, representatives of some of the country's largest corporations will gather in Washington today to present federal officials with their recommendations on how businesses can best prepare for and react to incidents of acquired immune deficiency syndrome in the workplace.

The report—"AIDS: Corporate America Responds"—is the product of a national conference sponsored last fall by Allstate Insurance Co., a unit of Sears, Roebuck & Co. The 100-page document urges companies to take the lead and develop AIDS policies "before a known AIDS case or problem arises (in order to) minimize crises and reduce employee fear, mistrust and uncertainty."

According to the report, only 5% of U.S. employers have developed an AIDS policy. Most companies have failed to address the issue, the report states, because of fears of image problems, client backlash, or qualms about appearing to condone homosexuality or intravenous drug abuse.

Setting the Pace

Although there is no guarantee that the report will prompt many—or any— companies to adopt policies on AIDS, the authors say it may succeed because corporations often take their cues from each other. Here, as in the early days of affirmative action, large corporations are attempting to set the pace for smaller companies.

"There is a need for this kind of support," says Benjamin Schatz, an attorney with National Gay Rights Advocates, a public interest law firm in San Francisco. "While we're making progress, major problems of AIDS-based discrimination still exist in the workplace." In one hour on Monday, he says, he received four telephone complaints from people who were fired or forced to take leaves of absence because they had or were rumored to have AIDS.

"Just because such practices are illegal," Mr. Schatz says, "doesn't mean they aren't happening."

Although the report suggests strategies for coping with the financial costs of AIDS, it primarily seeks to promote a model of humane corporate behavior toward those with the disease. Thus, the report recommends that companies ban mandatory AIDS testing and support confidentiality, continued employment and broad benefits—themes that homosexual rights groups have long sounded.

In the face of persistent public anxiety about how AIDS spreads, the report endorses the current medical consensus that AIDS is transmitted only through sexual relations, blood products or shared needles—not casual social or professional contact that occurs in the workplace. Outside the field of health care, the report says no special job modification is necessary for co-workers of AIDS patients.

However, job modification for people with AIDS is strongly urged by the report as a way of keeping them on the job for as long as they are able to work. Bank of America, for instance, approaches life-threatening illnesses with a flexible work plan, says Nancy L. Merritt, vice president and director of equal opportunity programs. Thus, one employee with AIDS—who feared public reaction to the purple lesions of Kaposi's sarcoma, an AIDS-linked cancer— was allowed to work at home on his personal computer. The report promotes similar uses of home work, flex-time, lightened workloads and rest breaks.

Treatment of employees with AIDS should be the same as that for others with a chronic or life-threatening illness, the report states, including eligibility for the same work privileges and medical benefits.

For example, International Business Machines Corp. drafted its AIDS policy in 1985 and followed it up last fall by mailing copies of the AIDS brochure written by the U.S. Centers for Disease Control to all 240,000 domestic employees. The brochure was prefaced by a "Dear IBMer" letter from the company's medical director, Glenn E. Haughie, who wrote: "IBMers affected by AIDS will be encouraged to work as long as they are able, and their privacy will be respected."

In a chapter on legal affairs, the Allstate report reminds corporate America that "all federal and state courts and state agencies which have considered the question have held that AIDS is a handicap entitled to protection (against) discrimination. . . ."

The report cites the Supreme Court's 1987 decision in the case of The School Board of Nassau County vs. Arline. Although that case addressed tuberculosis and not AIDS, the court's decision extended protection of federal handicap statutes to contagious diseases. Moreover, the report says that testing for antibodies to HIV, the AIDS virus, "is likely to be considered illegal since testing positive for HIV cannot be shown to be related to performance on the job."

Raising a Red Flag

The legal chapter raises one red flag that is bound to spark arguments. It cautions that companies that hand out written AIDS policies to all employees may create a new class of contractual rights for workers with AIDS. Employers who may make exceptions or allowances for victims of AIDS on a case-by-case basis may fear being legally bound to uphold such a standard universally, the report implies.

"Should a company wish to assure consistent treatment of employees with AIDS, but not wish to create contract rights," the report states, "it may want to issue guidelines to its managers instead of distributing a specific policy to all employees." Under some state laws, a policy given only to managers would avoid creating a special class of contract law.

James Gladden, author of the legal report and an attorney with the Chicago law firm of Mayer Brown & Platt, says the report counsels companies not to limit their ability to hire and fire with a written policy that "would lock a person in to being paid forever, no matter what they did."

"I find that troubling," says Mr. Schatz of the National Gay Rights Advocates. He says it is evidence of insincerity and "shortsighted desire to protect all options on the part of managers." Besides, he notes, "I've seen dozens of corporate policies, and none says an employee with AIDS can continue to work regardless of his or her performance."

AIDS and the Workplace

1) What would your company do if an employee had AIDS-related symptoms?

Give time off for medical treatment
47%

Provide counseling
32%

Work accommodation (i.e., allow work at home)
27%

Try to get the employee to resign
16%

Fire the employee
6%

Not promote the employee
5%

2) How would your management feel about instituting an AIDS-testing program for current employees?

Unfavorable
60%

Neutral
18%

No idea
14%

Favorable
8%

NOTE: Figures total more than 100% due to multiple responses.
Sources: Allstate Insurance and Fortune Magazine

Kodak Will Support Value of Homes at Rochester Chemical Site

ROCHESTER, June 3—Saying they wanted to "do the right thing," Eastman Kodak Company officials acted this week to stabilize real-estate values in two communities shaken by reports of possible chemical contamination.

Under a complex plan, which could affect as many as 700 houses in two communities near the industrial complex known as Kodak Park, the company would guarantee the value of at least 200 houses closest to the park for the next 10 years.

Owners of those homes, on Rand Street and Steko Avenue, would also be eligible for interest-free loans equal to the equity in their houses if they decided to sell. A loan would have to be repaid after a house was sold. Kodak has also said it would pay moving, closing and legal expenses, as well as $500 for miscellaneous expenses, to any family that left the area.

As an incentive to stay, Kodak is offering homeowners on Rand Street, the street closest to the possible contamination, $5,000 in home-improvement grants. Others in the area would be eligible to receive home-improvement loans at 2 percent interest. Kodak would also refinance existing mortgages at below-market interest rates, and would offer new buyers in the neighborhood below-market mortgage rates.

No Cost Estimate Yet

The plan, which has drawn initial praise from local and national officials, real-estate agents and some enviromentalists, also offers subsidies for landlords and tenants.

In announcing the plan Tuesday night, Robert L. Grose, director of site operations at Kodak Park, said the plan showed the company wants "to do the right thing."

"We view the program as an investment in the long-term stability of the neighborhood," Mr. Grose said.

He said it was too early to determine how much the program would cost.

Environmental officials said today that they were unaware of any comparable program in the nation. "This is the first arrangement of this type of which I have become aware," said Dr. J. Winston Porter, assistant administrator for solid waste and emergency response at the Federal Environmental Protection Agency in Washington. "It is a responsible action for the business community to address the welfare as well as the health needs of residents near facilities which handle hazardous materials."

"Generally, in the cases I've heard of, it's the Government forcing companies to buy houses," said Lois Epstein, an environmental engineer with the Environmental Defense Fund in Washington.

Tests Reveal Chemicals

The program was devised in response to reports in the last several months that chemicals have leaked from tanks at Kodak Park into ground water in the Rand Street area here, south of the industrial site. State testing revealed that those chemicals included methylene chloride, which is used in the film-making process and is considered by the environmental agency to be a carcinogen. Much lower levels of contamination have been found in a second community, Koda-Vista, in the town of Greece, which borders Kodak Park on the north.

Local health and environmental officials have said they do not know the extent of the contamination, or whether it poses any long-term health dangers to residents of the two communities, who receive their drinking water from the city, not from wells. Testing is expected to take at least several months.

"We continue to believe that the presence of chemicals in the bedrock poses no health hazard," said Mr. Grose of Kodak. "We are cooperating fully with local and state health authorities in environmental agencies in moving ahead quickly on a comprehensive testing and correction program."

Kodak agreed earlier this month to provide $50,000 for an independent consultant to advise citizens on what type of testing should be done.

Kodak's offer of financial assistance to homeowners and home buyers received mixed reviews from residents this week. Those eligible to receive the greatest aid generally praised it, while those who live further from the source of possible contamination and who would receive less support said it did not go far enough.

"You'd like to see the plan available to the whole neighborhood," said Alan D. Hall, spokesman for Concerned Neighbors of Kodak Park, a citizens group. "The other concern is encouraging people to move into the neighborhood when you're not sure of the level of contamination."

About 700 families could take advantage of some aspect of the plan. About 200 are on Rand Street or Steko Avenue, south of Kodak Park. Another 250 are on streets further south, in a neighborhood of mostly colonial and Cape Code-style single-family homes valued from $50,000 to $60,000. Another 250 families live in Koda-Vista, a well-kept neighborhood of mostly single-family colonial homes valued from $80,000 to $90,000.

The strongest criticism of the Kodak plan came from an environmentalist who questioned the ethics of trying to induce people to stay or move into the area before comprehensive testing determined the scope of the contamination.

"Basically Kodak is saying, 'We insure against your loss of property so take a risk with your lives and those of your families,' " said Will Collette, an environmentalist and the organizing director of the Citizens Clearing House for Hazardous Waste in Washington. "No matter what the circumstances, they'll tell you there's no cause for alarm. Do they guarantee against loss of life? If children start coming down with . . . illnesses, will Kodak be there for them?"

Indeed, homeowners have widely varying views on whether to stay, said Mr. Hall, who has lived in the area for eight years. "There are some families that just want to go now—no ifs, ands or buts—and there are families who have adopted a wait-and-see attitude for a variety of reasons," he said. "Some people like the neighborhood; they've lived there a number of years and, if it's safe, they'd like to stay."

10

Futures

Business organizations are powerful entities in our society and the world beyond. Organizations are major centers of power in all industrialized societies and are thoroughly interwoven with other aspects of human endeavor. Their influence is so strong that they can be said to *make* history. Their agendas shape our personalities, the forms of technologies that develop, the content of dominant ideologies, and the nature of government.[1] The influence of organizations seems likely to expand as the nature of economic activity becomes more global. In fact, one writer has predicted that the modern corporation will rival the nation state in the global affairs of the future.[2] Consequently, the role of managers appears likely to become both more important and more complex as we approach the next century.

Of course, predicting the future is difficult and even an intuitively obvious prediction such as the one made in the previous sentence can be quite erroneous. In thinking about the future, most people find it difficult to do much more than project trends of the present forward in time. At certain points in history, such projections may have been good guides for approaching decades, centuries, and even millennia. In view of the rapid changes in the contemporary world, it seems highly unlikely that such an approach will yield successful predictions beyond a very few years.

For the most part the articles in this section could very easily be little more than current trends and concerns projected forward. Consequently, it is risky to try to use them to look very far into the future. Nevertheless, the themes that run through these articles are widely believed to be important for the future. This perceived importance and the strong pressures that seem to be driving these trends make it difficult to imagine many scenarios (with the exception of a great nuclear war or other such catastrophe) where these matters would not be of central concern to managers—at least for the next decade.

Almost all of the articles, in one way or another, point to developments that will require organizations to be more flexible. Of course as organizations become more flexible, people who work in them will have to be more flexible. (The first article, "Einstein's Advice on Work in the Next Century," describes what the demand for flexibility may mean for how managers need to think.) Personal dislocations are likely as organizations merge and redivide to meet the new contingencies they face. Undoubtedly the effects of these dislocations will spill over into the character of individuals and their institutions. In addition, as organizations attempt to become more flexible, it seems highly likely that the rigid, mechanistic structures of the past will increasingly need the help of committed people to achieve coordination. (Falvey's "Best Corporate Culture Is a Melting Pot" describes some of these personal and organizational changes—many of which he sees happening already.)

Yet another trend that seems almost certain to continue is the use of technology to manage information and control organizations. It is possible that these systems may allow information to be managed so effectively that a central staff or person (recall the selection on Mrs. Fields) can combine sophisticated decisions and centralized control with the flexibility of a small, entrepreneurial firm of the distant past. In fact, in the concluding article, Drucker suggests that organizations may come to look much like they did a century ago. Prior to the industrial revolution, many people worked at home in what has come to be known as cottage industry. Modern information systems present the possibility that many people can once again work at home—telecommuting from their electronic cottages. If this happened on even a moderately large scale, consider some of the implications for our society. Begin by thinking about how many features of the way we live and the systems that have grown to serve us have developed around people working in settings some distance from their homes. (The effects of changes in real estate values alone could constitute a major social revolution.) The nature of organizations and what managers would do will undoubtedly differ markedly from today's patterns.

It also seems almost certain that business will become increasingly global. Exactly what demands this will place on managers is very difficult to know; however, various forms of joint ventures are currently being attempted. It seems very likely that as business becomes increasingly global, managers will be required to coordinate the efforts of people from diverse cultures within the bounds of an organization. Clearly, at first, these requirements will create significant challenges. Over time, however, one would expect that not only will effective forms for doing this be developed, but that greater homogeneity among people from various countries will increase.

Of course, new types of challenges can be expected to emerge. As we have tried to show throughout, the major constant in managing is the dialectical process created by the tensions produced as organizations attempt to coordinate human efforts by superimposing themselves on individuals. As human societies evolve, so will management. This we know from history. In the future, we expect the reverse direction will take on even greater importance—as the organizations and management evolve, so will human society.

References

1. C. E. Lindblom, *Politics and markets* (New York: Basic Books, 1977).
2. A. Madsen, *Private power* (New York: Quill, 1982).

Einstein's Advice on Work in the Next Century

Gerald Baxter and Nancy Kerber Baxter

Imagine a world in which your age depends on the speed you travel, or a world with a force so strong that it can alter the path of a beam of light—without the use of mirrors.

Imagine a world in which a 40-foot pole can fit inside a 20-foot barn, and square objects look round and round objects look elongated to observers who are rational and wide awake.

The world described is our own.

The phenomena above don't depend on magic, but rather on the physical laws that govern us. They are descriptions of how the world works based on the special and general theories of relativity published by Albert Einstein in 1905 and 1916.

Einstein's theories of relativity are appropriate to our era of revolution and tremendous changes—changes set in motion by the dynamics of going from an industrial society to a culture of information and ideas.

Industrialism and its assembly-line technology are analogous to the physics of Isaac Newton. Like the assembly line, space was conceived of as being straight. Space and matter were seen as constant and consistent in motion and appearance.

Our interactions with objective reality were routine, unchanging and regulated. There was a comfortable and easily recognizable set of criteria regimenting our behavior.

We are leaving this perceptual home of Newton and assembly-line thoughts forever. We cannot return. Problematically, our future home does not yet exist.

We are still on the pathway of transformation. Our ideas, attitudes and beliefs are being dissolved and reshaped as they are flung head-long into the new dimensions of experience provided by our innovative technology.

Millions of jobs are being replaced. Millions of jobs are being created.

Finding an Absolute Truth in Society Is Like Trying to Find a True Shape in Space

The psychological ability to cope with rapid change is a basic survival requirement. The ability to cope is, in turn, inextricably linked to personality traits of adaptation.

Just what are the personality traits that permit people to cope and to adapt—and are, therefore, desirable traits to possess in the future era of fantastic change?

The following is a guess at what answers and advice Einstein might have given, based on his specific and general theories.

Independent Self-concept. Be careful: the shortest distance between two points is not necessarily a straight line; the shortest distance between two points is a crooked (curved by gravity) light beam.

Just as a beam of light is curved by gravity, societal reference points are revised and replaced by change. Thus, an independent self-concept is a necessary corollary of crooked space.

The autonomous, inner-directed individual has an internal anchor that provides a core of stability in the midst of turmoil.

People who define their own self-image primarily in terms of their relationships to external institutions suffer a major handicap.

As external references dissolve, the "outer-directed" individual may find him- or herself a prisoner of the past and of nostalgia, with no sense of identity in the present.

Adaptation: Einstein might say that to develop "internal anchors" and, thereby, gain independence from external reference points, it is necessary to know yourself, and to have the courage to be oneself in the face of opposition.

Non-absolutist Belief System. At high speeds, objects are distorted in appearance. Even at earth-bound speeds, large objects appear smaller if one races past them. At the speed of light, this problem becomes even worse.

If you go past what appears to be a saucer-shaped disc in space, don't assume that that is its true shape. In fact, it doesn't have a true shape; that is partly what relativity is all about.

A society experiencing great change in its reference points resembles conditions at the speed of light: finding an absolute truth in society is like trying to find a true shape in space.

Thus, the person who wishes to adapt to our future must have a comparatively nonabsolutist belief system, in which a small number of fundamental principles are used to organize a great many, more or less tentative values and beliefs.

The advantages are that a "fact" found to be false can be discarded without threatening the integrity of the whole belief system, and that a means serving a valuable end in one context can be supplanted by another serving the same end better in a different context.

A more rigid personality, on the other hand, tends to look for truth and morality in the dictums of revealed authority. This greatly reduces flexibility, since questioning or revising any fact or moral judgment also questions the validity of the authority—and therefore threatens to undermine *all* the beliefs in the system.

Adaptation: If one possesses discretionary tools—the ability to analyze and be critical—one can confront complexity and ambiguity with interest. At ease in the world of abstraction, one can then hone his or her generalization skills and see the universal applications of ideas.

You Can Fit a Lincoln Continental into a Doghouse—but Only if You Keep Moving

Openness. There are four dimensions to our world: three spatial dimensions plus the dimension of time ("space-time"). Just as your odometer is useless to you in space, your own cultural perceptions preclude measuring and valuing another culture's objects, people and belief systems.

Those who possess an autonomous self-image and a non-absolutist belief system, however, are not threatened by new ideas or information. Thus a third important attribute is openness—being receptive to many different points of view.

Although everyone avoids unpleasant or threatening information to one extent or another, individuals who attempt to screen out all contrary viewpoints deprive themselves of the negative feedback that is essential for continuing adaptation.

Those who can accept differing opinions or differing cultural perceptions are more likely to be able to grow with the situation, to bridge the "space-time" dimension of intercultural exchanges of people and principles.

Adaptation: Developing the ability to be open to new experience and to see the familiar from an unfamiliar point of view, permits you to synthesize and integrate—to find order in disorder.

A unified physics was, after all, Einstein's goal.

Curiosity. On your journey through space, your Lincoln Continental has shrunk to the size of a Honda Civic. Simply put, objects traveling at extremely high speeds shrink, reaching half their original size at nine-tenths the speed of light.

Thus, you can fit your big car into a doghouse—but only if you keep on moving. If you attempt to park in the doghouse, your car will expand to its original size.

The need to "keep moving" is as important intellectually as it is physically. It is curiosity that spurs the mind to motion.

In our era, change means a constant flow of new information. The future is full of surprises, but the individual who delights in a wide-ranging game of "what-if?" is unlikely to be startled and stymied by unanticipated events.

Adaptation: Einstein personified the ability to wonder. Curiosity leads to the ability to visualize or imagine new possibilities. This permits one to view the world with child-like innocence, to delight in the novel and the unexpected.

Idealism. Don't worry about aging. You could be in space for 10 years—earth time—and your body probably wouldn't age more than 10 minutes. This phenomena is best known by the so-called "twin paradox" and can be explained by the fact that the faster an object moves, the slower its "biological clock" ticks.

The twin paradox is this: a pair of twins is separated at birth; one goes off into deep space traveling at nearly the speed of light, and the other stays home.

When the first twin returns in 20 years (Earth time), he is still an infant and his brother is in college studying physics. Neither feels he has aged either quickly or slowly, but they have definitely aged at a different rate.

This theory has been supported by flying atomic clocks at high speeds for short periods of time and comparing them with other atomic clocks on the ground.

Adaptation: Einstein was a child of the universe. Similarly, pragmatic idealism—the twin of youthfulness—is the child of light, motion, innocence and surprise.

Idealism, in fact, is a survival trait for anyone caught in a society facing as many fundamental problems as this one. It is also the source of a basic sense of mission, without which life seems meaningless.

But idealism means little unless it has some constructive impact on the world. Pragmatic idealism, then, involves choosing high leverage points within the system and acting effectively.

In this way, one gains a sense of control in the midst of great change—that one is not merely being swept along by the current, but has some say in the destination.

To remain idealistic, one must be enthusiastic, spontaneous and flexible. To remain pragmatic, one must be able to make one thing out of another by shifting its function and modifying ideas for more comprehensive applications.

To be pragmatically idealistic, one must be persistent and work hard for long periods in pursuit of a goal—even without guaranteed results.

Ten Traits Personify the Manager of the 21st Century

By learning to apply the following specific behavior traits, one is on the way to joining the ranks of the "new breed" of XXI Century managers:

1. *Generalization.* Generalization is the ability to use a limited number of general ideas to integrate a large number of specific ideas.

   Generalization allows one to maintain a nonabsolutist belief system because, if one can integrate ideas, even an incongruous one does not threaten the entire belief system.

2. *Intuition.* Intuition is an instantaneous cognitive process in which one recognizes familiar patterns in order to combine isolated bits of data and experience into an integrated picture.

Through intuition, flexibility is greatly enhanced and life, then, can be experienced innovatively.

3. *Networking.* Networking is defined as the ability to define problems by forming categories to see how individual problems interrelate.

The result is that you are able to see the old in a brand new way and gain a universal perspective. (Einstein's genius involved this very trait of being able to perceive a new vision from old matter.)

4. *Creative problem analysis.* Creative problem analysis is the ability to use multiple approaches to find a solution. This is an outgrowth of openness: being receptive to new ideas permits us to entertain multiple or opposing points of view, simultaneously.

This inner dialectic permits us to make a choice that represents the best idea. That choice making, in turn, is linked to using a number of approaches to problem solving.

It's an infinite loop of cybernetic qualities.

5. *Ambiguity.* This ability to simultaneously entertain opposing points of view—to accept ambiguity—and to select the best answer emergent from those, is a capacity that evolves from internal anchors.

It is the stability and independence gained from becoming inner directed, that permit one to consider ideas that oppose one another in order to choose the best one.

6. *Novelty.* Novelty is the ability to counteract the basic conservatism of the human mind—its thoughts, attitudes, and patterns that persist beyond their need.

This ability can be developed by paying attention to feelings of surprise when a particular fact does not fit a prior understanding and then by highlighting, rather than denying, that novelty.

This perceptual view allows us to imagine new possibilities and to see the world with fresh eyes.

7. *Structure.* Structure is based on the ability to establish information systems to create order and harmony out of entropy and, in so doing, direct attention away from the routine and mundane.

Freed from the routine, the mind is open to innovative perspectives and can embrace the capacity to wonder—curiosity. It is this curiosity that makes one susceptible to new ideas and to the use of the technology that makes the novel possible.

With well-structured information systems, the human mind is able to keep moving.

8. *Responsiveness.* Responsiveness means systematically and continually gleaning information about an organization's performance in both time-sequenced-linear and intuitive ways.

In order to be responsive to both external and internal environments and to discard false facts without threatening the entire belief system, one must possess a nonabsolutist belief system.

9. *Discretion.* Discretionary powers are essential to define problems, develop alternative solutions, make decisions, and communicate change to entire organizations.

This is dependent, in large measure, upon a well-developed sense of optimism and hopefulness—in short—idealism, the ability to view the world as it might be.

10. *Action.* Action can be defined as placing thinking and doing in close concert. It also involves analyzing a problem, in light of the experience gained while attempting to solve that problem.

Idealism is a fundamental component of action—one must believe in his or her ability to make some impact on the world.

By applying idealism through action, one gains a sense of direction and control and develops the stick-to-itiveness the modern world demands.

The world as we know it is undergoing a dramatic transformation and only Einstein's theories are challenging enough to describe it.

As societal reference points become distorted—much like physical properties become distorted in space—workers must take on new and different properties in order to survive the revolution.

Best Corporate Culture Is a Melting Pot

Jack Falvey

Promoting from within has been a policy of misguided company loyalty that has damaged the foundations of organizations it seeks to build.

Because of promote-from-within policies, many companies are headed today by organization men of the 1940s. Many of these inmates-turned-wardens have never worked outside of the corporations they head. Is it any wonder they are having difficulty adjusting to a world marketplace? Take this example:

A major company introduced a new consumer product. The market for that product accelerated and soon a foreign competitor entered the arena. As the company's share began to erode, top management met to determine strategy. The competitor's clever advertising was to be countered with trade deals and deep price cuts. The decision was unanimous. Why? Because everyone in the meeting was with the company 15 years before when a similar foreign product threatened another segment of the business. Everyone's experience was exactly the same. "We were successful before, so we will do the same things again."

Unfortunately, the foreign challenge was slightly different this time and so were the results. There were layoffs, then several plant closings and finally sale of the product, or what was left of it, to another company.

When I speak to management groups of established companies, the view from the podium is sometimes frightening. They look alike; they dress alike; unfortunately, they think alike. They are the products of a success profile. They are plain vanilla. But strength comes from diversity. When you face a problem, isn't it better to have five or six options rather than just one?

When, on the other hand, there is "cross-pollination," some wondrous things begin to happen: A consumer-goods president took over as chief executive officer of a computer company. He insisted that stock be available before a new product was launched, knowing that advertising backed by empty shelves was a waste. Consumer electronics companies usually had announced first, promoted and sold second, and delivered third. He reversed the order and filled the distribution pipeline first. He single-handedly caused a major shakeout of his competition by his product's success.

To compound the promote-from-within syndrome, companies have established traditional areas of the business from which all top managers will come. Organizations are headed by finance businessmen 20 years after they are no longer in the finance business. Engineers have headed computer companies that have consistently driven down prices and increased performance of their products with technical breakthroughs but that have failed to make the products usable in the marketplace. Family ownership imposes similar limitations when it gives each son a small division or sees to it that every cousin has an office somewhere.

Is it any wonder our industrial giants become targets of opportunity for anyone who chooses to pose a serious challenge to their products, services or marketplace? (In some cases the challenge is directly to those companies' management teams in the form of takeover bids or green mail.)

One of the major moves in our business environment is the formation of ventures by talented, aggressive, well-trained managers who have left their companies. Most could not survive or contribute within an in-bred organization. The proliferation of prospering companies that have been spun off should tell us something about the company men who were unable to make a success of those subsidiaries.

Between 20% and 30% of all openings should be filled from outside. The broader the mix the better. Every position should have outside talent included in the selection process. If inside people are not competitive, how can your organization be competitive in the marketplace?

Consultants who work across industry lines will confirm that the fundamentals in every industry are almost identical. There are no real barriers to mobility. Junior managers especially should be valued if they have three or four different work experiences, because they have found that managing their own careers produces far better returns than delegating that responsibility to a single organization.

The mobile manager of the 1960s, who did duty in six cities and then returned to the home office, should now be replaced by the mobile manager of the 1980s, who has worked across six different industries and deals comfortably in business in three different continents. The time of the generalist top manager is coming, and none too soon. Narrow specialists have always had difficulty with the big picture.

The rules of business have been shifting dramatically and rapidly for the past decade. Stable, secure management teams are remnants of the past. Dynamic, diverse management is needed for the present and the future. The rigid rules of organization construction must be broken.

The process of regenerating cannot be done overnight. Broaden your view and bring in more talent from nontraditional sources. Its addition will add new strength. It may already be long overdue.

●

Mixing Cultures on the Assembly Line

*U.S.-Japanese ventures give birth to a
host of new management problems.*

John Holusha

Flat Rock, Mich.
Two distinctly different car models are rolling off the assembly line at a gleaming new automobile plant here, about 15 miles south of Detroit. One bears the block letter badge of Mazda, the other the oval emblem of Ford.

The cars look different but they are, in fact, two versions of the same car, produced by American workers and mostly Japanese managers, using a design developed by Mazda.

More important, however, they are symbols of Detroit's new economics and the complex web of ties that have developed between Japanese car companies and their American rivals. Although there have been alliances of one sort or another between Detroit and the Japanese for years, most recent ones are joint ventures based on a simple economic strategy: Cars are produced for both companies, with a common structure but different appearances. The cars are built in American factories using Japanese management and designs.

These joint ventures, and other alliances ranging from investment in rival companies to the importation of Japanese vehicles for sale under American

Fords and Mazdas off the Same Assembly Line

Flat Rock, Mich., plant is owned and managed by Mazda and has produced more than 35,000 cars since Sept. 1.

Production Plan:
Ford Probe: 60%   *Mazda MX-6: 40%*

Engines and transmissions for both cars are designed and manufactured by Mazda in Japan. Seats, tires and batteries are American-made. Major stampings of both cars are done in the plant. The Probe's styling and dashboard design are by Ford.

Sticker Price:
Ford Probe: *Mazda MX-6:*
$10,500–$13,600   *$11,100–$15,100*

labels, are helping transform the way the domestic industry operates, changing the nature of competition worldwide and blurring the distinction between American and imported cars. It is a development that is only beginning to leave its mark on the industry's economic landscape.

"I think there will be more alliances and that they will intensify," said Malcolm S. Salter, a professor at the Harvard Business School. "They are less costly than full mergers, give the Japanese access to markets and reduce risks for all."

But the alliances, particularly those with hybrid factories that blend two very distinct cultures, are creating distinct managerial challenges: Management is hard enough in heavily competitive industries, but when culturally different companies are linked—and rival companies, at that—complications are bound to emerge.

Although the joint projects appear to be successful so far, some experts question whether American workers will adapt to the tightly disciplined Japanese system.

"There are two faces to the Japanese system," said Harley Shaiken, a former auto worker who is now a professor of economics at the University of California at San Diego. "One is the increased efficiency, better quality, the consulting with workers. But the other is increased pressure, stress, tightly strung manufacturing. The question is which face will prevail."

Already, some things are clear. "There's no issue that they will adapt some hybrid of the Japanese manufacturing system," said David Cole, director of the University of Michigan's Office for the Study of Automotive Transportation. "That decision has already been made by the competitive environment. It's adapt or get out of the game."

The alliances started to develop several years ago because Japan, faced with import restrictions, wanted greater access to the American automobile market and Detroit needed to tap Japan's skills in small-car making. Detroit so needed the low-cost high-mileage cars that it was willing to cede part of its lucrative domestic market. In doing so, it also ceded part of the culture on which the domestic auto industry was based.

In the Japanese-run ventures, distinctions between workers and their bosses are obscured by the identical uniforms worn by both, quite a shift from Detroit's rigid labor-management structure. Traditional management perks—reserved parking spaces, for example, and executive dining rooms—have been abolished. American workers with Midwest accents lace their conversations with Japanese words and business concepts, words like "kaizen" (continuous improvement) and "wa" (harmony among people), dropped casually into discussions.

At Flat Rock, where the Ford Probe and the Mazda MX-6 are being built, cross-cultural complications were evident from the start.

"Americans have a tendency to plan in more detail in the early stages regarding costs and sales; the Japanese are more vague about these things," said Osamu Nobuto, president of the Mazda Motor Manufacturing (USA) Corporation.

That caused clear frustration for the Ford Motor Company. "For Ford to proceed with a project, we want to know the price and return on investment," said Gary M. Heffernan, a Ford senior executive. "Mazda is run by engineers who didn't have to worry too much about the financial aspects while the yen was weak and they were expanding so rapidly." In the end, Ford decided it needed the new Mazda-designed car badly enough to go ahead with the project.

According to industry experts, dispute resolution is a big obstacle to joint projects, one made more difficult by barriers of language and distance. "You always have internal battles over any new car," Mr. Heffernan said. "Internally, it gets resolved by the boss. With Mazda, we had to try to work those things out at a lower level."

This problem appears to have been an important factor in Mazda's decision to build and operate the Flat Rock plant by itself rather than as a joint venture with Ford. "One of the disadvantages of a joint venture is that decision-making is slow," Mr. Nobuto observed.

In other ventures, cultural clashes have emerged over less important matters, but the scars show nonetheless. At Diamond-Star Motors, a joint venture between the Chrysler Corporation and the Mitsubishi Motors Corporation to assemble cars for sale by both companies, one issue was how the office was to be laid out. American executives prefer private offices; the Japanese think having everyone in a big room with no walls promotes better communication.

After much discussion, Diamond-Star officials settled on an open office layout at the plant in Normal, Ill., but with partitions between individuals' work areas. But Yoichi Nakane, the Mitsubishi executive who is Diamond-Star's president and chief executive, is not certain they did the right thing. The partitions, he said, "will create a different way of operating and may cause some problems. A consensus is not always right; it may not get a good result."

There have been other problems. The General Motors Corporation is reportedly unhappy with the sales performance of its imported and domestically made Japanese cars—the Nova, made at a California plant managed by the Toyota Motor Company; the Chevrolet Spectrum imported from Isuzu Motors

Ltd, and the Chevy Sprint, imported from the Suzuki Motor Company—and is preparing to shift marketing strategies.

This fall, all three cars will be sold under the Geo brand name, giving no indication that they are related to Chevrolet. The idea, Chevrolet officials have told dealers, is to increase advertising efficiency by promoting one name and to overcome the reluctance of some import buyers to consider a domestic nameplate.

In all the auto alliances, there are limits to cooperation. The Ford-Mazda deal is one example.

"Each company only tells the other what is necessary to explore future opportunities," said Robert R. Reilly, director of strategic planning for Ford. "It would be inappropriate for us to talk about plans for the Lincoln Town Car or Continental," the company's big luxury cars.

Nor is Mazda about to turn over details of its unique rotary engine used in its RX7 sports car. "The rotary engine is a special case," Mr. Nobuto said. "We do not share that with other companies, including Ford."

For every tie established between auto companies, dozens more are discussed and discarded, industry leaders say. The hard part, they say, is to find a project that allows two companies to share costs without cutting into each other's potential sales.

The change in the value of the dollar, particularly with respect to the yen, is bringing a new balance into the relationships between the American auto companies and their partners, allowing the Americans more say in what the new cars—and deals—will look like.

"During the extended period of artificial exchange rates we were forced into the hands of the Japanese to develop new products," said Michael N. Hammes, vice president for international operations at Chrysler.

G.M., according to trade sources, is already planning to supply Isuzu with American-made engines for trucks intended for export to this country. And Mr. Nobotu concedes that when the Probe and MX-6 are updated, they will probably be equipped with Ford rather than Mazda engines and drivetrains.

Mr. Hammes of Chrysler predicted that his company's relationship with the Mitsubishi Motor Company would continue, but on a more equal basis, "It's going to be a two-way street from now on," he said. But such shifting relationships have made the subject of auto joint ventures so sensitive that G.M., which has the most extensive network of alliances, refused to allow its executives to be interviewed for this article.

There is little question, however, that the American industry has learned valuable lessons from its day-to-day contact with Japanese manufacturing managers.

G.M. officials, for example, were shocked to find that the highest-quality car sold by G.M. was produced at the New United Manufacturing Motor plant in Fremont, Calif., the G.M.-Toyota joint venture known by its acronym, Nummi. And that was the case despite the plant's low level of automation and lack of high technology.

The plant had a reputation as a labor-relations headache when it was operated by G.M., and although it is staffed by the same ex-G.M. workers, Toyota has molded them into an efficient, quality-conscious workforce. G.M. executives with experience at Fremont have been sent by the company to other plants around the country, preaching the gospel of worker involvement.

"Nummi changed the direction of the American automobile industry," said Maryann N. Keller, an analyst with Furman Silz Mage Dietz & Birney. "Nummi proved that it was not machines, it was systems and software that created high quality. At G.M., you never admitted there was a problem. The Japanese look at problems as an opportunity and encouraged open discussion of problems."

Nummi produces models known as the Chevrolet Nova and Toyota Corolla FX16. There was no equity exchange in the deal and relations between the two companies are necessarily distant because of antitrust considerations: G.M., after all, is the world's largest auto maker and Toyota is No. 3.

Nummi is hardly the only alliance in which G.M. has a major role. G.M. owns 41.6 percent of Isuzu, mainly a truck maker, and imports an Isuzu model sold as the Chevrolet Spectrum. It owns 5.3 percent of the Suzuki, and imports a car sold as the Chevrolet Sprint.

Chrysler and Ford also have other alliances, but they are less scattershot. Chrysler linked up with Mitsubishi in the early 1970's to import small, fuel-efficient cars when its domestic lineup was large and thirsty; today it owns 24 percent of Mitsubishi stock.

It still sells the Mitsubishi-made Dodge Colt, Premier and Vista models to buyers who prefer imports, but the fuel economy of its domestic cars has improved dramatically. Later, the two companies developed the joint venture called Diamond-Star Motors.

Ford acquired a 25 percent interest in Mazda in 1979. Initially Ford sold Mazda cars under the Ford label in the Asia-Pacific market; now the Mercury Tracers that Ford makes in a plant in Hermosillo, Mexico, are based on Mazda designs. The arrangement at Flat Rock is the most recent arrangement.

The wave of alliances surprised the experts. A decade ago most auto executives and industry analysts were predicting a shakeout in the international industry, with just a handful of giant companies surviving into the 1990's. But, experts said, managers in car companies all over the world were unwilling to yield autonomy, which thwarted merger activity.

"It is very difficult to work out the details of mergers because most companies want to keep control of the business," said Ford's Mr. Heffernan. "So we found ways to get the benefits without actually merging."

The greatest benefit, of course, stems from the economics of the deals. In general, the cars produced for both partners have a common structure but a different look that enables them to be marketed as different vehicles.

The cars made at Flat Rock, for example, the Ford Probe and the Mazda MX-6, share the same basic understructure and engine, but the Probe is a sporty hatchback and the MX-6 a more conservative sedan.

"This is an example of where two interests come together," said Mazda's Mr. Nobuto. "We would not have done it if the cars were competing."

The Globalization of the American Car

Some of the ties U.S. auto makers have with their Japanese rivals. The companies also purchase various components from each other.

Ford

Owns 25% of Mazda.

Mazda plant in Flat Rock, Mich., produces Ford Probe and Mazda MX-6.

Assembles Mercury Tracer in a Ford plant in Hermosillo, Mexico, using Mazda components.

Mazda supplies Ford affiliates in Australia, New Zealand and Taiwan with sets of selected components for Lasser model, to be combined with components from local sources and sold under Ford label in Pacific markets.

Collaborating with Mazda on future models.

Nissan and Ford studying possibilities for production of a new vehicle in North America, to be marketed by both companies.

General Motors

Owns 41.6% of Isuzu.

United Motor Manufacturing Inc. is a 50-50 joint venture with Toyota Motor Corp. Its plant in Fremont, Calif., produces the Chevrolet Nova and Toyota Corolla Fx-16. Toyota manages the plant, with limited G.M. participation.

Imports an Isuzu car, sold as the Chevrolet Spectrum.

Isuzu and Fuji are building an assembly plant in Lafayette, Ind., and G.M. is expected to be a supplier of major components for the Isuzu vehicle.

Owns 5.3% of Suzuki, and imports a Suzuki car, sold as the Chevrolet Sprint.

Building a joint venture plant with Suzuki in Ingersoll, Ontario, to produce small sports utility vehicles for sale by both Chevrolet and Suzuki.

Chrysler

Owns 24% of Mitsubishi.

Diamond-Star Motors Corp. is a 50-50 joint venture with Mitsubishi. An assembly plant in Normal, Ill., is being built to produce one model for each company, starting late this summer. Management is joint, with Mitsubishi in the lead.

Has imported Mitsubishi-made small cars and trucks for sale as Plymouths and Dodges since the early 70's.

Buys V-6 engines from Mitsubishi for various Chrysler models.

●
_____

Face to Face with The Corporate World

Beverly Rubik

Everyone I knew thought I had finally "made it." I was praised by my family and friends and more highly esteemed by my colleagues than ever before. I had a new position as a highly paid senior scientist in a multi-billion dollar international high-technology corporation. I came to this place from a background in academia and more recently working in a struggling small firm and a start-up company that both went under. I was open to the possibility that this could be the right place for me. It was a fresh beginning with a lot of promises and benefits, and I was excited and ready for a new challenge.

Immediately I noticed differences. Security was tight with an employee badge system, a barbed wire fence encircled the grounds, and guards stood duty by the gate day and night. Everything was spotless and new—only the latest models of laboratory equipment, computer-automated, with many more instruments and computers than personnel. A refreshment station was situated every 50 feet which served not only beverages, but dispensed vitamins, antacids, and analgesics. People walked briskly down the long shining corridors in designer-wear covered by sparkling white lab coats that sported their names machined in blue over the pocket. It was the hallmark of large-scale efficiency that I had never before been intimately connected with. Little things which manifested automatically each day, like the dusting and straightening up of my desk and the fresh plastic lining in my waste basket, impressed me along with the larger, more obvious—the huge, sleek office-laboratory that I had all to myself—chock full of wonderful scientific instruments, like new toys, for my very own use! For a few weeks I floated around in somewhat of a daze, impressed by all the amenities, space, cleanliness, service, and wondrous laboratory delights.

Like a child propelled into adulthood, I was quickly brought down from this whirlwind of novelty, taught the corporate jargon and the gist of my contribution-to-be. I began to see more clearly where I was, beyond superficial appearances. My background in living systems theory prompted me to regard the corporation as an organism unto itself, a large living system highly organized around the reduction and compartmentalization of large, difficult tasks into department, group, and eventually people-sized tasks. The goal was to flourish and the ultimate task that sustained it all was product sales. When making sufficient profits the corporation was self-organizing and self-maintaining. But market conditions change; competition is fierce; raw materials fluctuate in quality; new products replace old; and new decisions and directions must reflect these constant fluctuations in environment. This corporation was nearly a century old, and like many older firms, originated from a small family business transformed into a huge conglomerate; suffered growing pains; survived surgeries in the form of cut-backs and lay-offs; and economically advantageous marriages with strange bedfellows in the form of several corporate mergers. Many of the problems I began to see could be traced to historical baggage or archaic ideology.

One of the first things I did on the new job was to take a managerial training course given by the company. It surprised me, for it taught the essence of enduring values and spiritual principles cloaked in a practical businesslike vocabulary. It dealt with mentoring, coaching, and inspiring others; communicating with compassion and understanding in problem-solving modes; empowering workers to develop their own work goals; enhancing workers' self-esteem; and fostering joint decision making with employees, to name a few themes. It was the antithesis of the cold, authoritarian managerial rule we were subjected to from the upper management. Unfortunately, only supervisors and middle managers were undertaking this enlightening course. I came to know the fear and loathing felt by my fellow employees for the powerful, threatening, invisible men at the top who operated from an archaic, reactionary style of management.

Taking a closer look at the faces of people passing by in the long corridors, I saw stern managerial faces, many serious faces, long doleful ones, blank ones, and smiles only rarely. Why so rare? I learned that business is serious stuff, and that if you're happy and smiling and obviously having a good time, you can't be too seriously involved in your work! When I genuinely smiled at the people I passed, I would see some attempt to return that smile—a curl of the lips with blank, smileless eyes. A forced smile, perhaps, but maybe they were genuinely trying to smile, but had forgotten how—in the workplace.

When the glitter and glamour of my new job wore off, I experienced the daily grind of highly specific, highly technical, but routinized tasks. Like a cog in a huge machine, I was utilized more as a grand technician in the scheme of things, already predetermined, than as the wealth and depth of person that I was, still unfolding. It was enough to permanently demolish my smile. It became maddening to me to be highly paid for being a mere minutia of all that I really was! Even worse, it occupied much of my time—up to 11 hours per day, indirectly interfering with my greater aspirations. The rift widened between my job and my growth-oriented personal and spiritual goals. I knew that I couldn't flourish here, not even survive.

Even fewer smiles were seen after a new corporate merger was suddenly announced one day by upper management. A new CEO had been appointed, an experienced "axe-man," who was to do the hacking and eliminate jobs— "pruning" for healthy future growth. The axe-man always spoke of eliminating jobs, but of course that translates to eliminating people. This smooth talker only succeeded in escalating fear of things to come. The old timers who had devoted their entire lives to this company, many who knew the original old family business, knew they were especially vulnerable. Being older with narrow job skills makes it very difficult to find new employment. Although some had survived the last merger, they remembered how their many colleagues, long dedicated to the company, were given only a few days' notice of termination. Fear and trepidation filled the air. Productivity was down. Production lots failed quality control like never before. Employees read newspaper job ads on their coffee breaks and talked in nervous whispers.

Months later, the decisions were announced. I was informed of my imminent lay-off along with 25% of my department. It was devastating for many, and some cried quietly. My feelings were mixed—relief, elation, and sadness—and I needed to let off steam. Meetings were arranged to inform, but there was no appropriate outlet for feelings. So I wrote a poem which I posted on all the bulletin boards:

> I used to think of. . . .
> Just like a mutter.
> But now I shutter
> worried I won't have any butter,
> or worse, end up in the gutter.
> This is no time for smutter.
> I'll just clean up my clutter
> and look for anutter.

My days numbered there, it felt a little like death approaching, awesome yet necessary. What to do? I began to pick up and re-direct my life-thread, but also to analyze what was wrong there. I saw an organization striving to be viable, growing, and responsive, but that was actually functionally modelled after a machine, with a rigid, linear, pyramidal hierarchy. Based on reductionism, the corporate function was broken down into tinier and tinier fragments which eventually got parcelled out to the people as tasks, and people became identified with those tasks. This process can be internalized, and the rift for many between personal and career goals which I experienced is resolved as people identify themselves with their jobs and salaries and forget who they are in a greater capacity. Cogs in a machine don't smile, or complain, or have feelings. Top-level managers rooted in an old mechanical world view don't smile, and their leadership pattern is reactive—self-centered, punitive, fragmented, and forced upon the rest. Although this company was growing progressively in middle management, "kick and shove" from the top was still the main strategy. It was an organization in pain after yet another surgery and strange marriage-merger, blindly unconscious of its deep ties to Mother Earth for all of its materials, energy supply, and dedicated workers. It was an organization that will no longer flourish unless it reaches out responsively, empowering its workers toward self-actualization and responsibly achieving its mission, which must include serving the whole Earth. It must plan for change in response to a changing economy, moving from local to globally diffuse.

Although my experience at this particular company is a unique one, I believe these observations hold true for many others. The corporate world, with a fragmented ideology, has suffered by its neglect of the whole—the whole person, the whole Earth which sustains all, the "wholly" spirit of aliveness—and causes all of us further suffering. The cure: a new perspective of wholeness and interconnectedness that will bring no small change—only a Global Renaissance!

The Coming of the New Organization

Peter F. Drucker

The typical large business 20 years hence will have fewer than half the levels of management of its counterpart today, and no more than a third the managers. In its structure, and in its management problems and concerns, it will bear little resemblance to the typical manufacturing company, circa 1950, which our textbooks still consider the norm. Instead it is far more likely to resemble organizations that neither the practicing manager nor the management scholar pays much attention to today: the hospital, the university, the symphony orchestra. For like them, the typical business will be knowledge-based, an organization composed largely of specialists who direct and discipline their own performance through organized feedback from colleagues, customers, and headquarters. For this reason, it will be what I call an information-based organization.

Businesses, especially large ones, have little choice but to become information-based. Demographics, for one, demands the shift. The center of gravity in employment is moving fast from manual and clerical workers to knowledge workers who resist the command-and-control model that business took from the military 100 years ago. Economics also dictates change, especially the need for large businesses to innovate and to be entrepreneurs. But above all, information technology demands the shift.

Advanced data-processing technology isn't necessary to create an information-based organization, of course. As we shall see, the British built just such an organization in India when "information technology" meant the quill pen, and barefoot runners were the "telecommunications" systems. But as advanced technology becomes more and more prevalent, we have to engage in analysis and diagnosis—that is, in "information"—even more intensively or risk being swamped by the data we generate.

So far most computer users still use the new technology only to do faster what they have always done before, crunch conventional numbers. But as soon as a company takes the first tentative steps from data to information, its decision processes, management structure, and even the way its work gets done begin to be transformed. In fact, this is already happening, quite fast, in a number of companies throughout the world.

We can readily see the first step in this transformation process when we consider the impact of computer technology on capital-investment decisions. We have known for a long time that there is no one right way to analyze a proposed capital investment. To understand it we need at least six analyses: the expected rate of return; the payout period and the investment's expected productive life; the discounted present value of all returns through the productive lifetime of the investment; the risk in not making the investment or deferring it; the cost and risk in case of failure; and finally, the opportunity cost. Every accounting student is taught these concepts. But before the advent of data-processing capacity, the actual analyses would have taken man-years of clerical toil to complete. Now anyone with a spreadsheet should be able to do them in a few hours.

The availability of this information transforms the capital-investment analysis from opinion into diagnosis, that is, into the rational weighing of alternative assumptions. Then the information transforms the capital-investment decision from an opportunistic, financial decision governed by the numbers into a business decision based on the probability of alternative strategic assumptions. So the decision both presupposes a business strategy and challenges that strategy and its assumptions. What was once a budget exercise becomes an analysis of policy.

The second area that is affected when a company focuses its data-processing capacity on producing information is its organization structure. Almost immediately, it becomes clear that both the number of management levels and the number of managers can be sharply cut. The reason is straightforward: it turns out that whole layers of management neither make decisions nor lead. Instead, their main, if not their only, function is to serve as "relays"—human boosters for the faint, unfocused signals that pass for communication in the traditional pre-information organization.

One of America's largest defense contractors made this discovery when it asked what information its top corporate and operating managers needed to do their jobs. Where did it come from? What form was it in? How did it flow? The search for answers soon revealed that whole layers of management—perhaps as many as 6 out of a total of 14—existed only because these questions had not been asked before. The company had had data galore. But it had always used its copious data for control rather than for information.

Information is data endowed with relevance and purpose. Converting data into information thus requires knowledge. And knowledge, by definition, is specialized. (In fact, truly knowledgeable people tend toward overspecialization, whatever their field, precisely because there is always so much more to know.)

The information-based organization requires far more specialists overall than the command-and-control companies we are accustomed to. Moreover, the specialists are found in operations, not at corporate headquarters. Indeed, the operating organization tends to become an organization of specialists of all kinds.

Information-based organizations need central operating work such as legal counsel, public relations, and labor relations as much as ever. But the need for service staffs—that is, for people without operating responsibilities who only advise, counsel, or coordinate—shrinks drastically. In its *central* management, the information-based organization needs few, if any, specialists.

Because of its flatter structure, the large, information-based organization will more closely resemble the businesses of a century ago than today's big companies. Back then, however, all the knowledge, such as it was, lay with the very top people. The rest were helpers or hands, who mostly did the same work and did as they were told. In the information-based organization, the knowledge will be primarily at the bottom, in the minds of the specialists who do different work and direct themselves. So today's typical organization in which knowledge tends to be concentrated in service staffs, perched rather insecurely between top management and the operating people, will likely be labeled a phase, an attempt to infuse knowledge from the top rather than obtain information from below.

Finally, a good deal of work will be done differently in the information-based organization. Traditional departments will serve as guardians of standards, as centers for training and the assignment of specialists; they won't be where the work gets done. That will happen largely in task-focused teams.

This change is already under way in what used to be the most clearly defined of all departments—research. In pharmaceuticals, in telecommunications, in papermaking, the traditional *sequence* of research, development, manufacturing, and marketing is being replaced by *synchrony:* specialists from all these functions work together as a team, from the inception of research to a product's establishment in the market.

How task forces will develop to tackle other business opportunities and problems remains to be seen. I suspect, however, that the need for a task force, its assignment, its composition, and its leadership will have to be decided on case by case. So the organization that will be developed will go beyond the matrix and may indeed be quite different from it. One thing is clear, though: it will require greater self-discipline and even greater emphasis on individual responsibility for relationships and for communications.

To say that information technology is transforming business enterprises is simple. What this transformation will require of companies and top management is much harder to decipher. That is why I find it helpful to look for clues in other kinds of information-based organizations, such as the hospital, the symphony orchestra, and the British administration in India.

A fair-sized hospital of about 400 beds will have a staff of several hundred physicians and 1,200 to 1,500 paramedics divided among some 60 medical and paramedical specialities. Each specialty has its own knowledge, its own training, its own language. In each specialty, especially the paramedical ones like the clinical lab and physical therapy, there is a head person who is a working specialist rather than a full-time manager. The head of each specialty reports directly to the top, and there is little middle management. A good deal of the work is done in ad hoc teams as required by an individual patient's diagnosis and condition.

A large symphony orchestra is even more instructive, since for some works there may be a few hundred musicians on stage playing together. According to organization theory then, there should be several group vice president conductors and perhaps a half-dozen division VP conductors. But that's not how it works. There is only the conductor-CEO—and every one of the musicians plays directly to that person without an intermediary. And each is a high-grade specialist, indeed an artist.

But the best example of a large and successful information-based organization, and one without any middle management at all, is the British civil administration in India.[1]

The British ran the Indian subcontinent for 200 years, from the middle of the eighteenth century through World War II, without making any fundamental changes in organization structure or administrative policy. The Indian civil service never had more than 1,000 members to administer the vast and densely populated subcontinent—a tiny fraction (at most 1%) of the legions of Confucian mandarins and palace eunuchs employed next door to administer a not-much-more populous China. Most of the Britishers were quite young; a 30-year-old was a survivor, especially in the early years. Most lived alone in isolated outposts with the nearest countryman a day or two of travel away, and for the first hundred years there was no telegraph or railroad.

The organization structure was totally flat. Each district officer reported directly to the "Coo," the provincial political secretary. And since there were nine provinces, each political secretary had at least 100 people reporting directly to him, many times what the doctrine of the span of control would allow. Nevertheless, the system worked remarkably well, in large part because it was designed to ensure that each of its members had the information he needed to do his job.

1. The standard account is Philip Woodruff, *The Men Who Ruled India,* especially the first volume, *The Founders of Modern India* (New York: St. Martin's, 1954). How the system worked day by day is charmingly told in *Sowing* (New York: Harcourt Brace Jovanovich, 1962), volume one of the autobiography of Leonard Woolf (Virginia Woolf's husband).

Each month the district officer spent a whole day writing a full report to the political secretary in the provincial capital. He discussed each of his principal tasks—there were only four, each clearly delineated. He put down in detail what he had expected would happen with respect to each of them, what actually did happen, and why, if there was a discrepancy, the two differed. Then he wrote down what he expected would happen in the ensuing month with respect to each key task and what he was going to do about it, asked questions about policy, and commented on long-term opportunities, threats, and needs. In turn, the political secretary "minuted" every one of those reports—that is, he wrote back a full comment.

On the basis of these examples, what can we say about the requirements of the information-based organization? And what are its management problems likely to be? Let's look first at the requirements. Several hundred musicians and their CEO, the conductor, can play together because they all have the same score. It tells both flutist and timpanist what to play and when. And it tells the conductor what to expect from each and when. Similarly, all the specialists in the hospital share a common mission: the care and cure of the sick. The diagnosis is their "score"; it dictates specific action for the X-ray lab, the dietitian, the physical therapist, and the rest of the medical team.

Information-based organizations, in other words, require clear, simple, common objectives that translate into particular actions. At the same time, however, as these examples indicate, information-based organizations also need concentration on one objective or, at most, on a few.

Because the "players" in an information-based organization are specialists, they cannot be told how to do their work. There are probably few orchestra conductors who could coax even one note out of a French horn, let alone show the horn player how to do it. But the conductor can focus the horn player's skill and knowledge on the musicians' joint performance. And this focus is what the leaders of an information-based business must be able to achieve.

Yet a business has no "score" to play by except the score it writes as it plays. And whereas neither a first-rate performance of a symphony nor a miserable one will change what the composer wrote, the performance of a business continually creates new and different scores against which its performance is assessed. So an information-based business must be structured around goals that clearly state management's performance expectations for the enterprise and for each part and specialist and around organized feedback that compares results with these performance expectations so that every member can exercise self-control.

The other requirement of an information-based organization is that everyone take information responsibility. The bassoonist in the orchestra does so every time she plays a note. Doctors and paramedics work with an elaborate system of reports and an information center, the nurse's station on the patient's floor. The district officer in India acted on this responsibility every time he filed a report.

The key to such a system is that everyone asks: Who in this organization depends on me for what information? And on whom, in turn, do I depend? Each person's list will always include superiors and subordinates. But the most important names on it will be those of colleagues, people with whom one's primary relationship is coordination. The relationship of the internist, the surgeon, and the anesthesiologist is one example. But the relationship of a biochemist, a pharmacologist, the medical director in charge of clinical testing, and a marketing specialist in a pharmaceutical company is no different. It, too, requires each party to take the fullest information responsibility.

Information responsibility to others is increasingly understood, especially in middle-sized companies. But information responsibility to oneself is still largely neglected. That is, everyone in an organization should constantly be thinking through what information he or she needs to do the job and to make a contribution.

This may well be the most radical break with the way even the most highly computerized businesses are still being run today. There, people either assume the more data, the more information—which was a perfectly valid assumption yesterday when data were scarce, but leads to data overload and information blackout now that they are plentiful. Or they believe that information specialists know what data executives and professionals need in order to have information. But information specialists are tool makers. They can tell us what tool to use to hammer upholstery nails into a chair. We need to decide whether we should be upholstering a chair at all.

Executives and professional specialists need to think through what information is for them, what data they need: first, to know what they are doing; then, to be able to decide what they should be doing; and finally, to appraise how well they are doing. Until this happens MIS departments are likely to remain cost centers rather than become the result centers they could be.

Most large businesses have little in common with the examples we have been looking at. Yet to remain competitive—maybe even to survive—they will have to convert themselves into information-based organizations, and fairly quickly. They will have to change old habits and acquire new ones. And the more successful a company has been, the more difficult and painful this process is apt to be. It will threaten the jobs, status, and opportunities of a good many people in the organization, especially the long-serving, middle-aged people in middle management who tend to be the least mobile and to feel most secure in their work, their positions, their relationships, and their behavior.

The information-based organization will also pose its own special management problems. I see as particularly critical:

1. Developing rewards, recognition, and career opportunities for specialists.
2. Creating unified vision in an organization of specialists.
3. Devising the management structure for an organization of task forces.
4. Ensuring the supply, preparation, and testing of top management people.

Bassoonists presumably neither want nor expect to be anything but bassoonists. Their career opportunities consist of moving from second bassoon to first bassoon and perhaps of moving from a second-rank orchestra to a better, more prestigious one. Similarly, many medical technologists neither expect nor want to be anything but medical technologists. Their career opportunities consist of a fairly good chance of moving up to senior technician, and a very slim chance of becoming lab director. For those who make it to lab director, about 1 out of every 25 or 30 technicians, there is also the opportunity to move to a bigger, richer hospital. The district officer in India had practically no chance for professional growth except possibly to be relocated, after a three-year stint, to a bigger district.

Opportunities for specialists in an information-based business organization should be more plentiful than they are in an orchestra or hospital, let alone in the Indian civil service. But as in these organizations, they will primarily be opportunities for advancement within the specialty, and for limited advancement at that. Advancement into "management" will be the exception, for the simple reason that there will be far fewer middle-management positions to move into. This contrasts sharply with the traditional organization where, except in the research lab, the main line of advancement in rank is out of the specialty and into general management.

More than 30 years ago General Electric tackled this problem by creating "parallel opportunities" for "individual professional contributors." Many companies have followed this example. But professional specialists themselves have largely rejected it as a solution. To them—and to their management colleagues—the only meaningful opportunities are promotions into management. And the prevailing compensation structure in practically all businesses reinforces this attitude because it is heavily biased towards managerial positions and titles.

There are no easy answers to this problem. Some help may come from looking at large law and consulting firms, where even the most senior partners tend to be specialists, and associates who will not make partner are outplaced fairly early on. But whatever scheme is eventually developed will work only if the values and compensation structure of business are drastically changed.

The second challenge that management faces is giving its organization of specialists a common vision, a view of the whole.

In the Indian civil service, the district officer was expected to see the "whole" of his district. But to enable him to concentrate on it, the government services that arose one after the other in the nineteenth century (forestry, irrigation, the archaeological survey, public health and sanitation, roads) were organized outside the administrative structure, and had virtually no contact with the district officer. This meant that the district officer became increasingly isolated from the activities that often had the greatest impact on—and the greatest importance for—his district. In the end, only the provincial government or the central government in Delhi had a view of the "whole," and it was an increasingly abstract one at that.

A business simply cannot function this way. It needs a view of the whole and a focus on the whole to be shared among a great many of its professional specialists, certainly among the senior ones. And yet it will have to accept, indeed will have to foster, the pride and professionalism of its specialists—if only because, in the absence of opportunities to move into middle management, their motivation must come from that pride and professionalism.

One way to foster professionalism, of course, is through assignments to task forces. And the information-based business will use more and more smaller self-governing units, assigning them tasks tidy enough for "a good man to get his arms around," as the old phrase has it. But to what extent should information-based businesses rotate performing specialists out of their specialties and into new ones? And to what extent will top management have to accept as its top priority making and maintaining a common vision across professional specialties?

Heavy reliance on task-force teams assuages one problem. But it aggravates another: the management structure of the information-based organization. Who will the business's managers be? Will they be task-force leaders? Or will there be a two-headed monster—a specialist structure, comparable, perhaps, to the way attending physicians function in a hospital, and an administrative structure of task-force leaders?

The decisions we face on the role and function of the task-force leaders are risky and controversial. Is theirs a permanent assignment, analogous to the job of the supervisory nurse in the hospital? Or is it a function of the task that changes as the task does? Is it an assignment or a position? Does it carry any rank at all? And if it does, will the task-force leaders become in time what the product managers have been at Proctor & Gamble: the basic units of management and the company's field officers? Might the task-force leaders eventually replace department heads and vice presidents?

Signs of every one of these developments exist, but there is neither a clear trend nor much understanding as to what each entails. Yet each would give rise to a different organizational structure from any we are familiar with.

Finally, the toughest problem will probably be to ensure the supply, preparation, and testing of top management people. This is, of course, an old and central dilemma as well as a major reason for the general acceptance of decentralization in large businesses in the last 40 years. But the existing business organization has a great many middle-management positions that are supposed to prepare and test a person. As a result, there are usually a good many people to choose from when filling a senior management slot. With the number of middle-management positions sharply cut, where will the information-based organization's top executives come from? What will be their preparation? How will they have been tested?

Decentralization into autonomous units will surely be even more critical than it is now. Perhaps we will even copy the German *Gruppe* in which the decentralized units are set up as separate companies with their own top managements. The Germans use this model precisely because of their tradition of promoting people in their specialties, especially in research and engineering; if they did not have available commands in near-independent subsidiaries to put people in, they would have little opportunity to train and test their most promising professionals. These subsidiaries are thus somewhat like the farm teams of a major-league baseball club.

We may also find that more and more top management jobs in big companies are filled by hiring people away from smaller companies. This is the way that major orchestras get their conductors—a young conductor earns his or her spurs in a small orchestra or opera house, only to be hired away by a larger one. And the heads of a good many large hospitals have had similar careers.

Can business follow the example of the orchestra and hospital where top management has become a separate career? Conductors and hospital administrators come out of courses in conducting or schools of hospital administration respectively. We see something of this sort in France, where large companies are often run by men who have spent their entire previous careers in government service. But in most countries this would be unacceptable to the organization (only France has the *mystique* of the *grandes écoles*). And even in France, businesses, especially large ones, are becoming too demanding to be run by people without firsthand experience and a proven success record.

Thus the entire top management process—preparation, testing, succession—will become even more problematic than it already is. There will be a growing need for experienced businesspeople to go back to school. And business schools will surely need to work out what successful professional specialists must know to prepare themselves for high-level positions as *business* executives and *business* leaders.

Since modern business enterprise first arose, after the Civil War in the United States and the Franco-Prussian War in Europe, there have been two major evolutions in the concept and structure of organizations. The first took place in the ten years between 1895 and 1905. It distinguished management from ownership and established management as work and task in its own right. This happened first in Germany, when Georg Siemens, the founder and head of Germany's premier bank, *Deutsche Bank,* saved the electrical apparatus company his cousin Werner had founded after Werner's sons and heirs had mismanaged it into near collapse. By threatening to cut off the bank's loans, he forced his cousins to turn the company's management over to professionals. A little later, J. P. Morgan, Andrew Carnegie, and John D. Rockefeller, Sr. followed suit in their massive restructurings of U.S. railroads and industries.

The second evolutionary change took place 20 years later. The development of what we still see as the modern corporation began with Pierre S. du Pont's restructuring of his family company in the early twenties and continued with Alfred P. Sloan's redesign of General Motors a few years later. This introduced the command-and-control organization of today, with its emphasis on decentralization, central service staffs, personnel management, the whole apparatus of budgets and controls, and the important distinction between policy and operations. This stage culminated in the massive reorganization of General Electric in the early 1950s, an action that perfected the model most big businesses around the world (including Japanese organizations) still follow.[2]

Now we are entering a third period of change: the shift from the command-and-control organization, the organization of departments and divisions, to the information-based organization, the organization of knowledge specialists. We can perceive, though perhaps only dimly, what this organization will look like. We can identify some of its main characteristics and requirements. We can point to central problems of values, structure, and behavior. But the job of actually building the information-based organization is still ahead of us—it is the managerial challenge of the future.

2. Alfred D. Chandler, Jr. has masterfully chronicled the process in his two books *Strategy and Structure* (Cambridge: MIT Press, 1962) and *The Visible Hand* (Cambridge: Harvard University Press, 1977)—surely the best studies of the administrative history of any major institution. The process itself and its results were presented and analyzed in two of my books: *The Concept of the Corporation* (New York:John Day, 1946) and *The Practice of Management* (New York: Harper Brothers, 1954).

Conclusion

W e intend this conclusion to be a transition—a few words that will bring some central themes into focus so that they may be transported by students into the future and into their management careers. Some of these themes have been explicit throughout and will be restated here. A few themes have been more implicit; in fact, they only became clear to us after we had put the various pieces of this volume together.

Taken together, the contributors to this volume make it very clear that the realities of management are interwoven with a broad spectrum of other human endeavors. At a very general level, organizations as we know them depend on certain biological characteristics (for example, language, abilities to write, potential for cooperation) as well as social and technological developments. At a more specific level, the characteristics of organizations at a particular point in time are influenced by a host of past, present, and anticipated future events. The demands on organizations, the resources they have available, how they are viewed by members of society, and the characteristics of managers themselves and the people they manage are all influenced by these events. Finally, we have seen that organizations themselves have come to make history. In short, organizations, management, and human society evolve together.

It goes without saying that what people who write about management have to say is part and parcel of the same evolution. The contents of this book are no exception. With this in mind, it is instructive to examine the major framework of the book critically. Let us reconsider Figure 1 (the triangle) in the Introduction and our assumption that management is above all else a complex balancing act.

The Triangle and Balancing Reconsidered. At an abstract level, the issues of technique, practice, and values that define the triangle seem likely to have rather enduring significance. The content and the emphasis given to each issue will vary over time. For example, had we put this collection together even a year or two earlier, it is doubtful that we would have given nearly as much attention to ethics as we did.

In addition, throughout the book, along with our contributors, we emphasized that management is a balancing act. It is worth noting that many recent books have used the same or a very similar metaphor. For example, Robert Lamb refers to management as a "balancing game,"[1] Gareth Morgan discusses the need for managers to "hook everything together,"[2] and Harold Leavitt writes of "keeping the whole act together."[3] It would be extremely inconsistent with the theme of relativity that we have seen throughout this book if we did not urge the reader to recognize that our metaphor too is a product of its time.

One other observation on the managerial balancing act is necessary. It is very unlikely that the three elements will be equally important to all managers at a given time or to the same manager at different times. Perhaps, for instance, matters of technique simply dominate one's attention either because they are so important or because the issues of practice and values seem so clearly defined that they simply are ignored. Moreover, while to some degree every individual needs to come to terms with the three issues in one way or another, it is possible to view the balance as something that must be achieved by the organization as a whole and not necessarily a problem for very many individuals most of the time. For example, it is possible to envision an organization assigning responsibility for each of the issues to different people and achieving balance by integrating the efforts of the "specialists." In other words, it is possible that the balancing act we have attributed to managers is something that is primarily achieved by organizations, not by each manager.

Regardless of how the attention to the three issues is divided, somehow managers must recognize their importance and see to it that their organizations address them. What implications does this fact have for preparing people to manage?

Preparing Managers. Our thoughts about preparing managers and the need for organizations to balance technique, practice, and values are linked to two sets of assumptions. One set concerns the nature of organizations in the future and the second involves our beliefs about how managers are currently being trained.

First, let us review the assumptions about modern organizations. As we have said, we see modern organizations as superimposed on other human activities. We also see organizations as playing increasingly important roles within nations and in the global political economy. Given the rapid change in technology and in the social, political, and economic relationships within and among nations, organizations will need to become increasingly more flexible and able to deal with complexity.

Second, it is our impression that managers are not being prepared to respond to these demands. As we have noted, managers have not been encouraged to see the tight relationships between organizations and other aspects of human endeavor. We believe that, more recently, there has been a strong inclination to prepare managers in matters of technique. Less attention has been given to practice and even less to values. Moreover, there has been a tendency for business education to be ethnocentric. Although there are some notable exceptions, business schools have given little attention to an in depth understanding of other nations and cultures.

The contrast between these sets of assumptions is clear. Unfortunately ways to close the gap are less so. We believe, however, that the contents of this book point towards a useful orientation. They suggest that managers must be prepared to deal with the full range of human beings and their institutions. This preparation can not be achieved through the study of science and technique alone. While this study is essential, it must be embedded in an understanding and appreciation of other aspects of human experience.

How can this understanding and appreciation be attained? Again, no simple answers, but two thoughts. First, the gap we have noted needs to be observed and taken seriously. Second, managers and those who attempt to develop them must draw on resources that help develop the breadth of knowledge that understanding and appreciating the complexity of human experience and social organization require. We suggest these resources include the arts, language, anthropology, the humanities, philosophy, and spirituality to name a few.

If organizations are the fully human systems we have described, their managers must have the capacity to relate to the full range of human experiences. There is much to draw on. The starting point is recognition that these seemingly tangential bodies of knowledge and experience are in fact part of the essence of management.

References

1. R. B. Lamb, *Running American business* (New York: Basic Books, 1987), p. 302.
2. G. Morgan, *Riding the waves of change* (San Francisco: Jossey-Bass, 1988), p. 154.
3. H. J. Leavitt, *Corporate pathfinders* (Homewood, Ill.: Dow Jones-Irwin, 1986), p. 209.